Least Privilege Security for Windows 7, Vista and XP

Secure desktops for regulatory compliance and business agility

Russell Smith

[PACKT] enterprise

PUBLISHING

professional expertise distilled

BIRMINGHAM - MUMBAI

Least Privilege Security for Windows 7, Vista and XP

First published: July 2010

Production Reference: 1290610

Published by Packt Publishing Ltd.
32 Lincoln Road
Olton
Birmingham, B27 6PA, UK.

ISBN 978-1-849680-04-2

www.packtpub.com

Cover Image by Tina Negus (tina_manthorpe@sky.com)

Credits

Author
Russell Smith

Reviewers
Alun Jones

Stephen Lamb B.Sc (Hons)

Marco Shaw

Acquisition Editor
James Lumsden

Development Editors
Kerry George

Reshma Sundaresan

Technical Editors
Vinodhan Nair

Gaurav Datar

Copy Editor
Sanchari Mukherjee

Editorial Team Leader
Gagandeep Singh

Project Team Leader
Priya Mukherji

Project Coordinator
Ashwin Shetty

Proofreader
Chris Smith

Indexer
Rekha Nair

Graphics
Geetanjali Sawant

Production Coordinator
Adline Swetha Jesuthas

Cover Work
Adline Swetha Jesuthas

About the Author

Russell Smith specializes in management and security of Microsoft-based IT systems and is a Contributing Editor for CDW's Biztech magazine and writes regularly for industry journal Windows IT Professional. Russell is also contributing author to *Supporting and Troubleshooting Applications on a Microsoft Windows Vista Client for Enterprise Support Technicians* from Microsoft's Official Academic Course (MOAC) series of books published by Wiley and Sons.

An independent IT consultant and MCSE with more than ten years of experience, Russell's recent projects include Active Directory Security Consultant for the UK Health Service National Programme for Information Technology (NPfIT) and Exchange Architect for Wipro Technologies. Russell also has extensive experience as an IT trainer.

About the Reviewers

Alun Jones (MVP, MCP) is the President of Texas Imperial Software (http://www.wftpd.com). Texas Imperial Software develops secure networking software and provides security engineering consulting services. Texas Imperial Software's flagship product is WFTPD Pro, a secure FTP server for Windows, written entirely by Alun.

Alun entered the security field as more and more of WFTPD's support needs indicated that few companies were able to meet their needs for security on the Internet without help. His current day job is as a Security Engineer for an online retailer.

The Information Security-related blog, Tales from the Crypto (http://msmvps.com/blogs/alunj) carries Alun's occasional thoughts on the topic of Computer Security.

Alun has attended University at Corpus Christi College, Cambridge, and Bath University, and now lives near Seattle, Washington with his wife Debbie and son Colin, both of whom he now wishes to thank for their patience in allowing him to review this book.

Stephen Lamb has worked as an Information Security Professional for fifteen years, working with clients throughout Europe. Stephen is a firm believer that effective information security enables people and businesses to be more effective. He found from experience that a successful security strategy must encompass user awareness together with meaningful processes and procedures. During his career, Stephen has designed, developed, and implemented technical solutions to complex information security challenges. Stephen is fascinated by the challenges and opportunities social media bring to the security posture of organizations and individuals.

Marco Shaw is currently working as an independent contractor. He has been working in the IT industry for over 12 years. He was awarded the Microsoft Most Valuable Professional award for his contributions to the Windows PowerShell community in 2008, 2009, and again in 2010.

Marco spoke at TechMentor at San Francisco in 2008, where he provided two popular sessions on PowerShell. He also provided two popular sessions on Windows Server 2008 R2 and System Center Operations Manager 2007 at TechDays 2009 in Halifax, Canada.

His recent authoring activities have included writing PowerShell content for a Windows Server 2008 book by Microsoft Press, a PowerShell-related article on System Center Operations Manager 2007 for TechNet Magazine, providing PowerShell content for a SQL Server 2008 book by Sams, and also for a revised edition of *System Center Operations Manager 2007 Unleashed* by Sams. He has also co-authored the second edition of *PowerShell Unleashed*, published by Sams released early in 2009.

Marco has also been the technical reviewer for other books covering Microsoft technologies.

Blog: http://marcoshaw.blogspot.com

Twitter: http://twitter.com/marcoshaw

E-mail: marco.shaw@gmail.com

Dedicated to St. Petersburg, Russia - where this book was written.

Table of Contents

Preface

In this, the first book to be entirely dedicated to the subject of running Least Privilege Security (or standard user accounts) on Windows operating systems in the enterprise, you will learn about the benefits Least Privilege brings organizations in terms of not only security, but regulatory compliance, improved manageability, and operational simplicity. The book provides a complete guide to implementing Least Privilege Security on the desktop, with step-by-step instructions and advice about how to overcome the most common technical and political challenges.

What this book covers

Chapter 1, An Overview of Least Privilege Security in Microsoft Windows, explores the principle of Least Privilege Security and shows how to implement it in different versions of Microsoft Windows. It also explains how to control and change system privileges, benefit from implementing Least Privilege Security on the desktop, and overcome the most common technical and political problems and challenges when implementing Least Privilege Security.

Chapter 2, Political and Cultural Challenges for Least Privilege Security, covers the reasons why users may not accept Least Privilege Security on the desktop. It also clearly explains and justifies the benefits of Least Privilege Security for your organization. The chapter also covers how to apply Least Privilege Security to different categories of users and get buy-in from management.

Chapter 3, Solving Least Privilege Problems with the Application Compatibility Toolkit, covers how to modify incompatible applications on the fly and achieve the best balance between compatibility and security by using Application Compatibility shims. It explains how to create shims using the Application Compatibility Toolkit 5.5 and distribute compatibility databases to devices across the enterprise.

Chapter 4, User Account Control, covers how to achieve a seamless user experience by using the different components and compatibility features of User Account Control. It also explains how to configure User Account Control on multiple computers using Group Policy and the inner workings of User Account Control's core components.

Chapter 5, Tools and Techniques for Solving Least Privilege Security Problems, covers how to set up a system for temporarily granting administrative privileges to standard users for support purposes. It also covers how to use Task Scheduler to run common processes without the need to elevate privileges and how to install third-party solutions to configure administrative privileges for applications and Windows processes on-the-fly.

Chapter 6, Software Distribution using Group Policy, explains how to prepare applications for Group Policy Software Installation (GPSI) and Windows Installer deployment. It also explains how to repackage legacy setup programs in Windows Installer .msi format and how to make GPSI more scalable and flexible using the Distributed File System (DFS). It covers how to target client computers using Windows Management Instrumentation (WMI) filters and Group Policy Scope of Management.

Chapter 7, Managing Internet Explorer Add-ons, covers how to support per-user and per-machine ActiveX controls and manage Internet Explorer add-ons via Group Policy. It also explains how to install per-machine ActiveX controls using the ActiveX Installer Service (AxIS) and how to implement best practices for working with ActiveX controls in a managed environment.

Chapter 8, Supporting Users Running with Least-Privilege, explains how to support Least-Privilege user accounts using reliable remote access solutions, how to connect to remote systems with administrative privileges using different techniques and enable remote access using Group Policy and Windows Firewall.

Chapter 9, Deploying Software Restriction Policies and AppLocker, explains how to deploy default Software Restriction Policy (SRP) or AppLocker rules to ensure only programs installed in protected locations can run. It discusses how to force an application to launch with standard user privileges even if the user is an administrator and how to blacklist an application using SRP or AppLocker.

Chapter 10, Least Privilege in Windows XP, covers how to redeploy Windows XP with Least Privilege Security configured and identify problems with applications caused by Least Privilege Security using the Microsoft Deployment Toolkit. It also explains how to mitigate the problems and limitations users may face when running with a Least Privilege Security account and how to handle ActiveX controls in Windows XP.

Chapter 11, Preparing Vista and Windows 7 for Least Privilege Security, explains how to collect and analyze data to identify any potential compatibility problems with Least Privilege Security and software installed on networked PCs using Microsoft's Application Compatibility Toolkit (ACT). The reader will learn how to analyze logon scripts for Least Privilege compatibility, how to prepare a desktop image with Least Privilege Security enabled from the start and deploy the new image while preserving users' files and settings.

Chapter 12, Provisioning Applications on Secure Desktops with Remote Desktop Services, explains how to install the core server roles for Remote Desktop Services in Windows Server 2008 R2 using Windows PowerShell. It also explains how to set up and understand Remote Desktop Licensing and configure Remote Desktop Gateway for secure remote access to applications over HTTPS. This chapter also discusses how to advertise published Remote Applications on Windows 7's Start menu using Remote Desktop Web Access.

Chapter 13, Balancing Flexibility and Security with Application Virtualization, covers how to sequence an application for streaming and virtualization, and how to set up the App-V Client to work with a server-less deployment model.

Chapter 14, Deploying XP Mode VMs with MED-V, explains how to deploy legacy applications that are not compatible with newer versions of Windows and how to set up Windows XP Mode for Windows 7. It also explains how to configure the different components of MED-V for managing and deploying VMs in a large corporate environment and how to prepare VMs for use with MED-V.

What you need for this book

The following software products are used in this book:

- Windows Server 2008 R2 (any edition)
- Windows XP Professional
- Windows Vista (Business, Enterprise, or Ultimate)
- Windows 7 (Professional, Enterprise, or Ultimate)
- Microsoft Desktop Optimization Pack (MDOP) 2010
- An application that is not compatible with a standard user account on Windows XP, Vista or 7

Who this book is for

This book is for System Administrators or desktop support staff who want to implement Least Privilege Security on Windows systems.

Conventions

In this book, you will find a number of styles of text that distinguish between different kinds of information. Here are some examples of these styles, and an explanation of their meaning.

Code words in text are shown as follows: "Now that we've got our machines configured with the WinRM service and listening on port 5985 (or port 80 for WinRM 1.1), we need to see if we can connect using the winrs command."

Any command-line input or output is written as follows:

```
net user Support1 ******** /expires:never /passwordchg:no /ADD
net localgroup Administrators Support1 /ADD
```

New terms and **important words** are shown in bold. Words that you see on the screen, in menus or dialog boxes for example, appear in the text like this: "The **Allow non-administrators to install drivers for these device setup classes** setting under **Computer Configuration | Policies | Administrative Templates | System | Driver Installation** in Vista and Windows 7 Group Policy allows administrators to stipulate devices that can be installed by standard users according to the device GUID as specified in the driver".

Warnings or important notes appear in a box like this.

Tips and tricks appear like this.

Reader feedback

Feedback from our readers is always welcome. Let us know what you think about this book—what you liked or may have disliked. Reader feedback is important for us to develop titles that you really get the most out of.

To send us general feedback, simply send an e-mail to feedback@packtpub.com, and mention the book title via the subject of your message.

If there is a book that you need and would like to see us publish, please send us a note in the **SUGGEST A TITLE** form on www.packtpub.com or e-mail suggest@packtpub.com.

If there is a topic that you have expertise in and you are interested in either writing or contributing to a book, see our author guide on www.packtpub.com/authors.

Customer support

Now that you are the proud owner of a Packt book, we have a number of things to help you to get the most from your purchase.

Errata

Although we have taken every care to ensure the accuracy of our content, mistakes do happen. If you find a mistake in one of our books—maybe a mistake in the text or the code—we would be grateful if you would report this to us. By doing so, you can save other readers from frustration and help us improve subsequent versions of this book. If you find any errata, please report them by visiting http://www.packtpub.com/support, selecting your book, clicking on the **let us know** link, and entering the details of your errata. Once your errata are verified, your submission will be accepted and the errata will be uploaded on our website, or added to any list of existing errata, under the Errata section of that title. Any existing errata can be viewed by selecting your title from http://www.packtpub.com/support.

Piracy

Piracy of copyright material on the Internet is an ongoing problem across all media. At Packt, we take the protection of our copyright and licenses very seriously. If you come across any illegal copies of our works, in any form, on the Internet, please provide us with the location address or website name immediately so that we can pursue a remedy.

Please contact us at copyright@packtpub.com with a link to the suspected pirated material.

We appreciate your help in protecting our authors, and our ability to bring you valuable content.

Questions

You can contact us at questions@packtpub.com if you are having a problem with any aspect of the book, and we will do our best to address it.

1
An Overview of Least Privilege Security in Microsoft Windows

If you've ever been responsible for implementing IT system security in an organization, whether for servers or any other networked devices, you'll know what a tough job it can be. While upper management expects the IT department to keep the company's data safe from hackers and unauthorized access, users and middle management often have other ideas about what constitutes good security, preferring to circumvent security policy or have themselves exempted, without a valid business reason. Sometimes complaints about security are justified, due to poor design or execution.

Security is often bolted on to projects as an afterthought, rather than being an integral part of a design from the outset. Poorly implemented security makes you, the IT guy, unpopular. So, where security isn't an absolute necessity, it's regularly omitted for the sake of an easy life. To make matters worse, many IT professionals have a limited understanding of security, not knowing their **ACLs (Access Control Lists)** from their integrity levels, making it difficult for uninitiated staff to support a properly secured environment.

To minimize problems, personal firewalls are often disabled and users' rights are elevated. While such actions may be acceptable as part of the troubleshooting process, such configuration changes frequently remain permanent. If effectively managing security on servers and network devices causes enough problems with uncooperative coworkers who demand unrestricted access 24/7, then security on the desktop is not only likely to start a mutiny (if not well implemented), but it also comes with a unique set of technical challenges that are difficult to surmount, even for seasoned system administrators.

Least Privilege Security may sound like a complicated principle that only those with a degree in computer science can comprehend. But the reality is that anyone who has configured a basic firewall or router is likely to have encountered this most basic security principle, consciously or not, and that it has a natural place in desktop computing, just as in any other IT sphere.

In this chapter we will cover the following topics:

- Exploring the principle of Least Privilege Security, and how it is implemented in different versions of Microsoft Windows.

- Understanding how system privileges are used to control the aspects of an operating system's configuration that users can change.

- Looking at the benefits of implementing Least Privilege Security on the desktop.

- Examining how to overcome the most common technical and political problems and challenges while implementing Least Privilege Security.

What is privilege?

Each user that logs in to NT-based versions of Microsoft Windows, does so with a set of system privileges. **Privileges** differ from permissions in that they give users the ability to perform an action, whereas **permissions** allow access to an object such as a file or registry key. There are many privileges used to control access to various system functions, ranging from the ability to change the system time to restoring files and directories. Rather than assigning each user account with privileges individually, a set of built-in groups are provided with pre-assigned privileges. Users are then added to groups, in a form of role-based access control, as the following table describing built-in groups in Windows 7 illustrates:

Group	Description
Administrators	Administrators have almost complete and unrestricted access to the computer domain.
Guests	Guests have the same access as members of the Users group by default, except that the Guest account is further restricted.
Network Configuration Operators	Members in this group have some administrative privileges to manage configuration of networking features.
Power Users	Power Users is included for backwards compatibility, but has been deprecated and has no administrative privileges.

Group	Description
Remote Desktop Users	Members in this group are granted the right to log on remotely.
Users	Users are prevented from making accidental or intentional system-wide changes and can run most applications.

The two most frequently used built-in groups are *Users* and *Administrators*. If your user account is assigned to the Administrators group, you have a high level of privilege on the system and can perform almost any task that isn't specially protected by the operating system.

[
While members of the administrators group in Windows aren't completely unrestricted, it is possible to override operating system protections and make any desired changes.
]

In contrast, if your user account is assigned to the Users Group, you can run installed programs and change settings that won't affect system stability, but you can't install software to the restricted Program Files directory, or modify protected areas of the registry or Windows directory. The *Power Users* group was often used in Windows NT, 2000, and XP, but was essentially an administrator with a few less privileges. Microsoft decided to deprecate this group in Windows Vista, preferring system administrators to assign users to either the users or administrators group, as it was easy for power users to escalate to administrative privilege. You should, however, note that the Power Users group still exists in Vista and Windows 7 for compatibility reasons, but isn't assigned any privileges.

[
The built-in administrator account is disabled out of the box in Vista and Windows 7, and UAC prompts are not triggered for this account by default. This behavior can be changed in Group Policy.
]

What is Least Privilege Security?

Least Privilege Security is the practice of assigning users and programs the minimum permissions required to complete a given task. For example, if your daily duties include checking e-mail, surfing the Internet, and running a human resources application, then your user account should not be granted administrator privileges on your desktop. None of these tasks warrant anything more than standard user privileges. A standard user does not have any administrative access to the local system, and as such is not able to change critical settings that might affect system stability, security, or other users on the same machine. While this is a simplification, as it's likely that less privileges are required to run these applications than those granted to a standard user, it becomes impractical to study the privileges required for each and every operation that a user might carry out. Today, Least Privilege Security is most often referred to when discussing the protection of systems, rather than information in computer systems. As we enter an age when regulatory compliance and protection of information becomes more prevalent, it's interesting to note that Least Privilege Security is just as much about protecting information as it is about protecting the system—both go hand in hand. Programs generally run with the same set of privileges that are granted to the user. So, if you accidently launch a piece of malware from the Internet while you are logged in with administrator privileges, the malware has the ability to make the same changes and access the same information as your high-privileged administrator account.

> Most current malware relies on users having administrative privileges to install. If more users run with non-admin accounts, the situation is likely to change. Least Privilege Security should be further secured with the use of antivirus software and other protection technologies, such as Software Restriction Policy and AppLocker.

Limiting the damage from accidental errors with Least Privilege Security

Considering the threat landscape has changed beyond recognition in recent years, users will often counter least privilege accounts, insisting that *I'll be careful* or *I know what I'm doing*. When users undertake risky activities such as browsing the Internet (computer expert or not), it's impossible to be sure that malevolent software won't be accidently launched through malicious code embedded in web pages, which is intended to launch silently without the user's knowledge, or exploit an unpatched vulnerability in the operating system. While antivirus software can provide a certain degree of protection, many exploits cannot be detected by even the best antivirus programs. A defense-in-depth strategy that includes both antivirus and Least Privilege Security, among other measures, is far more effective than any one protection mechanism alone. Users often have blind faith in antivirus, software believing it will protect them from all evil. Browsing the Internet is just one example of a risky activity. Malware can find its way into systems through removable media, CDs, and e-mail, and then propagate throughout a network, causing untold amounts of damage and lost productivity.

Reducing system access to the minimum with Least Privilege Security

A word processor is unlikely to need privileged access to a system. If we limit the level of privilege that an application has to a system, so users can perform only the tasks required to complete the job, then maintaining systems becomes much easier. Privileges can be assigned to user accounts through the built-in administrators and users groups in Windows NT, providing system administrators with an easy way to restrict privileges for the majority of users. While this doesn't necessarily achieve true Least Privilege Security — for example, why would a word processing application need to change a system's power scheme — it is a reasonable trade-off between security, manageability, and usability in most production environments.

Least Privilege Security in Windows

In 1993, Windows NT 3.1, which was designed for business use, introduced the NTFS filesystem and centralized security. Despite that, 9.x consumer editions of Windows existed in parallel with NT for some time, and the concept of securable objects was never introduced into the 9.x line. Starting with Windows XP, the distinction between consumer and business versions of Windows disappeared, at least from a technology point of view, as Windows XP was based on Windows 2000 and replaced Windows ME for home users.

Windows 9.x

The FAT/FAT32 (**F**ile **A**llocation **T**able) filesystem used in 9.x editions of Windows didn't support the use of access control lists. Therefore, there were no strict means of controlling access to specified files and registry keys for a set of defined users. All users were effectively administrators. There were some methods for controlling what users could do, but it was far from what was available in more sophisticated operating systems of the time.

Ease of use has always been one of Windows strong selling points, and the wide choice of applications has helped it become the most prevalent OS on the desktop.

Windows NT (New Technology)

Windows NT, which spawned Windows 2000, XP, Vista, and Windows 7 has many fundamental differences from DOS-based Windows. However, the most important point in this discussion is its use of NTFS—a filesystem that is considerably more reliable and flexible than FAT and supports the concept of access control. This provides NT-based systems with a foundation that can be secured and protected according to a user's role. Along with other features such as a stable kernel, the ability to assign users with system privileges, and computers with system policy, NT provided the stability and security features required from a true business-grade operating system.

NT had no built-in equivalent to the *switch user* (su) command in Unix, so it was common that all users would be assigned to the administrators group on any one system, or at a minimum power users, which was essentially the same as administrators with a few less privileges. This started the trend on Windows NT, despite a sound security model being in place, for all users to run with administrative privileges. The future merger of the NT line and DOS-based 9.x versions of Windows ensured that the practice of running with administrative privileges would be entrenched for years to come.

An unfortunate side effect was that application developers commonly ran with administrative privileges, meaning that their applications would not run correctly under a standard user account. Even to this day, there is much debate about secure application development and resistance from developers who refuse to work without administrative privileges.

> For an application to be awarded the **Certified for Vista trademark**, it must function properly without administrative privileges.

Windows 2000

Though the Windows NT 4 Resource Kit did include a tool called **SU (Switch User)**, similar to the Unix command-line tool, it was a separate product. Windows 2000 introduced for the first time a built-in command called runas that allows users to run an application under the context of a different user account without logging off. The runas command is an equivalent of the Unix su command and is facilitated through the secondary logon service. This new command-line tool and service were intended for administrators, in the hope that they would use a standard user account for everyday use, and elevate applications only when administrative access was required. It suffices to say that this never caught on. One of the biggest annoyances of runas is that it can't be used to launch Explorer or certain control panel applets, without using messy workarounds.

runas isn't limited to administrators, but for daily use its implementation is simply too clumsy and wouldn't gain user acceptance in most environments. Another major drawback of runas is that if a standard user needs to run an application under the context of another account, then all the access rights the standard user has to the network and local filesystem are lost if not shared with the elevated user. runas is best used in contexts where a standard user will elevate using an account that has access to all necessary resources, for example, when a sysadmin elevates from their standard user account to *Domain administrator*.

In Windows Vista and Server 2008, network drives mapped in one security context are not visible to processes running under a different account in the same logon session, regardless of the permissions assigned to the network drive. This behavior can, however, be changed by adding a REG_DWORD entry to the registry called EnableLinkedConnections, with a value of 1 under HKLM\Software\Microsoft\ Windows\CurrrentVersion\Policies\System and rebooting the system. runas has several command-line options, known as **switches**, which can be used to change the way elevated programs are launched. The /netonly switch allows users to retain access to resources on the local machine as specified by their primary account, but gives permission to networked resources according to the privileges of the account specified in the runas command. This can be useful for certain tasks where local administrative access is not required. Other switches such as /noprofile and /env allow users to control whether their own user profile or environmental variables will be used. While runas from the command line is likely the most convenient way for system administrators to use the full array of features, holding *Shift* while right-clicking on an executable file presents runas in the context menu.

Windows XP

If Windows 2000 was designed for business, then XP was a revolution for home users, finally merging the 9.x and NT range, thereby providing everyone with the security and stability of the NT kernel. This wasn't without its challenges, and to address problems with applications that weren't designed to run on NT, Microsoft created the **Application Compatibility Toolkit (ACT)**. ACT allows businesses to scan their networks, creating an inventory database of installed applications. Programs can then be tested, and if necessary, any problems resolved with the use of application compatibility shims (fixes). ACT comes with a series of predefined shims, several of which can be used to solve problems with applications that weren't designed to run as a standard user.

XP also includes new Group Policy settings called **Software Restriction Policy (SRP)**. While not intended to directly address Least Privilege Security problems, SRP does allow system administrators to dictate that given applications must run as a standard user. This is useful where users have to run with administrative privileges, but you want to restrict applications, such as Internet Explorer, to standard user privileges, minimizing the risk if users surf websites that host malware or browser exploits.

Windows Vista

While it has always been, in theory, possible for corporate users to run as a standard user on NT-based operating systems, it was always difficult and unrealistic for home users, largely because Windows wasn't designed with this in mind. Ease of use always prevailed over security.

For the first time, Microsoft tried to go some way to change this situation with the introduction of **User Account Control (UAC)** in Vista. Much derided and misunderstood, UAC is a collection of technologies designed to make it easier for users to run with Least Privilege Security and to persuade developers to design applications that work without administrative privileges. Before Windows Vista, many routine tasks required elevation of privilege. User Account Control addresses this problem by changing system privileges to allow standard users to change the time zone, power schemes, and other previously restricted settings. User Account Control includes file and registry virtualization that transparently diverts write operations for protected areas of the filesystem and registry to the user's profile, allowing applications that don't comply with the Windows security model to function correctly without any modification.

Finally, and most controversially, UAC prompts users before they're allowed to make any changes to the system that require administrative privileges. This behavior can be configured in several different ways depending on the organization's requirements. UAC have been criticized for being too ubiquitous, thereby increasing the chances that users will simply agree to elevation without considering the risks. Despite Microsoft's efforts to make it easier to run as a standard user, by default, the first account in Vista is an administrator, albeit protected by UAC. If users opt to create additional accounts, they are prompted to assign standard user privileges, though this is not mandatory.

Descriptions of UAC from Microsoft have been somewhat contradictory. One of UAC's original design goals was to make it a security boundary, providing a sandbox where privilege cannot be elevated without the user's explicit consent. However, after Vista's release Microsoft acknowledged that it was a security feature, and not a boundary when running in Admin Approval Mode, implying that it could be compromised and wasn't designed to be impenetrable.

Using least privilege concepts, Microsoft has tightened the security of system services. To reduce the attack surface, Vista's system services run with a minimum set of privileges. The service control (sc) command-line tool lets system administrators query and change the system privileges assigned to services. The following example shows how to use the command to determine what privileges are granted to the **Remote Procedure Call (RPC)** service:

```
sc qprivs rpcss
```

The following output shows just three privileges:

```
[SC] QueryServiceConfig2 SUCCESS
SERVICE_NAME: rpcSs
PRIVILEGES        : SeChangeNotifyPrivilege
                  : SeCreateGlobalPrivilege
                  : SeImpersonatePrivilege
```

Windows 7

Microsoft has attempted to improve UAC in Windows 7 by making it quieter and more configurable. While there is no doubt that UAC is more configurable in Windows 7, it is for you to decide whether or not it is improved. The default user in Windows 7 is still a Protected Administrator, but the UAC settings are not as stringent as those in Vista. Windows 7 provides users with a less annoying experience, but with the prospect that their systems could be silently compromised. When designing UAC for Windows 7, Microsoft endeavored to strike the right balance between usability and security. Windows 7 gives users more control over UAC behavior, and the new features can also be configured in Group Policy.

Professional, Enterprise, and Ultimate SKUs of Windows 7 include **XPM (XP Mode)**, which is intended to help smaller businesses migrate to Windows 7, while alleviating application compatibility concerns. It includes a license to run a virtualized instance of Windows XP and a new version of Virtual PC, which can integrate applications running inside a virtual machine with the Windows 7 desktop—blurring the line between installed and virtualized programs. Microsoft provides a managed version of XPM for larger organizations called **Microsoft Enterprise Desktop Virtualization (MED-V)**.

Least Privilege Security in Unix-based operating systems

In Unix-based operating systems it is common to log in with a restricted set of privileges for everyday use, and to switch to a different user account with administrative privileges, when required. Traditionally, Unix offered an all-or-nothing approach to privilege assignment. Accounts either had administrator or standard user privileges. This model has been supplemented in modern distributions with the ability to assign privileges in a more granular fashion.

Advanced Least Privilege Security concepts

Most operating systems, including Windows NT, use advanced Least Privilege Security concepts as follows:

Discretionary Access Control

Discretionary Access Control (DAC) is where system administrators assign access to a set of objects, such as a directory of files, and allow the user to change the security properties of those files. The user becomes the owner of the directory and can modify the security properties of all files within that directory.

Mandatory Access Control

Mandatory Access Control (MAC) allows system administrators to centrally control the changes users can make to objects they own. MAC helps prevent the flow of sensitive information from a high-privileged account to a lower one.

Mandatory Integrity Control

Windows Vista introduced a form of MAC through **Mandatory Integrity Control (MIC)** that prevents processes running with a low **Integrity Level (IL)** from writing to or deleting objects with a higher IL.

Role-based Access Control

Windows Server 2003 included **Role-based Access Control (RBAC)** that allows system administrators to control access, based on users' organizational roles. Focusing on users' roles rather than objects and resources, as with DAC, is a more natural way for system administrators to control access to data across an organization. DAC enforces basic least privilege concepts to protect operating system files and registry keys using groups, which are collections of users, whereas RBAC roles are collections of permissions.

Least Privilege Security in the real world

As servers are usually considered crucial to an organization, operators are often granted limited privileges to perform a restricted set of duties. A common example of this is management of backups in remote offices. Employees responsible for backup may have limited IT knowledge, but they need to change tapes and log on to the server to check for running backup jobs. It's preferable not to assign unqualified personnel administrative privileges on a server and create an additional significant risk.

In the same way that a firewall is supplied with all inbound ports blocked (requiring an admin to specifically open individual ports for Internet traffic to traverse one of the firewall's network interfaces to the corporate intranet) modern operating systems elevate privilege only when necessary. The firewall system of all ports closed, by default where the factory configuration prevents network traffic flowing from an untrusted to trusted network, also makes the device simple to configure. Issuing a command to open one or two ports is easier than trying to shut off hundreds of ports, leaving just a few open.

Benefits of Least Privilege Security on the desktop

Least Privilege Security is often applied to servers as a matter of course, but the idea of desktop security is regularly limited to the concept of antivirus software and possibly a personal firewall. The benefits that least privilege brings to servers also apply to desktops.

Change and configuration management

Though considered a security principle, the biggest benefit of Least Privilege Security is that it aids change and configuration management. Every time you log in to a computer with administrative privileges, there's the potential that the system's configuration may undergo unsanctioned changes, knowingly or otherwise. Least privilege helps to maintain the intended configuration of a system, but at the same time giving the flexibility to change it (if permitted by corporate policy enables System Administrators to maintain) and manage who can change what. Least Privilege Security enables system administrators maintain better standardized environments and reduce support costs. If the helpdesk can be reasonably certain of a system's configuration, it's much easier to support that system. If users are allowed to change important configuration settings without a good reason, the help desk faces a much tougher job, increasing the time required to resolve problems, thus driving up costs.

Least Privilege Security also prevents users from circumventing controls implemented by system administrators. If a user has administrative privileges, with the right knowledge, it's possible to circumvent Group Policy. Ultimately, if a user has administrative privileges, there's likely a way to break into a system even if other controls are in force.

Good change and configuration management provides stability. How often are support staff faced with queries such as *it was working ok yesterday*? Computers don't stop working without a reason. Something must have changed. If system administrators can prevent unwanted change, these types of queries can be reduced. Wouldn't it be nice to know that every time a user switches on their system, they can be sure that it will work as expected?

Damage limitation

If users are prevented from making unintentional changes to critical system components on the desktop, the risk of malicious or unsanctioned software finding its way onto corporate systems is significantly reduced. The likelihood of users being infected with drive-by internet attacks, rootkits, or worms is minimized as users need to specifically give permission for such software to run. A large number of today's malicious programs require administrative privileges to install. Therefore, a standard user is far less likely to infect a machine accidentally. Even if a standard user account becomes infected with a virus, the damage it can do is considerably less than if they had been granted administrative privileges.

You may be thinking that there are ways around some of the protections that Least Privilege Security provides, and you would be right. However, it must be understood that Least Privilege Security should be used as one layer of a comprehensive defense-in-depth strategy, and that other technologies such as Software Restriction Policies, Windows Firewall, and antivirus software, should be deployed to provide complete protection.

Regulatory compliance

Many organizations are subject to regulatory compliance, and all such regulations require that users are given only the privileges required to complete their work. Even if your business is not subject to regulation, it should be considered best practice to implement Least Privilege Security, to boost customer trust. Sensitive data is easily stolen from users if layered protection is not in place. If keylogging software is silently installed on a user's machine, then the program may be able to transmit captured data to its author without the user's knowledge. A comprehensive defense-in-depth security strategy would be almost certain to prevent such an attack.

Software licensing

Least Privilege Security can also help organizations to manage software licensing. While it doesn't necessarily remove the need to audit programs installed across an enterprise, enforcing a standard image using least privilege reduces the chances that your business will fall out of compliance through unauthorized or unlicensed applications being installed on desktops.

What problems does Least Privilege Security not solve?

Least Privilege Security shouldn't be viewed as a panacea for all security-related problems. It's perfectly possible that malware could install itself by exploiting an unpatched security vulnerability, which might have otherwise required administrative privileges to install. Freely available software on the Internet is often packaged in portable or a per-user form, which usually indicates that it can be installed without administrative privileges. Consequently, Least Privilege Security alone cannot prevent all unauthorized software appearing on your network, and should be used in conjunction with Software Restriction Policy. Least Privilege Security does a good job of protecting critical system components and configuration, but a virus could still infect a fully patched system. The damage would likely be limited to an individual user's profile, leaving the underlying system untouched. This damage limitation mechanism, provided by Least Privilege Security, makes any virus outbreak on your network less serious and easier to clean up.

Common challenges of Least Privilege Security on the desktop

The biggest reason to avoid least privilege on the desktop is that striking a balance between usability and security is much harder on a desktop than on a server. However, technologies do exist to help implement least privilege successfully on the desktop.

Application compatibility

The single biggest roadblock in running as a standard user is application compatibility. Windows developers have become used to logging in to their machines with administrative privileges. This inevitably results in software that requires administrative privileges to work correctly. One of Microsoft's goals with User Account Control is to try to change this practice, and force programmers into developing software as a standard user. Application compatibility problems with Least Privilege Security range from programs failing to launch, to not retaining user settings. Error messages appearing at inopportune moments, inconveniencing users, and making it appear that the application wasn't designed to run on the system where it's installed are a result of bad practice on the part of developers. Frequent UAC prompts in Vista led many users to think that the problem was with UAC rather than due to a poorly coded application.

Earlier versions of *Intuit's QuickBooks* software for small businesses were probably the most well-known Least Privilege Security compatibility offenders. Until recently, it was a requirement for users of *QuickBooks* to be a member of the administrators, or pre-Vista power users group, forcing many businesses to risk the integrity of their systems by allowing users to run with administrative privileges. Fortunately today, most commonly used off-the-shelf enterprise applications will run with least privilege user accounts. For legacy applications and other programs that are still incompatible with Least Privilege Security, there are many technologies that can be used to solve compatibility problems, such as virtualization techniques and compatibility shims, which will be covered in the second half of this book.

System integrity

Security is always a trade-off against usability, and least privilege is no exception. Implementing Least Privilege Security prior to Windows Vista involved a lot of work, and most system administrators simply didn't have the time, resources, or management backing to make it work in such a way that it would be accepted by end users. That's not to say that it's impossible to implement Least Privilege Security in Windows XP, but it does require time and testing on your part. There are many common settings that users can't change as a standard user in Windows XP. User Account Control has addressed most of these issues in Vista and Windows 7.

Let's take a look at the issue of changing a system's time zone, date, or time. As a standard user in Windows XP, you cannot change any of these settings. Changing the date and time is protected because *Kerberos*, the standard network authentication protocol in Windows 2000 and later, relies on date and time synchronization for successful authentication with a domain controller. If a system's date and time doesn't fall within close range of the domain controller, the user will not be able to log in. Hackers can manipulate the date and time to cover their tracks and as such this provides another reason to restrict access to these settings. For non-domain computers, Windows synchronizes the time and date with an Internet time server, so standard users don't require access to modify time and date settings.

Time zone is another matter as it simply changes the way the time is displayed to users, not affecting their ability to log in if the time zone is different to the server's. Prior to Windows Vista, standard users were not able to change the time zone, causing much frustration for notebook users. It may not seem such a big deal to most system administrators, but users are not likely to accept that they can't change the time zone on their notebook if they travel a lot, deeming it as a problem with their system. The time zone is just one example of a problem you will encounter when implementing Least Privilege Security in Windows XP.

In spite of it being considered a routine task by most users, standard users cannot burn data to a CD or DVD in Windows XP. As you can see, removing administrative privileges in Windows XP is likely to create problems very quickly if the change is not carefully planned.

End user support

Though Least Privilege Security makes it harder for users to break their systems, it also makes it more difficult for users to fix problems or make necessary changes without involving the help desk. This may not be a problem for desktops that are located in an office with easy access to IT support, but for remote workers without administrative privileges, should a serious problem occur, there could be a long wait before a solution is implemented. Help desks often rely on remote workers to change important system settings to fix serious problems. This is somewhat of a catch-22 situation, as it's likely that if a user doesn't have administrative privileges, those important settings can't be modified and the system will work reliably, but should something need to be changed, the user has to call the help desk.

It's commonplace for system administrators to rely on remote workers, who rarely visit the office, to install operating system updates and third-party software patches, which requires administrative privileges. Issues also arise when users want to install hardware. If a suitable driver isn't already available on the system, a standard user cannot add a new device driver. Many smaller businesses don't require users to adhere to a list of supported hardware, further exacerbating the problem. There are certain categories of employees, such as engineers and sales representatives, who may need to install or update software on a regular basis.

Even in a large organization, it may not be possible to deliver all such software automatically from a central distribution point. Help desks are not used to supporting Least Privilege Security as it's not the standard configuration in older versions of Windows. Along with many Windows professionals, first-level support and help desks often have little understanding of the Windows security model. To support Least Privilege Security, system administrators and help desks need to have a good understanding of basic security principles such as the Windows security model, User Account Control, and how to solve common problems related to Least Privilege Security. So, before implementing Least Privilege Security in your enterprise, you need to consider training costs for support staff.

Least Privilege and your organization's bottom line

While my own experience shows that in most cases implementing Least Privilege Security on the desktop is more than worth the effort, I'm not expecting you to take my word for it that least privilege is going to make a big difference to your organization's bottom line. Fortunately, there is independent evidence pointing to the fact that Least Privilege Security does make a difference.

Determining the affect of Least Privilege Security on productivity

Measuring the productivity of an information worker is much harder than for a traditional blue-collar worker. System performance and reliability plays only a small part in what constitutes user productivity, with usability, familiarity, and transactional efficiency also playing a role. While there is plenty of anecdotal evidence supporting the benefits of Least Privilege Security, getting hard figures is difficult. The best way to persuade management to adopt a desktop least privilege project in your organization is to conduct your own trials with a small but varied group of users, and compare variables such as the quantity of help desk tickets raised, user satisfaction, and productivity comparisons before and after least privilege is trialed. Running these tests will also give you some insight into the technical problems that will be specific to your organization. You should also set an example and run as a standard user, elevating to an administrative account only when necessary, to demonstrate to the users and management that least privilege is a feasible solution for everyone.

Reducing total cost of ownership

Without least privilege on the desktop, it's impossible to truly reap the benefits of a centrally managed infrastructure. Research by IDC covering 141 enterprises with 1,000 to 20,000 users shows that central management can save up to $190 per PC a year. Small businesses without a managed infrastructure benefit from improvements in Vista and User Account Control. While not all of Vista's security features can be emulated in XP, larger organizations can configure XP to run accounts as a standard user, and reap the benefits of Least Privilege Security.

Improved security

A study carried out by eWEEK before the release of Windows Vista showed that organizations that deployed least privilege for users on Windows 2000 and XP experienced a significant decrease in the number of successful security exploits. Vista was developed using the **Secure Development Lifecycle** (**SDL**) and with new features, such as UAC and service hardening, it is more secure than Windows XP. Microsoft's Security Intelligence Report for July to December 2008 (*SiRv6*) shows that malware infected Vista SP1 roughly 60 percent less than XP SP3. Changes in Vista make it more difficult to compromise the operating system and Internet Explorer. SiRv6 shows that Microsoft software was targeted 35 percent less in Vista than XP. This isn't without its downside, as attention has moved to exploiting third-party software. Research by BeyondTrust, a company that produces software to help enterprises eliminate administrative privileges, shows that running as a standard user mitigates 92 percent of known security vulnerabilities on Windows systems.

Summary

We should now have a full understanding of the principle of Least Privilege Security and its implementation in Windows, from the early days of no real security in consumer editions of the operation system to today's push towards Least Privilege Security in Windows 7. Before proceeding to the next chapter, we have:

- Understood how system privileges are used to control the aspects of an operating system's configuration that users can change
- Familiarized ourselves with the principle of Least Privilege Security, and how it is implemented in different versions of Microsoft Windows
- Become aware of the technical advantages and disadvantages that Least Privilege Security brings to desktop computing
- Understood the business benefits of Least Privilege Security on the desktop

In the next chapter, we will move on temporarily from the technical aspects of implementing Least Privilege Security on the desktop, to talk about the cultural and political challenges, which for many can be harder to overcome.

2
Political and Cultural Challenges for Least Privilege Security

While there's no doubt that Least Privilege Security on the desktop poses some technical difficulties, especially for older operating systems and legacy applications, the political and cultural challenges of implementing Least Privilege Security can be even harder to surmount. To help you plan a Least Privilege Security deployment and avoid unexpected surprises that you might encounter along the way, this chapter deals with the human aspect of security, and how the technical elements of a secure desktop can affect and upset the most important people in your organization—end users.

In this chapter, we will cover the following:

- Why users may not accept Least Privilege Security on the desktop
- How to clearly explain and justify the benefits of Least Privilege Security for your organization
- How to apply Least Privilege Security to different categories of users
- How to get buy-in from management

Company culture

Culture is often a roadblock to innovation and change, and understanding company culture is crucial to the success of any project, technical or otherwise. People resist change, and this is no less true in the area of computer security, as users almost universally perceive security as an inconvenience and something that hinders their work. Users' acceptance of new ideas and working methods largely depends on company culture.

During my career, I've worked for various organizations, each with its own unique culture. If you've never worked for a large corporation or have worked only for small businesses in a specific field, it may be difficult to appreciate the vast gap between cultures, how this affects what can be achieved, and how to go about doing it. Though it's possible (and maybe even desirable) to change your company's culture, that's not what this book is about. Instead, we need to determine what kind of culture exists in your company, and how to work with it so that Least Privilege Security will be accepted.

Defining company culture

Company culture determines how the employees and management of a company behave. For instance, to what extent do employees:

- Help one another and contribute to teamwork?
- Cooperate to achieve common goals that will benefit the company's bottom line?
- Respect each other?
- Understand the work profile of colleagues and other departments?

If your answer *to most of the above questions* is to a great extent, then it's likely that your company has a healthy culture. This will make deploying Least Privilege Security on the desktop easier in your organization, as users will make an effort to understand the reasons for the project, if properly explained to them.

Should your answer be not to a great extent, you're likely to have your work cut out. Employees may be defensive, unreasonable, have unrealistic expectations, or be aggressive. Also, if it's not deemed by users to be in their interests, IT is likely to struggle to get users on-side with any new project.

Culture shock

Assuming that users are currently running with administrative privileges on desktops and if you plan to take those away from them, then no matter what kind of culture your company has, you need to be well prepared to justify your actions. This is similar to taking a toy away from a small child. If users arrive at their desks one morning to find that they can no longer install the latest version of Quake, you're likely to have a mutiny on your hands.

While it may seem perfectly reasonable to remove privileges, you might be surprised at how quickly management backs out on support for your project, if faced with an unhappy workforce. Users may feel that such measures are draconian and that they are not trusted.

In large organizations, it's often the culture that such security measures are the norm, and employees rarely question security initiatives. However, it's still recommended to plan for the changes Least Privilege Security requires and be fully prepared for any cultural problems that might arise.

Culture case studies

The following case studies illustrate how culture affects daily IT operations. While they represent two extremes, both are common in the real world, including everything in between. It takes only a few days for a new employee to understand a company's culture, but understanding how it influences employee behavior is important for gauging the level of cooperation you're likely to receive.

Company A

Joe Ramsey works for Company A and is the IT department's biggest nightmare. He installs software downloaded from the Internet on his laptop, allows his 16-year-old son to surf the Web unsupervised, and changes settings on a daily basis. Joe calls the help desk two or three times a day, and the operating system on his laptop has to be reinstalled every three months. Joe's machine has been responsible for a denial-of-service attack against the company's e-mail server because of a worm that the antivirus software failed to detect, which cost his company $10,000 in lost revenue and damaged its professional reputation.

Company A is like the Wild West. Despite the costs to the business, users are allowed to use IT systems however they see fit, breaking IT policy at great expense to the company. Systems are not managed in any way and neither are users' expectations. The company's PCs are riddled with malware and illegally downloaded software. Users demand that new software and hardware be installed on their company PCs, whether or not approved by IT, and are perplexed if such requests are not fulfilled immediately.

Despite all the damage Joe has caused by ignoring IT policy, he is still employed. While other employees don't cause as much trouble, there could certainly be more employees like Joe. If the IT department rejects a request to install software or to make some change that doesn't fall into the category of business requirement, users get angry and often complain to their boss. This makes it very difficult for the IT department to manage systems and make changes based on business needs, as the culture allows aggressive behavior to take priority over genuine needs and requirements.

Unfortunately, employees that do comply with IT policy still experience problems with their PCs, with a high total cost of ownership and limited return on investment. PCs require constant maintenance, and the IT staff has little time to invest in improving systems for the benefit of the company's bottom line.

Implementing Least Privilege Security on the desktop in Company A is going to be tough. You will need to have a really strong personality, and be prepared to stick to your guns when the going gets tough.

Company B

In comparison, company B is paradise. Though there is limited management of PCs, users respect IT policy and rarely break the rules. Regular auditing allows IT to detect whether users have installed unauthorized software, and act accordingly.

Employees are used to following IT procedures for procurement of new software and hardware, and don't make requests that they know in advance are not business related. Users wait for the time specified in the service level agreement when requests are processed by IT, and don't use aggressive tactics to get their own way.

This orderly culture will make deploying Least Privilege Security on the desktop much easier, as all requests for service can be reviewed appropriately to make sure they work in harmony with Least Privilege Security. Company B's culture puts IT in a better position to manage systems effectively, invest more time in improving services, and help the company to stay ahead of the competition.

Getting support from management

The ultimate success of your Least Privilege Security project will be determined by user acceptance and support from management. A smooth and trouble-free implementation is in the interests of the business, and in the event that you should encounter resistance on the shop floor, it's good to know that you've got full backing from management.

In an economic downturn, you may find it easier to get the attention of management as they seek to cut costs as much as possible, and Least Privilege Security can certainly be considered a cost-cutting initiative, with many other benefits to help the company remain competitive during hard times.

Selling Least Privilege Security

Projects that implement some form of security measure are always a hard sell. This is especially true of Least Privilege Security, as business has little understanding of security beyond antivirus software and firewalls. It's assumed that if antivirus software and a firewall are installed, systems are fully protected against every eventuality. Those who are knowledgeable about IT security are aware of the fact that antivirus software is not completely effective and as threats become more sophisticated, security becomes less effective.

Security is like insurance, much easier to sell as a part of another product. Consumers expect cars to come supplied with seatbelts, and would no doubt prefer that PCs come already protected from common threats. Physical security is easy to see; everyone wants a lock on their front door as it's clear what the consequences of not having one might be. IT security is harder to quantify for those not well versed in computer science. Therefore, it's especially hard to sell as a separate entity. If users can't see a problem, they're not worried about it. The same applies to management; you have to present security as a real business problem that affects the company's bottom line, for it to be taken seriously.

It's best not to sell security directly, but include it as part of another project. The ideal platform for promoting Least Privilege Security is the deployment of a new desktop image, sometimes referred to as desktop refresh.

> A **desktop refresh** is a preconfigured copy of an operating system that's used for deployment to many desktops. Images help reduce costs by cutting out the manual steps required to install an operating system on individual PCs and help IT departments standardize configuration.

Many initiatives can be packaged along with a desktop refresh, improving the return on investment. You will need to demonstrate to management what benefits a desktop refresh will bring and how your project will help meet business needs. Some of the technical benefits of a desktop refresh are:

- Standardized image

- Upgraded operating system or service pack

- Least Privilege Security

- A move towards a properly managed desktop infrastructure that has Group Policy settings and other management technologies

- Changes to users' systems can be explained more easily as part of a desktop refresh

- Updated software

- Improved performance and security by removing unnecessary software and components

Communicating technical details to business managers is not effective as they don't understand the language. When a serious virus outbreak is discussed by management, you will hear statements such as *But we've got a firewall, haven't we?* This is a clear demonstration of lack of technical understanding and that management doesn't want or need to learn the technical ins and outs of computer networking. Many of us drive cars, but that doesn't mean that we understand or care how the engine works.

Use business language when communicating with management. Only present figures on how many viruses infected the network if specifically requested, or as a last resort. The fact that your network was infected by a hundred viruses in one week is of little interest to most managers. They want to know how this affected the company's bottom line. Having this data to hand is useful, if you're required to back up your claims, but using it as the basis for a presentation will not be effective.

Using key performance indicators

It is a good idea to identify Key Performance Indicators (KPIs) using your organization's business goals and map them to security risks. Mapping security risks to key performance indicators helps to get acceptance from management for your Least Privilege Security project.

> A **Key Performance Indicator** (**KPI**) is a metric used to measure the success of a process that helps a business reach a predetermined goal or objective.

Show management how Least Privilege Security, or preferably its parent project, will help you better manage security incidents. While it's useful to have data about how many security incidents the IT department has dealt with in a given time period, you should present this information only if it's demanded by management. Try to focus on how efficiently you manage security rather than the number of incidents that were dealt with.

Using key risk indicators

While security incidents on PCs often remain isolated and disrupt activity only for a short time, if you add together all these incidents, the loss in productivity over a long period of time can be considerable.

> **Key Risk Indicators** (**KRIs**) show the likelihood of a security incident disrupting business activity, and so directly affecting the company's bottom line.

For instance, if sales people need to sell a certain number of units in a given time frame, identify how a security incident might prevent that target from being met. This is part of demonstrating that security is a business problem, and not something that is just an issue for IT.

It may be useful to create your own KPIs based on how IT supports business processes, rather than relying on those stated in business documentation, making it easier to map KRIs to KPIs. You'll need to have a good knowledge of your business and the industry in which it operates to truly understand the motivations for particular KPIs.

Mapping CSFs to KPIs

Rather than looking at a list of key performance indicators for your company, it may be easier to examine security issues faced by your IT infrastructure, identify how they might affect **Critical Success Factors** (**CSFs**), and then map them back to the appropriate KPIs.

> A **Critical Success Factor** is an important activity that ensures a business will meet a goal or objective.

As someone who is knowledgeable about your company's IT infrastructure, you know what the security issues are. Looking at a list of KPIs and trying to map them to security issues could be a daunting task. Security incidents affect productivity, compliance, and business continuity on a micro level, making it hard to map security risks to high-level key performance indicators.

Computer systems create operational and compliance risks for your business. IT systems are so critical to the operation of most modern businesses that almost any risk introduced into a computer network has the potential to affect a large percentage of a company's KPIs. When presenting information to management, try to avoid using IT KPIs as the main focus, and if they must be included, do it sparingly and as the last example.

The following diagram shows how IT security risks can negatively affect the business bottom line using two terms that business leaders understand — key performance indicators and critical success factors.

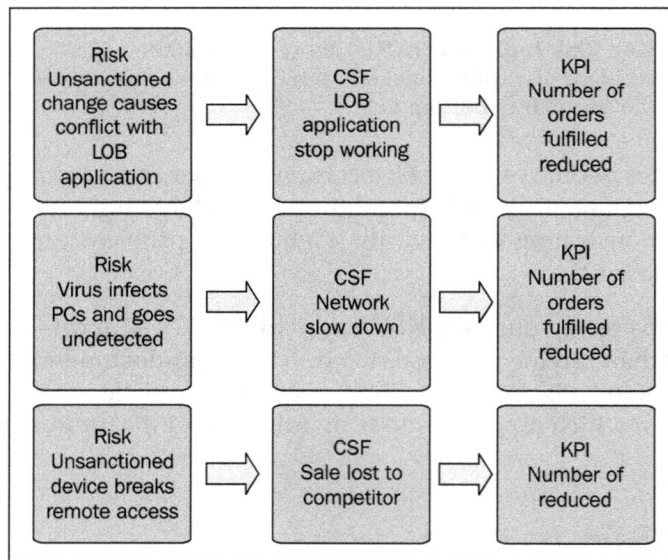

Risk	CSF	KPI
Unsanctioned change causes conflict with LOB application	LOB application stop working	Number of orders fulfilled reduced
Virus infects PCs and goes undetected	Network slow down	Number of orders fulfilled reduced
Unsanctioned device breaks remote access	Sale lost to competitor	Number of reduced

Security metrics

Data from **Intrusion Detection Systems (IDS)**, firewalls, and antivirus software can be used to help security professionals improve service and provide evidence for the need to implement new systems and projects. Data can be collected automatically and reports can be generated by security systems to show the extent to which security risks are a problem across the enterprise.

Threat modeling

Threat modeling may also be used as a means to show the effect of security incidents on critical business processes. Applications such as Amenaza's SecureITree can help you build detailed threat models to help promote security initiatives to management.

Reducing costs

Show management how future costs will be reduced by implementing Least Privilege Security or its parent project. A simple graph, based on data that you've collected might be used to prove how your project can save money and help improve productivity.

Instead of trying to forecast how much such a project could save the business, if you can get backing, try to conduct a trial on a small number of users. You can then compare before and after data to demonstrate that your project will make a difference, if implemented throughout the enterprise. Running a trial is more effective than presenting facts and figures without any real evidence of the benefits to your company. Obtaining hardcore data to show how Least Privilege Security improves IT services is not easy, so it's likely that you will have to prove the benefits to management yourself.

The following graph is an example of how you might demonstrate to management the benefits of a desktop refresh project in reducing help desk costs and increasing productivity over a three-year period.

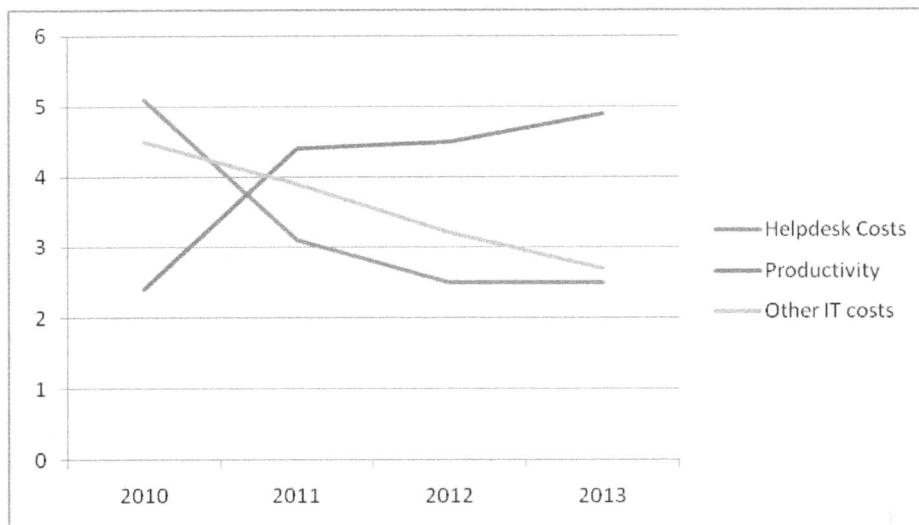

Security adds business value

Tell managers how Least Privilege Security, or its parent project, is going to add business value. Strong security helps business continuity. In the event of a serious virus outbreak, Least Privilege Security on the desktop can help minimize or even prevent systems from crashing and being subject to data loss.

If you formulate a security risk programme, it's useful to include governance on how security decisions are made. If the final say is down to upper management, record that fact. So, when security issues arise, it's clear who was ultimately responsible if the decision to ignore key risk indicators was taken.

Setting an example

Employees take the lead from their managers, so if a project to implement Least Privilege Security is to be successful, you must have management buy-in. Not only should management support your initiative, but they must also be prepared to set an example and opt in as well. Only too often, managers decide to exclude themselves from Least Privilege Security, on the basis that being a part of management is a good enough reason to be exempted. If managers don't think a scheme is important, then employees won't follow suit. Managers should also be held accountable, as they often like to exempt not only themselves but also the staff in their charge, without a solid justification.

Sysadmin standard user accounts

Sysadmins should also run with Least Privilege Security, thereby helping to set an example and catch problems related to standard user accounts in advance of its deployment across your enterprise.

User acceptance

Users are more likely to accept Least Privilege Security on the desktop if they understand how changes to their PC can help the company as a whole. Therefore it's important to make sure you not only communicate how their computing experience will change and improve, but also explain the benefits for the company.

Well-designed security is a business enabler. Just like seatbelts and good brakes in a car allow us to drive faster, Least Privilege Security on the desktop, as part of a defense-in-depth strategy, allows users to fulfill their responsibilities without being exposed to unnecessary risks and maintains performance and reliability, thereby allowing tasks to completed as quickly as possible. Information and systems security is in the interests of the company, ensuring it can remain competitive and survive an economic downturn.

Least Privilege Security terminology

If you need to justify the reasons for implementing Least Privilege Security, avoid using language such as lockdown and restricted privileges. Such terms don't go down well with users, and create the feeling that draconian controls are being put in place.

If users can no longer perform a particular task on their PC, be ready to provide some justification. An example might be the inability to change the system time. Explain that the time zone can be changed while travelling, but the system time must match that of the servers at head office in order to log on to the network successfully. You could also add that it reduces the amount of calls related to logon problems to the help desk. Ultimately, in a modern system, there shouldn't be any need for users to change the system time. If time synchronization is not working correctly on your network, it's likely to manifest itself in other ways such as logon failures. Therefore, you should nevertheless check that time synchronization is in order before removing the ability from users to change the time and date.

If you decide to implement a parent project such as a desktop refresh, you should try to avoid mentioning Least Privilege Security directly. Following are some more examples of how you can sell Least Privilege Security to users:

- **A faster and more reliable PC**: Least Privilege Security will help keep your PC running at optimal levels throughout its lifetime, thus helping you improve productivity.

- **Regulatory compliance**: The company is required to run secured desktop and notebook computers for all employees due to regulatory constraints. Though not all companies are subject to regulatory compliance, this is one of the most important justifications for implementing Least Privilege Security on the desktop. Your company will not be able to operate legally in the marketplace if you cannot prove to auditors that your systems are secure according to regulatory requirements. All the major regulatory doctrines require Least Privilege Security on the desktop.

If your company is not subject to regulatory compliance:

- **Best practices**: Regulatory requirements are based on best practices, which are developed to secure and minimize operational problems with IT equipment. While our company is not subject to regulatory compliance, we adhere to regulations as a best practice, which helps customers gain greater confidence in our business.

- **PC total cost of ownership (TCO)**: The cost of maintaining and supporting each desktop and notebook PC on the network counts for a considerable percentage of IT costs. Least Privilege Security is proven to reduce total cost of ownership and improve return on investment.

- **Financial savings**: The financial savings reaped from Least Privilege Security on the desktop will be invested in other areas of IT, to help improve services and contribute to the success of the company.

- **Network security**: Every desktop and notebook PC that connects to the corporate network is part of that network and cannot be completely isolated. Therefore, PCs must be secured using a defense-in-depth strategy that includes Least Privilege Security. Due to the complex nature of viruses and malware, one PC can infect all other devices connected to the same network, including servers that store valuable business data. Remote users can also infect the corporate network with malware. Comprehensive, layered protection is necessary because some viruses can cause complete data loss, and such an event could prove potentially devastating for the company.

  Viruses can also cause denial-of-service attacks on the network, meaning that if your PC becomes infected, it can attack servers, PCs, and other network devices, making the entire network run slowly and even disrupt service completely. Such downtime is embarrassing and costly for the company. Viruses can also be spread if you connect to the corporate network using your notebook from a remote location.

- **Software Licensing**: USA and European law states that the company must provide a valid license for all software installed on company-owned computers. This means you cannot install your own software on company computers, even if you have a valid license. Least Privilege Security on the desktop helps us enforce software licensing. Additionally, free software downloaded from untrusted sources on the Internet poses a security risk, as these free programs can contain viruses and can conflict with line-of-business applications, thereby rendering systems unstable. Such software is also unsupported by the IT department.

- **Competitive advantage**: Least Privilege Security on the desktop helps improve service and free up IT resources, helping the company remain competitive.

- **Downtime is expensive**: Least Privilege Security is proven to help prevent viruses, malware, illegal software, and unwanted configuration changes that create problems for employees and often result in expensive downtime.

- **Improved service from IT**: Least Privilege Security on the desktop helps IT maintain standardized desktop configurations across the enterprise. This in turn makes it easier for the help desk to resolve queries.

Justifying the decision to implement Least Privilege Security

Users may also appreciate understanding how and why the decision to implement Least Privilege Security was taken. Again, if you are implementing Least Privilege as part of another project, offering this information directly may not be necessary, but it should be available if need be.

As no security mechanism alone can prove completely effective, the company considered the various options and came to the conclusion that Least Security Privilege on the desktop was one of the most effective security devices when used as part of a defense-in-depth strategy.

IT has designed desktop images with Least Privilege Security so that systems can be managed with confidence, giving employees flexibility and security at the same time. Users will be empowered to work as productively as possible, benefiting the company as a whole.

Applying Least Privilege Security throughout the enterprise

While it would be great if it were possible to apply Least Privilege Security to all PCs in the enterprise, it's unlikely to be a realistic goal; there will always be employees who need to be excluded for solid business reasons. For example, consider an engineer who visits customer sites to repair telecom systems. The engineer's notebook is not only a tool for checking e-mail and writing customer reports, but is also used as part of their onsite toolkit. When faced with problems at a customer's site, it may be that engineers are required to install software that's not part of the IT department's approved list—for example, to connect a notebook to a telecom system or some other device.

Least Privilege Security doesn't accommodate such job roles easily. Though the engineer could run with Least Privilege Security most of the time, some tasks will require elevated rights. This may not be an issue if running Vista or Windows 7, as User Account Control accommodates such situations by allowing users to run with restricted privileges and elevate only when required. However, in Windows XP, the business will have to decide whether a particular group of users should run with Least Privilege Security or upgrade to Vista or Windows 7.

Deciding whom to exempt from running with a standard user account

In Windows Vista and later, users can reap the benefits of Least Privilege most of the time as a Protected Administrator. However, there are benefits in running as a standard user over a Protected Administrator, and you should aim to use standard user accounts whenever possible.

The following table summarizes the key differences in functionality when running with different types of user account in XP, Vista, and Windows 7. Use this table to help you decide what kind of user account to assign users in your organization.

	Standard User (Vista or Windows 7)	Protected Administrator (Vista or Windows 7)	Standard User (Windows XP)	Administrator (Windows XP)
Install software	No	Yes	No	Yes
Integrity levels	Yes	Limited	N/A	N/A
Modify important system settings	No	Yes	No	Yes

What not to do

Don't ask users what access they need to their systems. The inevitable answer will be full access. Start by making a list of job roles in your organization that are likely to require administrator privileges to complete some business-related process. The list is likely to be quite small, for instance just engineers. All other employees should be able to run with a standard user account.

The main tasks that require administrator privileges are:

- Installing per-machine software
- Changing domain or workgroup membership
- Installing device drivers
- Changing Windows Firewall properties
- Changing some network settings
- Manually installing Windows or third-party updates
- Changing power management settings (Windows XP only)

While the last point may seem relatively trivial, a bug in Windows XP sometimes resets power settings when a Windows update is applied. This can be frustrating for notebook users who don't have administrative privileges—when they find the notebook automatically entering sleep mode or closing the lid exhibits different behavior—as they cannot change these settings without calling the help desk.

Other tasks such as burning data to a CD or changing the system time have been omitted from the list as, under normal circumstances, these activities do require administrative privileges (Windows XP only). There are workarounds that can be used to avoid granting such high privileges to perform a single task.

If any of your users need to perform any of the listed tasks on a regular basis without intervention from IT, then you should consider allowing them to run with administrative privileges in Windows XP or as a Protected Administrator in Vista and Windows 7, and rely on other defense-in-depth security mechanisms to provide protection.

Managing expectations

Once you've got over the initial hurdles of getting your Least Privilege Security or parent project implemented, you may continue to face problems as users discover the restrictions placed on them that prevent them from carrying out non-business related tasks.

Service catalog

Creating a catalog of services that your IT department offers helps set expectations and manage Least Privilege Security on the desktop. All software, configurations, and hardware devices in the catalog can be tested against your Least Privilege Security settings, and give users a clear idea of what they can expect from IT.

Your service catalog should show users and management how IT services map to business needs, and so helping to establish trust between IT and the business, by showing users and management the value of IT services.

Chargebacks

If business is able to utilize IT services free of charge, there is the risk of abuse. For instance, users and their managers will think nothing of making requests for services if they know that there is no direct financial consequence. This situation can be changed by charging for services, and so creating an internal market.

Least Privilege Security on the desktop is affected because most problems are created by requests for services that don't fall within IT policy, such as for a piece of software or hardware that has not been tested with Least Privilege Security as it's not part of the IT department's service catalog. Requests for unauthorized services can create the perception that IT systems are broken because they are not able to support certain applications or devices. When chargebacks are implemented, requests for services that are not business related are minimized due to the direct cost involved, and managers think twice before authorizing employees to make unnecessary demands on IT.

If creating an internal market is a step too far for your organization, you could consider implementing a virtual internal market. This system involves charging for IT services using virtual currency or a points system. The idea is to show management how much each department, or even employee, costs the organization in terms of IT.

Maintaining flexibility

While security is a necessary evil in modern computing, you should remember that Least Privilege Security on the desktop may inhibit the IT department's ability to respond to changing business needs in a timely manner if not planned carefully or if the IT staff is not adequately trained. When Least Privilege Security is deemed to inhibit flexibility or the speed at which IT can respond, the project may fail.

Fortifying IT systems to provide business continuity has to be balanced with the ability to respond to changing business needs, and must not stifle the ability to innovate. Organizations that move slowly and are not able to respond in a timely manner often lose out to the competition, as IT systems play a key role in the ability to respond.

User education

While controls such as Least Privilege Security are arguably more important than educating users about security risks, education helps to establish trust and get users on-side so that they are aware of why security initiatives are important, how they are relevant to their own roles, and how security issues affect the business's bottom line.

Failure to communicate creates an environment of suspicion and control. It's important that users understand what IT is trying to achieve, and how you will help them perform their jobs better. If you can communicate the issues at hand, while promoting the fact that IT is offering users a service to meet real business needs, it's far more likely that your project will be accepted.

Summary

You should now be aware of the main political and cultural challenges that lie ahead for Least Privilege Security, and have identified what kind of culture exists in your organization. Before reading the next chapter you should:

- Understand the culture in your company and identify potential problems that may prevent Least Privilege Security from being accepted by management or users
- Know how to sell Least Privilege Security to management
- Prepare users for the change to Least Privilege Security
- Identify which users cannot run without access to administrative privileges
- Map IT services to business needs

In the next chapter we'll look more closely at the **Application Compatibility Toolkit (ACT)** and how to create application compatibility shims to resolve problems with applications that are created by least privilege security and/or **User Account Control**.

3
Solving Least Privilege Problems with the Application Compatibility Toolkit

The launch of Windows XP in 2001 heralded the long-awaited transition of consumer-orientated editions of Windows to the NT codebase. Microsoft designed the **Windows Application Compatibility Infrastructure** as part of Windows XP to help system administrators and home users solve compatibility problems with applications that were designed to run in Windows 98 or earlier versions of the 9x range.

In this chapter we will learn:

- How the Application Compatibility Infrastructure uses **shims** to modify incompatible applications on the fly
- Why using shims provides the best balance between compatibility and security
- How to create shims using **Application Compatibility Toolkit 5.5**
- Distributing compatibility databases to devices across the enterprise

Quick compatibility fixes using the Program Compatibility Wizard

In small enterprise environments or on home computers, compatibility fixes can be applied without using the Application Compatibility Toolkit through the user interface. If you want to know how the Windows Application Compatibility Infrastructure works in detail or if you want to deploy fixes to multiple devices, skip straight to the second part of this chapter: *Achieving application compatibility in enterprise environments*.

Applying compatibility modes to legacy applications

Compatibility fixes can be grouped together to form **compatibility modes**. Windows XP, Vista, and Windows 7 all come with a default set of compatibility modes out of the box. System administrators can also use **Compatibility Administrator** to create their own compatibility modes.

Compatibility modes can be applied directly from the user interface either by using the **Program Compatibility Wizard** in Windows XP, or by right-clicking on an executable file, or a shortcut to an executable file, and selecting **Properties** from the menu.

Windows XP contains the following compatibility modes:

- Windows 95
- Windows 98 / Windows ME
- Windows NT 4.0 (Service Pack 5)
- Windows 2000

As shown in the following screenshot, the **Compatibility** tab in Vista and Windows 7 (left) looks a little different from Windows XP (right).

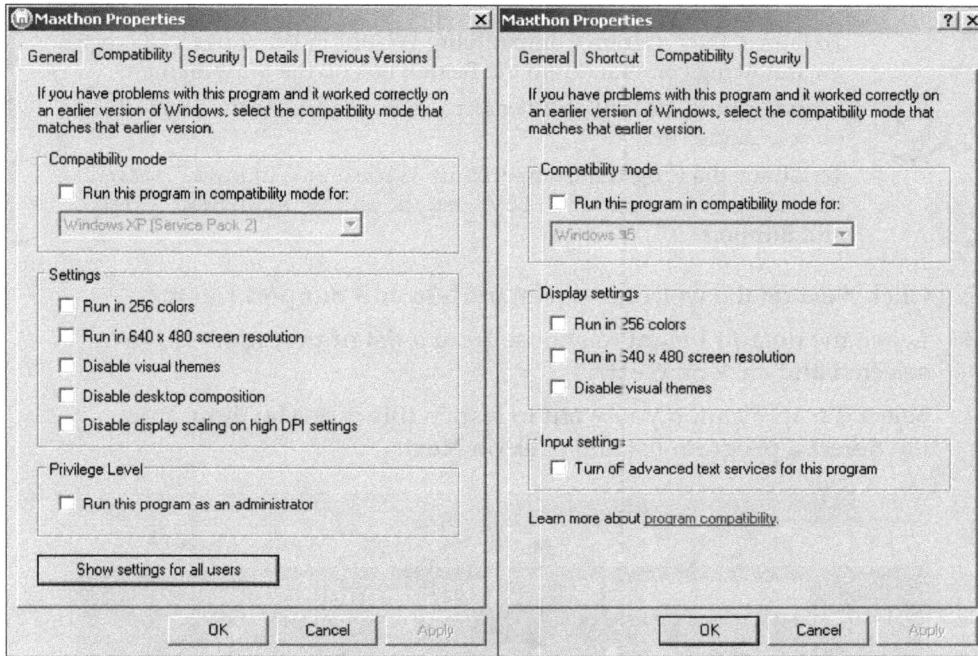

> Privilege level in Vista and Windows 7
>
> Note that the **Run this program as an administrator** option will be grayed out if an application manifest is included with the program.

Program Compatibility Wizard

Included in Windows Vista and later, the Program Compatibility Wizard allows users or system administrators to test legacy applications running against different compatibility modes.

1. To launch the **Program Compatibility Wizard** in Windows XP, select **Start | Accessories | Program Compatibility Wizard**.

> To launch the Program Compatibility Wizard in Windows Vista, type the following command into the **Search** box on the **Start** menu:
>
> `%systemroot%\System32\mshta.exe res://acprgwiz.dll/compatmode.hta`
>
> To launch the Program Compatibility Wizard in Windows 7, search for `program compatibility troubleshooter` in **Start | Help and Support**.

2. Click **Next** on the welcome screen in **Help and Support Center**.

3. Leave the default **I want to choose from a list of programs** option selected and click on **Next**.

4. Select the application you want to test, in this case **Maxthon**, from the **Select a program** list and click on **Next**.

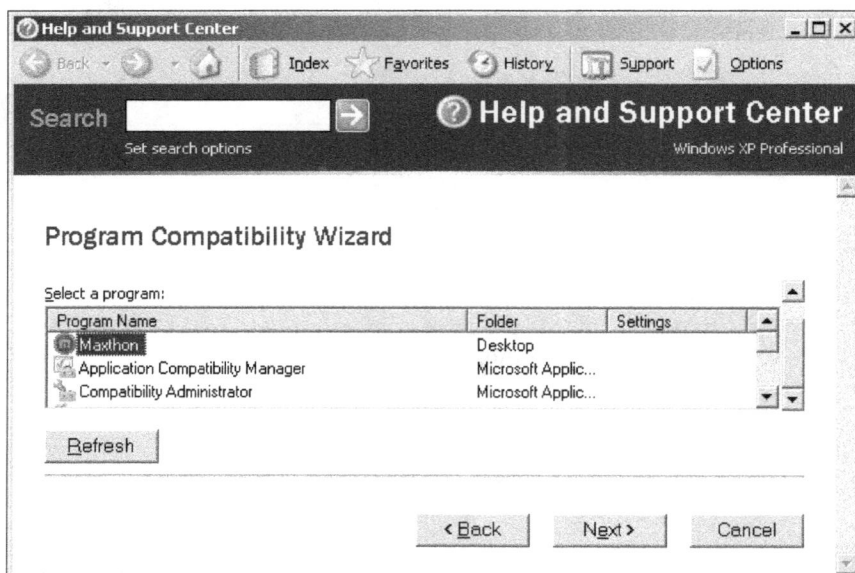

5. Choose a compatibility mode from the list, such as Microsoft Windows 95 or Windows 2000, and click on **Next**.

Compatibility modes set using the **Program Compatibility Wizard** only apply to the currently logged in user. Compatibility settings in Vista and Windows 7 can be applied to the logged in user or to all users. Administrative privileges are required to apply compatibility settings for a given application to all users of a system.

6. If required, select display settings (256 colors or 640 x 480 screen resolution) to be used with the program and then click on **Next**.

7. Click **Next** to test the compatibility mode against your application.

The application will launch and you can test it to see if the selected compatibility mode resolves the identified problems. Once you've finished testing, close the application. Back in the **Help and Support Center**, choose to either apply the compatibility settings or try different settings.

Browsing compatibility settings for each user

If compatibility modes are set on programs for specific users, you can use **Compatibility Administrator** to browse the settings for each user under the **Per User Compatibility Settings** node. This node only appears if per user settings are found on the system.

Program Compatibility Assistant

Introduced in Windows Vista, the **Program Compatibility Assistant** helps to automate the process of applying compatibility fixes to legacy applications by monitoring for known problems when programs are running. This feature runs as a service, and prompts users to apply suggested fixes for applications, either during the setup phase or when running an installed application. The Program Compatibility Assistant can detect the following problems automatically:

- Errors when launching setup programs
- Failures in install routines
- Failures caused by **User Account Control**
- An install needing to run as an administrator
- A control panel applet requiring administrative privileges
- Errors caused because a component is not present in the current version of Windows

- Notifying users about unsigned drivers on 64-bit versions of Windows
- Matching applications against a list of programs with known problems and notifying the user at program startup

The **Program Compatibility Assistant** intercepts an installation routine, prompting the user to try again using recommended settings.

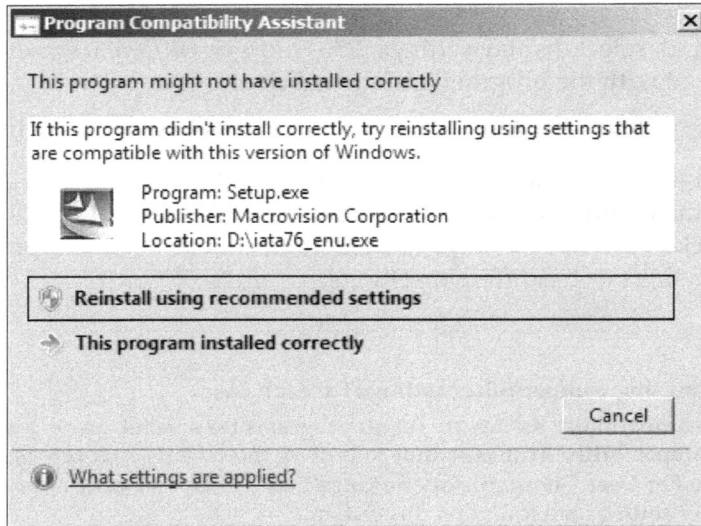

Disabling the Program Compatibility Assistant

The Program Compatibility Assistant is intended to help home users resolve problems with legacy applications. In an enterprise environment, to avoid potential problems with messages generated by the Program Compatibility Assistant, you should consider disabling the service in **Group Policy**. The **Turn off Program Compatibility Assistant** setting can be found in the **Group Policy Management Editor** under **Computer** or **User Configuration | Policies | Administrative Templates | Windows Components | Application Compatibility**.

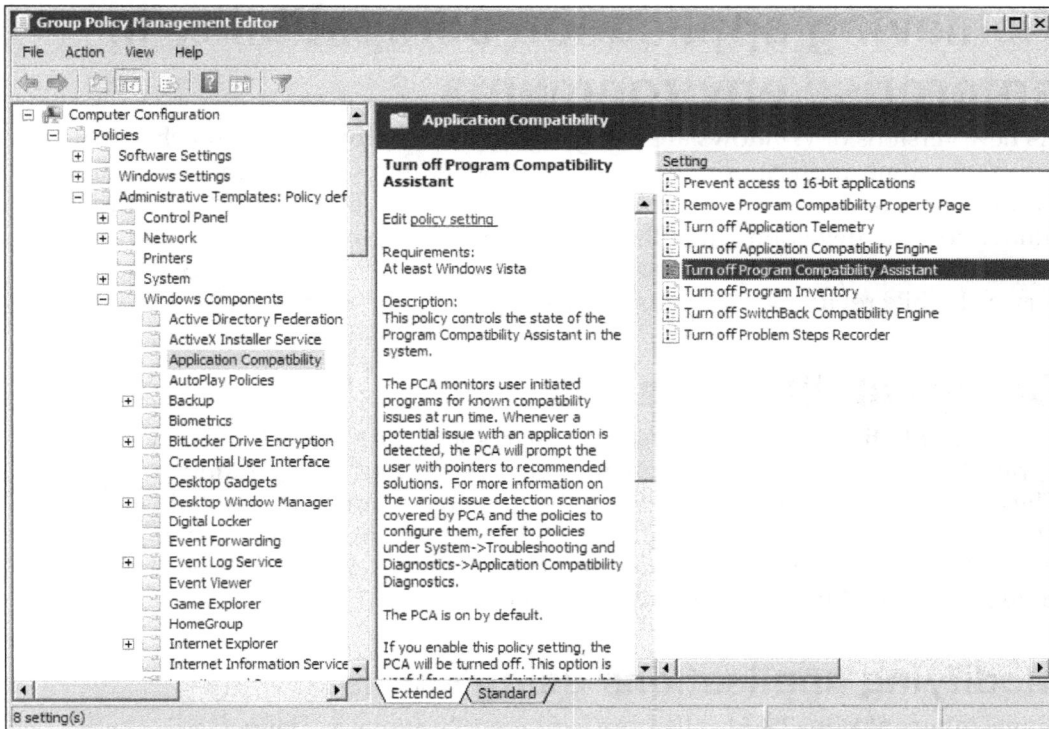

Excluding executables from the Program Compatibility Assistant

The Program Compatibility Assistant doesn't monitor programs that have an application manifest that marks them as compatible with Vista or Windows 7. However, if you want to exclude a program but don t want to disable the Program Compatibility Assistant completely, you can create a REG_MULTI_SZ registry value named ExecutablesToExclude under the following key:

```
HKLM\ Software\Microsoft\Windows NT\CurrentVersion\Compatibility
Assistant
```

Achieving application compatibility in enterprise environments

As new versions of Windows are being developed, improvements and changes mean that some applications designed for earlier editions of the operating system may experience compatibility problems in the later versions. Rather than restricting innovation and development of the OS in favor of compatibility, the Windows Application Compatibility Infrastructure was designed to allow the OS to move forward while retaining compatibility with legacy applications.

Compatibility fixes

Compatibility fixes, sometimes also known as shims, target specific legacy applications and allow them to run in current versions of the operating system. The advantage of using shims is that rather than maintaining legacy code in the operating system to ensure that all applications run without modification, which in turn makes the OS inherently more complicated and insecure, the legacy application code is modified by a shim instead of the OS.

Modifying applications using shims

Shims intercept Win32 API calls from legacy applications, as defined by system administrators, and then modify the call before passing the code to Windows for execution.

A legacy application fails to run in Windows Vista:

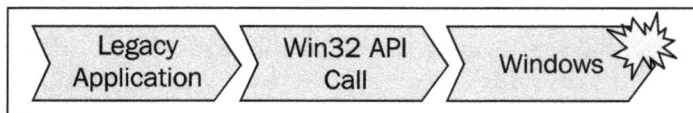

A legacy application successfully runs in Windows Vista:

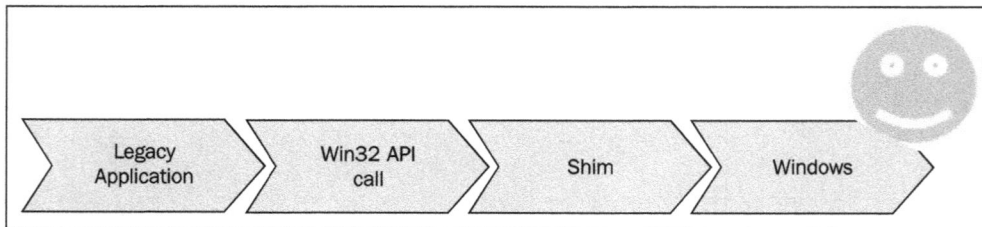

> **Shims** are bundled with the operating system in the system database, but are not part of Windows code itself. As such, shims are updated by Microsoft via **Windows Update**.

Enhancing security using compatibility shims

As far as Windows is concerned, the modified code presented to it by the shim is code from the application itself. Therefore, it's important to note that any application code modified by a shim runs in the same security context as the application. As shim code is not part of the operating system, it can't be used to bypass Windows security features.

It's common place for system administrators to either grant administrative rights to users or loosen **Access Control Lists** (**ACLs**) on files, directories, or registry keys to force legacy applications to run on newer versions of Windows. This increases the attack surface and makes it more likely that systems will fall prey to some kind of security threat. Shims on the other hand, don't require users to hold any additional privileges or modification of security principals. Therefore, shims are inherently more secure than workarounds such as relaxing ACLs.

One example of improved security when using shims is if an application needs to write to a protected area of the file system. Rather than loosening the ACLs on the given directory to ensure that write operations made by the application succeed, a shim can be used to redirect the request to a virtualized copy of the protected directory.

Deciding whether to use a shim to solve a compatibility problem

From a security standpoint, a shim is always preferable to loosening ACLs on security principals for solving compatibility problems. While failed I/O operations made by applications are the most common reason why legacy programs fail in Windows XP, shims provide a solution for many additional compatibility problems that loosening ACLs alone cannot solve.

Vendor support

Bear in mind, when considering whether to deploy shims in your organization, that because the application's behavior will essentially be modified, you may invalidate any support agreement with the vendor. If vendor support is absolutely critical for your line-of-business application, you should check in advance whether support will be provided if a shim is used to solve a compatibility problem. Better still, ask the vendor if they will modify the application to support the current version of Windows.

In-house applications

In the same way that shims are preferable to loosening ACLs, modifying the original application code is better than using a shim, as it removes an extra layer of complexity. Applications developed in-house should be modified by the developers and then redeployed. Shims can be used as a temporary solution if compatibility problems with line-of-business applications are likely to block an upgrade project for a significant time period.

Kernel-mode applications

Shims cannot be used to solve compatibility problems with drivers and other software that hooks deep into the operating system, such as antivirus programs. Shims run in user-mode, so drivers and kernel-mode software must be modified at source if there are compatibility problems with the latest version of Windows.

Creating shims for your legacy applications

Custom databases are created using Compatibility Administrator, part of the Application Compatibility Toolkit, and contain:

- **Compatibility fixes (shims)**: Compatibility fixes can be applied to specific applications installed on devices across your organization.
- **Custom compatibility modes**: Custom compatibility modes can be added to the default list that ships with Windows.
- **Apphelp messages**: Apphelp messages inform users about compatibility problems with specific software and optionally block programs from running.

Shims can be packaged with each application as you deploy software on your network, or you can manage a central database that contains all the shims required for your applications and deploy the database to every machine.

[Compatibility Modes are collections of shims used to address problems with legacy applications that were designed to run on a specific platform.]

> **Viewing the fixes included in a compatibility mode**
>
> Follow the instructions to add a compatibility fix to a custom database using **Compatibility Manager**, but instead of pressing *Ctrl+P* to add a fix, press *Ctrl+L* to add a compatibility mode. At the bottom of the **Create a Custom Compatibility Mode** dialog box, click on **Copy Mode**. The fixes included in the selected compatibility mode are then displayed under **Compatibility fixes for the mode** on the right.

On small networks, where only a handful of legacy applications require shims for compatibility purposes, it may be feasible to package a **custom database** with each application. This requires a developer or system administrator who is familiar with application packaging technology, and each package must be tested thoroughly. Shims can be difficult to track if they're embedded into application installer packages. If many applications require shims, a more scalable solution is to maintain a single central custom database and update it on client machines as necessary. Your custom database can be deployed using a Group Policy startup script. Very large organizations can manage several sets of custom databases and deploy them to defined categories of users for ease of administration.

> Custom databases must be deployed under the security context of a user with administrative privileges.

You could consider adding a custom database to the OS image that your organization uses to deploy Windows. Custom databases then only need to be updated using Group Policy when a change is made to the central database.

Solving compatibility problems with shims

This section describes the compatibility fixes that are most commonly used to solve application compatibility problems caused by least privilege security.

> You should note that you cannot create your own compatibility fixes, only compile collections of fixes (custom databases) modified to work with specific applications in addition to the default system database of customized fixes.

LUA compatibility mode fixes in Windows XP

The `LUARedirectFS` and `LUARedirectReg` compatibility fixes provide the two main workarounds for forcing legacy applications that write to protected areas of the file system and registry to work correctly using a standard user account.

LUARedirectFS

If a legacy application tries to write to a protected system folder such as `c:\windows` or `c:\program files`, the `LUARedirectFS` compatibility fix can be used to redirect all writes and subsequent read operations to the user's profile: `%systemDrive%\ Documents and Settings\%username%\LocalAppData\Redirected\drive\ filepath`. When configuring this fix for a specific application, you need to launch and run the program during the configuration process so that the Compatibility Administrator can detect which files should be redirected.

LUARedirectFS_Cleanup

Intended for use when an application is removed from a computer, the `LUARedirectFS_Cleanup` compatibility fix can be used to remove application files that were redirected to user profiles.

LUARedirectReg

Similar to `LUARedirectFS`, `LUARedirectReg` can be used to detect when a legacy application tries to write to the protected `HKEY_LOCAL_MACHINE` registry hive and redirect the write and subsequent read operations to the user's `HKEY_CURRENT_USER` hive. The application being fixed must be launched and run during the configuration process so that Compatibility Administrator can detect which keys should be redirected.

LUARedirectReg_Cleanup

For use when an application is being uninstalled, the `LUARedirectReg_Cleanup` fix removes redirected registry keys from users' profiles.

LUATrackFS

The `LUATrackFS` compatibility fix is for monitoring which files and folders a legacy application accesses when run. This information is recorded in a file so that developers can modify the application to work with a standard user account.

Creating your own custom database

Start by installing the **Application Compatibility Toolkit 5.5 (ACT)**. Refer to *Chapter 11, Preparing Vista and Windows 7 for Least Privilege Security*, for installation instructions. The only component of ACT required to create a custom database is the Compatibility Administrator. There's no need to install SQL, SQL Express, or AppVerifier to run the Compatibility Administrator tool.

Compatibility fixes are specific to different versions of Windows, so if you want to create a custom database with shims for Windows XP, you should create your custom database using Compatibility Administrator installed on Windows XP.

> Windows XP-specific compatibility fixes are not available when Compatibility Administrator is installed on Vista or Windows 7.

Maxthon on Windows XP

A legacy version of Maxthon, a replacement shell for Internet Explorer, doesn't retain customizations made by standard users because settings are stored in files in the protected `Program Files` directory. Let's create a custom database with compatibility fixes configured to target Maxthon that redirects file and registry I/O operations to virtualized per-user file and registry stores.

1. Log in to Windows XP as an administrator and select **Start | All Programs | Microsoft Application Compatibility Toolkit 5.5 | Compatibility Administrator**.

2. In the left pane of **Compatibility Administrator**, you'll see **System Database**, which contains **Applications** (see the following information box), **Compatibility Fixes**, and **Compatibility Modes**, and a new custom database.

> The **Applications** folder in the **System Database** contains customized compatibility fixes that address known problems with commonly used programs.

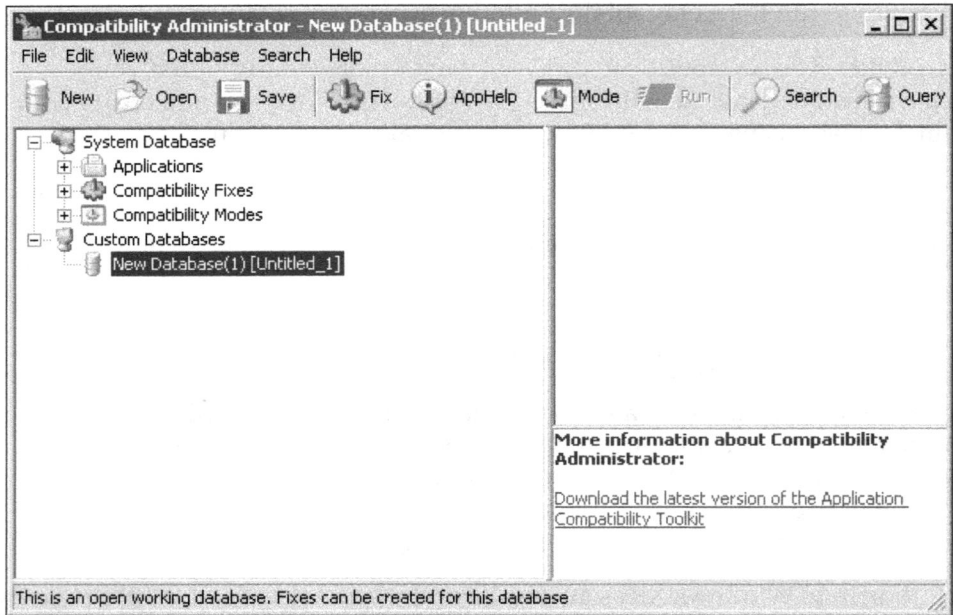

3. Under **Custom Databases**, select **New Database** and press *Ctrl+R*. Type `Maxthon` and press *Enter*. Now, press *Ctrl+P* to create a new application fix.

4. In the **Create new Application Fix** dialog box, type `Maxthon` in the **Name of the program to be fixed** field.

5. To the right of **Program file location**, click on **Browse** and locate the Maxthon executable file in the `Program Files` directory. Select it and click on **Open**.

6. In the **Create new Application Fix** dialog box, click on **Next**.

7. We're going to apply specific compatibility fixes to Maxthon, so under **Operating System Modes** select **None** and in the **additional compatibility modes** list on the right select **LUA** and then click on **Next**.

8. As we have already selected **LUA** (Least privilege User Account) in the previous dialog box, the appropriate compatibility fixes, `LUARedirectFS`, and `LUARedirectReg` are already selected for us. Therefore, no configuration is required on this screen and we can click on **Next** to continue.

> LUARedirectFS and LUARedirectReg are specific to Windows XP. Starting in Vista, UAC File and Registry Virtualization provides automatic redirection. The CorrectFilePaths or VirtualRegistry compatibility fixes can be used for more granular control over redirection.

9. On the **Matching Information** screen, we can control how the shim identifies the Maxthon executable. Let's leave the default settings and click **Next**.

10. Select **Yes, Customize these fixes now** and then click **Finish**.

11. Click **Next** on the **Monitor the Program** screen.

12. In the **Test run application** dialog box, click **OK** to launch Maxthon.

13. Once Maxthon has been launched, select **Maxthon Options** from the **Options** menu, check **Allow only one instance of Maxthon**, and click **OK**.

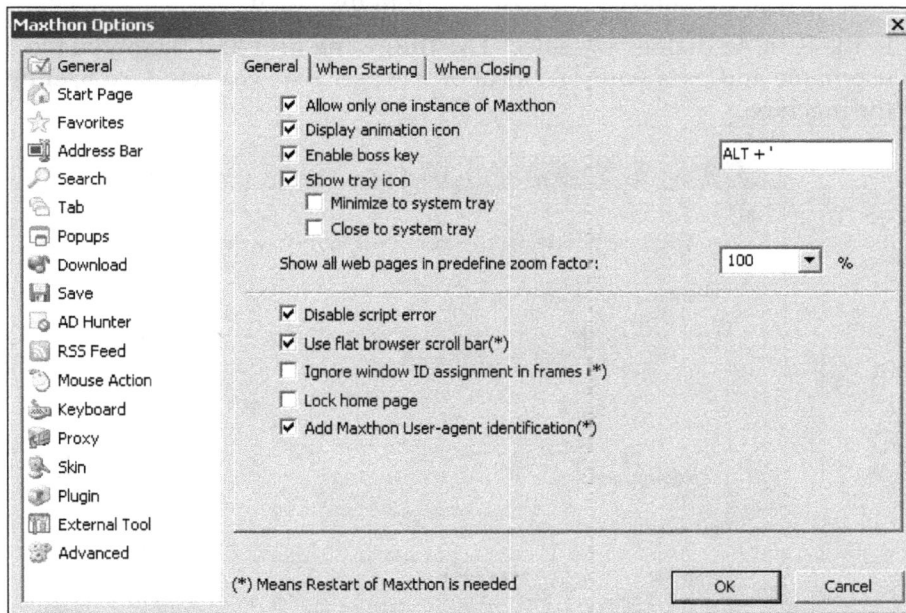

14. Now, close Maxthon. On the **Exclude File Extensions** screen, leave the **File extensions to be excluded** field blank and click **Next**.

15. The **Edit the File Redirection List** screen shows us all the files that **Compatibility Administrator** has determined to be redirected to a per-user location. Let's select all the files listed and click **Next**.

16. Click **Finish** on the **Redirection Locations** screen.

> As **Compatibility Administrator** didn't detect any failed registry I/O operations, there was no screen showing a list of registry key redirections.

17. Maxthon will now appear under the **Applications** node in the Maxthon custom database. Let's save the Maxthon database by pressing *Ctrl+S*. Name the database `Maxthon` and save it to your desktop.

18. Right-click on the Maxthon database in **Compatibility Administrator** and select **Install** from the menu.

19. Click **OK** in the **Compatibility Administrator** dialog box. This confirms that the database was successfully installed.

20. To test whether the shim is being applied, we need to start Maxthon as a standard user and see if it retains our customizations. Right-click on the Maxthon shortcut on your desktop, or the `maxthon.exe` file in `c:\program` files and select **Run as...** from the menu.

21. In the **Run As** dialog box, select **The following user** and then type the username and password of a local or AD user who is a standard user on the machine.

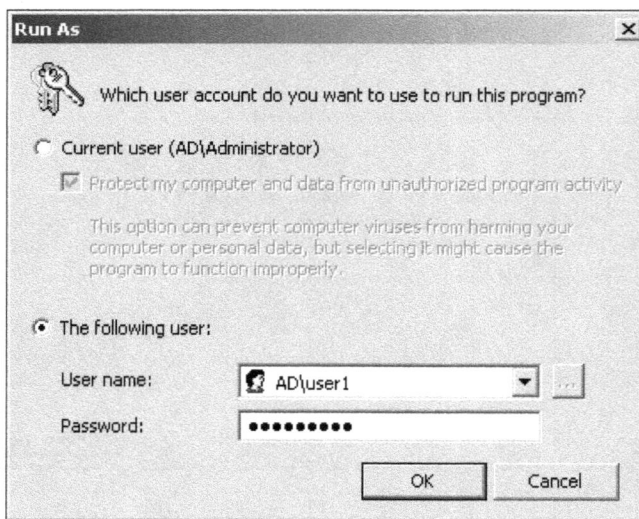

22. Maxthon will start. Select **Maxthon Options** from the **Options** menu, check or uncheck **Allow only one instance of Maxthon**, and click **OK**.

23. Close Maxthon and then restart it using **Run As** and the same limited user account.

You should now see that Maxthon retains configuration changes made by a standard user as the shim is redirecting the file I/O operations to a per-user location.

Working with other commonly used compatibility fixes

The compatibility fixes demonstrated in this section are available in all versions of Windows, starting with XP, unless otherwise stated.

ForceAdminAccess

Problem	The application has a hard-coded check to see if the logged in user is a member of the local Administrators group.
Fix	Apply the `ForceAdminAccess` compatibility fix using Compatibility Administrator.

1. Log in to Windows as a standard user. Start **Standard User Analyzer (SUA)** in **Developer and Tester Tools** in the Application Compatibility Toolkit under **All Programs** in the **Start** menu.

2. On the **App Info** tab, click on **Browse** and locate the **CorporateApp** executable file.

> **AppVerifier**
>
> Remember that **AppVerfier**, which comes with the Application Compatibility Toolkit 5.5, must be installed to use **Standard User Analyzer**.

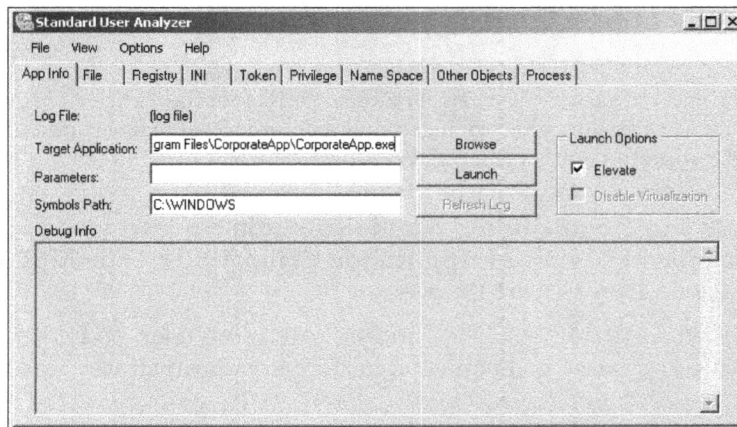

3. Click **Launch,** enter administrator credentials into the **Run As** dialog box, and click **OK** to elevate the SUA service. If SUA prompts that **All existing AppVerifier logs will be deleted, do you want to continue?,** click **Yes.**

4. Enter administrator credentials into the **Run As** dialog box and click **OK** again to elevate the **CorporateApp** executable file.

5. Run **CorporateApp** and make sure that the function that checks for administrative privileges runs. Now, close **CorporateApp.**

6. Return to the **Standard User Analyzer** program and you'll see that the issue count on the **Token** tab has increased to **1.**

7. Click the **Token** tab to see detailed information about the problem. Double-click the entry on the **Token** tab and three extra windows will appear with details about the problem.

In the **Detailed Information** box, you'll see that SUA has identified that **CorporateApp** calls the **IsUserAnAdmin** API to check for administrative privileges. This information is important, because the ForceAdminAccess check fix in Windows XP only intercepts the CheckTokenInformation API. The ForceAdminAccess fix in Vista and Windows 7 can intercept the following APIs that might be used by applications to check whether the user is a member of the local Administrators group:

- AccessCheck
- CheckTokenMembership (CheckTokenInformation in Windows XP)
- RegOpenKeyExA
- GetTokenInformation
- IsUserAnAdmin
- NetUserGetInfo
- SetActivePwrScheme

> **ForceAdminAccess**
>
> The ForceAdminAccess fix will not intercept the IsUserAnAdmin API in Windows XP. So, it can only be used to solve our problem with **CorporateApp** in Vista and Windows 7.

1. Right-click on **Compatibility Administrator** in the **Start** menu under **All Programs | Microsoft Application Compatibility Toolkit 5.5** and then click on **Run as** from the menu.

2. In the **Run As** dialog box, click on **The following user:** and enter the username and password of a local or domain administrator account.

3. Under the **Custom Databases** node in **Compatibility Administrator**, click **New Database**, press *Ctrl+R*, and rename it as **CorporateApp**.

4. Click on the **CorporateApp** database and press *Ctrl+P* to create a new fix. Under **Program information**, enter the application's details including the path to the main executable file.

5. Click on **Next** to continue. As we know the specific compatibility fix that we want to apply, select **None** under **Operating System Modes** on the **Compatibility Modes** screen and then click **Next**.

6. On the **Compatibility Fixes** screen, scroll down the list of fixes and check **ForceAdminAccess**.

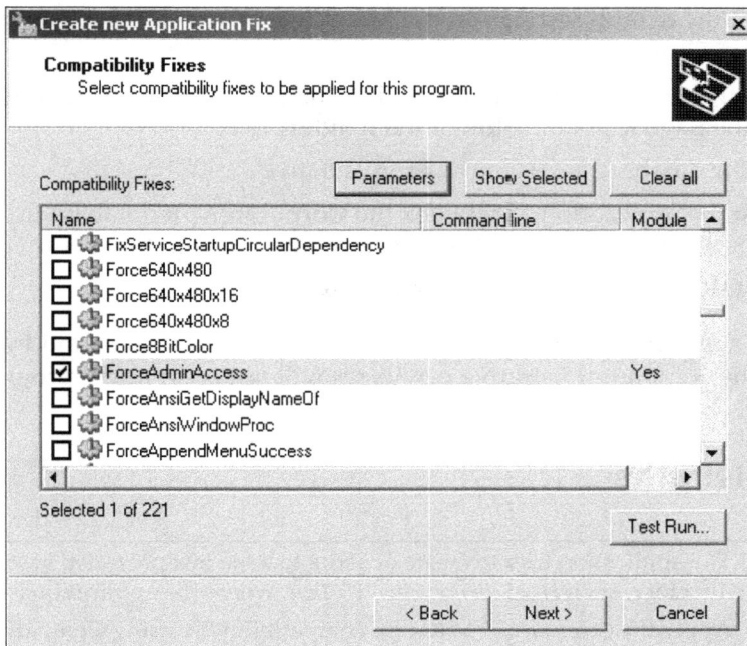

7. Now, click **Parameters** and then type an asterisk (*) in the **Module name** field and click **Add**.

> Files located in `C:\windows\system32` are excluded from the compatibility infrastructure by default. So if an application calls an API from a file located in the `system32` folder, any shims you've configured will be ignored. While this default configuration doesn't usually cause a problem, applications coded with **Visual Basic (VB) 6** or earlier may ignore shims as the VB runtime is located in `system32`. CorporateApp is a Visual Basic application, so we must ensure that all modules launched from the `system32` folder are included.

8. Click **OK** in the **Options for ForceAdminAccess** dialog box and then click on **Next** to continue in the **Create new Application Fix** wizard.

9. Accept the default settings on the **Matching Information** screen by clicking **Finish**.

10. Select the **CorporateApp** database in **Compatibility Administrator** and click the **Save** icon at the top of the window.

11. Save the database as `corporateapp.sdb` to `C:\`.

12. To test the application, right-click the **CorporateApp** database in **Compatibility Administrator** and select **Install** from the menu.

13. Click **OK** in the confirmation dialog box.

You can now run CorporateApp as a standard user on this system and the hard-coded check for administrative privileges will not prevent the program from running.

CorrectFilePaths

Problem	The application tries to create or write to a file in a protected system directory, such as `C:\Program Files`, where the application is installed.
Fix	Apply the `CorrectFilePaths` compatibility fix using **Compatibility Administrator**.

Log in as a standard user but start **Compatibility Administrator** with administrative privileges, as described in the steps for configuring `ForceAdminAccess` fix and follow these instructions::

1. Click **Open** at the top of **Compatibility Administrator** and open the **CorporateApp** database (`c:\corporateapp.sdb`).

2. Expand the **CorporateApp** database under the **Custom Databases** node and click **CorporateApp** in the **Applications** folder in the left pane.

3. Click **CorporateApp.exe** at the top of the right pane. Now select **Edit | Modify | Edit Application Fix.**

4. Click **Next** past the **Program information** screen, and **Next** again past **Compatibility Modes.**

5. On the **Compatibility Fixes** screen, scroll down the list of fixes and check **CorrectFilePaths.**

6. Click **Parameters** and then type the path of the file to be redirected and its new location as follows: old path;new path into the **Command line** field. For example, **CorporateApp** is trying to create and write to a file called config.ini in c:\program files\CorporateApp. We need to redirect the file to a location where standard users have permission to write. So an example redirection might be as follows:

   %programfiles%\CorporateApp\config.ini;%userappdata%\config.ini

> **Multiple file redirections**
> One CorrectFilePaths application fix can contain multiple redirections on the command line separated by a space.

7. Once you've added the file redirection, type an asterisk (*) in the **Module name** field and click **Add** to include all modules in the system32 folder.

8. Click **OK** in the **Edit Application Fix** dialog box and then click **Next** to continue in the **Create new Application Fix** wizard.

9. Accept the default settings on the **Matching Information** screen by clicking **Finish.**

10. Click **Save** at the top of the **Compatibility Administrator** window and then right-click the **CorporateApp** database and select **Install** from the menu.

11. Click **OK** in the confirmation dialog box.

VirtualRegistry

The VirtualRegistry fix is one of the most flexible compatibility fixes and can be modified by specifying command-line options. In this section, we'll look at the functions of VirtualRegistry that are of most interest in solving problems related to least privilege security.

ADDREDIRECT

The ADDREDIRECT option was introduced in Windows Vista. It allows you to redirect a specific registry key to a different location as specified in the command-line options. Let's have a look at how to add command-line options to the VirtualRegistry fix. In this example, we'll redirect a registry key that reads and writes to the protected HKEY_LOCAL_MACHINE hive to the HKEY_CURRENT_USER hive, which standard users have read and write access to.

Follow these instructions, logged in as a standard user but running **Compatibility Administrator** with administrative privileges:

1. Click **Open** at the top of **Compatibility Administrator** and open the **CorporateApp** database (c:\corporateapp.sdb).

2. Expand the **CorporateApp** database under the **Custom Databases** node and click **CorporateApp** in the **Applications** folder in the left pane.

3. Click on **CorporateApp.exe** at the top of the right pane. Now select **Edit | Modify | Edit Application Fix**.

4. Click **Next** past the **Program information** screen, and **Next** again past **Compatibility Modes**.

5. On the **Compatibility Fixes** screen, scroll down the list of fixes and check **VirtualRegistry**.

6. Click **Parameters** at the top of the screen and type the following option into the command line field:

   ```
   ADDREDIRECT (HKLM\SOFTWARE\Microsoft\PCHealth\ErrorReporting\
       DW^HKCU\Software\DemoApp\DW)
   ```

7. Type an asterisk (*) in the **Module name** field and click **Add** to include all modules in the system32 folder. Click **OK** to continue.

You'll now see the command line added to **VirtualRegistry** on the **Compatibility Fixes** screen and you can continue as per the instructions in the *Create your own custom database* section.

> **RedirectFiles and RedirectRegistry**
>
> The RedirectFiles and RedirectRegistry compatibility fixes are designed specifically for Internet Explorer. CorrectFilePaths and VirtualRegistry should be used to redirect files and registry keys.

Working with custom databases

When updating or maintaining a central custom database in your organization, you may need to deploy or redeploy the database, and merge new applications fixes.

Adding new shims to your custom database (merging custom databases)

If you decide to maintain a central custom database that contains all your application shims, it's likely that you'll need to update it from time to time when new programs are deployed. Compatibility Administrator allows you to open two databases simultaneously and copy and paste fixes between them. Let's create a new application fix and add it to a custom database. First you should follow the steps described in *Creating your own custom database* to add a new shim to a custom database and save it. You cannot create a shim without a database.

1. In **Compatibility Administrator**, open the database that contains the shim you want to add to the central database, in this case **Shim to merge**, and open the central database.

2. In this example, we want to merge the fix for **Demoapp** into the central database that already contains a fix for **Maxthon**. Right-click on the **Demoapp** fix under **Applications** and select **Copy** from the menu.

3. Now, right-click the **Applications** folder under the central database node and select **Paste** from the menu.

4. The fixes for **Demoapp** and **Maxthon** now appear together in the central database and you can click **Save** at the top of **Compatibility Administrator** to save changes to the central database.

Temporarily disabling compatibility fixes

If an application is updated to address a known compatibility problem that one of your shims addresses, you may want to temporarily disable a fix in the custom database while testing the new version of the program.

1. Click **Open** at the top of **Compatibility Administrator**, locate your central database .sdb file and click **Open**.

2. Select the fix you want to disable in the **Applications** folder in the left
   pane and then select **Disable Entry** from the **Database** menu at the top
   of the window.

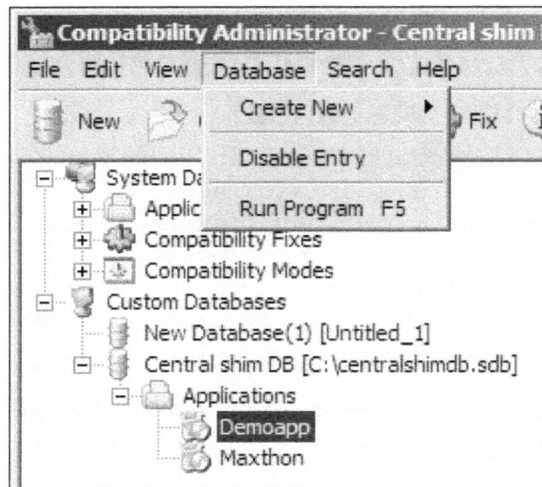

3. To re-enable the disabled fix, repeat the procedure as described earlier, but
   select **Enable Entry** from the **Database** menu instead.

Installing a custom database from Compatibility Administrator

When developing shims using Compatibility Administrator, you will need to test
if the fixes solve the issue(s) at hand. To do this on the same machine on which
Compatibility Administrator is running, you must install the custom database that
contains the fixes.

1. To install a custom database locally, right-click on your database in the left
   pane of Compatibility Administrator and select **Install** from the menu.

2. To uninstall a custom database, expand the **Installed Databases** node in
   the left pane of Compatibility Administrator, right-click on the database
   to remove, and select **Uninstall** from the menu.

> **Database locations**
>
> The System Database, which is included as part of the operating system and contains shims that resolve known compatibility problems with popular applications, is located in the AppPatch directory in c:\ windows and is updated by Microsoft via Windows Update. The AppPatch directory contains a subdirectory called Custom, which contains any custom databases installed on a machine.

Deploying a database to multiple devices

While Compatibility Administrator can be used to install or remove a database on the machine where it's installed, Microsoft provides a command-line utility called sdbinst.exe for deploying custom databases across multiple machines.

Finding the GUID of custom database

Once a custom database has been saved in Compatibility Administrator, it's assigned a **Globally Unique Identifier (GUID)** that can be referenced from the command line when installing or removing databases. To find the GUID of a given database, right-click the database in the left pane of Compatibility Administrator and select **Properties** from the menu. The database's GUID will be shown in the **Database Properties** window.

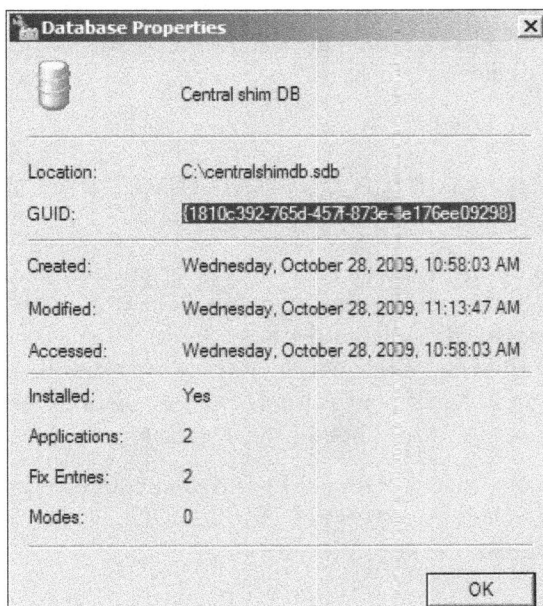

Database Properties		✕
	Central shim DB	
Location:	C:\centralshimdb.sdb	
GUID:	{1810c392-765d-457f-873e-4e176ee09298}	
Created:	Wednesday, October 28, 2009, 10:58:03 AM	
Modified:	Wednesday, October 28, 2009, 11:13:47 AM	
Accessed:	Wednesday, October 28, 2009, 10:58:03 AM	
Installed:	Yes	
Applications:	2	
Fix Entries:	2	
Modes:	0	
		OK

SDBINST command-line switches

There are four basic switches that can be used with `sdbinst.exe` and they are outlined in the following table:

Switch	Description
`-n "filename"`	Used to specify the filename of the custom database to install or uninstall.
`-g GUID`	Used to specify the custom database by GUID to install or uninstall.
`-q`	Silent install. No information is presented to the user during an install or uninstall operation. Used mainly for scripts.
`-u`	Performs an uninstall operation as opposed to the default install.

For example, we can install our custom central database from the command line using the following switches:

```
sdbinst.exe -g {1810c392-765d-457f-873e-8e176ee09298}
```

Alternatively, we can uninstall the same database by filename silently:

```
sdbinst.exe -u -q -n "\\networkshare\centralshimdb.sdb
```

[SDBINST must be run with administrative privileges to install and remove custom databases.]

Distributing or updating a custom database using Group Policy

Custom databases can be included as part of your organization's standard image. Alternatively, SDBINST can be distributed using a Group Policy computer startup script. The following batch file calls `reg.exe` and `sdbinst.exe`, both command-line programs that are included in Windows XP and later by default, to first check the existence of a custom database by verifying the presence of an uninstall registry key, and if the registry key is not found, install the database:

```
reg.exe query "HKLM\SOFTWARE\Microsoft\Windows\CurrentVersion
  \Uninstall\{GUID}.sdb" && (goto:eof)
sdbinst.exe -q %~dp0centralshimdb.sdb
```

```
:eof
exit
```

> **The %~dp0 variable**
>
> %~dp0 sets the working directory to the same path as the location of the
> batch file. This enables us to drop the centralshimdb.sdb file into the
> same location as the batch file called from the Group Policy startup script
> without having to specify the exact path.

If you want to update an installed custom database, as long as the new version
of the database has the same GUID as the one to be replaced, sdbinst.exe will
automatically remove the database and install the new version. In an update
situation, you will need to remove the logic in the batch file that checks for the
presence of an installed database with the specified GUID. This can be easily
achieved by adding a hash (#) in front of the reg.exe command to temporarily
prevent it from running.

```
#reg.exe query "HKLM\SOFTWARE\Microsoft\Windows\CurrentVersion
  \Uninstall\{GUID}.sdb" && (goto:eof)

sdbinst.exe -q %~dp0centralshimdb.sdb

:eof
exit
```

Now that we've got our batch file ready, let's create a Group Policy Object and
add it as a computer startup script. First, save the batch file in Notepad and call
it installdb.bat.

1. Open the **Group Policy Management Console** as a domain administrator
   from **Administrative Tools** on the **Start** menu and expand your **Active
   Directory** forest and domain in the left pane.

2. Locate your **Clients** OU, right-click it, and select **Create a GPO in this
   domain, and Link it here** from the menu.

3. In the **New GPO** dialog box, type App Compat DB startup script in
   the **Name** field and click **OK**.

4. Expand the **Clients** OU in the left pane, right-click the **App Compat DB
   startup script** GPO, and select **Edit** from the menu.

5. In the **Group Policy Management Editor** window, expand **Policies** under
   Computer Configuration in the left pane.

6. Expand **Windows Settings** and click **Scripts (Startup/Shutdown)**.

7. Double-click **Startup** in the right pane and click **Show Files...**.

8. A new window will open with the location of script files for this Group Policy Object. Copy the `installdb.bat` and `centralshimdb.sdb` to the **Startup** folder and then close the window.

9. Click **Add...** in the **Startup Properties** dialog box and then **Browse...** to the right of the **Script Name** field.

10. Select the `installdb.bat` file in the **Browse** dialog box and click **Open**.

11. Click **OK** in the **Add a Script** dialog box and the `installdb.bat` file should now appear in the **Startup Properties** window.

12. Click **OK** in the **Startup Properties** dialog box and close the **Group Policy Management Editor**.

Now if you restart a machine in Clients OU, the Startup Script will run as the computer boots.

> **Always wait for the network at computer startup and logon to the computer**
>
> Unless configured otherwise, it may take several reboots before the Startup Script runs. This is because, by default, Windows does not wait for the network to respond to all requests, speeding up the boot process. The **Always wait for the network at computer startup and logon to the computer** policy setting is located in **Computer Configuration | Administrative Templates | System | Logon**. If a device is configured to connect to a wireless network only after a user logs on, Group Policy startup scripts will not run.

Summary

In this chapter, we've discussed all the basic concepts of the Windows Application Compatibility Infrastructure and how to manage compatibility fixes in an enterprise environment. Before continuing to the next chapter you should:

- Understand how to use **Compatibility Administrator** to create a **custom database**

- Be able to deploy and update a **custom database** to multiple devices across a network using **Group Policy** in conjunction with the `sdbinst.exe` command-line utility

- Know how to update and add shims to a **custom database** using **Compatibility Administrator**
- Be familiar with the most common compatibility fixes used for solving least privilege security problems in legacy applications and how to deploy them

In the next chapter we'll look more closely at the technologies which compromise **User Account Control** in Vista and Windows 7.

4

User Account Control

User Account Control (UAC), introduced in Windows Vista, is a collection of technologies designed to make it easier to run as a standard user, and to help programmers develop applications that work without administrative privileges. In this chapter we'll cover:

- How the different components of User Account Control work together to provide a seamless user experience
- User Account Control's application compatibility features
- How to configure User Account Control on multiple computers using Group Policy
- The inner workings of User Account Control's core components

Running with standard user privileges was indeed possible before Vista, but required significant work. Limitations in Windows prevented standard users from performing many common everyday tasks. The additional skills required to manage a software distribution system to install applications meant that only the largest organizations or those with the greatest need were able to deploy Least Privilege Security on the desktop.

Windows 2000 alleviated the problem somewhat with Active Directory, which included Group Policy Software Installation as a method for small and medium-sized businesses to distribute software. Furthermore, Windows 2000 introduced the Secondary Logon Service and runas command, which were intended for system administrators in the hope that they'd log on as a standard user and elevate privileges only when required for administrative tasks.

> **Elevated privileges or elevation**
> When we refer to elevation or elevated privileges, it relates to the practice of giving a process or application consent to run with administrative privileges from a standard user or protected administrator account (we shall define protected administrator later).

With Windows XP came an application compatibility engine that allowed sysadmins to manually create application compatibility shims for legacy programs that failed to work correctly with standard user accounts. Again, from all but the largest organizations, this functionality remained hidden; many sysadmins were either not aware of its existence or did not know how to use shims.

Microsoft recognized that if running as a standard user requires extra steps, such as switching to a secondary user account to perform common tasks, it's likely that users will continue to run with administrative privileges. User Account Control is designed to make it more convenient for users and sysadmins to run, most of the time, with standard user privileges.

In most cases, sysadmins no longer need to identify which processes or applications require administrative privileges, as User Account Control can automatically determine if a process requires administrative privileges and elevate once consent has been given. This new workflow helps ensure that there is a balance between security and convenience. Home users also benefit, as User Account Control reduces the risks of running as an administrator by ensuring that elevated privileges are only activated for non-Windows binaries when a user gives explicit consent.

Similarly, assuming User Account Control is enabled, when a programmer is developing an application on Windows, it doesn't look good if UAC elevation prompts appear when the application under development is being run. In this sense, User Account Control encourages developers to follow best practices when creating programs for Windows.

User Account Control components

Let's look at the different technologies that constitute User Account Control. The following is a list of UAC's core components:

- Elevation prompts and auto-elevation
- Protected administrator accounts and Admin Approval Mode
- Windows Integrity Mechanism and User Interface Privilege Isolation
- Application Information Service
- Filesystem and registry virtualization

- Internet Explorer Protected Mode
- ActiveX Installer Service

We'll learn about these components in detail later in this chapter (except the ActiveX Installer Service, which is covered in *Chapter 7*). Here is a brief description of each component and how it relates to Least Privilege Security.

Elevation prompts

User Account Control automates the process of elevating privileges for convenience in many circumstances, and provides two different types of elevation prompt depending on whether the user is running as a standard user or a protected administrator. **Auto-elevation** means users don't usually have to decide which processes should run with administrative privileges. Also, it removes the need to right-click on an executable and select **Run as administrator** from the context menu to elevate a program.

Protected administrator (PA)

Protected Administrator accounts were introduced as part of User Account Control in Vista. They are intended to reduce the risks associated with logging on as an administrator, by issuing a filtered security access token that runs with standard user privileges until the user gives consent for a process to run with full administrative rights.

Access tokens

Access tokens contain security information for processes such as the initiating user's group membership, privileges, and other security related details.

The ability to elevate to administrative privileges at the click of a button makes it very convenient for home users and system administrators to run with standard user privileges most of the time and elevate only when necessary, thereby considerably reducing the risks involved in running with an administrative account. This UAC mode is sometimes known as **Admin Approval Mode** (**AAM**), as it requires the user to approve a process's elevation to administrative privileges.

Windows Integrity Control and User Interface Privilege Isolation

Windows Integrity Control and **User Interface Privilege Isolation (UIPI)** were introduced to help prevent malicious processes (that run using the filtered access token of a protected administrator account) from injecting code into processes that have been elevated to run under the same PA account with an unfiltered administrative token. The standard Windows security model prevents this when processes run using different user accounts. But as protected administrators have what is sometimes referred to as a *split token*, when a PA gives a process consent to run with full administrative privileges, it does so using the same user account.

> UIPI is not a security boundary. While it helps to block certain vectors such as shatter attacks, some Windows messages can be sent from processes running under the same account with low integrity to those running with high integrity. The only way to create a true security boundary that completely isolates running processes is to use the switch user function, sometimes known as Fast User Switching, which was introduced in Windows XP.

Application Information Service

The **Application Information Service (AIS)** invokes elevation prompts for users' convenience, allowing users to launch processes with administrative privileges as easily as possible.

Filesystem and registry virtualization

Windows XP contains an application compatibility engine that allows system administrators to apply shims. These shims can be used to redirect failed registry and filesystem I/O operations to locations that are accessible to standard users. However, the process of applying shims is not automatic.

UAC's filesystem and registry virtualization helps mitigate problems with legacy applications run as a standard user by automatically redirecting write operations and subsequent reads to protected areas of the filesystem and registry to a per-user virtual store. This helps ensure that many applications that would not run on earlier versions of Windows as a standard user will work without any intervention from system administrators.

Internet Explorer Protected Mode

Protected Mode in Internet Explorer helps to defend against threats using **Windows Integrity Control**. When IE Protected Mode is enabled, IE runs with low integrity, meaning that it can't write to or read from processes that are running with medium or any higher level of integrity, protecting processes from malware that may launch from an infected website. Protected Mode is the default mode for Internet-zone websites, and it prevents malicious websites from changing users' account settings.

The shield icon

Many settings, once that could be changed only with the help of administrative privileges, such as modifying the time zone, can now be accessed by standard users. The ability to change the system time is still restricted to users with administrative rights, as a synchronization error can cause logon failures in a corporate setting where the time is automatically synchronized with a domain controller. The time zone, however, simply changes the way Windows displays the system time to users. Notebook users may also need to change the time zone setting when travelling.

To make it easier for users to understand what functionality requires administrative privileges in Windows, the entire user interface has been revised to include a shield icon wherever elevation is needed to complete a task. The **Date and Time** control panel applet shows the shield icon next to **Change date and time** but not next to **Change time zone**. Similar examples can be found throughout the user interface in Vista and Windows 7.

User Account Control access token model

The concept of a protected administrator account is new to Windows, and the access token model needs to be understood to support and troubleshoot **UAC** effectively.

Standard user access token

When a standard user logs in to Vista, Explorer is launched with the standard user's access token. However, when the user wants to elevate an application, as in Windows XP and Windows 2000, the **Run as administrator** command can be invoked through a right-click in Explorer and alternative credentials must be entered to start the process with a user account that has administrative privileges. There is no split or filtered token. Therefore, the elevated process is running with a different access token than that of the standard user who logged in and started the desktop session.

> **Explorer**
>
> Explorer is the process that is used to present the desktop, sometimes referred to as the **Windows Shell**, to the end user. Explorer also refers to the application that is used to view and manage files in Windows.

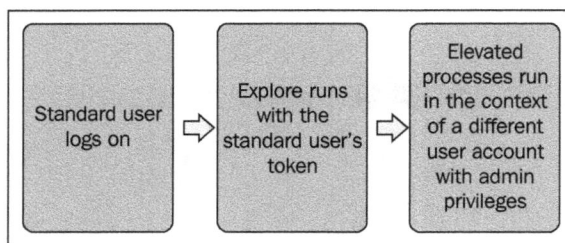

The previous figure illustrates the access token for standard users. Due to the fact that the elevated process will run in the context of another user account with a different security access token, standard users should bear in mind that when elevating a process to run with administrative privileges, the elevated process may not have access to the same local and remote resources as the standard user. This illustrates one good reason why applications should be designed not to require use of **Run as administrator** when logged on as a standard user, as functionality may be impaired.

The following screenshot shows how privileges are assigned to a standard user access token:

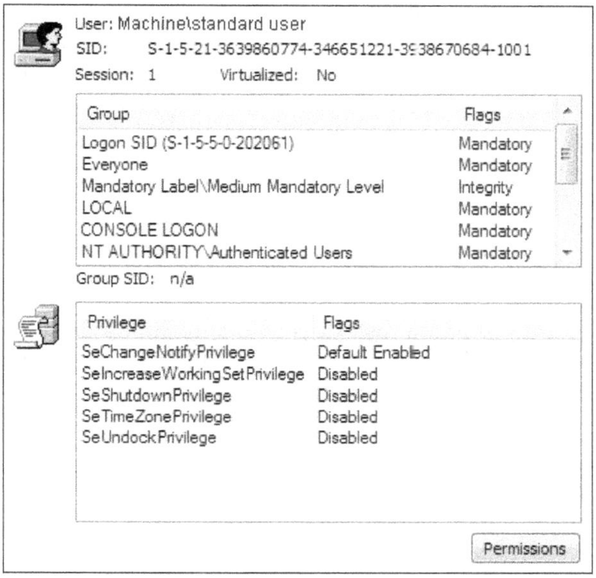

The next screenshot shows the change in username and privileges when a process is elevated from a standard user account with UAC enabled.

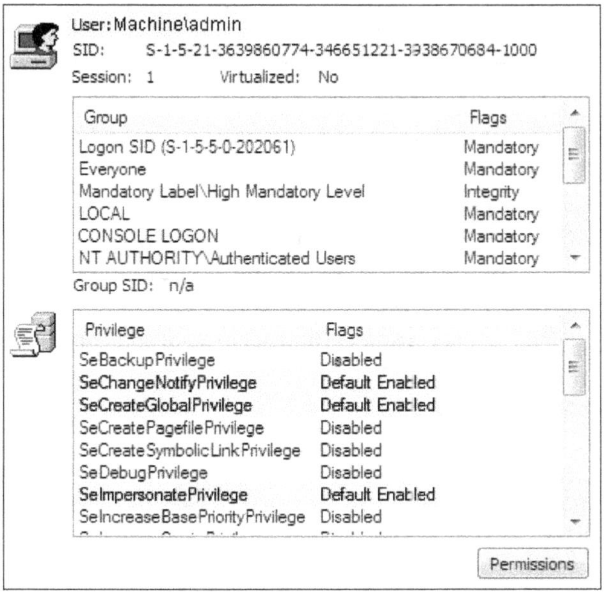

Protected administrator access token

If UAC is configured for Admin Approval Mode when a protected administrator logs on, Explorer is launched with a filtered version of the user's access token. This filtered access token removes all administrative privileges and renders it effectively the same as an access token issued to a standard user. Any processes the user launches are also run with the filtered token, unless a request for elevation is made and the user gives consent, or in the case of Windows 7, where auto-elevation occurs for certain Windows binaries.

> **Protected administrators (PA)**
>
> When UAC is configured for Admin Approval Mode, which is the default setting, all administrators who log in to a system are referred to as protected administrators, because their security access token is filtered to remove administrative privileges.

The following flowchart shows how access tokens are handled in Admin Approval Mode:

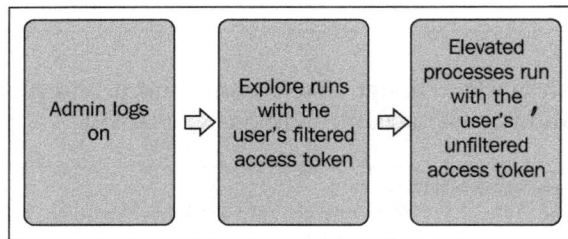

As Admin Approval Mode runs elevated processes with the same user account and security access token as the user who logged in and started the desktop session, the default configuration is to provide consent for elevation and alternative credentials are not required. However, UAC can be configured so that when a protected administrator wants to elevate a process, their credentials must be confirmed. This can be useful to force users to stop and think for a moment about what they're doing, rather than blindly clicking in a consent elevation prompt.

> **Consent versus credentials**
>
> Consent elevation prompts require a user to simply give permission for elevation to occur by clicking **Continue** or **Cancel**. On the other hand, credential elevation prompts require the user to either enter their own administrative credentials or those of another user.

If a system administrator launches a process and gives it consent to run with administrative privileges, any child processes spawned from the parent process will also run with administrative privileges, as long as they are marked with the same integrity level. For example, if a system administrator launches a command prompt with administrative privileges, and then launches `notepad.exe` from the command prompt, `notepad.exe` also runs with administrative privileges. Child processes also inherit the privileges of the parent if the parent process was launched by a standard user.

The following screenshot shows the privileges of a protected administrator running with a filtered security access token:

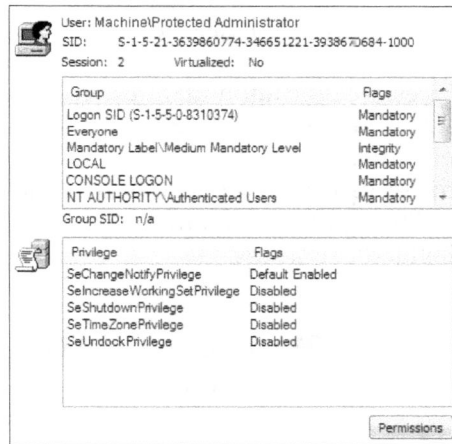

The next screenshot shows the same user after consent has been granted to run a process with elevated privileges:

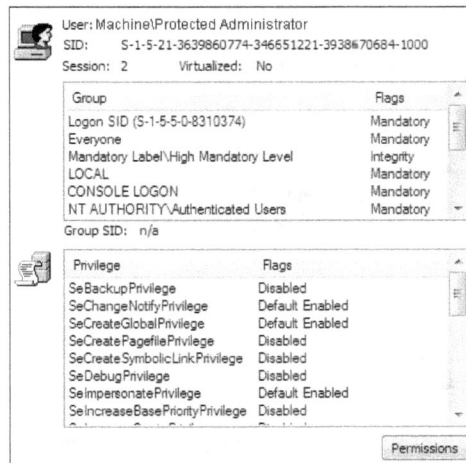

Conveniently elevating to admin privileges

To make it as convenient as possible to elevate to admin privileges when running as a standard user or protected administrator in Windows Vista, Microsoft designed a system of automatic elevation in certain scenarios.

Automatically launching applications with admin privileges

When a process is launched as a standard user, the CreateProcess function calls the AppCompat, Fusion, and Installer Detection functions to determine if the process requires elevation. The process's application manifest is also checked to establish the value of the requestedExecutionLevel tag. If any of these variables determine that the process requires elevation, the CreateProcess function returns an error and the ShellExecute process calls the Application Information Service to launch the process with elevation. The Application Information Service is responsible for creating processes with elevated privileges.

Consent and credential elevation prompts

UAC introduced two types of elevation prompts in Windows Vista—consent and elevation prompts.

Consent prompts

With the default configuration of Vista and Windows 7, when a user is running with a protected administrator account in Admin Approval Mode, if a process is elevated, a consent prompt is presented to the user. This requires the user to either grant or deny permission for the process to run with administrative privileges by clicking **Continue** or **Cancel**.

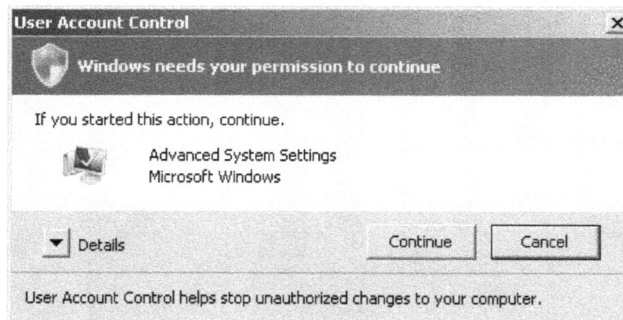

Credential prompts

Sometimes referred to as **Over the Shoulder** (OTS) prompts, when a user is running as a standard user, they are required to enter the credentials of an administrative account to launch a process with elevated privileges.

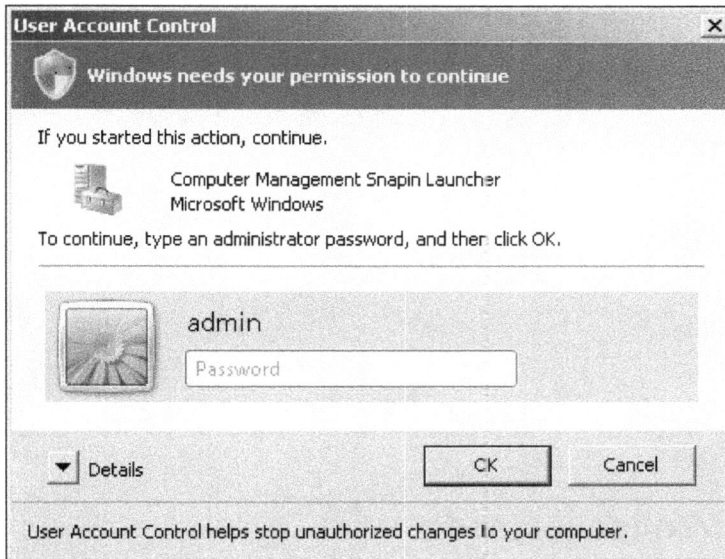

> **Why Over the Shoulder (OTS)?**
>
> At least in corporate environments, the credentials for administrative accounts shouldn't be made known to standard users, so a sysadmin is required to physically enter the credentials on behalf of the user.

Application-aware elevation prompts

Besides the two main types of elevation prompts that we just discussed, UAC also changes the color-coding and look of prompts depending on the type of process or application being launched. These visual clues are designed to draw the user's attention to the level of risk involved in allowing the executable to run with elevated privileges.

Windows Vista

If the publisher of an executable is determined as the operating system, then the elevation prompt is color coded with a blue/green background with a shield icon. cmd.exe is an example of an application that is signed with a certificate published by the operating system.

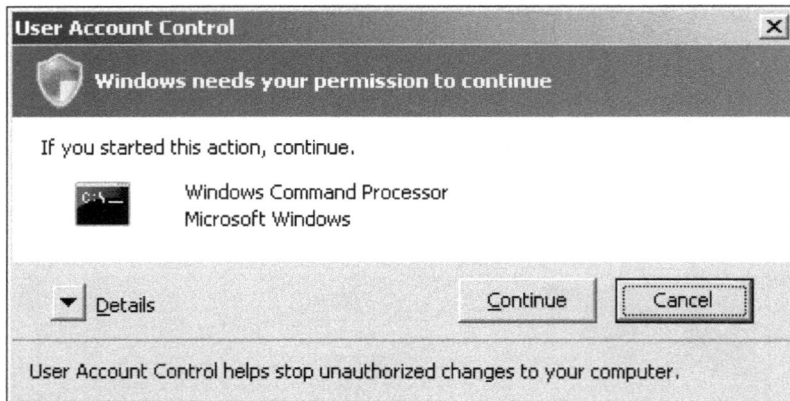

Publisher verified (signed)

If the publisher of the application can be verified from the executable's digital certificate, the elevation prompt is color-coded with a grey background and a gold shield.

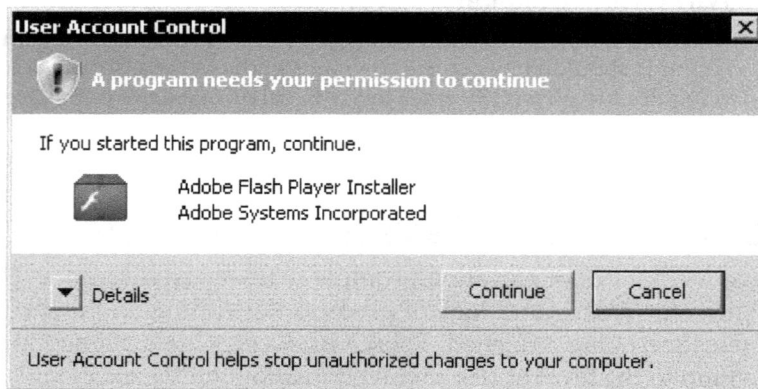

Publisher not verified (unsigned)

If the executable is neither signed by the operating system nor has a valid publisher's digital certificate, then the elevation prompt is color-coded in yellow with a gold shield.

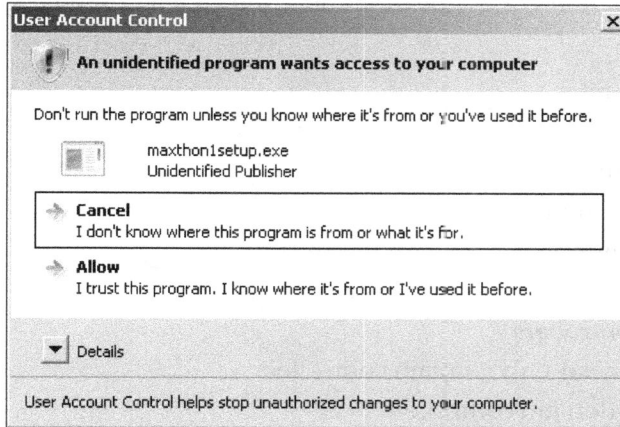

Trusting signed applications

Note that an application may be signed, but if the certificate is not trusted by the local computer, an elevation prompt with a yellow background will still be displayed. For a publisher-verified elevation prompt, the local computer must trust the certificate used to sign the application.

Publisher blocked

If the publisher is blocked by Group Policy, a red background and shield icon are displayed.

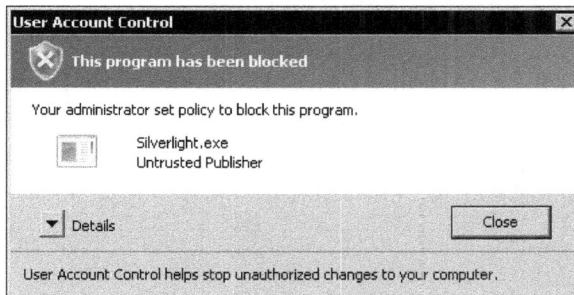

Administrator accounts

Vista considers all members of the groups listed below to be administrators, but not all of the groups give members full local administrative rights to a system. If a user is not a member of the local Administrators group, but is a member of one of the admin groups listed below, then OTS elevations are used instead of the usual consent elevation prompts.

- Built-in admins
- Certificate admins
- Domain admins
- Enterprise admins
- Policy admins
- Schema admins
- Domain controllers
- Enterprise read-only domain controllers
- Read-only domain controllers
- Account operators
- Backup operators
- Cryptographic operators
- Network configuration operators
- Print operators
- System operators
- RAS servers
- Power users
- Pre-Windows 2000 compatible access

Elevation prompt security

User Account Control, while being a welcome addition in Vista and Windows 7, cannot ensure complete protection to computers. The only computer that is completely secure is one that is never switched on, and never used. As such, there are several elements of User Account Control where potential security risks are apparent. As an example, elevation prompts could potentially be initiated by applications that the user didn't intend, or could be emulated by malware that in turn captures the user's logon credentials.

Securing the desktop

To help minimize the risks involved, User Account Control switches to a **Secure Desktop** by default whenever an elevation prompt is initiated. The secure desktop displays a darkened version of the interactive desktop with the elevation prompt displayed brightly to draw the user's attention. Only Windows processes can access the secure desktop. A fake secure desktop in Admin Approval Mode is no risk to the user, as the malware cannot harvest the user's credentials or elevate to run with admin privileges even if consent is given by clicking **Continue**.

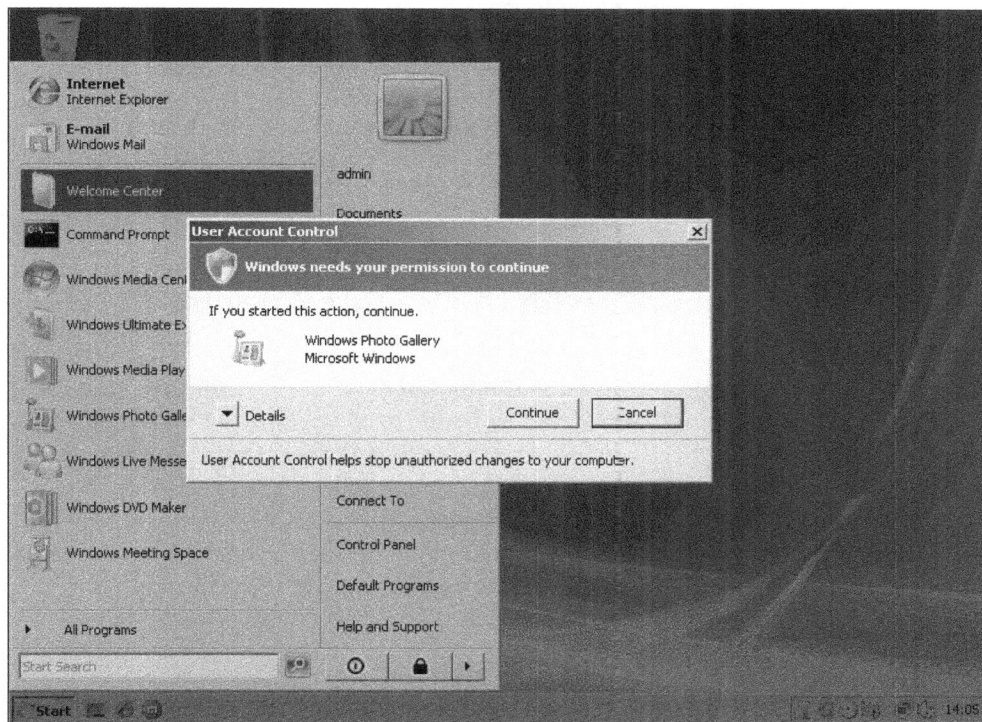

If malware emulates the secure desktop and manages to obtain the user's password and username from a credential elevation prompt, this still doesn't automatically lead to privilege elevation. Vista and later versions of Windows include **Windows Defender**, which is designed to prevent malware from infecting a system in the first instance, and other defenses that prevent malware from elevating to run with admin privileges such as the **Windows Integrity Mechanism** and **User Interface Privilege Isolation (UIPI)**. However, that's not to say that it's completely impossible to get access to a privileged account and take control of the system.

> **Automatically deny elevation requests**
>
> Microsoft recommends that in corporate environments, system administrators should configure UAC to automatically deny elevation requests using the **User Account Control: Behavior of the elevation prompt for standard users** local or Group Policy setting. This ensures that malware can't intercept an elevation prompt and harvest the credentials of an admin account.

Providing extra security with the Secure Attention Sequence (SAS)

If, for some reason you need to leave the credential elevation prompt for standard users enabled, User Account Control can be configured to require that users invoke the secure desktop through the **Secure Attention Sequence**, otherwise known as pressing the *Ctrl*, *Alt*, and *Delete* keys simultaneously. This is the only way to ensure that users are interacting with a real elevation prompt and not something that has been emulated by malware. When Windows boots, the `winlogon` process reserves the *Ctrl+Alt+Delete* key sequence to make sure other processes cannot use it.

> **Require the Secure Attention Sequence**
>
> Enable the **Require trusted path for credential entry** setting in local or Group Policy under **Computer Configuration | Administrative Templates | Windows Components | Credential User Interface**.

Securing elevated applications

In an attempt to prevent malware from injecting code into elevated applications, Microsoft introduced the Windows Integrity Mechanism and User Interface Privilege Isolation in Windows Vista. UIPI relies on Windows Integrity Mechanism to prevent malware from driving the user interface to inject commands into applications with higher privileges.

Windows Integrity Mechanism

Sometimes referred to as *Integrity Levels* or *Windows Integrity Control*, **Windows Integrity Mechanism** assigns a level of trust to all objects and processes to prevent those with a low level of trust from accessing objects and process with a higher level of integrity. Even if you decide to disable User Account Control, Windows Integrity Mechanism is part of the Windows security model and cannot be disabled.

Integrity policies

Mandatory policies are assigned to processes and set in the security access token, and in the mandatory label **Access Control Entry (ACE)** for objects. Both types of policy define how access is restricted from lower integrity processes to higher level integrity objects or processes. The standard policy for an object is NO_WRITE_UP, which means lower integrity processes cannot write to any object that has a higher level of integrity. Two other policies (listed next) can also be assigned to objects:

- NO_READ_UP: This policy prevents read access from processes with a lower level of integrity than the object.

- NO_EXECUTE_UP: This policy prevents launch access from processes with a lower level of integrity than the object.

> Processes and threads by default contain the NO_READ_UP and NO_WRITE_UP policy.

> **Why mandatory?**
>
> Access Control Lists can be set by system administrators on files and folders, and can be modified by users to control access. The Windows Integrity Mechanism has mandatory labels and policies that are set by the operating system, and while system administrators can manipulate them, it is not intended that these policies and labels be changed. The mandatory policies override ACLs and are designed to help protect users.

Assigning integrity levels

There are essentially five different levels of integrity in Windows, which are represented by **Security Identifiers** (**SIDs**).

- Untrusted
- Low
- Medium
- High
- System

When a local administrator launches a process, the access token for that process is assigned a high integrity level, but a medium integrity level is assigned when a standard user launches a process.

Integrity levels assigned to processes launched by different categories of user are listed as follows:

User	Integrity level assigned to launched processes
LocalSystem	System
LocalService	System
NetworkService	System
Administrators	High
Backup Operators	High
Network Configuration Operators	High
Cryptographic Operators	High
Authenticated Users	Medium
Everyone	Low
Anonymous	Untrusted

Internet Explorer Protected Mode

One exception to processes running with a medium level of integrity when launched by a standard user or protected administrator, is Internet Explorer in Protected Mode, which runs with low integrity.

When an object is created, it is assigned the same integrity level as the process that created it; however, there are some exceptions to this rule. For instance, when a file (NTFS only) or registry key is created by a process running with medium or higher integrity, it is not assigned an integrity level automatically.

> Files stored on a FAT32 partition are not securable, and therefore cannot be assigned an integrity level.

If no integrity level is defined for an object, medium integrity is implicitly assigned when the Windows security subsystem performs its mandatory policy check. In contrast, objects created by processes running with an integrity level less than the default of medium are explicitly assigned an integrity level.

> **Viewing the integrity level of a running process**
> Process Explorer from TechNet's Sysinternals tools can be used to view the integrity level of a running process and is available from: `http://technet.microsoft.com/en-us/sysinternals/default.aspx`.

A new command-line tool called `icacls` is built into Vista and Windows 7, and it allows you to view the integrity level of an object. For example, open a command prompt and type `icacls`, followed by the full path of the file:

```
icacls "c:\textfile.txt"
```

If the resulting output doesn't give any specific information about the file's integrity level, it means that an implicit level of the system's medium integrity will be assigned during a mandatory policy check.

> All securable objects have either an explicit or implicit integrity level.

The next screenshot shows a folder in the LocalLow folder that exists in all user profiles in the hidden AppData folder. All files in the LocalLow folder have low integrity. In this case, icacls shows the explicit label in its output.

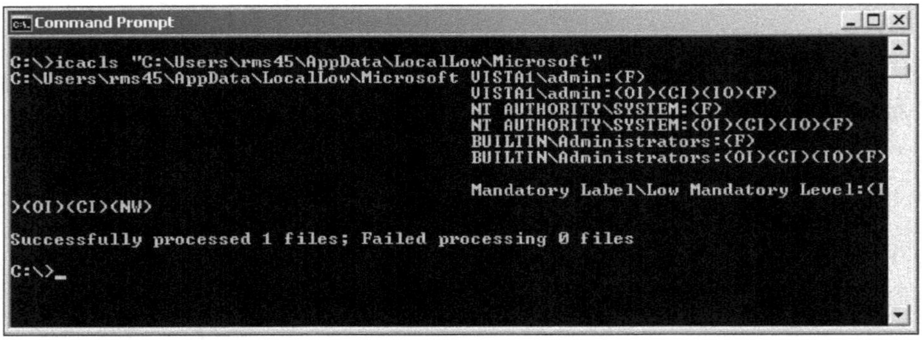

```
Command Prompt                                                    _ |□| x|
C:\>icacls "C:\Users\rms45\AppData\LocalLow\Microsoft"
C:\Users\rms45\AppData\LocalLow\Microsoft VISTA1\admin:(F)
                                         VISTA1\admin:(OI)(CI)(IO)(F)
                                         NT AUTHORITY\SYSTEM:(F)
                                         NT AUTHORITY\SYSTEM:(OI)(CI)(IO)(F)
                                         BUILTIN\Administrators:(F)
                                         BUILTIN\Administrators:(OI)(CI)(IO)(F)

                                         Mandatory Label\Low Mandatory Level:(I
)(OI)(CI)(NW)

Successfully processed 1 files; Failed processing 0 files

C:\>_
```

Integrity levels are inherited by objects in a folder hierarchy in the same way as NTFS Access Control Lists. Suppose a process running with medium integrity creates a file in a folder that's set so that all child objects inherit low integrity from the parent object. A file created in this location by the medium integrity process will be set with low integrity. An exception to this rule is if the process creating the object wants to set an explicit level of integrity, in which case the object won't inherit an integrity level from the parent container. However, the process cannot assign an integrity level higher than that with which it runs, but it can be higher than that of the folder where the new object is created.

> Processes, threads, and tokens are always assigned an explicit integrity level.

User Interface Privilege Isolation

UIPI works with the Windows Integrity Mechanism to stop processes that run with low integrity from communicating with or injecting code into processes that run with a higher level of integrity. This generally applies to *write* Windows messages that are sent between processes running with low and high integrity, but doesn't include *read* messages.

User Interface Privilege Level

When a process initiates a *User Interface* (*UI*), the windowing and graphics subsystem (User subsystem) assigns an integrity level to the UI, equal to that of the initiating process's primary security access token. Processes running with lower integrity cannot perform the following actions on processes running with a higher integrity:

- Inject dynamic link libraries (DLLs)
- Perform window handle validation
- Monitor a process with journal hooks
- Use `SendMessage` or `PostMessage` functions
- Attach to a process using thread hooks

> **Shared windowing and graphics subsystem (USER) resources**
> When UIPI is enabled, certain resources such as information stored on the clipboard can still be shared between processes running with lower integrity and higher integrity.

UIPI and accessibility

User Interface Privilege Isolation may prevent accessibility tools, such as the onscreen keyboard, from driving applications that are started with elevated privileges (for instance when a user is running as a protected administrator in Admin Approval Mode). If an application is launched with elevated privileges, a tool such as the onscreen keyboard may not be able to send messages to the elevated application.

Application manifests can set the `UIaccess` security attribute to `true`, which permits an application to bypass UIPI if the following conditions are met:

- The application is signed and trusted by the local computer.
- The program must be installed in a protected location such as `%ProgramFiles%` or `%WinDir%`.

User Account Control Group Policy includes the setting: **User Account Control: Only elevate UIAccess applications that are installed in secure locations**. Enabled by default, this setting can be disabled to allow applications that are located outside protected locations to bypass UIPI.

Achieving application compatibility

The introduction of User Account Control in Windows Vista meant that some changes had to be made to the operating system to allow applications to work correctly, and in some cases, minor changes to program code.

Application manifest

Windows application manifests are XML files that list the side-by-side assemblies that a program should call when executed, and also include information about how to work with User Account Control. If an application's manifest file doesn't include UAC-specific information, it should still work without any problems.

> **Application manifest** files are usually embedded into executables as a Win32 Resource, so you may not be able to see the XML file.

Manifest files can include the `requestedElevationLevel` tag that specifies a value defining the level of privilege the application should be launched with. The three values are:

requestedElevationLevel **value**	**Resulting launch condition**
asInvoker	Launches an application in the same security context as the user's logon session and is recommended for applications that should run as a standard user.
requireAdministrator	Forces elevation and the application to run with an administrator's unfiltered access token when the program is launched.
highestAvailable	Launches a program with the highest privileges available to a user — if the user is a standard user, no elevation will not be attempted; if the user is a protected administrator, elevation will be triggered.

The following example of an application manifest XML file for `exampleapp.exe` shows the `requireAdministrator` value set for the `requestedElevationLevel` tag to force elevation at runtime:

```
<?xml version="1.0" encoding="UTF-8" standalone="yes"?>
<assembly xmlns="urn:schemas-microsoft-com:asm.v1"
                          manifestVersion="1.0">
<assemblyIdentity version="1.0.0.0" processorArchitecture="X86"
                          name="ExampleApp" type="win32"/>
```

```
<trustInfo xmlns="urn:schemas-microsoft-com:asm.v3">
  <security>
    <requestedPrivileges>
      <requestedExecutionLevel level="requireAdministrator"
        uiAccess="false"/>
    </requestedPrivileges>
  </security>
</trustInfo>
</assembly>
```

uiAccess

Also note, in the highlighted section of the manifest code, a variable called uiAccess is set to false. This can be used if the application needs to bypass User Interface Privilege Isolation.

Internal elevation points

If an application, such as an installer, is started with standard user privileges, it's possible for the developer to include internal elevation points that require the user to elevate to administrative privileges after the initial launch of the executable.

Disabled file and registry virtualization

When an application includes an application manifest file, this indicates that it is designed for Windows Vista (or Windows 7) and as such does not require write access to protected areas of the filesystem and registry. Therefore, file and registry virtualization is disabled.

Power Users

The Power Users group has been deprecated in Vista but remains for the purposes of backward compatibility. If you need to re-enable privileges that were once assigned to the power users group for an application to work correctly, you'll have to apply an appropriate security template to your systems to assign permissions and privileges to power users, or manually re-instate privileges and permissions to the power users group.

Windows Logo Program

The Windows Logo Program gives consumers an indication of whether hardware or software is compatible with a particular version of Windows. The *Certified for Windows Vista* software logo can be used only on programs that are compatible with User Account Control.

Certification requirements

There is a list of basic requirements that software developers must adhere to when developing programs that are to be certified for Windows Vista:

- Unless an application is genuinely intended for use by administrators only, it should work seamlessly for a standard user.

- Application manifests must be embedded into all of the application's executable files and include the requestedExecutionLevel tag.

- All related .exe, .dll, .sys, .drv, .ocx, .cpl, or .scr files should be signed with an *Authenticode* certificate.

- Installers must include internal elevation points if designed to be launched by a standard user who can then choose to install the program just for himself/herself (no elevation required) or for all users (elevation required).

- If the installer uses a bootstrapper, an executable used to unpack and launch an .msi file or secondary executable, the bootstrapper must include an embedded application manifest that includes the requestedExecutionLevel tag.

- Applications must be tested by a Microsoft-approved testing vendor.

Filesystem and registry virtualization

The most common application compatibility issue when running legacy applications as a standard user is that they require unrestricted access to areas of the filesystem or registry that standard users have limited rights to. Windows XP includes an application compatibility engine that allows system administrators to deploy application compatibility shims that can redirect or 'virtualize' writes directed to protected file and registry locations to a specially designated writeable area of the user's profile. User Account Control in Vista takes this concept one step further by detecting when an application is trying to write to protected locations, and automatically redirects writes and subsequent reads to a virtualized area of the user's profile. This enables legacy applications that wouldn't have worked on Windows XP as a standard user without an application compatibility shim to run on Vista and Windows 7 without errors and with no intervention from system administrators.

Filesystem virtualization

Vista (and Windows 7) includes the UAC File Virtualization Driver (luafv.sys), which monitors all file operations, but modifies only the destination path for write/read operations on files in system-global locations if an application is deemed to be legacy. It doesn't affect native 64-bit applications, programs run from network shares or applications that have been marked as Vista/Windows 7 compatible with an application manifest.

> **System-global locations**
>
> System-global locations are areas of the filesystem and registry that can only be written to or modified by processes running with system or administrative-level privileges. %ProgramFiles%, %ProgramData%, and %SystemRoot% are the system-global locations that luafv.sys monitors for access denied errors generated by legacy applications.

Virtual root directory

Each user profile has a **virtual root directory**, where luafv.sys redirects write/read operations if access is denied to a system-global location. During read operations, the user's virtual root directory is checked first for the required file, and if it is not found is redirected to the equivalent system-global location.

> **Virtual root directory path**
> %userprofile%\AppData\Local\VirtualStore

For example, a legacy application writes information to the %ProgramFiles% directory, but luafv.sys intercepts the write operation when an access denied message is received and modifies the path as follows from C:\Program Files (x86)\real\realplayer\deviceinfo to C:\users\user name\appdata\local\virtualstore\Program Files (x86)\real\realplayer\deviceinfo.

> **AppData**
> You should note that the AppData folder is hidden, so to view this folder and the virtual store, you must enable **Show hidden files, folders and drives** in **Folder and search options** on Explorer's **Organize** menu.

> **Local versus roaming profiles**
> The virtual store is located in the local part of a user's profile, and therefore is not available in roaming profiles.

Registry virtualization

Only the HKEY_LOCAL_MACHINE\Software part of the registry is subject to virtualization, with the following exceptions:

- HKEY_LOCAL_MACHINE\Software\Microsoft\Windows
- HKEY_LOCAL_MACHINE\Software\Microsoft\WindowsNT
- HKEY_LOCAL_MACHINE\Software\Classes
- Keys that a user with administrative privileges cannot write to

> As with filesystem virtualization, native 64-bit applications are not subject to registry virtualization, as well as services and kernel-mode processes (drivers and so on).

There is no definitive list of registry locations that should be virtualized for legacy applications, but each key maintains three flags that determine how virtualization should be handled:

Registry Key Flag	Virtualization
REG_KEY_DONT_VIRTUALIZE	Not enabled as standard. If set, the registry key is excluded from virtualization.
REG_KEY_DONT_SILENT_FAIL	Not enabled by default. If virtualization for a registry key is disabled, the default setting of this flag allows a silent failure, should an application receive an access denied message due to a lack of access rights.
REG_KEY_RECURSE_FLAG	Cleared as standard and controls whether new sub-keys inherit the flags of the parent object, or the default flags.

The status of the three flags outlined above can be determined using the reg.exe command-line tool. For example, to see the flag statuses for the HKLM\Software\Realtek key type the following command line:

```
reg flags "hklm\software\realtek"
```

```
HKEY_LOCAL_MACHINE\software\realtek
        REG_KEY_DONT_VIRTUALIZE: CLEAR
        REG_KEY_DONT_SILENT_FAIL: CLEAR
        REG_KEY_RECURSE_FLAG: CLEAR

The operation completed successfully.
```

Virtual root registry

Each user profile has a virtual root registry that is stored in the user's `Classes` hive:

`HKEY_CURRENT_USER\Software\Classes\VirtualStore`

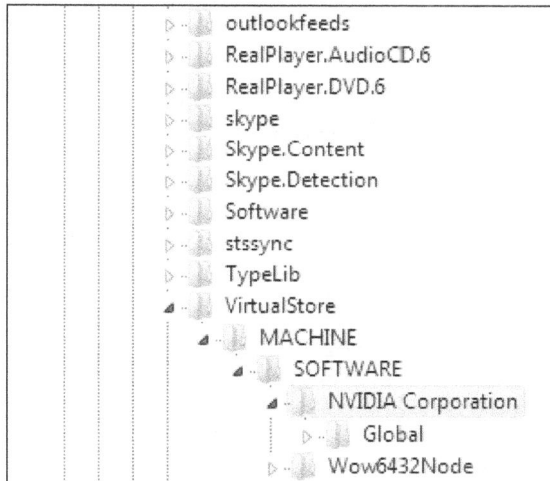

> **User's Classes hive**
>
> The user's `Classes` hive is stored in a file called `usrclass.dat` in `%userprofile%\AppData\Local\Microsoft\Windows`. As the path suggests, this information is not included in roaming profiles.

When a process reads a key stored in the virtual root registry, a combined view of the key using values from the virtual root registry and real registry is presented to the application.

> Note that the registry editor itself is an application, and so if you are running as a restricted user or protected administrator and you have not elevated, you will be looking at the combined view of data that would be made available to an application.

Using Task Manager to determine whether a process is using UAC filesystem and registry virtualization

Log in to Vista or Windows 7 as a standard user or administrator:

1. In Windows Task Manager, go to **View | Select Columns** from the menu, check **User Account Control (UAC) Virtualization** (or just **Virtualization** in Vista), and click **OK**.

2. You'll now see an extra column in Task Manager showing the status of virtualization for the listed processes.

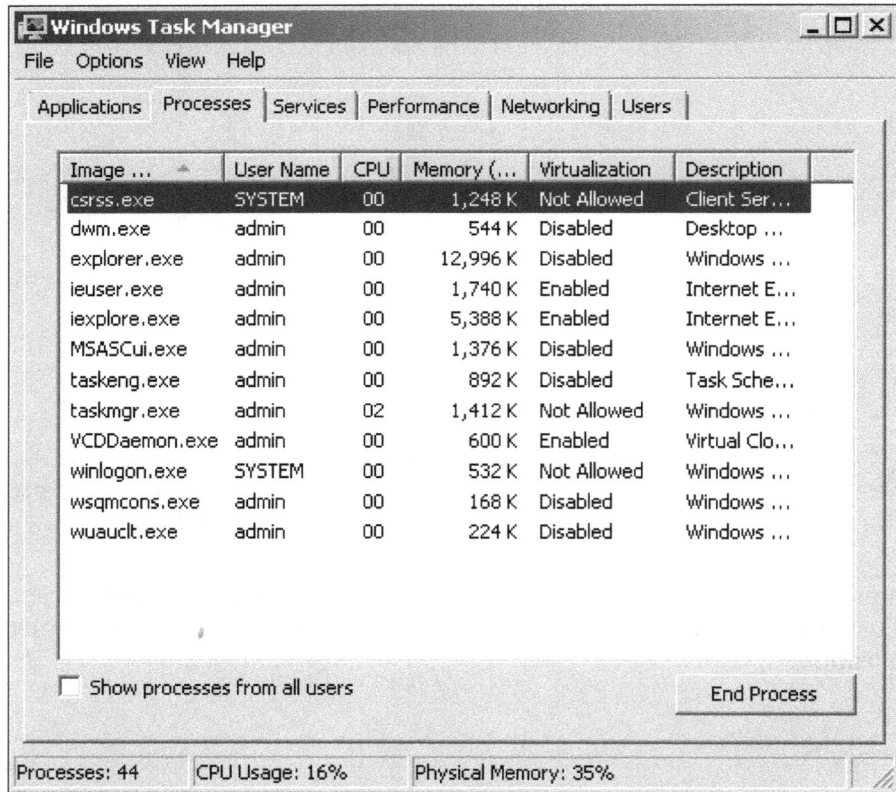

Windows Task Manager _ □ ×

File   Options   View   Help

Applications | Processes | Services | Performance | Networking | Users |

Image ... ▲	User Name	CPU	Memory (...	Virtualization	Description
csrss.exe	SYSTEM	00	1,248 K	Not Allowed	Client Ser...
dwm.exe	admin	00	544 K	Disabled	Desktop ...
explorer.exe	admin	00	12,996 K	Disabled	Windows ...
ieuser.exe	admin	00	1,740 K	Enabled	Internet E...
iexplore.exe	admin	00	5,388 K	Enabled	Internet E...
MSASCui.exe	admin	00	1,376 K	Disabled	Windows ...
taskeng.exe	admin	00	892 K	Disabled	Task Sche...
taskmgr.exe	admin	02	1,412 K	Not Allowed	Windows ...
VCDDaemon.exe	admin	00	600 K	Enabled	Virtual Clo...
winlogon.exe	SYSTEM	00	532 K	Not Allowed	Windows ...
wsqmcons.exe	admin	00	168 K	Disabled	Windows ...
wuauclt.exe	admin	00	224 K	Disabled	Windows ...

☐ Show processes from all users   End Process

Processes: 44   CPU Usage: 16%   Physical Memory: 35%

Windows Installer and User Account Control

While one of the design goals of User Account Control is to prevent software from silently installing without the user's knowledge, the shipping version of Windows Installer in Vista was designed to be compliant with User Account Control. Just like Linux has the **RPM Package Manager** for software distribution, Windows has Windows Installer. Standardizing on a format for the Windows platform makes it easier for system administrators to distribute software using Group Policy Software Installation or System Center Configuration Manager. You should note that, while Group Policy Software Installation can be used to install software that isn't packaged in Windows Installer format (.msi file), only Windows Installer packages can be distributed to users who don't have administrative privileges.

> **Prevent users from installing software from removable media**
>
> You can additionally configure Windows Installer through Group Policy, and prevent users from running Windows Installer packages from removable media such as CD ROM. The **Prevent removable media source for any install** setting is located in local and Group Policy under **User Configuration | Administrative | Templates | Windows Components | Windows Installer**.

While it is possible to grant standard users the ability to install all Windows Installer packages with administrative rights by enabling the **Always install with elevated privileges** Group Policy setting under **User Configuration | Administrative | Templates | Windows Components | Windows Installer**, it's preferable to restrict application installations to those approved by the corporate IT department.

Automatically detecting application installers

Mainly intended for the convenience of home users and system administrators, **Installer Detection** was introduced as part of User Account Control in Vista, and attempts to automatically detect when a user launches an executable that installs software on the local computer. Most software requires administrative privileges to install correctly, as the installer package writes to protected areas of the filesystem and registry, amongst other administrative operations such as registering **Dynamic Link Libraries (DLLs)**.

Application manifests for programs that are deemed to be compatible with Vista, and therefore User Account Control, should include the appropriate requestedExecutionLevel tag to ensure that the installer prompts for elevated privileges, in which case, Installer Detection is not required. As with other User Account Control technologies, Installer Detection doesn't apply to 64-bit executables.

Installer Detection uses heuristics to determine if a 32-bit process should be elevated to run with administrative privileges based on the follow criteria:

- *Install, setup,* or *update* included in the executable's filename
- Specific keywords in the executable's *Versioning Resource* fields
- Keywords in the embedded application manifest for side-by-side assemblies
- Specific sequences of bytes in the executable that were found to be common in various installer technologies
- Key attributes in the resource file data

Turn off Installer Detection

In a corporate environment, it may be desirable to turn off Installer Detection. This can be achieved in User Account Control Group Policy settings.

Controlling User Account Control through Group Policy

User Account Control can be configured specifically for your organization's needs using Group Policy. All the settings for User Account Control are located under **Computer Configuration | Security Settings | Local Policies | Security Options** in local and Group Policy:

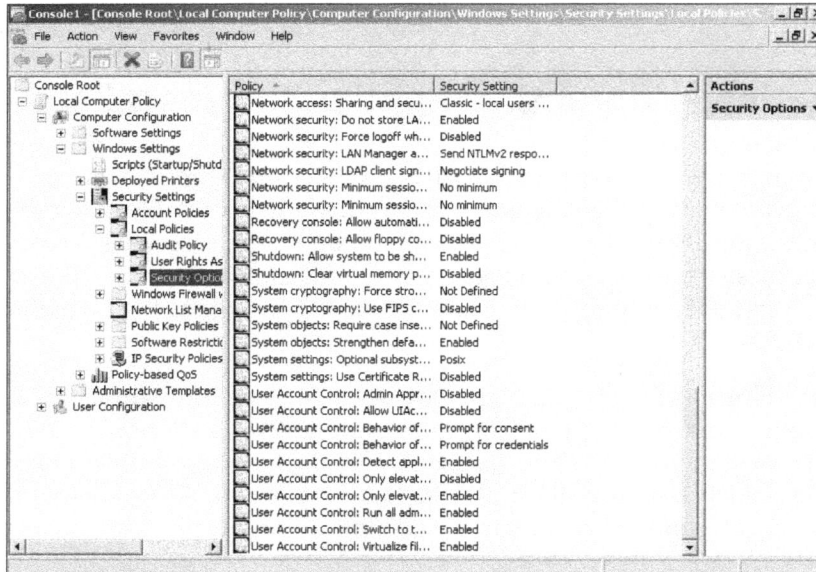

The descriptions of policy settings listed here are for Windows 7. Vista UAC Group Policy settings differ in subtle ways and any differences are highlighted in each section that follows.

Admin Approval Mode for the built-in administrator account

Both this policy and the built-in administrator account in Vista and Windows 7 are disabled by default. If you enable the built-in administrator account, it runs all processes with a full administrative access token unless this policy is enabled.

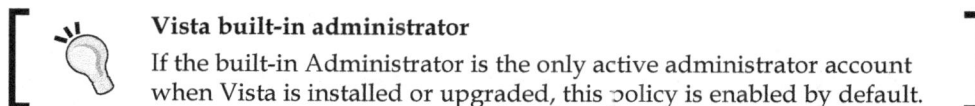

Vista built-in administrator

If the built-in Administrator is the only active administrator account when Vista is installed or upgraded, this policy is enabled by default.

Allowing UIAccess applications to prompt for elevation without using the secure desktop

This setting was introduced in Vista Service Pack 1 to resolve a problem with Remote Assistance where system administrators could not enter administrative credentials during a Remote Assistance session in an elevation prompt on a secure desktop. This setting is disabled by default in both Vista and Windows 7.

Behavior of the elevation prompt for administrators in Admin Approval Mode

This setting changes how and when elevation prompts are presented to protected administrators. There are five different options:

Group policy setting	Description
Elevate without prompting	Allows protected administrators to run processes with administrative privileges without giving consent
Prompt for consent on the secure desktop (Windows 7 only)	Presents elevation prompts on the secure desktop as opposed to the user's interactive desktop
Prompt for credentials	Changes from the default consent elevation prompt and requires protected administrators to enter credentials before elevation is permitted

Group Policy Setting	Description
Prompt for consent	The default setting in Vista; presents protected administrators with the standard consent elevation prompt
Prompt for consent for non-Windows binaries (Windows 7 only)	The default setting in Windows 7; presents protected administrators with the standard consent elevation prompt when administrative privileges are required for executables that are not part of the operating system

Secure Desktop

You should note that the **Switch to the secure desktop when prompting for elevation** setting forces all elevation prompts to the secure desktop if enabled, despite what may be set in behavior polices for administrators and standard users.

Behavior of the elevation prompt for standard users

This setting changes how and when elevation prompts are presented to standard users. Again there are several options for this Group Policy setting:

Group Policy Setting	Description
Automatically deny elevation requests	Presents standard users with an error message if a process requires elevated privileges.
Prompt for credentials on the secure desktop (Windows 7 only)	For Windows 7 only. Requires administrative credentials to be entered to elevate a process.
Prompt for credentials	The same as the previous setting, but doesn't force a secure desktop. This is the default setting in Vista and Windows 7.

Detect application installations and prompt for elevation

This policy is enabled by default for home users but disabled for domain-joined computers. Installer Detection is switched off by disabling this policy. In Vista, this setting is enabled by default regardless of whether the machine is joined to a domain.

Only elevate executables that are signed and validated

This policy is disabled by default. If it is enabled, executables to be elevated must be signed with a certificate that the local computer can validate.

Only elevate UIAccess applications that are installed in secure locations

Enabled by default, UIAccess applications, such as Remote Assistance, must be installed in one of the following locations:

- \Program Files or a subfolder
- \Program Files (x86) or a subfolder in 64-bit versions of Windows 7
- \Windows\system32

Run all administrators in Admin Approval Mode

This setting is enabled by default and switches Admin Approval Mode on and off. If you change this setting, you'll have to reboot the machine before it takes effect. When it is enabled, additional UAC Group Policy settings related to AAM must be configured and when disabled, all AAM UAC Group Policy settings are rendered ineffective.

Switch to the secure desktop when prompting for elevation

Enabled by default, all elevation prompts are presented to administrators and standard users on the secure desktop. This setting overrides prompt behavior settings for administrators and standard users.

Virtualize file and registry write failures to per-user locations

This setting is enabled by default, and virtualizes file and registry write operations that generate an access denied failure and subsequent read requests to the appropriate per-user virtual stores for legacy applications.

What's new in Windows 7 User Account Control

Apart from the differences in Group Policy settings that we looked at in the last section, the basic engineering of User Account Control in Windows 7 remains unchanged.

User Account Control slider

The most visible change to User Account Control in Windows 7 is the addition of a slider to control the level of protection that UAC exercises over the system, ranging from **Always notify**, which is the equivalent of **UAC** in Vista, to **Never notify**. Along with this, the design of UAC has changed slightly to accommodate two new modes:

- Permitting certain Windows binaries to elevate silently under protected administrator accounts
- Presenting elevation prompts either on the secure desktop or on the PA's interactive desktop

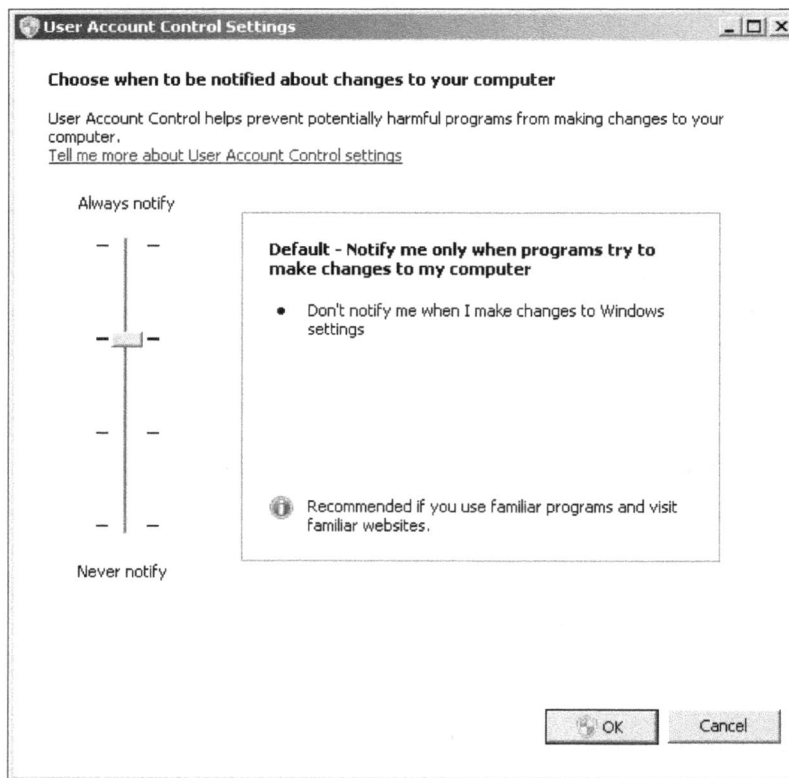

Auto-elevation for Windows binaries

Certain Windows binaries are silently elevated when using a protected administrator account if they meet the following conditions:

- They must be digitally signed by the Windows publisher
- They should be located in a designated secure directory that cannot be modified by standard users

Executables

Windows binaries of the `.exe` variety auto-elevate if their manifest includes the `autoElevate` tag. Some Windows 7 executables that are also required to operate on other versions of Windows, such as the Migration Wizard (`migwiz.exe`), are hardcoded to auto-elevate to avoid errors being generated by the `autoElevate` tag in the executable's application manifest.

Microsoft Management Console (MMC)

When the MMC is started from a protected administrator account, it runs a command line that includes an `.msc` file that lists all the snap-ins that will be loaded into the console. The `mmc.exe` file and `.msc` file are checked to make sure they are compliant for auto-elevation as per a standard executable, and additionally the `.msc` file must be included in Windows 7's list of `.msc` files that are allowed to auto-elevate.

Component Object Model (COM) objects

With User Account Control's default settings, if a protected administrator uses **Explorer** to modify areas of the registry or filesystem that are restricted for standard users, the operations will succeed because the COM objects used by **Explorer** to complete the tasks are marked for auto-elevation. COM Objects are flagged in the registry for auto-elevation and must be called from a Windows executable.

> **SigCheck**
>
> Sysinternal's SigCheck command-line tool can be used to examine embedded application manifest files in executables. The example command line below displays the application manifest for Task Manager in Windows 7 64-bit edition: `sigcheck -m "C:\Windows\SysWOW64\taskmgr.exe"`
>
> SigCheck download: `http://technet.microsoft.com/en-us/sysinternals/bb897441.aspx`.

More settings accessible to standard users

Windows 7 continues the work started in Vista by making more settings available to standard users. For instance, it's now possible for a standard user to refresh TCP/IP settings from a DHCP server, use Windows Update to install optional updates and change display DPI settings.

Summary

In this chapter, we've learned about the design goals of User Account Control, how the main components are intended to make it more convenient to run Windows as a standard user, and that User Account Control cannot be considered a security boundary, but works with other defense-in-depth security technologies to help protect the operating system. Before continuing to the next chapter, you should:

- Understand the differences between standard user and Admin Approval Mode (AAM)
- Be familiar with the changes to User Account Control in Windows 7
- Be able to configure User Account Control using Group Policy
- Understand in what scenarios the different components of User Account Control apply

In the next chapter, we'll look at some additional tools that can be used to help deploy least privilege security on the desktop.

5

Tools and Techniques for Solving Least Privilege Security Problems

We've covered most of the main techniques for resolving issues with legacy applications that fail to run for users who don't have administrative privileges. However, there may be situations where you need to support standard users and have no choice but to temporarily grant administrative privileges. This chapter includes information about tools and techniques that can be used to solve Least Privilege Security problems.

In this chapter we'll learn to:

- Set up a system for temporarily granting administrative privileges to standard users for support purposes
- Use Task Scheduler to run common processes without the need to elevate privileges
- Use third-party solutions to configure administrative privileges for applications and Windows processes on-the-fly
- Suppress UAC elevation prompts

Granting temporary administrative privileges

One of the primary concerns for system administrators when implementing Least Privilege Security on notebook computers is how to solve problems that require administrative access if a remote connection cannot be established. Consider a scenario where a user arrives at a conference center but can't connect their notebook to the local network because there isn't a DHCP server available. The only way to make a successful connection is to manually configure an IP address.

While we could add users to the Network Configuration Operators group on each notebook so that they can configure local network settings, the requirement to manually configure network options is rare and granting this access is likely to create more support problems than it solves. If you've ever worked on a help desk, you'll know that a high percentage of calls from mobile workers are related to network connection problems, often caused by a misconfiguration.

Windows doesn't have any built-in mechanism that allows system administrators to temporarily grant administrative privileges, leaving IT nervous to commit to Least Privilege on notebook computers. In this section, we'll look at a couple of simple techniques that can be used to grant temporary administrative access to mobile users when all else fails. Neither method is perfect, and could potentially be hijacked by savvy users to install unsanctioned software or grant themselves permanent administrative access, but there must be a back door for system administrators to ensure confidence in the ability to provide support in any situation.

The instructions that follow use local user accounts and local policy settings, but are intended for use in a domain environment. If you wish to manage the accounts and policy settings centrally, domain users and domain-based Group Policy Objects can be used as an alternative. The following techniques shouldn't be used in high security environments.

Granting temporary administrative access using a separate logon (Vista and Windows 7 only)

For each notebook in our organization, we need to create a set of accounts that have administrative access. Let's create three accounts on each notebook—Support1, Support2, and Support 3.

Creating three support accounts

You can do this easily from the command prompt or by adding the appropriate commands to a batch file. Log on to the notebook as an administrator and run the following two commands from the command prompt:

```
net user Support1 ******** /expires:never /passwordchg:no /ADD
net localgroup Administrators Support1 /ADD
```

Replace ******** with a random password for each account. The passwords for each support account must be recorded somewhere for future reference. The password for each account should be completely random and differ on every notebook.

Creating a policy setting to automatically delete the support account at logoff

To ensure that the support account is deleted at log off, we need to create a local policy setting for each support account.

1. Type MMC into the **Search programs and files** box on the Start menu and press *Enter*.
2. Press *Ctrl+M* to add a snap-in.
3. In the **Add or Remove Snap-ins** dialog box select **Group Policy Object Editor** from the list on the left and click **Add**.
4. In the **Select Group Policy Object** dialog box, click **Browse**.
5. In the **Browse for a Group Policy Object** window, switch to the **Users** tab.
6. Select **Support1** in the list and click **OK**.
7. In the **Select Group Policy Object** dialog box, the Group Policy Object will now read **Local Computer\Support1**. Click **Finish**.

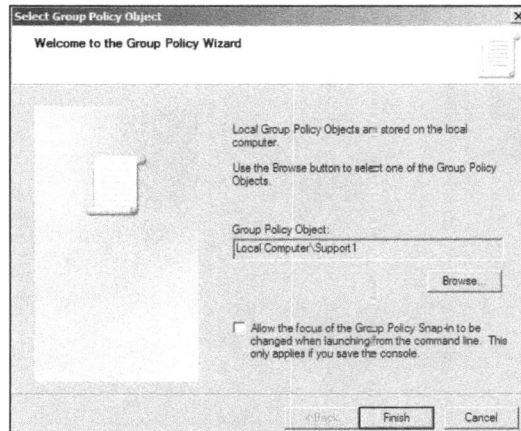

8. In the **Add or Remove Snap-ins** dialog box, click **OK**.

9. In the MMC console window, expand **Local Computer\Support1 Policy, User Configuration, Windows Settings** under **Console Root** in the left pane.

10. Click **Scripts (Logon/Logoff)** under **Windows Settings**.

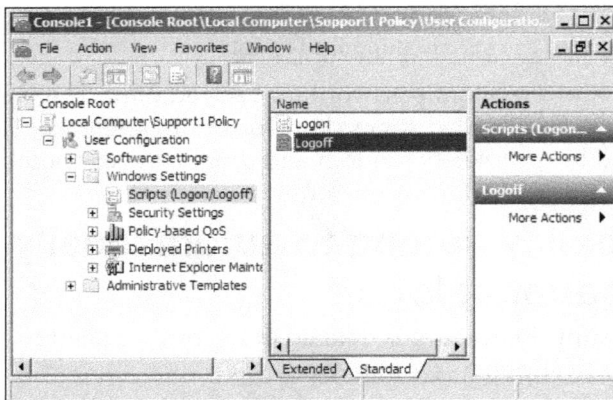

11. In the central pane, double-click **Logoff**.

12. In the **Logoff Properties** dialog box, click **Add**.

13. In the **Add a Script** window, type net in the **Script Name** field.

14. In the **Script Parameters** field type user support1 /delete and click **OK**.

15. Click **OK** in the **Logoff Properties** dialog box.

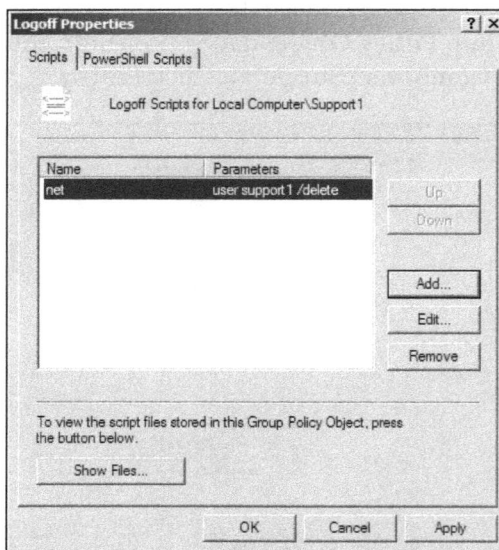

16. Close the MMC window.

These steps need to be repeated for each support account.

Testing the support accounts

To test the configuration, log in to Windows using the Support1 account.

1. You'll need to click **Switch User** on the log on screen and then select **Other User**.

2. When entering the username, specify that it's a local user account using the format COMPUTERNAME\USERNAME. In this case, the computer is called **WIN7**.

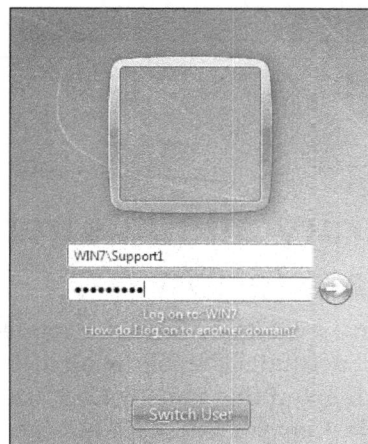

3. Check that **Support1** has administrative access by performing a task such as changing the date or time. If **Support1** has administrative privileges, UAC will not prompt for elevation.

4. Log off **Support1** and then try to log in again using the same account. This time you should be presented with **The user name or password is incorrect** as an error message because the **Support1** account no longer exists.

To repeat the support procedure, the password for **Support2** must be known by the user.

Putting into practice

The procedure outlined here can be used by help desk staff when a user requires a temporary administrative login for support:

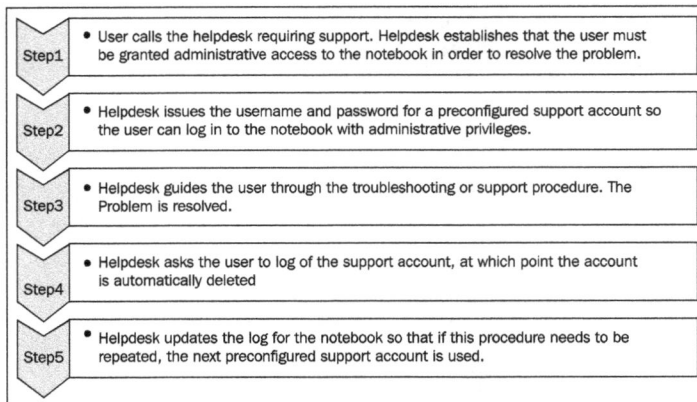

Step1	• User calls the helpdesk requiring support. Helpdesk establishes that the user must be granted administrative access to the notebook in order to resolve the problem.
Step2	• Helpdesk issues the username and password for a preconfigured support account so the user can log in to the notebook with administrative privileges.
Step3	• Helpdesk guides the user through the troubleshooting or support procedure. The Problem is resolved.
Step4	• Helpdesk asks the user to log of the support account, at which point the account is automatically deleted
Step5	• Helpdesk updates the log for the notebook so that if this procedure needs to be repeated, the next preconfigured support account is used.

Granting temporary administrative access without a separate logon

Sometimes we just need to give the logged in user administrative privileges without asking them to use a different account. The following technique uses the same three support accounts created earlier, but this time instead of asking the logged in user to switch user and start a new desktop session, we'll ask them to launch a preinstalled batch file using the *support* user's credentials supplied by the help desk.

Creating a batch file to elevate the privileges of the logged in user

We're going to create three batch files, one for use with each of the three support user accounts. The batch files are also unique for the logged in user. As this elevation technique will generally only be used for mobile users, and notebooks tend to have only one regular user, this limitation shouldn't prove too much of a problem. This technique could be developed further to accommodate more complex requirements.

Using Notepad, save the following commands as Support1.cmd:

```
@echo off
net localgroup Administrators AD\user /ADD
@ping 127.0.0.1 -n 60 -w 1000 > nul

@ping 127.0.0.1 -n %1% -w 1000 > nul
```

```
net localgroup Administrators AD\user /DELETE
net user support1 /DELETE
exit
```

So what does the batch file do?

1. The logged in user, in this case user@ad.contoso.com, is added to the notebook's local Administrators group.
2. The two ping commands are used as a means of creating a timed delay in the batch file of 60 seconds. This value can be changed to meet your needs and gives user@ad.contoso.com a time-limited chance to elevate his/her account.
3. Once the timer has stopped, user@ad.contoso.com is removed from the local Administrators group and the support1 user account is deleted to ensure the user can't repeat the procedure.

You should create three batch files, one for each support user account, modifying the commands as necessary— Support1.cmd, Support2.cmd, and Support3.cmd. The files should be saved to a trusted location on the user's notebook, for instance to a dedicated folder in C:\Program Files or C:\Windows, to help ensure that the user can't modify commands in the batch files. when they are running without administrative privileges.

Testing the procedure

Log in to a notebook with a standard user account and follow these instructions:

1. Locate the support batch files in C:\Program Files or C:\Windows.
2. Select Support1.cmd, right-click on the file, and select **Run as administrator** from the menu.
3. User Account Control will prompt for administrative credentials. Enter the credentials for the Support1 account, remembering to use the following format: COMPUTERNAME\USERNAME.

4. A command-line window will appear. Now attempt to change the time or date. UAC will still prompt for administrative credentials, but this time user@ad.contoso.com can enter their **own** credentials to elevate and successfully change the date or time.

5. After 60 seconds, the batch file will continue processing and remove user@ad.contoso.com from the local Administrators group.

6. Try again to change the time or date; enter user@ad.contoso.com credentials into the UAC prompt and this time the request will be denied as user@ad.contoso.com has been demoted back to a standard user.

Limitations of the procedure

OK, so this seems to work well, but you may have noticed some limitations. The user could close the command-line window and prevent the batch file from completing, effectively leaving user@ad.contoso.com in the local Administrators group. While there's no simple way to prevent this, you can use Group Policy Restricted Groups to ensure that only approved accounts remain permanently in the Administrators group on each notebook.

user@ad.contoso.com could also log out and log in before the batch file completes processing, again elevating themselves to a permanent administrative status if Group Policy Restricted Groups is not configured. Ultimately, it's important to understand that even in granting a user temporary administrative privileges lies the possibility that they could change system-wide configuration to prevent Group Policy settings applying or grant themselves permanent administrative access to the PC.

Help desk procedure for granting temporary administrative access:

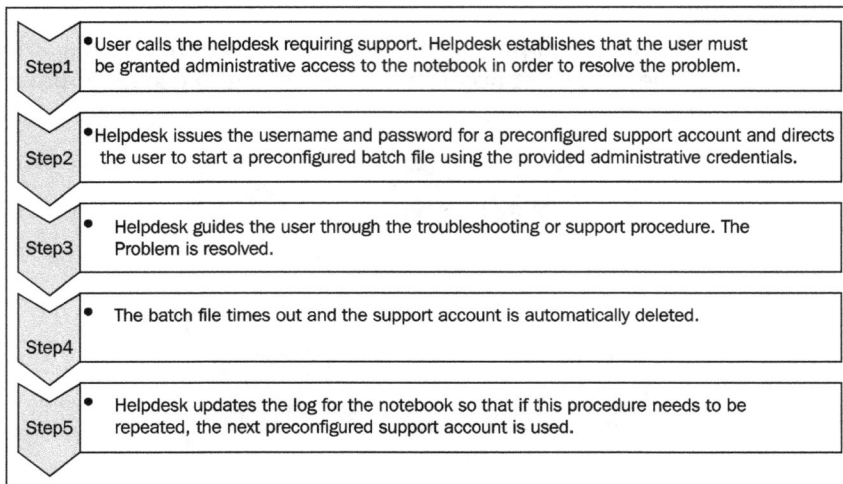

Step1	• User calls the helpdesk requiring support. Helpdesk establishes that the user must be granted administrative access to the notebook in order to resolve the problem.
Step2	• Helpdesk issues the username and password for a preconfigured support account and directs the user to start a preconfigured batch file using the provided administrative credentials.
Step3	• Helpdesk guides the user through the troubleshooting or support procedure. The Problem is resolved.
Step4	• The batch file times out and the support account is automatically deleted.
Step5	• Helpdesk updates the log for the notebook so that if this procedure needs to be repeated, the next preconfigured support account is used.

> **Restricting access to firecall accounts**
>
> Consider restricting the number of help desk staff who have access to usernames and passwords for firecall accounts, to limit the reporting requirements for the purposes of SOX and PCI compliance, should these credentials be abused.

Bypassing user account control for selected operations

It may be necessary for a mobile user to perform an operation that requires administrative privileges on a regular basis. A real-world example of this that I encountered was on a notebook with a faulty wireless adapter. After the notebook resumed from hibernation, it was quite common that the adapter would not work. The only solutions were to reboot the notebook, a considerable nuisance for the user, or to disable and then enable the adapter in the Network and Sharing Center, but this operation requires administrative privileges.

Using Task Scheduler to run commands with elevated privileges

To solve this problem, log in to the notebook as an administrator and create a batch file that contains the necessary commands to disable and enable the wireless adapter.

```
@echo off
echo --- Restarting Wireless Adapter
netsh interface set interface
  name="Wireless Network Connection" admin=disabled
netsh interface set interface
  name="Wireless Network Connection" admin=enabled
```

Save the file, `wireless.bat`, to a trusted location on the user's notebook; for instance to a dedicated folder in `C:\Program Files` or `C:\Windows`. In this case, I've created a folder called `Support` in `C:\Program Files`.

1. Type **Task Scheduler** in the **Search programs and files** box on the Start menu and press *Enter*.
2. In the left pane of Task Scheduler, select **Task Scheduler Library**.
3. Right-click on **Task Scheduler Library** and select **New Folder** from the menu.
4. Call the folder **Support** and click **OK**.

5. Expand **Task Scheduler Library**, right-click the **Support** folder, and select **Create Task** from the menu.

6. In the **Create Task** dialog box, name the task **Wireless**.

7. Click **Change User or Group** and in the **Select User or Group** dialog box, type SYSTEM and click **OK**.

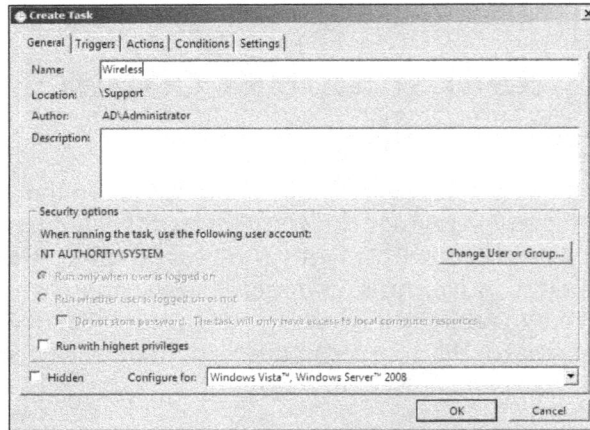

8. Switch to the **Actions** tab and click **New**.

9. In the **New Action** dialog box, enter the local path of the `wireless.bat` file in the **Program/script** box under **Settings** and click **OK**.

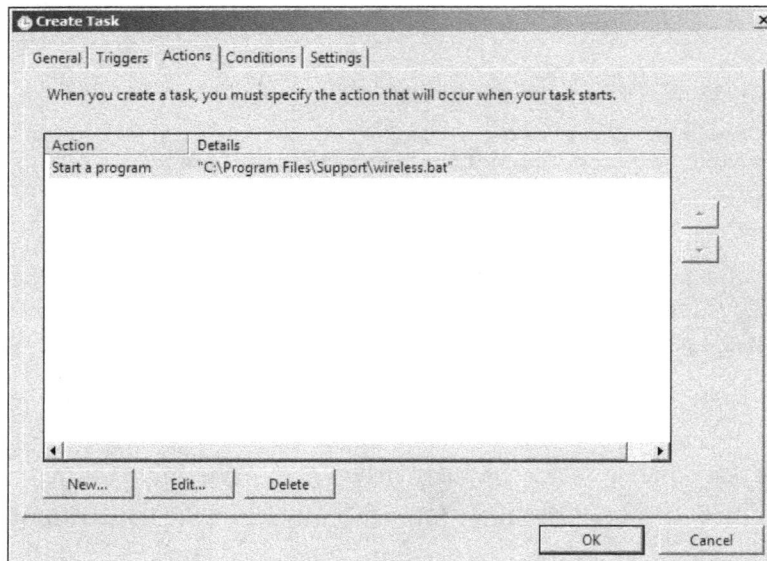

10. Switch to the **Conditions** tab and under **Power**, uncheck **Start the task only if the computer is on AC power**.

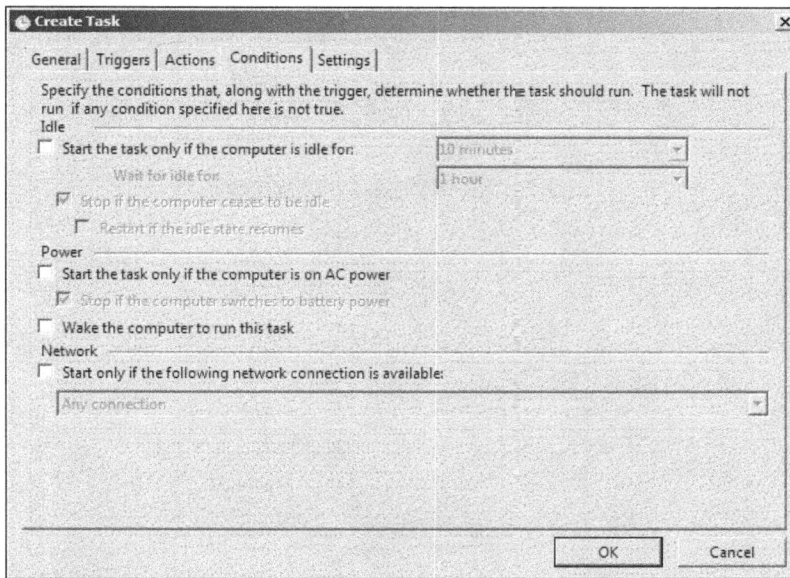

11. Click OK. In the central pane of Task Scheduler, right-click the **Wireless** task and select **Run** from the menu. Make sure that the wireless adapter is restarted as expected.

The challenge is now to allow a standard user to run this task, because, by default, standard users can't run tasks on demand that are created by an administrator. We need to change permissions on the *Wireless* task using Windows Explorer to allow **Authenticated Users** to run it.

1. Launch **Windows Explorer** by pressing the Windows Key + *E*. Navigate to C:\Windows\System32\Tasks\Support, right-click on the **Wireless** file, and select **Properties** from the menu.

2. In the **Wireless Properties** dialog box, switch to the **Security** tab.

3. Click on **Edit** and in the **Permissions for Wireless** window, click **Add**.

4. In the **Selected Users, Computers, Service Accounts, or Groups** dialog box, click on **Locations**, select the local computer, and click **OK**.

5. Type **Authenticated Users** into the box and click **OK**.

6. In the **Permissions for Wireless** window, select **Authenticated Users** and check **Allow** for **Read & Execute and Read** permissions.

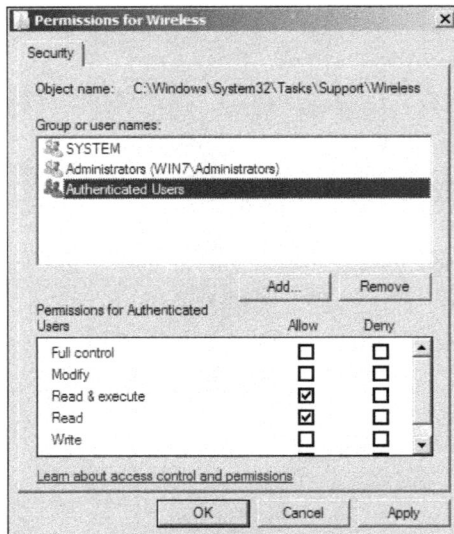

7. Click **OK** and then **Yes** in the **Windows Security** dialog box.
8. Click **OK** in the **Wireless Properties** dialog box.

Running the Scheduled Task as a standard user

Now that the task is in place and permissions have been set, let's set up a shortcut to allow the user to run the task on demand. Log in to the notebook using a standard user account, in this case user@ad.contoso.com.

1. Open a command prompt and type schtasks /run /TN "Support\ Wireless" and press *Enter*.

2. Schtasks should respond with SUCCESS: Attempted to run the scheduled task "Support\Wireless".

3. Check that the wireless adapter has been restarted as expected.

4. Right-click the user's desktop and select **New | Shortcut** from the menu.

5. In the **Create Shortcut** dialog box, type schtasks /run /TN "Support\ Wireless" into the box and click **Next**.

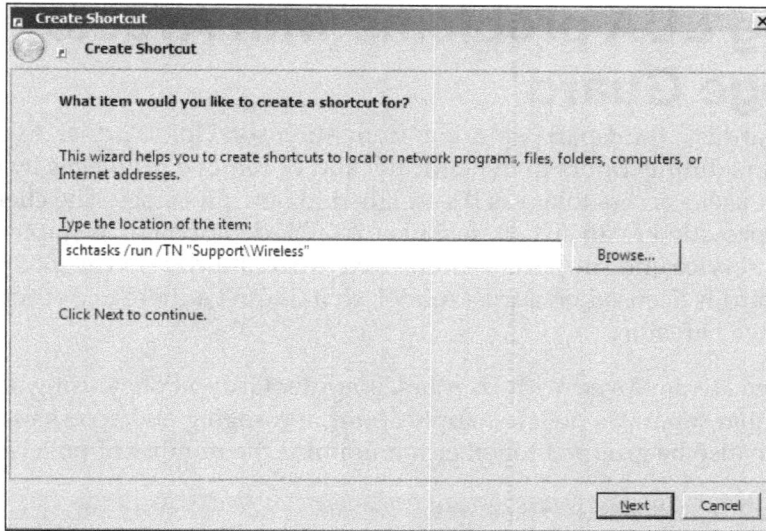

6. Give the shortcut a name and click **Finish**.

Configuring applications to run with elevated privileges on-the-fly

Despite all the possible workarounds to launch an application or set of commands with elevated privileges from a standard user account, Windows doesn't provide any built-in means of allowing system administrators to configure a particular application to launch as the currently logged in standard user, but with an administrative token. Consider a situation where you don't have time to fix an application that won't run as a standard user, but don't want to grant administrative privileges just for the sake of one application. While it may be possible to start the application using a secondary logon, this is impractical in most cases.

Solving LUA problems with Avecto Privilege Guard

Privilege Guard is a third-party solution, from Microsoft Gold Partner Avecto, that allows system administrators to dynamically add or remove privileges by modifying the logged in user's access token as it's assigned to new processes. The client-side component, provided as an .exe or .msi file for GPSI deployment, is implemented as a user-mode service and supports Windows XP (or Windows Server 2003) and later. Privilege Guard is licensed on a trust model, so it doesn't adhere to a strict object count in Active Directory.

Client settings are deployed with User or Computer Group Policy using a flexible architecture that separates policies, applications, messaging and access tokens. Programs can also be grouped together to minimize the number of policies applied.

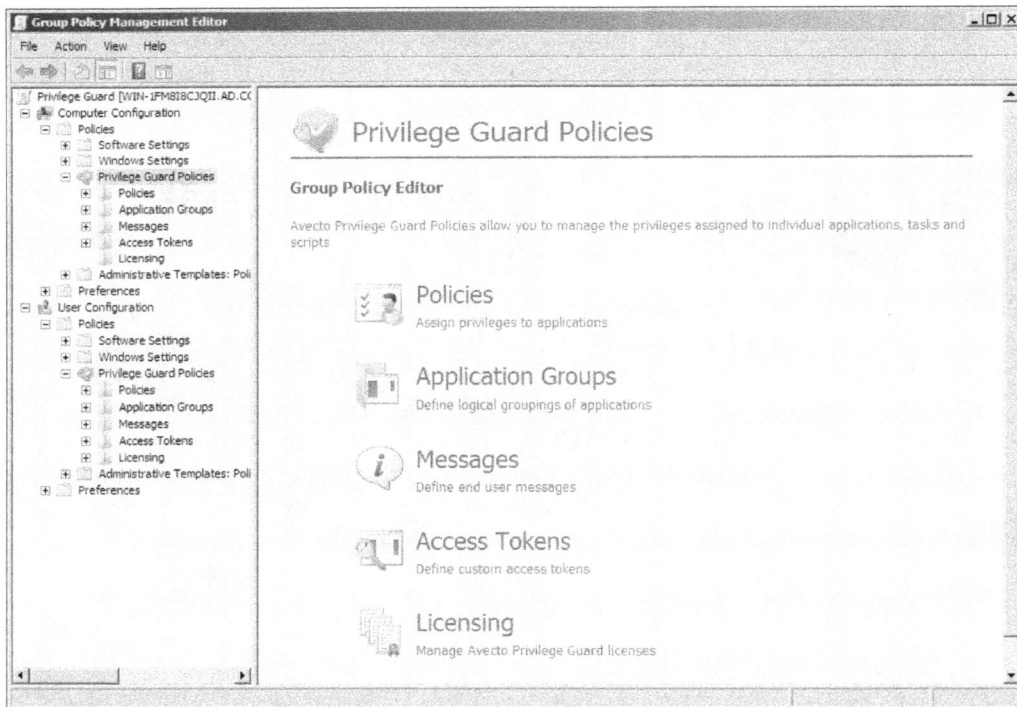

Defining application groups

For each Application Group, you can define one or more programs using the following categories:

- Executables
- Control Panel Applets
- Management Console snap-ins
- Windows Installer Packages
- Windows Scripting Host (WSH), PowerShell scripts and batch files
- Registry Editor files
- ActiveX controls (matched by URL or CLSID)

Application Templates can also be used to quickly locate built-in Windows tools such as Performance Monitor or System Restore. In the screenshot that follows, I used an Application Template to locate the Disk Management console (diskmgmt. msc) in Windows 7. The default setting is to match processes by file or folder name, but processes can also be matched by command line switch, file hash, publisher or any combination thereof. Privilege Guard supports matching by publisher certificate when Windows binaries are indirectly signed using Windows Security Catalogs.

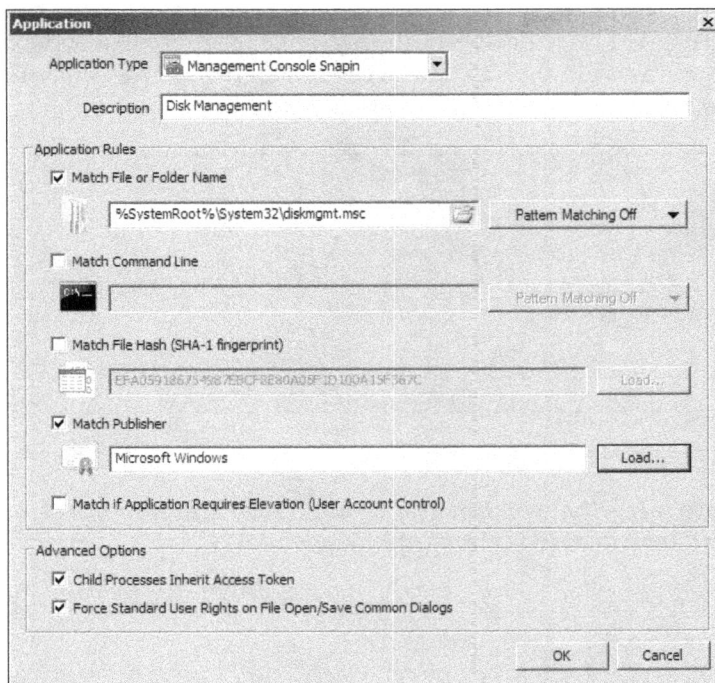

Additional options include:

- The ability to match processes if Privilege Guard detects that an application will trigger UAC.
- To determine whether child processes spawned by the matched parent process inherit the privileges of the user's modified access token.
- To suppress elevated privileges on File Open/Save common dialogs to prevent users from modifying protected files.

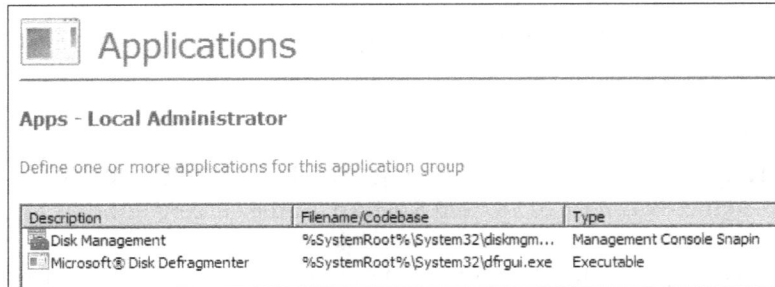

Applications

Apps - Local Administrator

Define one or more applications for this application group

Description	Filename/Codebase	Type
Disk Management	%SystemRoot%\System32\diskmgm...	Management Console Snapin
Microsoft® Disk Defragmenter	%SystemRoot%\System32\dfrgui.exe	Executable

Defining access tokens

We can define the rights allotted to access tokens in Privilege Guard based on the privileges assigned to Windows built-in groups. Rights can also be added or removed on an individual basis. The access token below uses the built-in Administrators group as the basis for assigning privileges.

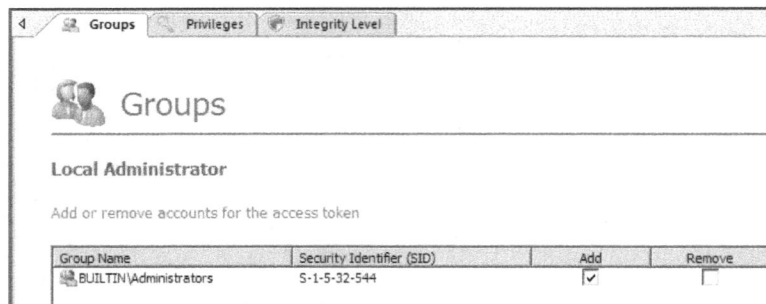

| ◁ | Groups | Privileges | Integrity Level |

Groups

Local Administrator

Add or remove accounts for the access token

Group Name	Security Identifier (SID)	Add	Remove
BUILTIN\Administrators	S-1-5-32-544	✓	☐

An access token's integrity level can also be overridden. See *Chapter 4, User Account Control,* for more information on integrity levels.

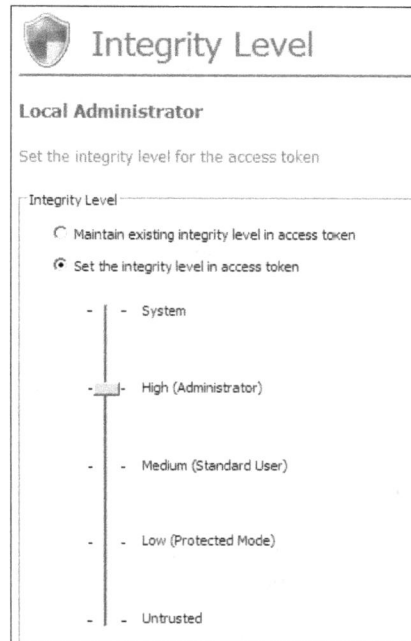

Any combination of groups, privileges or integrity levels can be added or removed in an access token.

Configuring messages

While it may be preferable in many situations to silently elevate privileges when a user starts a legacy application, organizations can use Privilege Guard to generate fully customizable messages, in multiple languages if necessary, that are displayed when applications are blocked, or if users are required to confirm their credentials or provide a reason for launching a process with elevated privileges.

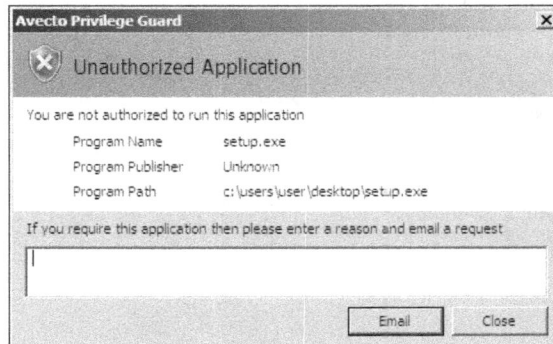

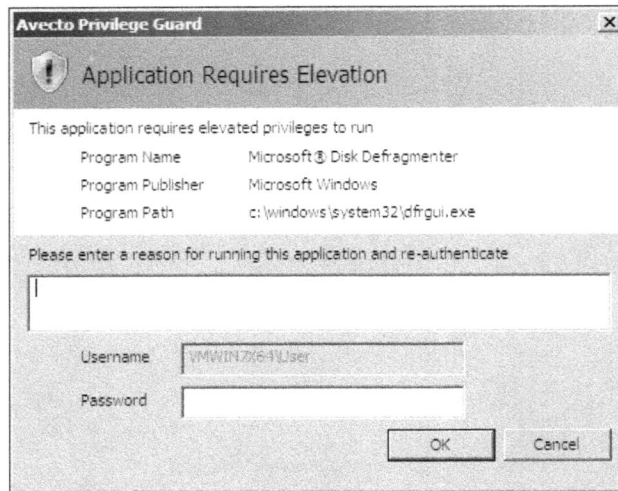

The drop-down menu under Message Type can be set to Allow or Block Execution, and determines not only the type of message that's displayed, but enforces the corresponding block/allow action.

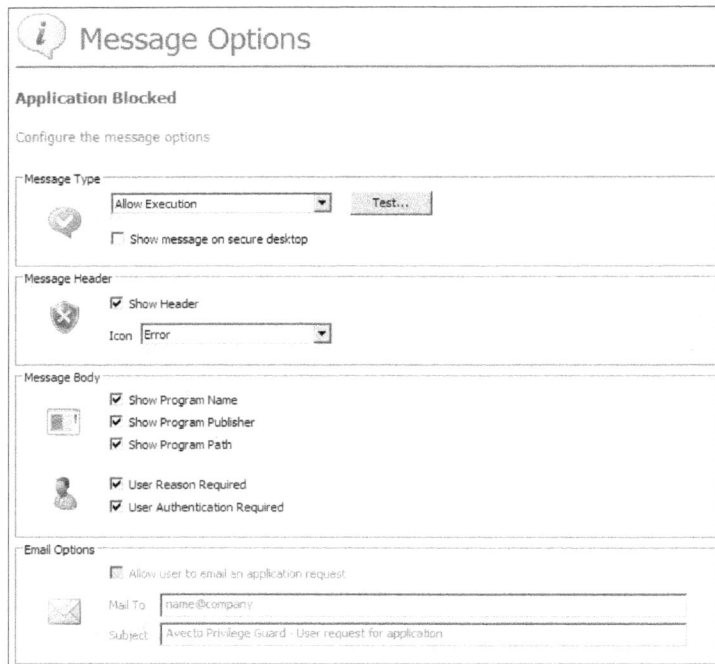

Defining policies

The final task is to define a policy to bring the entire configuration together and determine how it is applied. Here we can choose to apply our policy to all users (using the built-in Everyone group), or select individual users and groups; set the application group, access token and optionally message included in the policy. We can configure multiple sets of actions for application groups, access tokens, messages and auditing (Application Group Actions and Auditing).

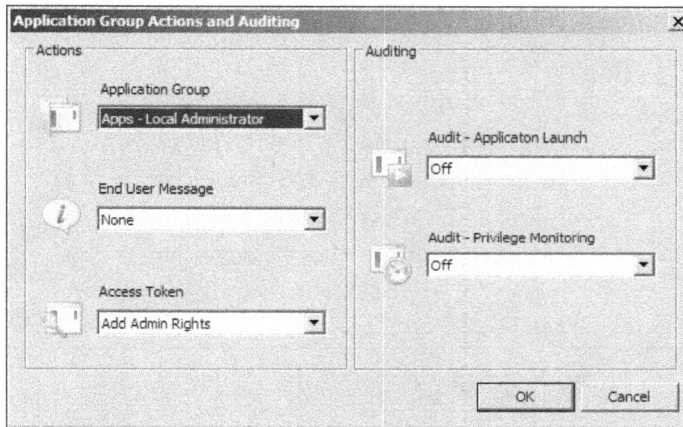

Optional settings include the ability to configure Privilege Guard shell integration for specified application groups so that a process can be launched from Explorer's context menu with a modified access token, allowing advanced users to elevate applications on demand. System administrators can also enable logging options for the purposes of software metering or monitoring privilege use.

Solving LUA problems with Privilege Manager

BeyondTrust's **Privilege Manager** provides system administrators with a solution that allows them to define applications or processes that launch as the logged in user, but with an administrative-level access token. Privilege Manager is divided into client and server software. The server software, or snap-in software as it's referred to, installs on a server in your organization and updates Group Policy Object Editor for policy configuration and provides Group Policy Management Console integration. The client software installs on each device to which Privilege Manager policies will apply.

Let's take a simple example of how Privilege Manager might be used. We'll configure a policy that allows standard users to start Notepad with administrative rights.

Defining Privilege Manager rules

We start by deciding what kind of rule we want to apply, in a similar vein to Software Restriction Policy (or AppLocker in Windows 7), but the options for targeting applications are slightly expanded:

Privilege Manager Rules:

Rule name	Function
Path rule	Target an application by its program file path
Hash rule	Target an application by a hash of its file
Folder rule	Target all applications in a folder
MSI Path rule	Target installations by MSI file path
MSI Folder rule	Target installations by MSI file folder
ActiveX rule	Target an IE ActiveX control installation
Certificate rule	Target an application by its certificate
Shell rule	Target any application started from Explorer
CD\DVD rule	Target a CD-ROM or DVD

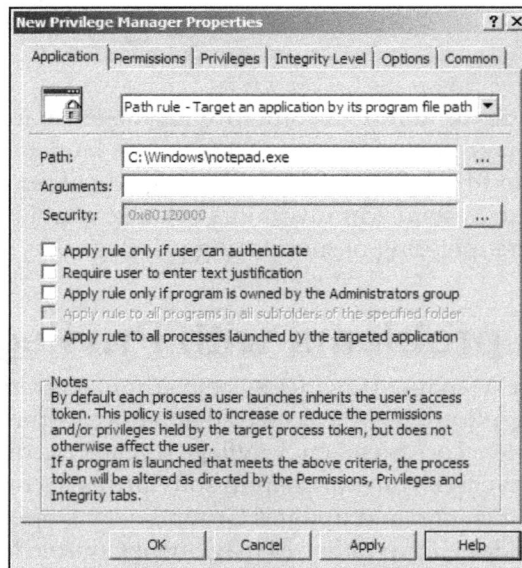

Once we've chosen the rule type, we can enter the path to our application manually or use the browse button to choose from a list of predefined Windows applications, control panel applets, and wizards.

> **Per-Computer or Per-User Policies**
> Policy Maker policy settings can be applied to the computer or to specific users. Additionally, Policy Maker can be used with local policy settings or Group Policy.

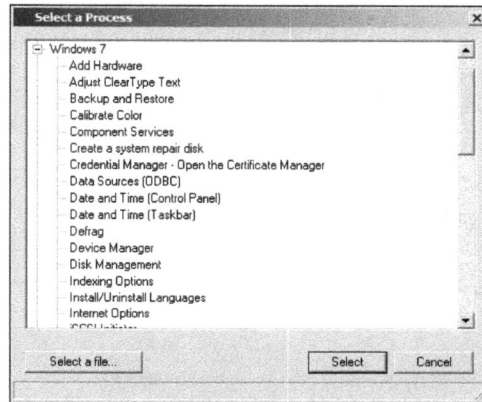

Two additional options require users to enter their credentials again before the process or application is launched (**apply rule only if user can authenticate**) or require users to provide an explanation for launching the application, which is logged by Privilege Manager (**require user to enter text justification**).

Assigning permissions

Here we get to choose the permission level with which the process or application will launch. You can choose to add or remove a group from the logged in user's access token.

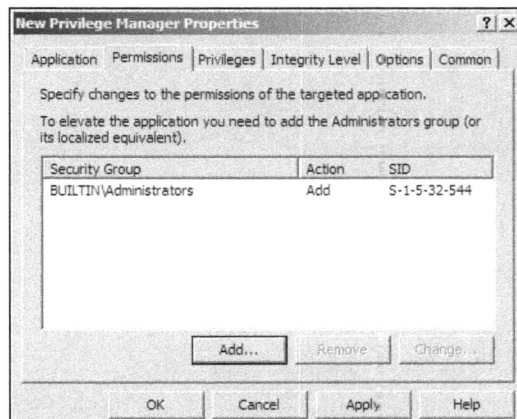

Adding or removing individual privileges

The **Privileges** tab gives us more granular control to add or remove individual rights.

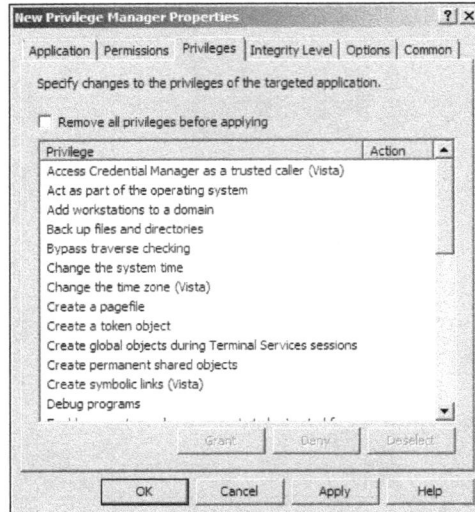

Specifying integrity levels

We have the opportunity to specify the integrity level with which the process should launch under Vista and Windows 7. See *Chapter 4, User Account Control*, for more details on integrity levels.

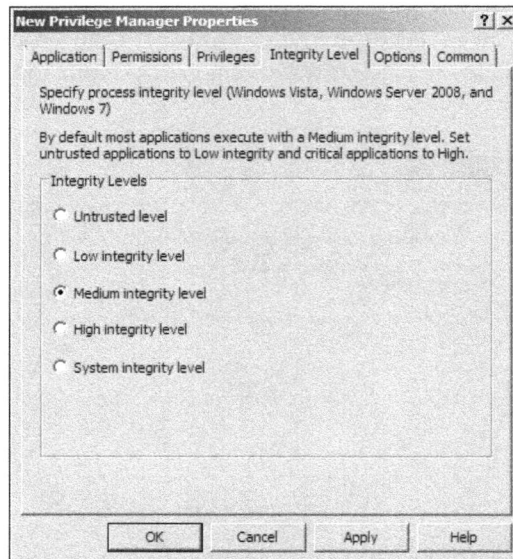

Suppressing unwanted User Account Control prompts

As we learned in *Chapter 3*, the privilege level at which a program runs can be specified in the application's manifest. There are some applications that insist, via the manifest, that they run with elevated privileges. If an application requires administrative privileges via the manifest, it's not possible for a standard user to run the application without providing alternative login credentials.

This can be a rather frustrating situation for system administrators, who want to issue standard user accounts but are forced to provide administrative credentials because of applications that specify only to be run with administrator credentials in their manifest. There are two possible solutions—modify the application's manifest to specify the RunAsInvoker value, or use the Application Compatibility Toolkit to apply the RunAsInvoker shim. Some applications insist on being run as an administrator via the manifest, but in reality, don't require administrative privileges for normal everyday operation.

Modifying application manifest files

As per Microsoft's best practice advice, if there's a compatibility problem with an application, it's always preferable to fix the problem with the application, rather than apply a compatibility fix. While some application manifests are included separately from the main executable file as an XML file, many applications embed the manifest in the .exe, making it difficult to edit. For example, Microsoft Office 2007 uses separate XML manifest files for each application in the suite, making it easier to edit the manifests in the unlikely event you should need to.

Editing manifests using Resource Tuner

For applications that embed the manifest into the main .exe, one solution for editing the manifest is to use a third-party application called Resource Tuner (http://www.heaventools.com/resource-tuner.htm) from Heaventools.com.

> **MT.exe**
> Microsoft has a tool that is part of the **Windows Software Development Kit (SDK)** that's designed to add or modify manifests, but is not always reliable at parsing precompiled .exe files.

Update Notifier (`updatenotifier.exe`) is a small portable executable that scans the applications on a PC and checks against an Internet database to check that the latest versions are installed. When run as a standard user, it triggers User Account Control to prompt for administrative privileges. However, simply to scan applications and run a report against them doesn't require anything more than standard user privileges. Resource Tuner can be used to edit the manifest, which is embedded in the application's main `.exe` file, to provide trust information that specifies the program should be launched with the privilege level of the currently logged in user (asInvoker).

The following screenshot shows the application's original manifest in Resource Tuner without a section for trust information:

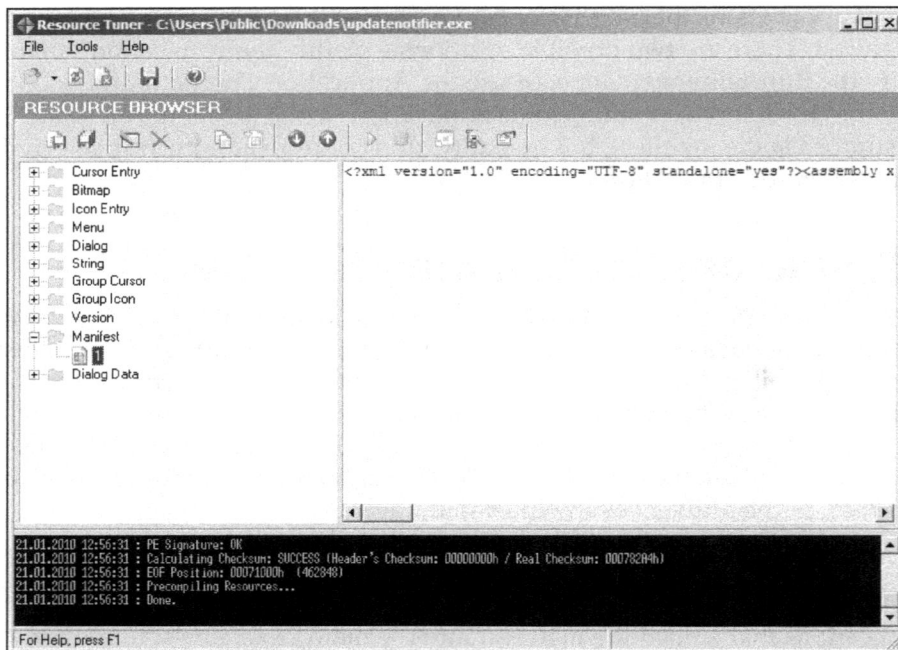

I was able to use Resource Tuner's editor to modify the manifest to include the appropriate trust information as shown in this screenshot:

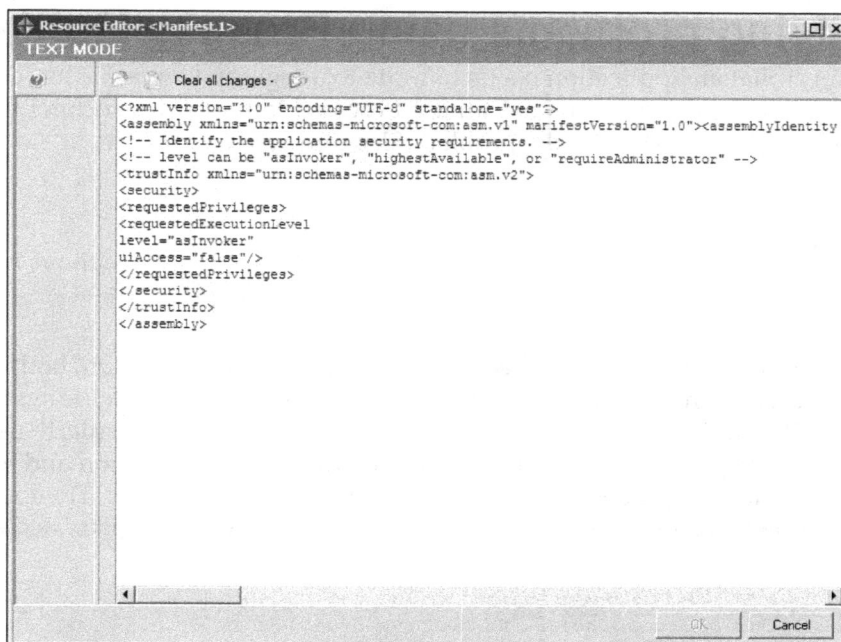

```
<?xml version="1.0" encoding="UTF-8" standalone="yes"?>
<assembly xmlns="urn:schemas-microsoft-com:asm.v1" manifestVersion="1.0"><assemblyIdentity
<!-- Identify the application security requirements. -->
<!-- level can be "asInvoker", "highestAvailable", or "requireAdministrator" -->
<trustInfo xmlns:schemas-microsoft-com:asm.v2">
<security>
<requestedPrivileges>
<requestedExecutionLevel
level="asInvoker"
uiAccess="false"/>
</requestedPrivileges>
</security>
</trustInfo>
</assembly>
```

The application now starts without triggering a UAC prompt for elevation.

Modifying manifests using the RunAsInvoker shim

For applications that are permanently installed on PCs, that is not portable, the Application Compatibility Toolkit can be used to apply the RunAsInvoker shim, with the same result as the previous solution, but without the need to modify the executable or manifest files. Before applying this shim, you should consider modifying the application's installer if developed in-house, or contact the software company for a fix. For more information about distributing compatibility shims, see *Chapter 3*.

Setting permissions on files and registry keys

It's always preferable to leverage the compatibility features built into Windows via the Application Compatibility Toolkit to avoid relaxing permissions that could lead to security or support issues. However, Least Privilege Security problems related to permissions on files, folders, and registry keys can be solved by loosening permissions using Windows Sysinternals tools and Group Policy.

Identifying problems using Process Monitor

If you suspect that an application needs to write to a registry key or file but doesn't have the necessary permissions, you can use Process Monitor from Technet's Sysinternals website to identify the problem files or registry keys.

> **Process Monitor**
>
> Download Process Monitor from Technet here: `http://technet.microsoft.com/en-us/sysinternals/bb896645.aspx`.

Process Monitor combines two deprecated tools, RegMon and FileMon, both of which were used to monitor how processes accessed the registry and file system. Process Monitor adds to the features of these two applications. Particularly useful is the ability to filter processes, so you can remove unwanted information and focus on what's important by right-clicking an item to filter out similar entries. The following screenshot shows Process Monitor in action, monitoring file and registry access for `updatenotifier.exe`:

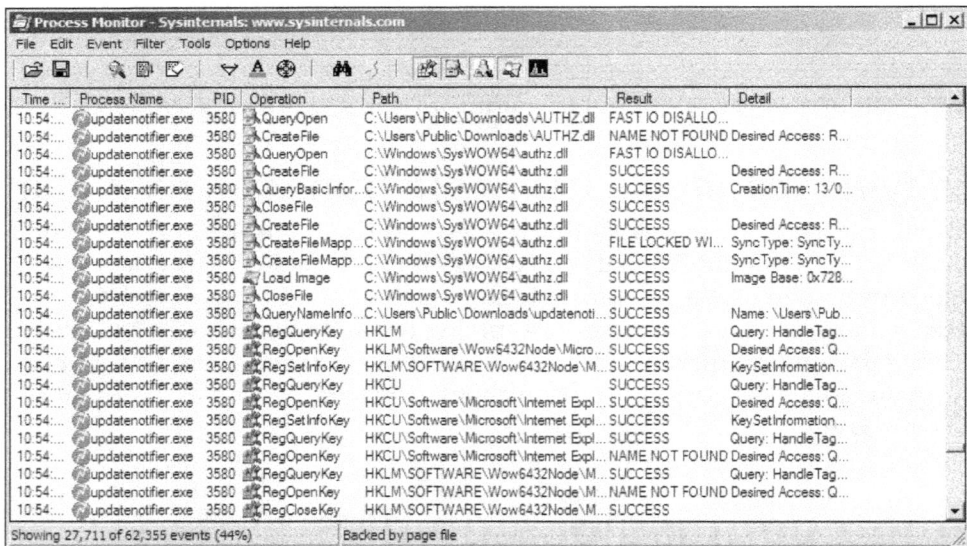

Modifying permissions on registry keys and files with Group Policy

Once you've decided on and tested the permissions that need to be modified, Group Policy can be used to make and enforce those changes across multiple computers. Create a new Group Policy Object linked to the Organizational Unit that contains the computer accounts of the PCs that need their configuration modified.

1. In **Group Policy Management Editor**, expand **Computer Configuration, Windows Settings, Security Settings**.

2. Right-click **File System** and select **Add File** from the menu.

3. In the **Add a file or folder** dialog box, browse for the file or folder on which you want to modify and/or enforce permissions and click **OK**.

4. In the **Database Security** dialog box, set the required permissions and click **OK**.

Permissions

You should note that the permissions presented in the Database Security dialog box may not necessarily be those that are currently set on the file or folder. You should check what permissions currently exist on your systems to ensure that any changes you make or enforce through Group Policy don't break important functionality.

5. In the **Add Object** window, choose whether to **Propagate inheritable permissions to all subfolders and files, Replace existing permissions on all subfolders and files with inheritable permissions**, or **Do not allow permissions on this file or folder to be replaced**.

6. Click **OK** and the new configuration will appear in the right pane.

The procedure for configuring or enforcing permissions on registry keys is identical to the procedure for files and folders as outlined here.

Fixing problems with the HKey Classes Root registry hive

Some older applications, such as earlier versions of AutoCad, write to HKCR every time the application starts, to ensure that file associations and COM registration information is still present before the program starts. This data should, in principle, already be present in the registry, as it is written when the application is installed, but access violations will occur if a standard user starts the program, despite the fact that the information doesn't usually need to be rewritten.

> **Changes to HKCR in Windows 2000 and later**
>
> Windows 2000 and later operating systems use per-user registration for file associations and COM objects in HKCU\Software\Classes, and the HKCR registry hive is a merged view of HKLM\Software\Classes and HKCU\Software\Classes.

Using Registry Editor to copy keys from HKCR to HKCU

Identify which HKCR keys your application is attempting to write to when it starts up using Process Monitor or LUA Buglight and export them to a file using Regedit.

1. Log in as a local administrator and type Regedit into the **Search for programs and files** box on the Start menu.

2. In the left pane of Registry Editor, expand **Computer**, **HKEY_CLASSES_ ROOT** and find the first key that you need to export to a file.

3. Right-click the key and select **Export** from the menu.

4. In the **Export Registry File** dialog box, save the file to an accessible location and click on **Save**.

5. Locate the saved .reg file, right-click on it and select **Edit** from the menu.

6. Replace all cases of **[HKEY_CLASSES_ROOT** with **[HKEY_CURRENT_ USER\Software\Classes** and save the file.

7. Right-click the saved .reg file again and select **Merge** from the menu.

8. In the **Registry Editor** dialog box, click **Yes** to confirm that you want to go ahead with the operation.

9. Click **OK** in the **Registry Editor** window.

You may need to repeat this procedure several times depending on how many keys need to be copied to HKCU, and how many users you want to do this operation for.

Mapping .ini files to the registry

Despite the fact that the use of .ini files for application configuration information was phased out as early as Windows NT 3.1, the APIs for use with .ini files still exist in Windows and are used by some applications. If an application attempts to use the APIs to find .ini file information but cannot find an entry under HKLM\ SOFTWARE\Microsoft\Windows NT\CurrentVersion\IniFileMapping\ for its configuration data, it may try to write to the file system, generating an access violation error for standard users. This problem can be rectified by logging in to a system as an administrator and adding the necessary information to the IniFileMapping key in the registry.

> For more information on the IniFileMapping registry key, see the following information on Technet:
>
> http://technet.microsoft.com/en-us/library/
> cc722567.aspx

Using LUA Buglight to identify file and registry access violations

A tool for identifying file system and registry access violations when programs run as a standard user, LUA Buglight 2.1, has been updated to support Windows 7.

> **Downloading LUA Buglight 2.1**
>
> LUA Buglight can be downloaded from here:
>
> http://blogs.msdn.com/aaron_margosis/
> archive/2006/08/07/LuaBuglight.aspx

LUA Buglight intercepts an application when an operation fails due to standard user rights. The operation is then repeated and information logged in the LUA Buglight Reporter for analysis.

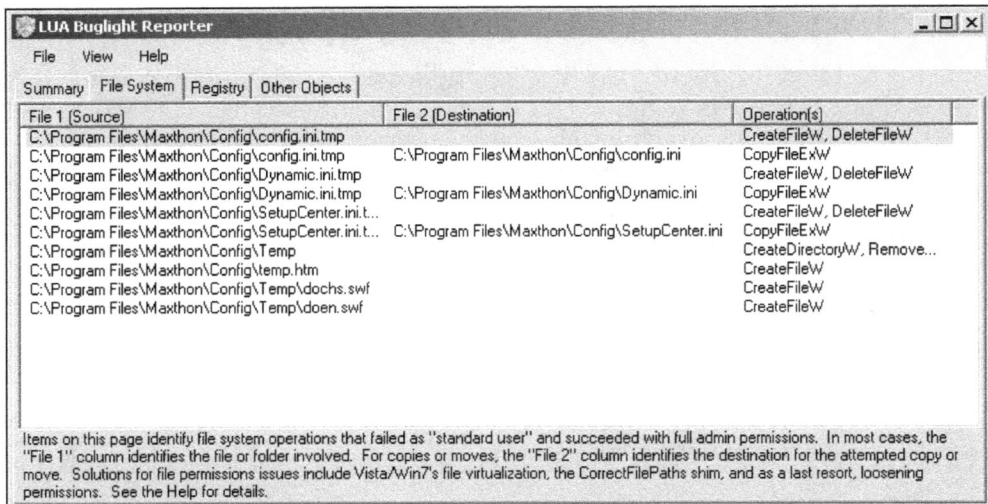

Summary

In this chapter, we've learned how to cope with difficult support situations for standard users, run common processes without the need to elevate with administrative privileges all the time, and about additional third-party tools that can be used to solve common Least Privilege Security problems. Before continuing to the next chapter, you should be able to:

- Implement a support solution for mobile users who run with standard user privileges

- Configure common tasks to run without the need to enter an administrator username and password

- Solve Least Privilege Security problems with legacy applications on Windows XP that write to the HKCR registry hive on startup

- Be aware of some of the third-party tools available for solving Least Privilege Security problems

In the next chapter, we'll learn how to deploy software across networks that run with least privilege user accounts

6

Software Distribution using Group Policy

One of the biggest barriers to implementing Least Privilege Security on the desktop is software installation. Removing administrative privileges from end users gives IT more control over what software is installed on the network, but users must rely on an administrator or a software distribution system to install or update authorized programs. In this chapter, we'll learn how to distribute software using Group Policy to computers where users run with Least Privilege Security. We will cover:

- Preparing applications for deployment using **Group Policy Software Installation (GPSI)** and **Windows Installer**
- Creating .msi **wrappers** for legacy setup programs
- **Repackage** legacy setup programs in Windows Installer .msi format
- Making GPSI more scalable and flexible using the **Distributed File System (DFS)**
- Targeting client computers using **Windows Management Instrumentation (WMI) filters** and **Group Policy Scope of Management**

Installing software using Group Policy

If your organization doesn't have an enterprise-class software distribution system, such as System Center Configuration Manager (previously known as Systems Management Server) or System Center Essentials, Group Policy Software Installation (GPSI) can be used to distribute applications to computers where users run without administrative privileges.

GPSI was introduced as part of **IntelliMirror** technology in Windows 2000, but hasn't been widely adopted by SMEs. Large organizations use more scalable software management systems like **Systems Center Configuration Manager (SCCM)**.

Microsoft System Center Configuration Manager offers several advantages for software distribution over Group Policy Software Installation, such as the ability to stream packages over slow network connections using the **Background Intelligent Transfer Service (BITS)** and more efficient targeting using **Collections**. System Center Essentials, which provides a subset of SCCM's features, can also take the pain out of repackaging legacy applications by accepting .exe files for deployment.

Installing software using Windows Installer

Windows Installer packages (.msi files) are relational databases that contain information about the files and configuration changes that need to be made to a system for successful installation. When an application is installed from an .msi file, all operations are recorded, so that changes can be rolled back in the event of an error or for removing the program.

Many new applications come packaged in .msi format, which is ideal for use with GPSI, as it enables you to take advantage of Windows Installer and its ability to distribute software to users who run without administrative privileges. Windows Installer has other advantages, such as built-in resiliency and repair functionality. In many cases, software manufacturers provide customization programs that are used to generate transform (.mst) files that allow the installation to be customized without modifying the original .msi file.

Using an .msi file supplied by the manufacturer

Try to get an .msi file directly from the software manufacturer, as producing your own installer packages is something of an art and requires a lot of background knowledge and time for testing.

Deploying software using Group Policy

To install software without administrative privileges, GPSI requires applications to be packaged in Windows Installer .msi format. While many programs come packaged in .msi format, there are still numerous legacy applications that rely on older setup technologies. Legacy setup programs, which usually end with the .exe file extension and don't contain an .msi file, can be published using GPSI .zap files, but the logged-in user must be an administrator to complete the installation process.

> **Group Policy Software Installation .zap files**
>
> .zap files are simple scripts, which GPSI calls to publish a program in the **Add/Remove Programs** control panel applet. The application isn't installed unless the user selects it from the control panel or tries to open a file that is associated with the published application. Users must have administrative privileges to install applications published using .zap files.

If an .msi file isn't available for the application, you ll need to investigate one of the following methods:

- **Create an .msi wrapper for setup.exe**: An .msi wrapper is a Windows Installer database that uses a custom action to launch a legacy setup.exe file.

- **Use a Group Policy startup script**: Launch setup.exe with administrative privileges from a batch file using command-line switches to invoke a silent install and customizations.

- **Repackage the software in .msi format**: Repackaging involves using third-party software to monitor an application installer and generate a Windows Installer database. However, it should be considered a last resort, as without the appropriate tools and experience on hand, it's difficult to produce reliable installers using this method. Some repackaging solutions take snapshots of the operating system before and after an application is installed to produce .msi files. This method is less reliable than monitoring low-level changes that the installer makes while it's in progress.

> **Office 2007**
>
> Prior to Office 2007, Microsoft utilized .msi files and transform files (.mst) for Office customization. In Office 2007, patch files (.msp) are used for customization, but are not supported by GPSI. The recommended method for deploying Office 2007 is Microsoft System Center Configuration Manager or Group Policy startup scripts.

Comparing Group Policy Software Installation with system images for software distribution

Larger organizations often make use of imaging technologies, such as Windows Deployment Services or Symantec Ghost, that allow the operating system and applications to be pre-configured and deployed over the network from a dedicated server.

Choosing between thin and fat images

So called thin images contain just the operating system and the minimum of additional components. All remaining configuration is managed via Group Policy and/or a dedicated management system, such as Microsoft System Center Configuration Manager. Fat images contain the operating system and all the required applications are pre-installed. When new applications are required, the image is updated and redeployed.

Larger organizations, that can afford the necessary infrastructure and have the required skills, can use imaging solutions to overcome some of the problems associated with deploying software to users running with Least Privilege Security. Many companies choose a combination of imaging and other management systems for maximum flexibility.

Preparing applications for deployment

It's always preferable to use a Windows Installer package (.msi file) supplied by the manufacturer. Creating your own installer package for a legacy application is a complicated process that requires a lot of testing. In this section, we'll look at how to inspect installer packages for embedded .msi files, and in a worst case scenario, how to create an .msi file using a third-party repackaging tool.

> **Ask the vendor**
>
> Before looking at any of the following information, always approach the vendor directly and ask if they have an .msi installer for the software if you can't find one on their website.

Extracting .msi files from setup packages

If an application is not supplied as an .msi file, it may be that the .exe is simply a wrapper for an .msi package and other associated files. In this case, you should check the manufacturer's website to see if the files inside the .exe can be extracted using a command-line switch. For example, Adobe supplies its free Acrobat Reader software as an .exe file. The .msi package and associated files can be extracted by specifying the -nos_ne switch:

```
adberdr90_en_us_std.exe -nos_ne
```

Once the files have been extracted, they can be found in the %userprofile%\AppData\Local\Adobe\Reader 9.0\Setup Files folder.

> **Acrobat Reader in the Enterprise**
>
> While Acrobat Reader is a free product, if you want to distribute the program in a corporate environment, you must apply for a free enterprise license at:
>
> `http://www.adobe.com/products/acrobat/distribute.html`
>
> The standalone installer package for Acrobat 9.0 can be downloaded from Adobe's FTP site:
>
> `ftp://ftp.adobe.com/pub/adobe/reader/win/9.x/9.0/enu/`
> `AdbeRdr90_en_US_Std.exe`

Using WinRAR or 7-Zip to extract .msi files

If the manufacturer hasn't enabled any switches for extracting the contents of an `.exe` package, there are a couple of other methods you might use to inspect the contents of an `.exe`. On a test machine, run the supplied `setup.exe` file and use a monitoring utility, such as Process Monitor from SysInternals, to see where the files are being extracted to; usually somewhere in the user's temporary directory. There you might find an `.msi` file to install the software. Depending on the compression algorithm, you could also try to use decompression/compression utilities like WinRAR or 7-Zip to extract the contents of the `.exe`.

> **Links to tools**
>
> SysInternals Process Monitor:
>
> `http://technet.microsoft.com/en-us/sysinternals/`
> `bb896645.aspx`
>
> WinRAR:
>
> `http://www.win-rar.com/`
>
> 7-Zip:
>
> `http://www.7-zip.org/`

Using command-line switches for silent installs and customization

Legacy setup programs often come with a series of switches that can be specified on the command line after the main executable to change the way the application installs or customize certain features. You should refer to the manufacturer's documentation as switches are often specific to the application. Common examples are the use of the `/quiet` switch for a silent install, where the user interface is suppressed while the application is installing.

> **Each application is individual**
>
> While certain packaging solutions, such as InstallShield and Wise, have switches that are common to the given technology, you should expect that every application you need to deploy is likely to require different treatment. There is no one standard for specifying command-line switches after `setup.exe` and the industry has yet to standardize solely on Windows Installer.

The msiexec application can also be used to launch `.msi` files with switches. This can be useful if you want to install an application from within a script or from the command line and need to specify a silent install or other options. Here's an example command line for msiexec that applies a transform file to customize Acrobat Reader and install the application silently:

```
msiexec.exe /i "acroread.msi" TRANSFORMS="acroread.mst" /qn
```

> **Msiexec command-line switches**
>
> A full list of command-line switches for msiexec can be found at:
> `http://technet.microsoft.com/en-us/library/cc759262(WS.10).aspx`

Deploying system changes using Group Policy startup scripts

While GPSI has advantages over scripted deployment, such as the ability to manage the application's full lifecycle and awareness of the installation state, the complexities of repackaging or creating an `.msi` wrapper for a legacy application might outweigh the advantages of GPSI. Therefore, you may want to consider using a simple batch file to deploy software from the command line using a Group Policy startup script.

Startup scripts are covered, which run in the context of the local system account with full administrative privileges, in *Chapter 10*, *Least Privilege in Windows XP*, to deploy Group Policy Preferences client-side extensions. Microsoft also supports Office 2007 deployment using startup scripts. For more detailed information on deploying Office 2007 using Group Policy, see `http://technet.microsoft.com/en-us/library/cc179134.aspx`.

Maximum wait time for Group Policy scripts

Group Policy startup scripts time out by default after 10 minutes. If you're deploying large applications using startup scripts, such as Office 2007, you should test your scripts in a lab environment to ensure that the default timeout value allows enough time for installs to complete. The **Maximum wait time for Group Policy scripts** policy setting can be found under **Computer Configuration | Administrative Templates | System | Scripts** in the Group Policy Management Editor and should be specified in seconds.

Creating an .msi wrapper

While repackaging a legacy setup program attempts to create a Windows Installer `.msi` file that replaces the original setup executable, an `.msi` wrapper launches the supplied setup executable, with or without customizations using switches, purely for the purposes of leveraging Windows Installer's ability to deploy an application without the need for the end user to have administrative privileges.

The main advantage of using a wrapper over repackaging is that it requires less testing because we're using the original setup routine to install the application. Secondly, we can use the original setup executable's switches to perform customizations with minimal testing. Third, when a new version of the application is released, it is easier to reuse our wrapper process than to repackage.

Wrappers versus repackaging

If you choose to create an `.msi` wrapper instead of repackaging the installer, you should note that you lose some of the benefits inherent to standard Windows Installer packages, such as resiliency and transactional operations.

In this section, I'm going to show you how to use a free utility called **Windows Installer Wrapper Wizard (WIWW)** (`http://www.vinsvision.com/Downloads/tabid/57/Default.aspx`) to create an `.msi` file that launches our legacy setup program using a custom action. The resulting `.msi` file can then be used with Group Policy Software Installation. Log in to a client machine as a local or domain administrator and install WIWW. In the instructions below, corporateapp should be replaced with a legacy installer of your choice. Once the installation has completed, do the following:

1. Launch WIWW from **All Programs** on the **Start** menu and click **Next** on the welcome screen.

2. On the **Windows Installer File** screen, click **Browse** to create a new `.msi` file.

3. In the **Save As** dialog box, create a folder called `CorporateAppSetup` to hold the installer files (`corporateappsetup.exe` and `corporateappsetup.msi`) on the desktop by clicking the new folder icon in the top right.

4. In the **Save As** dialog box, double-click the new **CorporateAppSetup** folder, type **corporateappsetup** in the **File name** box, and click **Save**.

5. On the **Windows Installer File** screen, click **Next**. On the **Install Commands** screen, click **Add**.

6. In the **Program to run** dialog box, on the right of **Select a Windows Installer folder property** check **Use [SourceDir]** and then click **Browse**.

7. Select the `coporateappsetup.exe` file in the `CorporateAppSetup` folder and click **Open**.

8. In the **Program to run** dialog box, add any switches required to install the application silently in the **Specify any program parameters field** and click **OK**.

9. On the **Install Commands** screen, click **Next**.

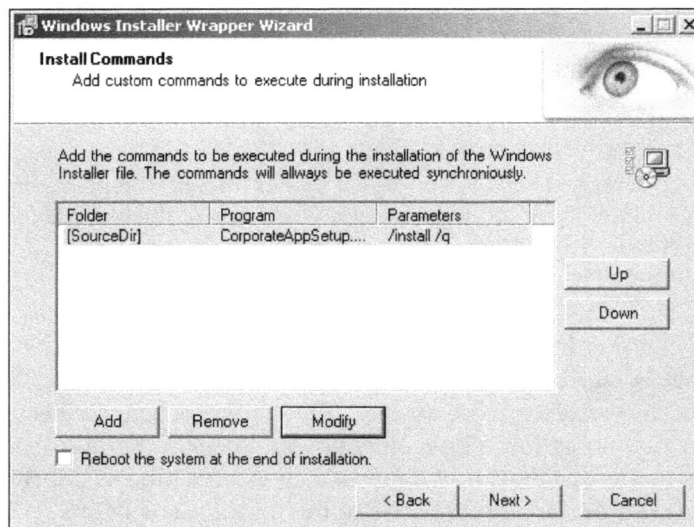

10. Repeat the same procedure for specifying the executable and switches for uninstall and click **Next**.

11. On the **Product Appearance and Requirements screen**, select any additional options regarding how the program is displayed in the **Add/Remove Programs** control panel applet and operating system requirements before clicking **Next**.

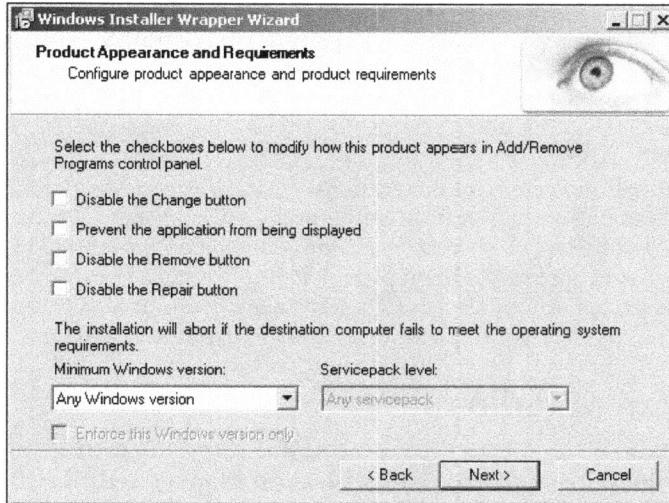

12. On the **Package MetaData and Language** screen, enter the product name, select the correct language and click **Next**.

13. Check the summary details and click **Next**.

14. Wait for processing to complete and click **Finish**.

15. Move `corporateappsetup.exe` to the `corporateappsetup` folder. When the `.msi` wrapper runs, it needs to have access to the original setup file (`corporateappsetup.exe`) in the `corporateappsetup` folder.

Double-click the `corporateappsetup.msi` file in the `CorporateAppSetup` folder to test the install. Repeat the procedure to remove CorporateApp.

Create an .msi wrapper with InstallShield

InstallShield can be used to create `.msi` wrappers for legacy setup programs but the process is more complicated than using WIWW. You need to start with a **Basic MSI** template in InstallShield, generate an `.msi` package and then add a custom action to launch the `setup.exe` file. InstallShield is available as part of AdminStudio or as a separate product.

Repackaging an application with a legacy installer

If all else fails and you're unable to obtain an `.msi` file directly from the manufacturer or extract one from whatever installer package is available, you can use a third-party solution to repackage legacy installers. In this section, I'll show you how to repackage a legacy installer using Flexera's AdminStudio, a product for administrators who manage installation packages on corporate networks and which is based on the popular InstallShield technology.

> ### Flexera's AdminStudio
>
> AdminStudio comes in four editions—Configuration Manager, Standard, Professional, and Enterprise. Configuration Manager is a limited free edition for users of Microsoft's System Center Configuration Manager server, and Standard edition provides simple repackaging and editing for those using Group Policy Software Installation. For more information, see: http://www.flexerasoftware.com/products/adminstudio.htm.

Installing AdminStudio

AdminStudio can be installed on Windows XP (SP1 and later) or Windows Server 2003 or later. If you're installing the Configuration Manager edition, make sure that SCCM or SMS is available in your domain. In the following demonstration, AdminStudio was installed on Windows Server 2008. Instructions may vary slightly for different versions of Windows.

Configuring AdminStudio's Repackager to run on a remote machine

Once AdminStudio is installed, you should configure the remote repackager to run on a cleanly installed operating system so that an installation routine can be successfully monitored and repackaged.

> ### Using a clean machine
>
> For best results, make sure that you have a clean machine available on which to install the application that will be repackaged. A clean machine has the operating system, any currently available service packs and updates, but nothing else. The repackaging wizard can be run from a network share to avoid installing the Repackager tool on the clean machine. Virtual Machines are useful in repacking scenarios as changes can easily be rolled back.

On the machine where AdminStudio is installed, do the following:

1. Right-click the **Repackager** folder under `c:\program files\adminstudio\9.0.1\` and select **Properties** from the menu. Switch to the **Sharing** tab and click **Advanced Sharing**.

2. In the **Advanced Sharing** dialog box, check **Share this folder** and click **Permissions**.

3. In the **Permissions for Repackager** dialog box, click **Add**.

4. In the **Select Users, Computers, Service Accounts, or Groups** dialog box, type **Authenticated Users**, click **Check Names** and then **OK**.

5. In the **Permissions for Repackager** dialog box, under **Group or user names**, select **Authenticated Users** and select **Allow** permissions for **Full Control** and **Change**.

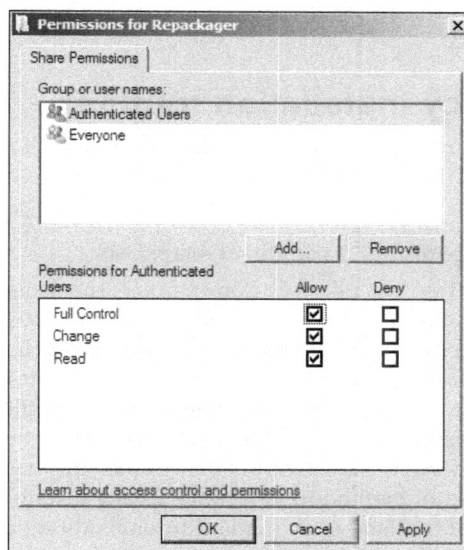

6. Click **OK** in the **Advanced Sharing** and **Repackager Properties** dialog box. Repeat the sharing process for the `c:\adminstudio shared` directory.

Installing the remote repackager

Log in to your clean machine that will be used to monitor the installation process and follow these instructions to install the remote repackager binaries:

1. Open the shared **Repackager** folder from the machine where AdminStudio is installed on the clean machine and run `setup.exe` in the **Remote Repackager** folder.

2. In the **Remote Repackager – InstallShield Wizard** dialog box, click **Next**.

3. Accept the licence, agree, and click **Next**.

4. On the **Customer Information** screen, enter appropriate details and click **Next**.

5. On the **AdminStudio Shared location** screen, enter the UNC path (`\\servername \adminstudio shared`) for the **AdminStudio Shared location** and click **Next**.

6. On the **Repackager Location** screen, enter the UNC path (`\\servername \repackager`) for the **Repackager Location** and click **Next**.

7. On the **Ready to Install the Program** screen, click **Install**. Click **Finish** once the process has completed.

Three new shortcuts will appear on the desktop—**Repackaging Wizard**, **Repackager**, and **OS Snapshot Wizard**.

Monitoring a legacy installation routine

Now that we can run the repackager on a remote machine, it's time to launch the repackaging wizard.

The advantage of monitoring over snapshots

I recommend that you choose a commercial repackaging solution that supports monitoring low-level changes (for example, Installation Monitoring in AdminStudio that an installer makes to a system), as opposed to the *snapshot* method where the system state is recorded before and after to generate an `.msi` file. The snapshot method tends to produce less reliable results, and while free software such as Scalable's WinInstall LE (`http://www.scalable.com/softwaredownload/ledownload`) uses the snapshot method to repackage legacy installers in `.msi` format, many hours of trial and error, and additional editing of the `.msi` file will often be required before it can be used in a production environment.

Launch the **Repackager Wizard** from the shortcut created on the desktop of the remote machine. In the **Repackaging Wizard** dialog box, on the **Method Selection** screen, select **Installation Monitoring** and click **Next**.

Self-extracting installers

If the installer package is of the self-extracting variety, that is it is a compressed ZIP file that extracts a legacy setup package and related files when run, exclude the file in the **Repackaging Wizard** dialog box by clicking on **Advanced Settings** and then click on the folder icon to the right of **Excluded Processes** and add the name of the legacy installer package, in this case **corporateappsetup.exe**, to the list and click **OK**.

1. On the **Method Selection** screen, click **Next**. On the **Collect Product Information** screen enter the path of the legacy installer in the **Program File** field. Enter appropriate information in the **Product Name** and **Company Name** fields and then click **Next**.

Edit Setup List

The **Edit Setup List** option allows you to add several legacy installers to one package. This might be useful in situations where an application has several components that must be installed separately. While it may seem tempting to roll up many applications into one .msi file, in practice this is difficult to manage and not recommended.

2. Change the default location for the project path on the **Set Target Project Information and Capture Settings** screen to a shared location on the AdminStudio machine and click **Start** to launch the corporateappsetup. exe installer.

3. Install the legacy application, and once the setup process has terminated, go back to the **Repackaging Wizard** dialog box and click **Process**.

4. On the **Summary** screen, click **Finish** to launch Repackager.

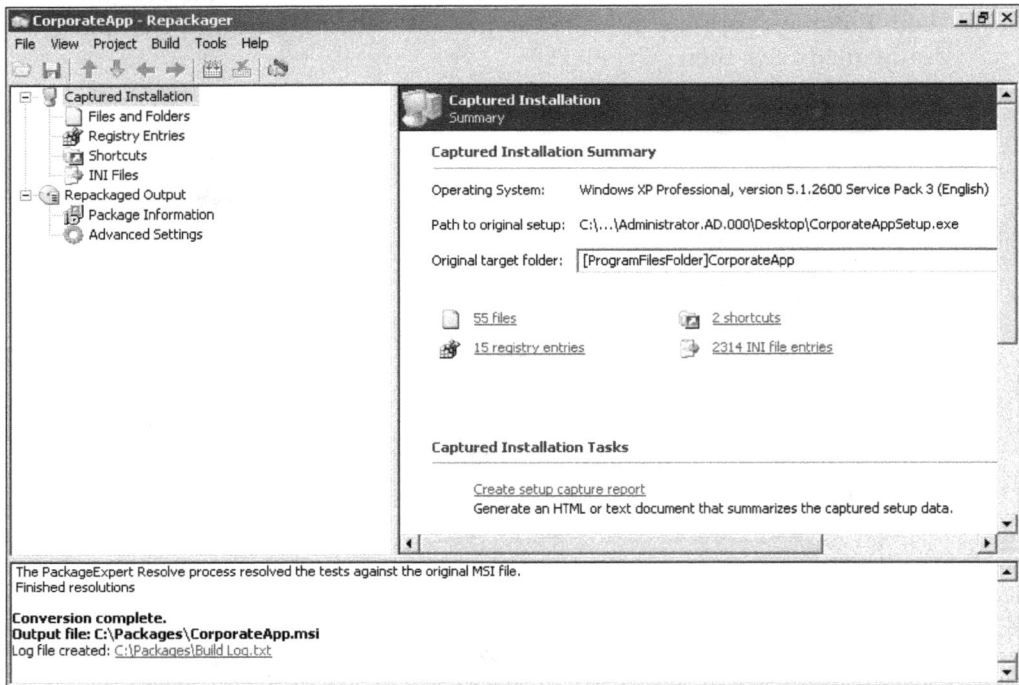

5. In the **CorporateApp – Repackager** window, press *F7* to build the `.msi` file.

Once the build process is complete, you'll see **Conversion complete** displayed in the messages window at the bottom of Repackager. The new `.msi` file is located in the shared directory specified in step 3. You should copy the `corporateappsetup.msi` and related files to another computer and test the installer by checking the application functions as expected.

Customizing an installation package

It's likely that you'll want to configure applications for your organization's specific needs. While some setup programs allow limited customization from the command line or using configuration files, others have dedicated customization applications that can be used to create transform (`.mst`) files for use with GPSI. Examples include the **Office Customization Tool (OCT)** for Microsoft Office, the **Internet Explorer Administration Kit (IEAK)** and Adobe Customization Wizard for Acrobat and Acrobat Reader.

Customizing Acrobat Reader's MSI installer using Adobe Customization Wizard 9

For this section, we need to download Adobe Customization Wizard 9 from `http://www.adobe.com/go/reader_wizard`.

1. Install Adobe Customization Wizard 9 and launch it from **All Programs** on the **Start** menu. In the **Adobe Customization Wizard 9** window, click the open icon under the **File** menu.

2. In the **Open** dialog box, locate the `.msi` for Acrobat Reader 9 that you want to modify and then click **Open**.

3. In the left pane of the customization wizard, click on **Installation Options**. Under **Run Installation** in the right pane select **Silently (no interface)** and **Reboot without prompt** under **If reboot required at the end of installation**.

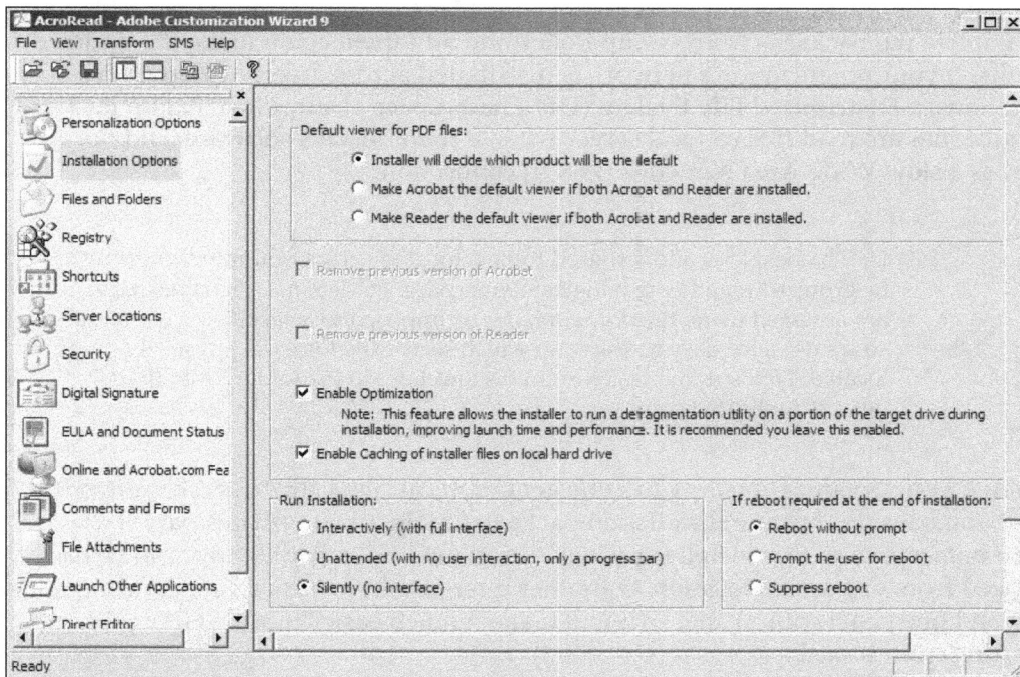

4. In the left pane of the customization wizard, click **Online and Acrobat.com Features**. In the right pane, check **Disable all updates** and **Disable Product Improvement Program** under **Online Features**.

5. Click *Ctrl+S* to save the package (`acroread.mst`) and then close the customization wizard.

Editing .msi files

If you want to edit .msi files without paying for third-party software, Microsoft provides an application called ORCA that can be used to edit the tables in .msi files. ORCA is part of the Windows Installer SDK and can be downloaded from:

http://www.microsoft.com/downloads/details. aspx?FamilyID=71deb800-c591-4f97-a900- bea146e4fae1&displaylang=en

Using the Distributed File System with GPSI

One disadvantage of Group Policy Software Installation is that once a package has been configured for deployment, it's not possible to change the path for the installation package source files. While this may not seem so much of a problem initially, if in the future you need to move the files to another server, you will need to remove the packages from Group Policy and add them again using the updated paths. If your organization's network is distributed across diverse geographic locations, a **Distributed File System (DFS)** namespace ensures installation package source files are read from a local server when a client installs software, and not across a slow **Wide Area Network (WAN)** connection.

DFS namespaces allow shared folders located across multiple servers to be grouped together in a logical namespace. Folders in DFS namespaces are accessed using the domain name as opposed to a specific server name, so it's not necessary to know on which server the folder is physically located. DFS automatically redirects the client to the folder, or to the nearest replicated copy.

Even if your organization only has one geographical site, I strongly recommend that you consider hosting installation package files in a folder that is part of a DFS namespace so that installer packages used in GPSI policy settings can be easily moved from one server location to another if required. If your organization expands beyond one geographical site, DFS will make it much easier to scale GPSI without starting from scratch.

Creating a DFS namespace

Let's start by installing the DFS Namespace role service:

1. Log in to the Windows Server 2008 R2 system that you want to designate as a namespace server with a domain administrator account.

2. Install the DFS Namespace role service using PowerShell, which can be launched from the taskbar or by typing `PowerShell` into the **Search programs and files** box on the **Start** menu.

3. Before running the following commands, you'll need to import the Server Manager module into PowerShell by typing `Import-Module servermanager` and pressing *Enter*. First add the DFS Namespace role service:

```
Add-WindowsFeature FS-DFS-Namespace
```

If your organization has more than one geographical site, you should also add the DFS Replication role service:

```
Add-WindowsFeature FS-DFS-Replication
```

> **Using PowerShell to show installed roles and features**
>
> Type `WindowsFeature` at the PowerShell prompt to display a list of available and installed roles and features. The Server Manager module must be imported (`Import-Module servermanager`) into PowerShell before you can run the `WindowsFeature` command.

Now that the DFS Namespace role service is installed, let's configure DFS using the DFS Management MMC.

1. Open **DFS Management** from **Administrative Tools** on the **Start** menu. Right-click the **Namespaces** node in the left pane and select **New Namespace** from the menu.

2. In the **New Namespace Wizard** click **Browse**.

3. Type the name of the server to host the DFS namespace in the **Select Computer** box (in this example, **WINADMIN**) and click **OK**. Alternatively, click **Advanced** and then **Find Now** to list computers in the domain.

4. In the **New Namespace Wizard** click **Next**. On the **Namespace Name and Settings** screen, type `Software` in the **Name** field and click **Next**.

> The **New Namespace Wizard** will create the Software folder (`c:\ dfsroots\software`) and share for us if it doesn't already exist.

5. On the **Namespace Type** screen, accept the default settings by clicking **Next**.

Windows Server 2008 mode

DFS Windows Server 2008 mode supports access-based enumeration and better scalability. To use Windows Server 2008 mode, the forest functional level must be set to Windows Server 2003 or higher, the domain must use the Windows Server 2008 domain functional level, and all namespace servers in the domain must be running Windows Server 2008.

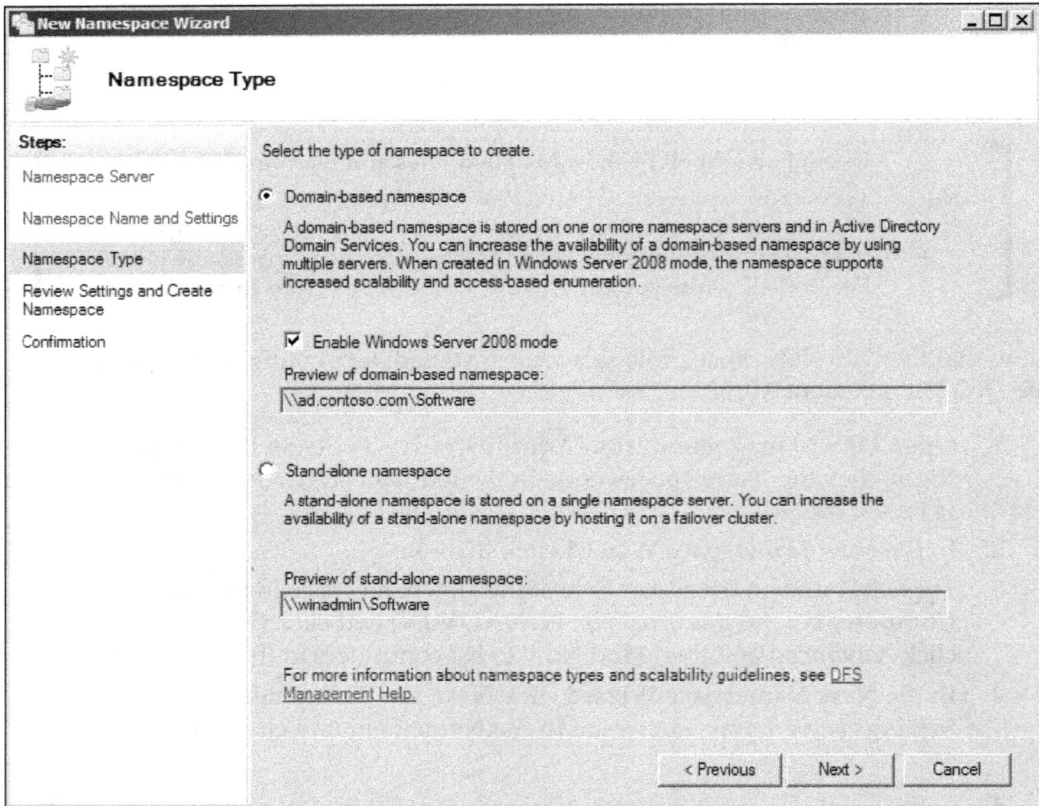

6. On the **Review Settings and Create Namespace** screen, click **Create** to complete the process.

New Namespace Wizard

Review Settings and Create Namespace

Steps:

Namespace Server

Namespace Name and Settings

Namespace Type

Review Settings and Create Namespace

Confirmation

You selected the following settings for the new namespace. If the settings are correct, click Create to create your new namespace. To change a setting, click Previous, or select the appropriate page in the orientation pane.

Namespace settings:

Namespace
    Namespace name: \\ad.contoso.com\Software
    Namespace type: Domain (Windows Server 2008 mode)
    Namespace server: winadmin
    Root shared folder: A shared folder will be created if one does not exist.
    Local path of namespace shared folder: C:\DFSRoots\Software
    Permissions for namespace shared folder: Everyone read only

< Previous   Create   Cancel

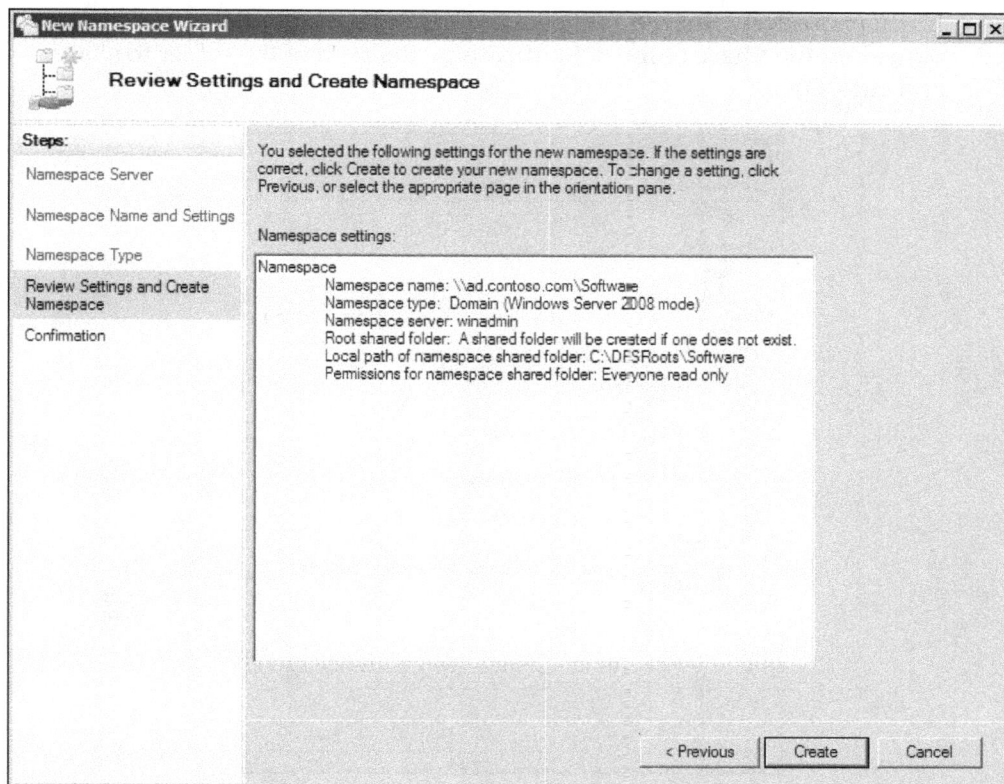

7. On the **Confirmation** screen, click **Close**.

Adding a folder to the namespace

Now, let's add a dedicated folder for storing our installer packages to the DFS namespace:

1. In the left pane of **DFS Management**, expand the **Namespaces** node, right-click the **\\ad.contoso.com\software** namespace, and select **New Folder** from the menu.

2. In the **New Folder** dialog type **Installers** in the **Name** field. Click **Add** under **Folder targets**.

3. In the **Add Folder Target** dialog box, click **Browse**. In the **Browse for Shared Folders** dialog box locate an existing share on the server where you host your installation package files or click **New Shared Folder** to create a new shared folder on the server.

4. If you chose **New Shared Folder...**, in the **Create Share** dialog box type a name into the **Share name** field, then type the path of the folder to share and click **OK**.

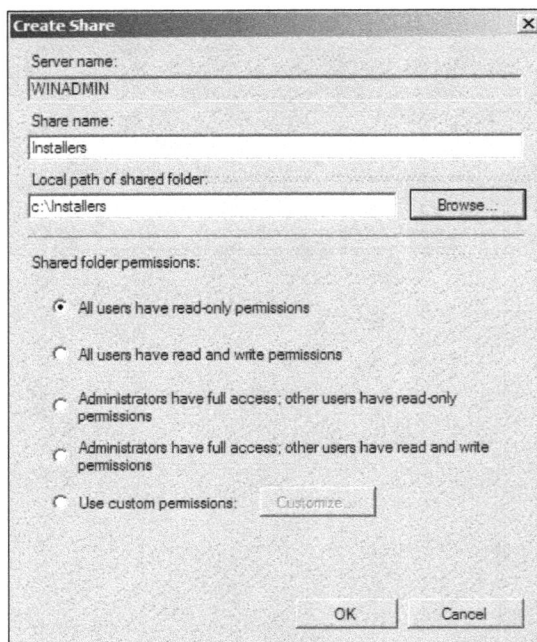

5. Click **OK** again in the **Browse for Shared Folders** and the **Add Folder Target** dialog boxes. The share path should now appear under **Folder targets**.
6. Click **OK** in the **New Folder** dialog box to complete the process.

Deploying software using GPSI

Now that we've prepared an .msi package and any customizations we want to apply in an .mst file, we need to add the package to a GPO so that it can be deployed to machines in our Clients OU.

Configuring software installation settings

Let's add a software installation package to a GPO:

1. Open the **Group Policy Management Console** as a domain administrator from **Administrative Tools** on the **Start** menu and expand your Active Directory forest and domain in the left pane. Right-click the **Clients** OU and select **Create a GPO in this domain, and Link it here** from the menu. In the **New GPO** dialog box, type **Acrobat Reader** in the **Name** field and click **OK**.

2. Expand the **Clients** OU in the left pane, right-click the **Acrobat Reader** GPO and select **Edit** from the menu. In the **Group Policy Management Editor** window, expand **Policies | Software Settings** under **Computer Configuration** in the left pane. Under **Software Settings**, right-click **Software installation** and select **New, Package** from the menu.

3. In the **Open** dialog box, enter the path of the DFS namespace (`\\ad.contoso.com\software`), select the `acroread.msi` file in the **Adobe9** folder, and click **Open**.

4. In the **Deploy Software** dialog box, select **Advanced** and click **OK**.

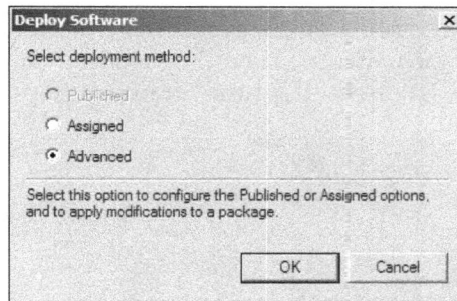

> **Modifications (transforms)**
>
> If the `.msi` being deployed needs to be customized with a transform (`.mst`) file, in the **Deploy Software** dialog box you must select **Advanced** and specify the transform file now. If you select **Assigned**, modifications cannot be added at a later stage.

5. In the **Adobe Reader 9 Properties** dialog box, switch to the **Modifications** tab and click **Add...**.

6. In the **Open** dialog box, select **acroread.mst** and click **Open**.

The **acroread.mst** file will now appear in the list of modifications.

> Make sure that the path used to specify `acroread.mst` uses the DFS namespace and not a server name.

7. In the **Adobe Reader 9 Properties** dialog box, click **OK**. You'll now see **Adobe Reader 9** appear in the right of the **Group Policy Management Editor** window. Note that the **Source** path uses the DFS namespace and not a server name in the UNC path.

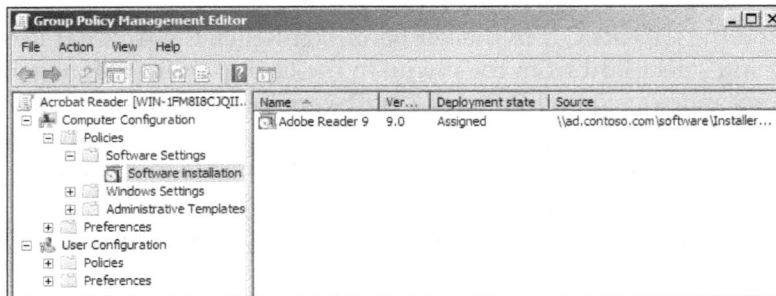

Computers located in the Clients OU will have Acrobat Reader installed the next time the device reboots. It may require a couple of reboots if machines in the Clients OU are not configured to wait for the network at computer startup and logon in Group Policy (**Computer Configuration** | **Policies** | **Administrative Templates** | **System** | **Logon**).

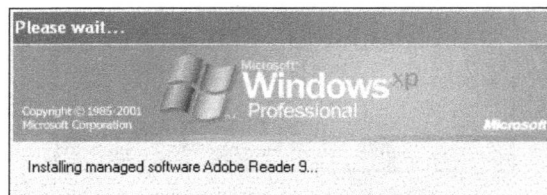

Targeting devices using WMI filters and security groups

Now that we have learned how to deploy Acrobat Reader to machines in our Clients OU, what happens if we need more control over the machines that receive the .msi package? There are two ways in which you can control how a Group Policy Object is deployed to computer accounts in a given OU.

Active Directory security groups

We can control which machines have software deployed to them using Active Directory security groups. For instance, we can create a security group called Acrobat Reader and make all the computer account objects in AD, where we want to install Acrobat, members of that group. We can then change security filtering on the Acrobat Reader GPO to make sure that only computers in the Acrobat Reader group can read and apply the GPO.

Creating a security group to filter a GPO

Let's create an AD group to control which computers have Acrobat Reader installed. In this section, we'll use PowerShell to perform the administration tasks, but it's also possible to use the Active Directory Users and Computers and Group Policy Management MMC consoles.

1. Log in to a Windows Server 2008 R2 domain controller and start Windows PowerShell from the shortcut on the taskbar or by typing `powershell` into the search box on the Start menu.

2. Before running the following cmdlet, you'll need to issue the `Import-Module activedirectory` command in the PowerShell console.

3. The `New-ADGroup` command (shown below) creates a new global security group in the **Users** container called Acrobat Reader. Change the **Distinguished Name (DN)** in the path string to match that of your Active Directory.

   ```
   New-ADGroup -Name "Acrobat Reader" -SamAccountName "Acrobat
   Reader"
     -GroupCategory Security -GroupScope Global -DisplayName
     "Acrobat Reader" -Path "cn=users,dc=ad,dc=contoso,dc=com"
     -Description "GPSI filter"
   ```

4. Now let's add a computer account to the new Acrobat Reader group. In this example, we'll add a computer account called XP1 to the group. Use the SAM account name and computer name for identity and member parameters, which means adding a dollar sign after the computer account name to designate a computer account.

   ```
   Add-ADGroupMember -Identity "Acrobat Reader" -Member XP1$
   ```

5. To check that XP1 has been added to the Acrobat Reader group, issue the following `Get-ADGroupMember` command. `FT Name` formats the table output to show only the names of the computer accounts in the Acrobat Reader group.

   ```
   Get-ADGroupMember "Acrobat Reader" | FT Name
   ```

6. Next, we need a security filter for the Acrobat Reader GPO. Type `Import-Module grouppolicy` in the PowerShell console to activate the Group Policy cmdlets. The name parameter specifies the name of the GPO to be modified and targetname the name of the group to be added to the ACL.

   ```
   Set-GPPermissions -Name "Acrobat Reader" -TargetName
     "Acrobat Reader" -TargetType Group -PermissionLevel GpoApply
   ```

   The group name and `SAMAccountName` must match to permissions programmatically set on a GPO using the `Set-GPPermissions` cmdlet.

7. Finally, remove the default GpoApply permissions for the authenticated users group on the Acrobat Reader GPO.

```
Set-GPPermissions -Name "Acrobat Reader" -TargetName
   "Authenticated Users" -TargetType Group -PermissionLevel None
```

To check security filtering permissions on the Acrobat Reader GPO, run the following command:

```
Get-GPPermissions –Name "Acrobat Reader" –All
```

Apart from the standard permissions issued to **Domain Admins**, **Enterprise Admins**, **ENTERPRISE DOMAIN CONTROLLERS**, and **SYSTEM**, the only other listed trustee should be **Acrobat Reader** with **GpoApply** permission.

```
Trustee      : Acrobat Reader
TrusteeType  : Group
Permission   : GpoApply
Inherited    : False

Trustee      : Domain Admins
TrusteeType  : Group
Permission   : GpoEditDeleteModifySecurity
Inherited    : False

Trustee      : Enterprise Admins
TrusteeType  : Group
Permission   : GpoEditDeleteModifySecurity
Inherited    : False

Trustee      : ENTERPRISE DOMAIN CONTROLLERS
TrusteeType  : WellKnownGroup
Permission   : GpoRead
Inherited    : False

Trustee      : SYSTEM
TrusteeType  : WellKnownGroup
Permission   : GpoEditDeleteModifySecurity
Inherited    : False
```

Windows Management Instrumentation filtering

While I'd recommend using security filtering to target machines for software deployment, you can add extra conditions to check target devices for suitability. For instance, to ensure that software installations don't fail, you might want to check that there's enough free disk space or that some other requirement is met. The disadvantage of using WMI filters with Group Policy is that WMI queries are processed every time policy is refreshed and not just at computer startup. Consequently, there's a slight performance hit for every WMI filter applied; so you should use filters sparingly.

Chapter 8, Supporting Non-Administrative Users, gives detailed instructions on how to add WMI filters to Group Policy Objects. Here are a couple of example filters that could be useful with GPOs that contain software installation settings. The first filter checks that there is at least 1GB of free disk space. The free space must be specified in bytes.

```
Select * from Win32_LogicalDisk where FreeSpace > 1073741824
```

This filter checks whether Acrobat Reader is already installed or not:

```
Select * from Win32_Product where name = "Acrobat Reader"
```

Upgrading software with GPSI

Let's upgrade Acrobat Reader 9.0 with version 9.2. Adobe provides this version as an .msi file on its FTP site, but to customize the application using the Adobe Customization Wizard, you should download the standard .exe file from the following link and extract the .msi and related files:

```
ftp://ftp.adobe.com/pub/adobe/reader/win/9.x/9.2/enu/AdbeRdr920_en
_US.exe
```

Create a new folder in the installers directory called Adobe9_2 and copy the extracted setup files and a new acroread.mst generated using the Adobe Customization Wizard.

1. Open the **Group Policy Management Console** as a domain administrator from **Administrative Tools** on the **Start** menu and expand your Active Directory forest and domain in the left pane.

2. Expand the **Clients** OU in the left pane, right-click on the **Acrobat Reader** GPO, and select **Edit** from the menu.

3. In the **Group Policy Management Editor** window, expand **Policies** under **Computer Configuration** in the left pane, **Software Settings**, right-click **Software installation**, and select **New, Package** from the menu.

4. In the **Open** dialog box, select **adberdr920_en_us.msi** in the Adobe9_2 folder and click **Open**.

5. In the **Deploy Software** dialog box, select **Advanced** and click **OK**.

6. In the **Adobe Reader 9.2 Properties** dialog box, switch to the **Modifications** tab and click **Add**.

7. In the **Open** dialog box, select **acroread.mst** in the Adobe9.2 folder and click **Open**. Switch to the **Upgrades** tab and you'll see that this package is already set to **Upgrade Adobe Reader 9**.

8. Click **OK** to continue. In the **Group Policy Management Editor** window, double-click **Adobe Reader 9** in the right pane. In the **Adobe Reader 9 Properties** dialog box, switch to the **Upgrades** tab. You'll see **Adobe Reader 9.2** list under **Packages** in the current GPO that will upgrade this package.

9. Click **OK**.

Computers located in the Clients OU will have Acrobat Reader 9.2 installed, or upgraded from version 9.0 the next time the device reboots. It may require a couple of reboots if machines in the Clients OU are not configured to wait for the network at computer startup and logon in Group Policy (**Computer Configuration | Policies | Administrative Templates | System | Logon**).

Uninstalling software with GPSI

One of the advantages of using a software distribution system such as Group Policy Software Installation or Systems Center Configuration Manager as opposed to fat images is that it's possible to manage the full lifecycle of software without the need to redeploy images. The full lifecycle of software includes the initial installation, upgrades and patches, and uninstalling software if it's no longer required. Group Policy Software Installation includes the ability to uninstall software.

Removing software when it falls out of scope of management

In the previous section, we looked at how to target software packages to particular devices using Group Policy security filtering. Each .msi package in a Group Policy Object can be set to automatically uninstall itself if the target device no longer falls within the GPO's scope of management. The **Uninstall this application when it falls out of the scope of management** option is set in Group Policy Software Installation on the **Deployment** tab of the package's **Properties** dialog box.

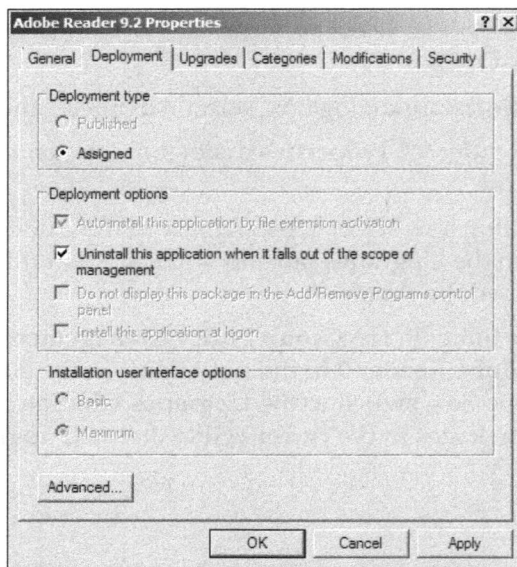

If the **Uninstall this application when it falls out of the scope of management** option is set, when you remove a computer account from an AD security group that's used for security filtering on the given GPO or out of the CU that the GPO is linked to, the next time the computer restarts, the affected software will be removed. Therefore, installation and removal of software can be controlled by AD group membership. Similarly, if a computer account falls out of scope of management for a particular GPO due to the fact that it no longer matches a WMI filter, software packages contained in the GPO will also be removed.

Removing .msi packages from Group Policy Objects

While you can't modify most properties of a software package once it's been configured in a Group Policy Object, you can choose to remove a package from a GPO, opting to either have the software removed or leave it installed so the user can continue working with it.

1. In Group Policy Management, open the GPO for editing and expand **Computer Configuration | Policies | Software Settings** and click **Software installation**.

2. In the right pane, right-click the package you want to remove and select **All Tasks, Remove** from the menu.

3. In the **Remove Software** dialog box, select **Immediately uninstall the software from users and computers** or **Allow users to continue to use the software, but prevent new installations** and click **OK**.

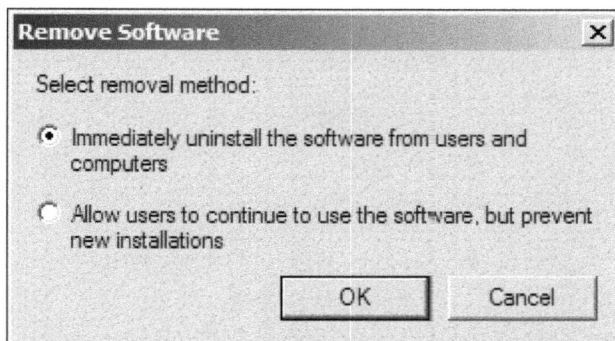

Summary

In this chapter, we've learned how to leverage Group Policy Software Installation to deploy software to computers where users run without administrative privileges. Before moving to the next chapter, you should be able to:

- Set up the infrastructure required to support Group Policy Software Installation
- Determine the best method for deploying your application
- Create repackaged legacy installers or .msi wrappers if necessary
- Deploy an application using a Group Policy startup script
- Target software to computers using WMI filters and security filtering

In the next chapter, we learn how to use the ActiveX Installer Service in Vista and Windows 7 to install ActiveX controls on behalf of standard users.

7
Managing Internet Explorer Add-ons

There's one more pain point that system administrators face on a daily basis when users run with least privilege accounts. Internet Explorer add-ons, such as toolbars and **ActiveX controls**, enable extra functionality in the browser such as the ability to display animations, add controls to web pages for uploading content, or display non-standard media formats. In this chapter we'll learn:

- To support per-user and per-machine ActiveX controls
- To manage Internet Explorer add-ons via Group Policy
- To install per-machine ActiveX controls using the **ActiveX Installer Service (AxIS)**
- Best practices for working with ActiveX controls in a managed environment

ActiveX controls

ActiveX controls are small add-on programs for Internet Explorer that enhance the functionality of a website. Emphasis should be placed on the fact that these controls are programs, and can be misused in the same way as any other piece of software. Users often think that there is no risk involved in installing these small add-on components, but the reality is that ActiveX controls have proved to be one of the biggest security headaches in Internet Explorer. Add-ons, like any other piece of code, need to be updated from time to time, especially commonly used controls such as Adobe **Flash**, which is regularly patched to address critical security flaws. Failure to manage add-on components leaves you wide open to drive-by attacks from infected websites.

Per-user ActiveX controls

Legacy ActiveX controls are considered to be per-machine, meaning that a user needs administrative privileges to install a control as the necessary files are added to the protected `Windows` or `Program Files` directory. With Internet Explorer 7 in Windows Vista, Microsoft introduced the concept of per-user controls, which are installed to user profiles and hence don't require elevated privileges.

While most public websites still publish ActiveX controls as per-machine, meaning that the control is installed for all users under the context of an administrative account, enterprises can package ActiveX controls hosted on intranet sites for per-user installation. This requires some simple changes to be made to the installation package, not the control itself.

> Per-site ActiveX controls were introduced as part of Internet Explorer 8 and allow controls to be restricted for operation on specified sites, reducing the risk that a control can be used for malicious purposes.

ActiveX controls are installed according to the instructions in their associated `.inf` file. Per-user ActiveX controls contain an extra section in the `.inf` file that directs them to be installed to the user's profile rather than a protected file system location. In turn, this means that ActiveX controls don't need to be installed on multiple systems if users have roaming profiles. ActiveX controls used on your corporate intranet should be packaged with a modified `.inf` to allow them to be installed as a per-user control.

Changing the installation scope to per-user

To change the installation scope to per-user in the `.inf` file, you need to add a new section called `Deployment` as shown below:

```
[Deployment]
    InstallScope=user
```

The `InstallScope` variable can be set to `user`, `machine`, or `user|machine`.

> **Add-on management**
>
> You can block the installation of per-user controls by denying all ActiveX controls that don't have explicit administrator approval using add-on management settings in Group Policy. See *Add-on Management* later in this chapter.

Best practices

Due to the security risks involved in allowing users to install unsanctioned ActiveX controls, and the difficulties associated with unmanaged controls and add-ons, you should think carefully before allowing users to install controls, approved or otherwise, unless you have a means of tracking installations and keeping them up to date.

Here is a list of best practices to consider when deciding how to manage ActiveX controls and other Internet Explorer add-ons:

- **Deploy commonly used controls**: The best way to manage ActiveX controls is to treat them like any other program and use a software deployment technology, such as Group Policy Software Installation, to distribute controls automatically. This allows full lifecycle management of controls and ensures they can be easily tracked and updated.

- **Deploy intranet ActiveX controls using an HTTPS URL**: If any of your company's intranet web applications use ActiveX controls, centralize their deployment from a web server that uses SSL. This means the control's host URL is `https://`, and set the Server Certificate Policy in **ActiveX Installer Service** configuration to abort installation if there are any certificate errors. This helps prevent man-in-the-middle attacks by ensuring that the control is installed from a verified source signed by an internal **Certification Authority (CA)**.

- **Provide access to a virtual machine or remote desktop for ad-hoc ActiveX controls**: When users inevitably demand access to a control that isn't authorized for use on your network, provide access to a virtual machine or remote desktop where the user can have temporary administrative privilege to install the control and complete the necessary work.

Deploying commonly used ActiveX controls

Controls such as Adobe Flash player, which are ubiquitous on the Web today, should be deployed and managed in your organization like any other piece of software, either using Group Policy Software Installation, or another software deployment system, such as System Center Configuration Manager. While the technologies outlined in this chapter give users the flexibility to install ActiveX controls without assistance from a system administrator, unless you have some means of detecting where controls have been installed and a system for ensuring they are kept up to date or removed, deploying all controls using a centrally managed system is the best option in most cases.

> **Manually removing ActiveX controls**
>
> Just like any other piece of software, most ActiveX controls can be removed via the **Add/Remove Programs** control panel applet.

Deploying Adobe Flash and Shockwave Player

In *Chapter 6, Software Distribution using Group Policy*, we learned how to use **Group Policy Software Installation (GPSI)** to deploy software and the issues involved. Deploying ActiveX controls such as Flash or Shockwave Player is the same as for any other piece of software. You can apply for an enterprise license from Adobe to distribute their ActiveX controls, and download them in .msi format for use with Group Policy Software Installation.

Deploying Microsoft Silverlight

Silverlight is becoming more common, and you might want to consider deploying it to avoid requests later down the line for ad hoc installations. Silverlight brings animations and a subset of .NET Framework features to the Web. Silverlight is supplied as a downloadable .exe file, which contains a Windows Installer .msi file.

1. Use the following link to download Silverlight.exe: http://www.microsoft.com/silverlight/. Save Silverlight.exe to your local C: drive.

2. If you want to run a silent install of Silverlight from a script, call the executable with the /q switch to suppress the GUI during installation:

   Silverlight.exe /q

3. If you need more flexibility during the installation process, you'll need to extract the Windows Installer database (.msi) and patch (.msp) files from Silverlight.exe. Start by running Silverlight.exe with the /extract switch:

   Silverlight.exe /extract

You'll then be prompted to specify a location for the extracted files. You'll find silverlight.msi amongst the extracted files. Unfortunately, you cannot simply add the .msi to a GPSI policy. To install Silverlight, a patch file (.msp), which is compressed in the Silverlight.7z file, must be applied to the .msi file. Therefore, in order to distribute Silverlight using Group Policy, you'll have to run msiexec in a startup script.

> Refer to *Chapter 6, Software Distribution using Group Policy*, for more information about distributing software using Group Policy.

The following command line only works when called from a batch file due to the inclusion of the %~dp0 variable in the file paths. The installation fails if the full path for the .msp file is not specified. See the, *Distributing or updating a custom database using Group Policy* section from *Chapter 3* for more information on using the %~dp0 variable. The /qn switch suppresses the installer's GUI during installation and /LiV provides verbose logging of installation events.

```
msiexec /i %~dp0silverlight.msi /update %~dp0Silverlight.msp
    ALLUSERS=1 /qn /LiV %temp%\silverlight3.log
```

> **ALLUSERS**
> The ALLUSERS parameter determines whether an application is installed only for the current user (if its value is set to 2) or for all users of a system (if its value is set to 1). For more information visit: http://msdn.microsoft.com/en-us/library/aa367559(VS.85).aspx

ActiveX Installer Service

The ActiveX Installer Service was introduced as part of Internet Explorer 7 in Windows Vista, and installs per-machine ActiveX controls on demand specified in Group Policy on behalf of standard users. Internet Explorer in Windows XP does not support the ActiveX Installer Service because it's part of Vista and Windows 7 User Account Control technology.

Enabling the ActiveX Installer Service

In Windows Vista Business, Enterprise, and Ultimate SKUs, the ActiveX Installer Service is an optional component and therefore must be installed. You can either install the service and make it part of your organization's default system image, or install it programmatically from a Group Policy startup script.

> In Windows 7, the ActiveX Installer Service is installed and enabled by default.

Using the GUI to install the ActiveX Installer Service

Log in to Vista Business, Enterprise, or Ultimate as a domain or local administrator:

1. Open the **Control Panel** from the **Start** menu.

2. In the top-right of the control panel window, type *features* into the search box and click **Turn Windows features on or off** under **Programs and Features**.

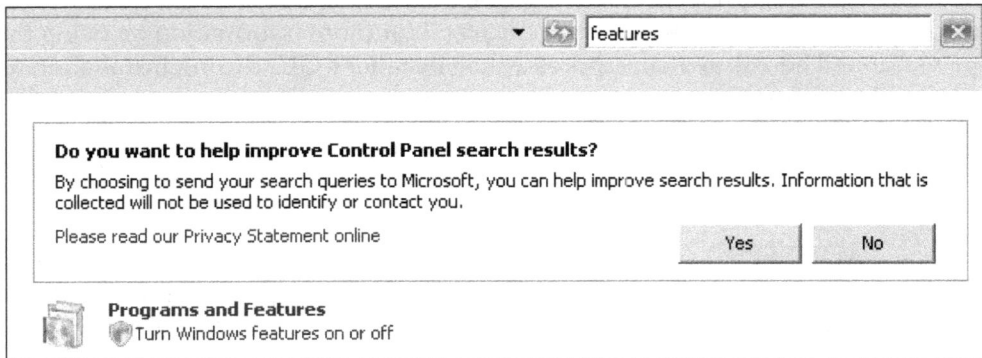

3. In the **Windows Features** dialog, check **ActiveX Installer Service** and click **OK**.

4. In the top-right of the control panel window, type *services* into the search box and click **View local services** under **Administrative Tools**.

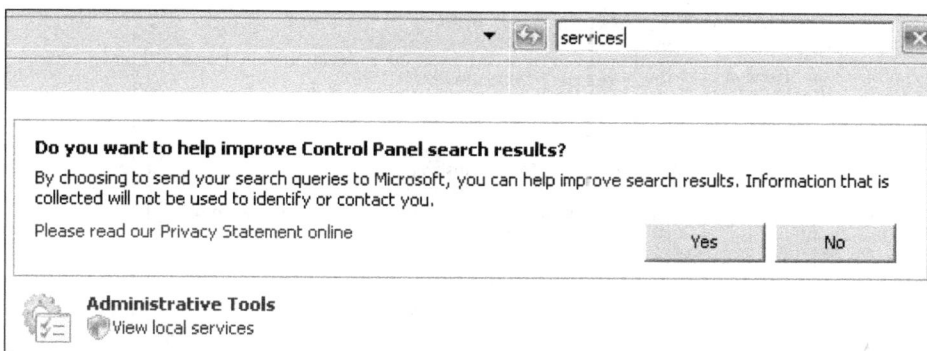

5. In the **Services** window, double-click **ActiveX Installer (AxInstSV)**.

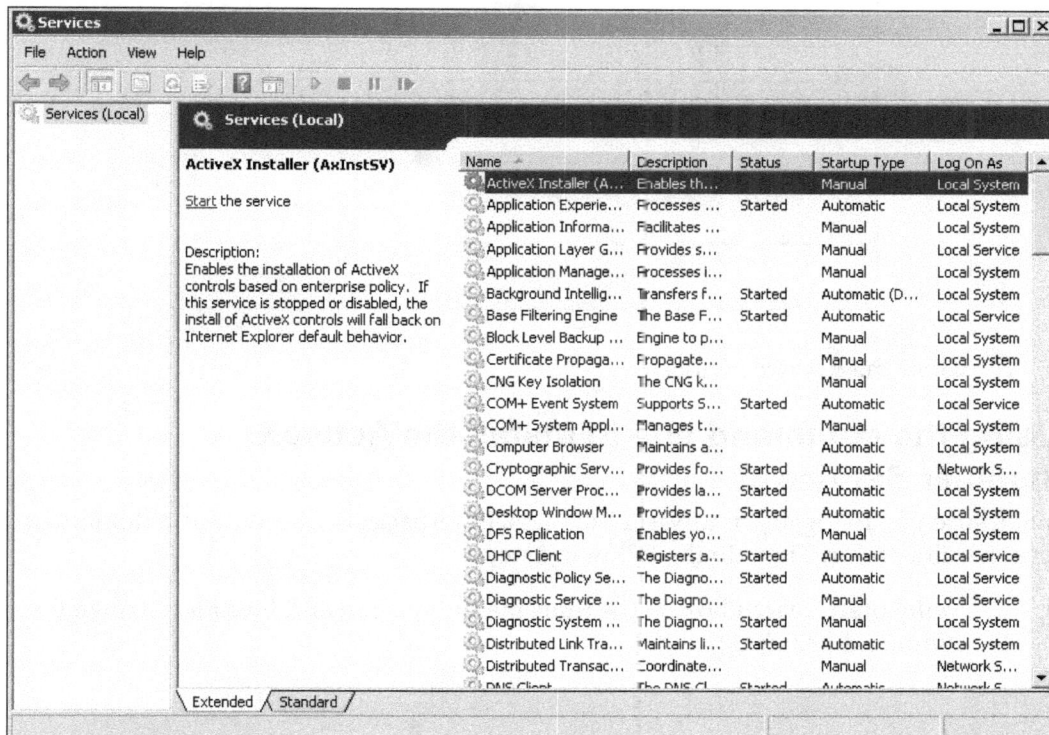

6. In the **ActiveX Installer (AxInstSV) Properties** dialog, change the **Startup type** to **Automatic**, click **Start**, and then **OK**.

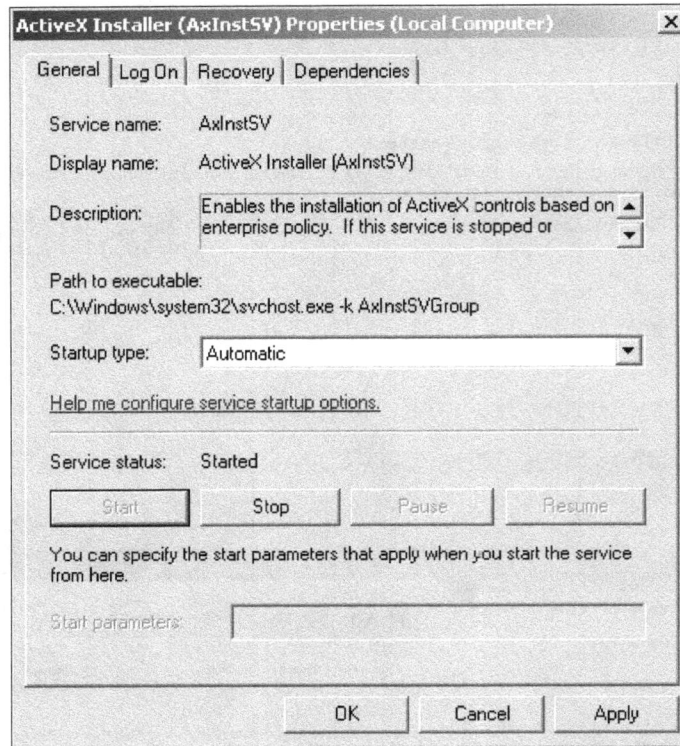

7. Close the **Services** window.

Using the command line to install the ActiveX Installer Service

Make sure you're logged in to Vista Business, Enterprise, or Ultimate as a domain or local administrator. Then do the following steps:

1. In the **Start Search** box on the **Start** menu type cmd and hit *Enter* to open the command prompt.

2. Enter the following command to install the ActiveX Installer Service.

```
start /wait ocsetup.exe AxInstallService
```

> **start /wait**
>
> Here we launch `ocsetup.exe` using the `start` command with the `/wait` switch so that it's clear from within the command prompt when `ocsetup.exe` has exited, and the installation of the ActiveX Installer Service is complete.

3. Now issue a command to change the ActiveX Installer Service startup type to automatic, **noting the space between the equals sign and** `auto`. Once completed, `[SC] ChangeServiceConfig SUCCESS` will be displayed in the command prompt window.

```
sc config axinstsv start= auto
```

4. Finally, start the ActiveX Installer Service using the `net start` command.

```
net start axinstsv
```

> In Windows 7, the ActiveX Installer Service startup type is *manual* by default and will be started automatically as required.

Determining the ActiveX control host URL in Windows 7

Before we can configure the ActiveX Installer Service in Group Policy, we need to decide which per-machine ActiveX control we want the service to install and find the host URL. For the purposes of this demonstration, let's configure the ActiveX Installer Service to install Facebook's Photo Uploader ActiveX control, which is packaged as a `.cab` file. Log in to Windows 7 as a standard user:

1. Open Internet Explorer and log in to a Facebook account. Prepare to upload photos to a new or existing album in the browser window and you'll be prompted to install the Uploader ActiveX control in the Information Bar.

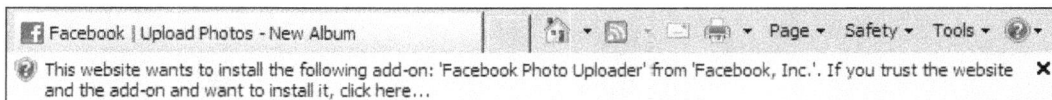

2. Click on the Information Bar and select **Install This Add-on for All Users on This Computer** from the menu.

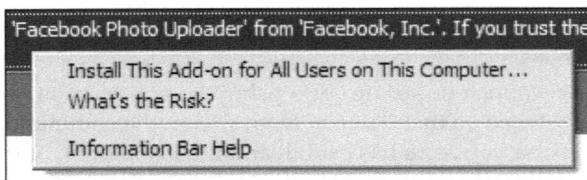

3. Wait a few seconds for the control to download and then in the **User Account Control** dialog, click **Show details**.

4. In the **User Account Control** dialog, you'll now be able to see the **Program location**, which specifies the full URL for the .cab file (http://upload.facebook.com/controls/2009.07.28v_5.5.8.1/FacebookPhotoUploader55.cab).

5. In the **User Account Control** dialog, click **No** to cancel the installation.

We're interested in the first part of the URL, `http://upload.facebook.com`. and that the control publisher has been verified. This means that the `.cab` file has been signed and the source, Facebook, Inc., has been verified as genuine.

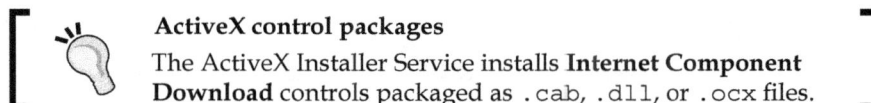

> **ActiveX control packages**
> The ActiveX Installer Service installs **Internet Component Download** controls packaged as `.cab`, `.dll`, or `.ocx` files.

Determining the ActiveX control host URL in Windows Vista

The User Account Control dialog in Windows Vista doesn't give as much information as in Windows 7, so to determine the control's URL, follow through steps 1 to 5 as outlined for Windows 7, and then open **Event Viewer** as an administrator to determine the URL:

1. In the **Start Search** box on the **Start** menu, type `eventvwr` and press *Ctrl+Shift+Enter* simultaneously. Enter administrative credentials into the **User Account Control** dialog and click **OK**.

2. In the left pane under **Event Viewer (Local)**, expand **Windows Logs** and click **Application**.

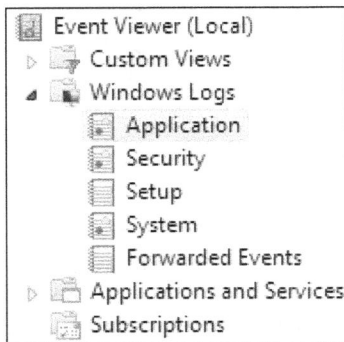

3. Search for error event ID 4097 in the central pane and double-click the event to see the host URL details.

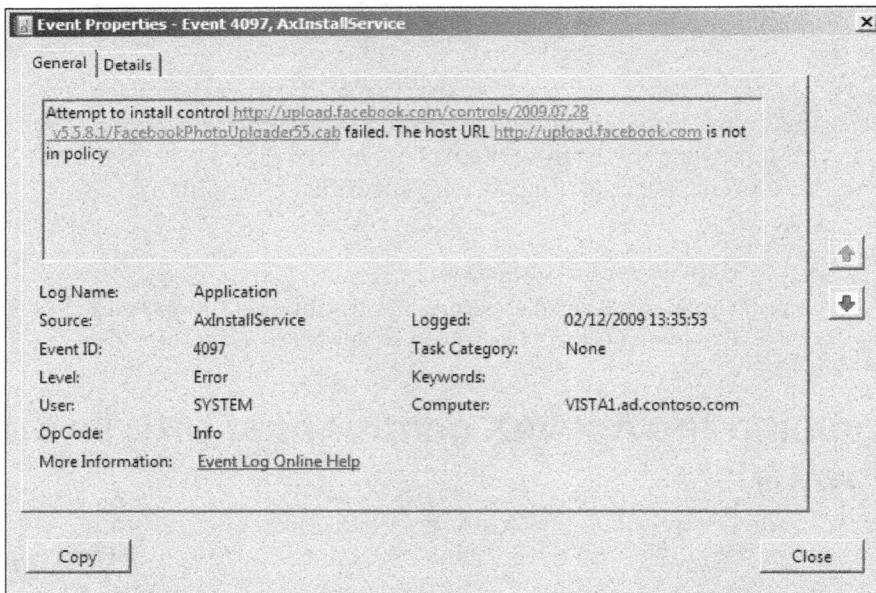

Tracking attempted ActiveX control installations

If you're interesting in finding out what ActiveX controls users regularly try to install on your network, you can configure **Event Triggers** to track instances of Event ID 4097.

Configuring the ActiveX Installer Service with Group Policy

Now that we've gathered all the necessary information about the Uploader ActiveX control, we can configure the ActiveX Installer Service in Group Policy on a domain controller as follows:

1. Open the **Group Policy Management Console** as a domain administrator from **Administrative Tools** on the **Start** menu and expand your **Active Directory** forest and domain in the left pane.

2. Right-click the **Clients** OU and select **Create a GPO in this domain, and Link it here** from the menu. In the **New GPO** dialog, type **AXIS** in the **Name** field and click **OK**.

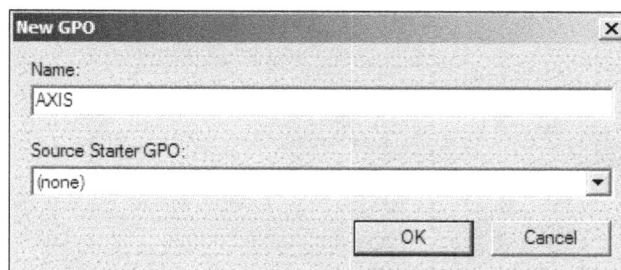

3. Expand the **Clients** OU in the left pane, right-click the **AXIS** GPO, and select **Edit** from the menu.

4. In the **Group Policy Management Editor** window, expand **Policies** under **Computer Configuration** in the left pane and then **Administrative Templates**. Under it expand **Windows Components** and select **ActiveX Installer Service**.

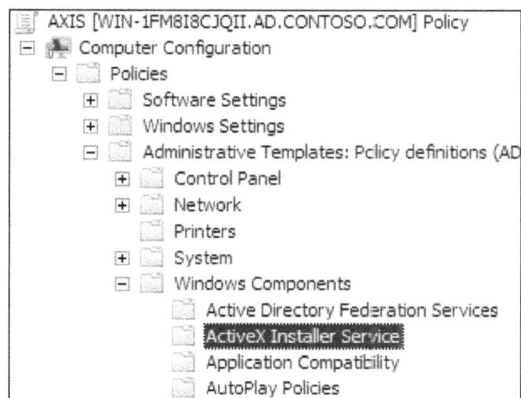

5. In the right pane, double-click **Approved Installation Sites for ActiveX controls**.

6. In the **Approved Installation Sites for ActiveX controls** dialog, select **Enabled** and then click **Show** to the right of **Host URLs**.

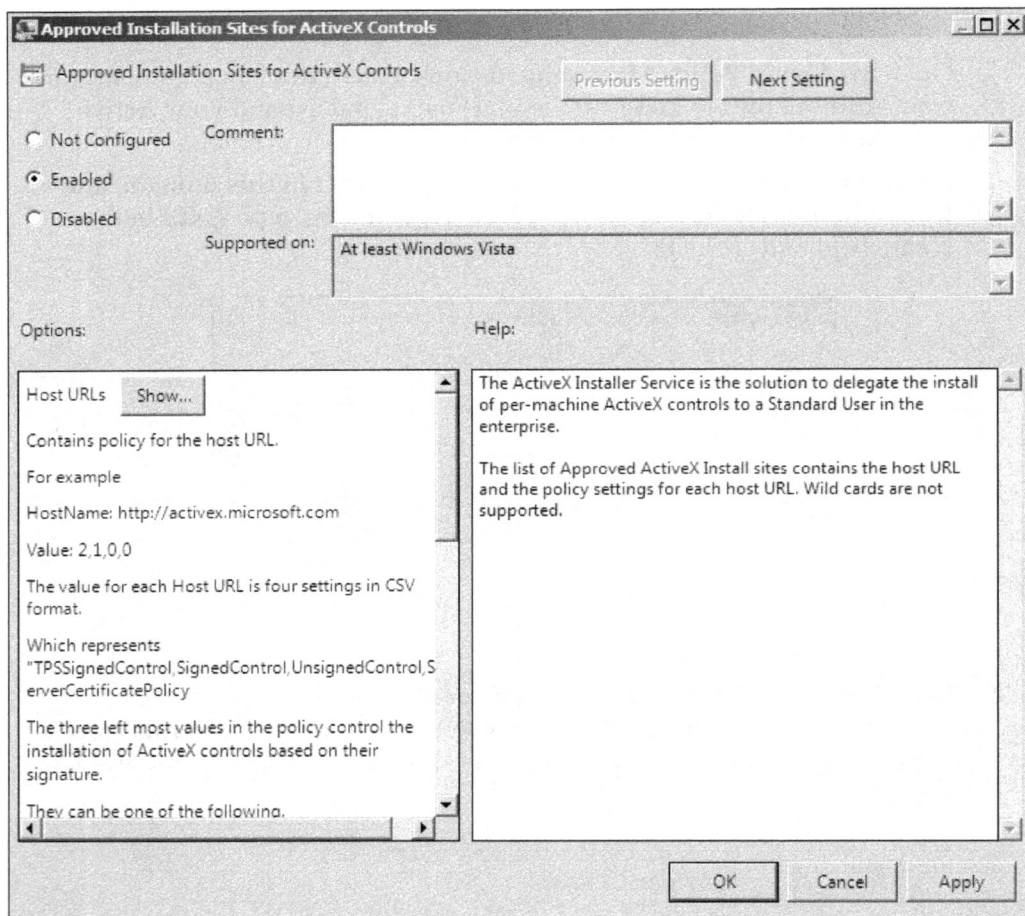

7. In the **Show Contents** dialog, type the URL of the site that hosts the ActiveX control (in this case `http://upload.facebook.com`) in the **Value name** field. In the **Value** field type `2,2,1,0` and then click **OK**.

Show Contents

Host URLs

	Value name	Value
▶	http://upload.facebook.com	2.2.1.0
*		

OK   Cancel

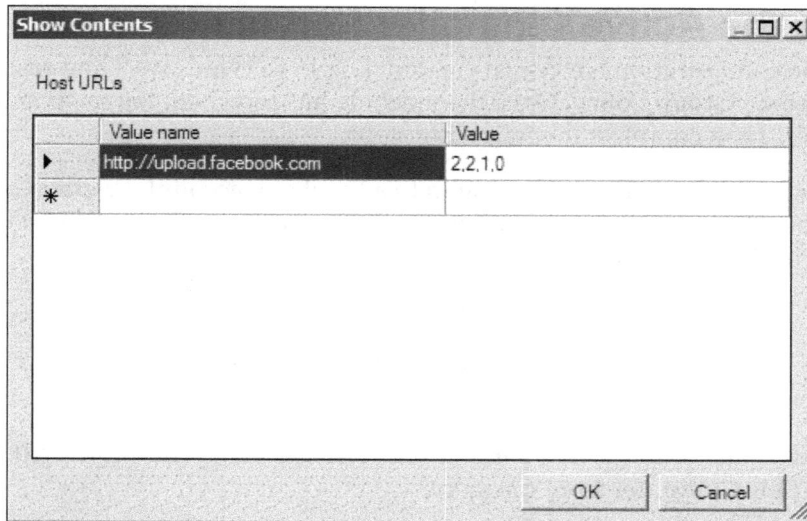

8. Click **OK** in the **Approved Installation Sites for ActiveX controls** dialog to complete the process.

The cryptic list of comma delimited numbers in the **Value** field controls various aspects of security when a control is installed. The first three digits regulate Trusted ActiveX controls, Signed ActiveX controls, and Unsigned ActiveX controls respectively. All three settings can be configured as 0 to block the install, 1 to prompt the user, and (with the exception of unsigned controls, which cannot be set to install automatically) 2 to install without prompting the user. The fourth digit controls Server Certificate Policy and should be set to 0 unless you want to ignore HTTPS certificate errors. The errors are as follows:

- 256 to continue installation if the Certification Authority is unknown to the client
- 512 to ignore invalid certificate usage
- 4096 to ignore an unknown common name (CN)
- 8192 to ignore a certificate that's expired

If you want to ignore a certificate that's expired and also any invalid certificate usage, add together 512 and 8192, or any other combination you require.

Testing the ActiveX Installer Service

Let's test the configuration we've just created. Log in to Windows 7 and restart it to refresh machine Group Policy. Once the machine has rebooted, log on as standard domain user. Then complete the following steps:

1. Open Internet Explorer and log in to a Facebook account. Prepare to upload photos to a new or existing album in the browser window and you'll be prompted to install an ActiveX control in the Information Bar.

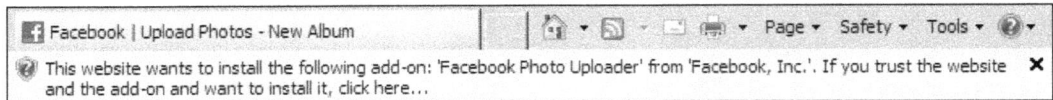

2. Click on the Information Bar and select **Install This Add-on for All Users on This Computer** from the menu.

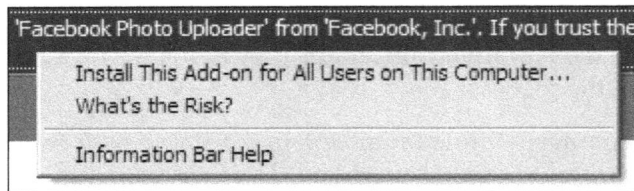

3. Wait for a few seconds. **You may be prompted with the Information Bar for a second time.**

4. Wait for the ActiveX control to download. This time, the installation should complete without any **User Account Control** prompt.

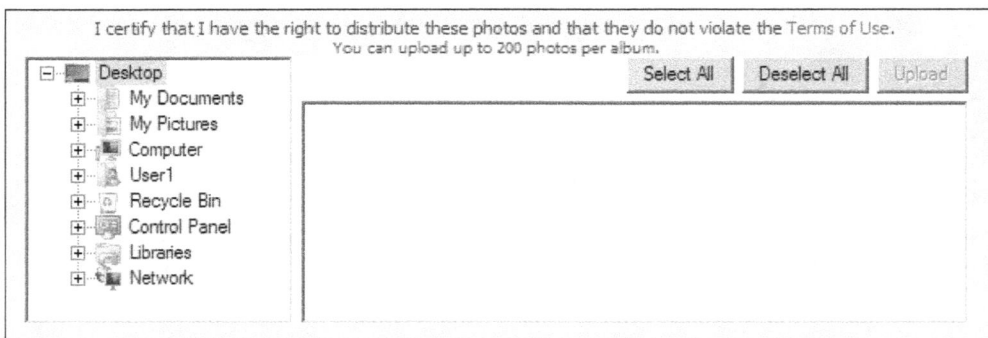

Managing add-ons

Toolbars and ActiveX controls present a challenge for system administrators. While deploying software using Group Policy Software Installation or a third-party solution is the best way to control add-ons through their full lifecycle—Internet Explorer comes with the **Manage Add-ons** console for enabling or disabling installed add-ons. Add-ons can also be enabled and disabled using Group Policy.

Administrator approved controls

You can disable ActiveX controls that were installed using the ActiveX Installer Service once they are no longer needed or have been superseded by an updated version. While this is not an ideal way to manage the lifecycle of add-ons, it can be used as the next best method. As of Internet Explorer 6 in Windows XP Service Pack 2, the Administrator Approved Controls setting in Group Policy is called Add-on Management. Let's edit our AXIS Group Policy Object to include settings for Internet Explorer Add-on Management. Log in to Windows Server 2008 R2 as a domain administrator:

1. Open the **Group Policy Management Console** from **Administrative Tools** in the **Start** menu and expand your Active Directory forest and domain in the left pane.

2. Expand the **Clients** OU, right-click the **AXIS** GPO, and select **Edit** from the menu.

3. In the **Group Policy Management Editor** window, expand **Policies** under **Computer Configuration** in the left pane and select **Administrative Templates**. Next expand **Windows Components**, then **Internet Explorer**, and finally **Security Features**.

4. Under **Security Features**, select **Add-on Management**. In the right pane, double-click **Deny all add-ons unless specifically allowed in the Add-on List**.

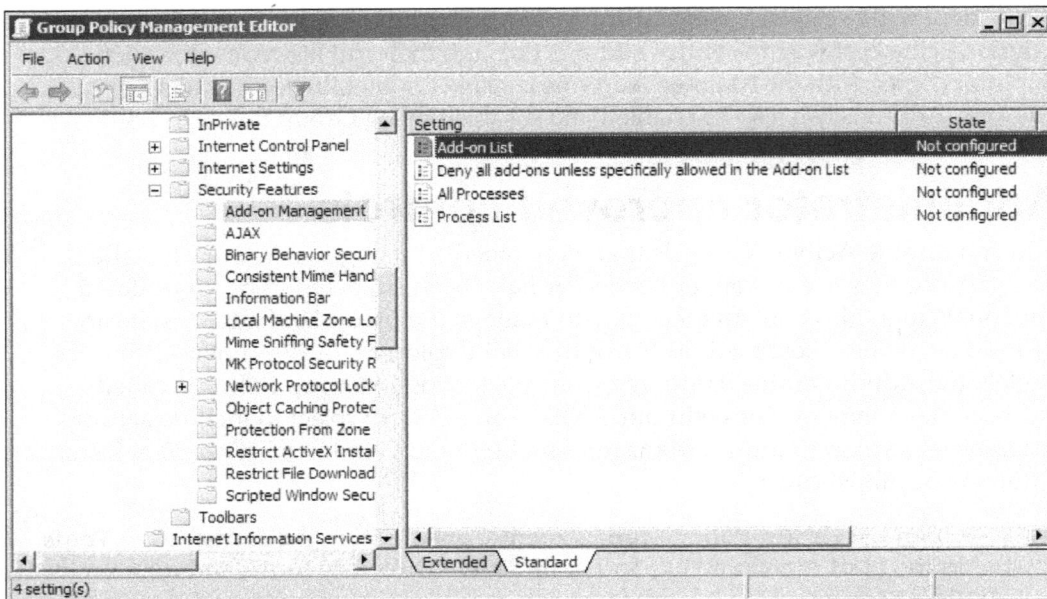

5. In the **Deny all add-ons unless specifically allowed in the Add-on List** dialog, select **Enabled** and click **OK**.

> **Per-user ActiveX controls and the ActiveX Installer Service**
>
> In Internet Explorer 8, per-user ActiveX controls are denied access to the ActiveX Installer Service. Per-user ActiveX controls redirected to AxIS in IE7 will fail to install.

Determining the Class Identifier CLSID of an installed ActiveX control

ActiveX controls are identified in the registry by a string called a **Class ID (CLSID)**. ActiveX controls must be specified in the add-on list by their CLSID. In this example, let's add the Facebook Photo Uploader 5.5 control to the add-on list.

Open Internet Explorer 8 on a client machine and install the Facebook Photo Uploader control. If the ActiveX Installer Service is not set up to install the control on behalf of standard users, you must be logged in as an administrator to complete the installation. Once the control has been successfully installed:

1. Select **Manage Add-ons** from the **Tools** menu in Internet Explorer.

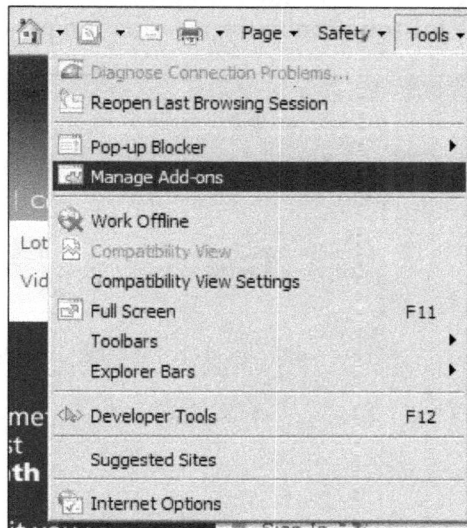

2. In the **Manage Add-ons** window, select **Downloaded controls** from the **Show** drop-down menu and select the **Facebook Photo Uploader 5 Control** on the right.

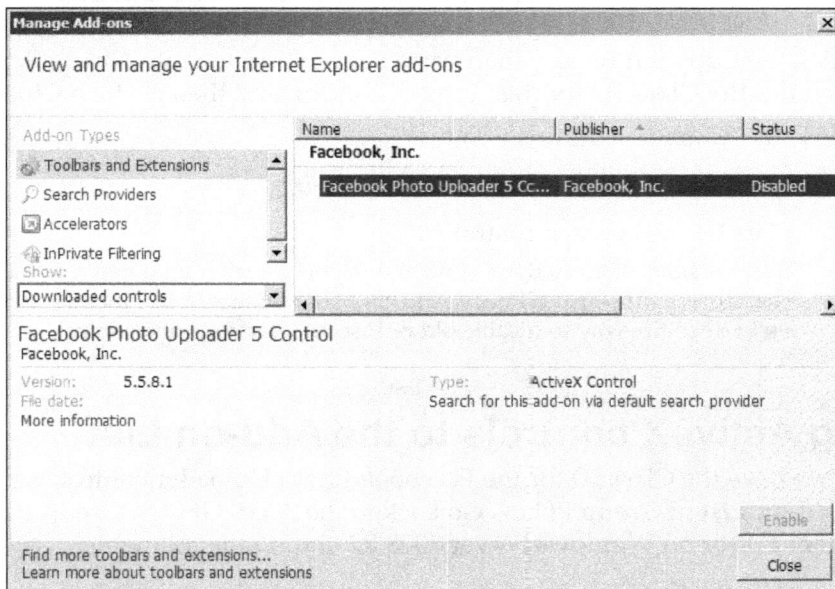

3. Notice that the control is disabled because the enabled **Deny all add-ons unless specifically allowed in the Add-on List** policy has already taken effect. Click **More information** in the information pane.

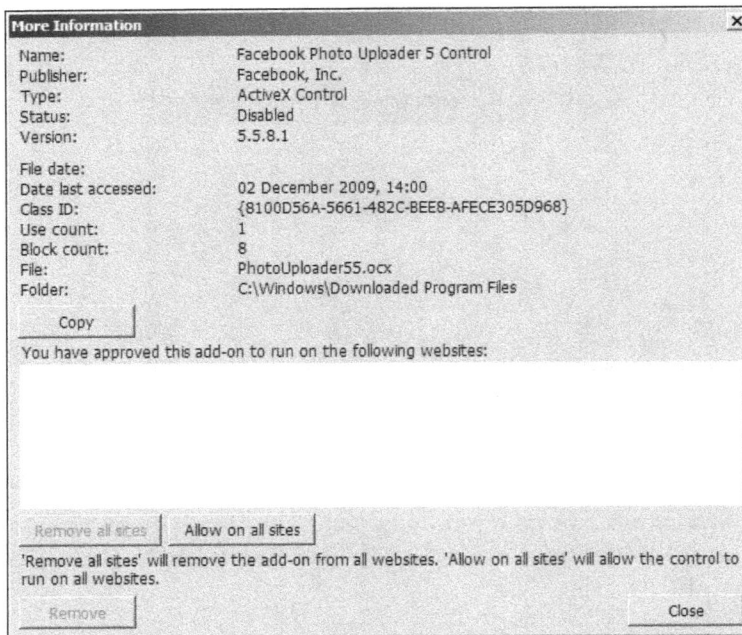

```
More Information                                            [x]

Name:              Facebook Photo Uploader 5 Control
Publisher:         Facebook, Inc.
Type:              ActiveX Control
Status:            Disabled
Version:           5.5.8.1

File date:
Date last accessed: 02 December 2009, 14:00
Class ID:          {8100D56A-5661-482C-BEE8-AFECE305D968}
Use count:         1
Block count:       8
File:              PhotoUploader55.ocx
Folder:            C:\Windows\Downloaded Program Files

    Copy

You have approved this add-on to run on the following websites:




 Remove all sites    Allow on all sites

'Remove all sites' will remove the add-on from all websites. 'Allow on all sites' will allow the control to
run on all websites.

    Remove                                            Close
```

4. Click the **Copy** button and then paste the information into Notepad, which includes **the Class ID** for this ActiveX control, and then click on **Close**.

5. Close the **Manage Add-ons** window.

Class IDs and version control

New versions of an ActiveX control don't necessarily use a new Class ID. Therefore, using Group Policy Add-on Management in Internet Explorer isn't a sure-fire way to disable old or insecure versions of a control.

Adding ActiveX controls to the Add-on List

Now that we have the Class ID for the Facebook Photo Uploader control, we can add it to the **Add-on List** in Group Policy. Go back to the **AXIS** GPO in **Group Policy Management Editor** on Windows Server 2008 R2 and do the following:

1. Double-click **Add-on List** in the **Setting** column.

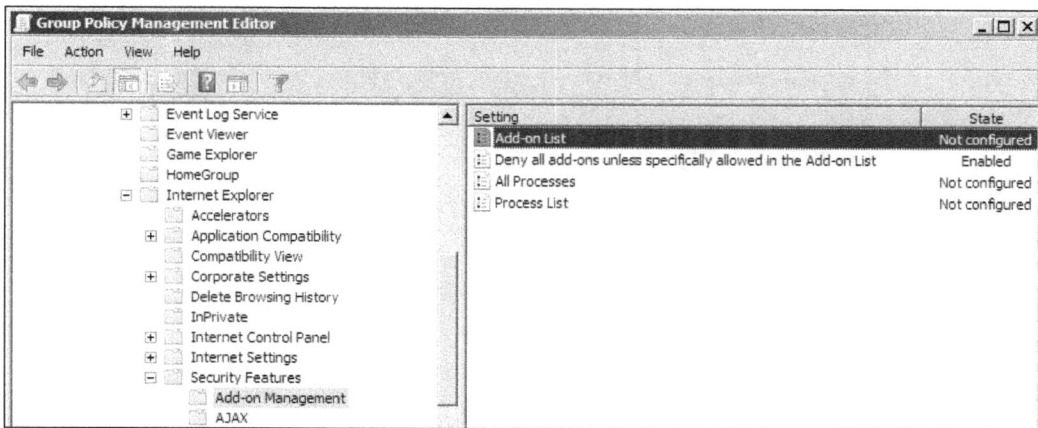

2. Select **Enabled** in the **Add-on List** dialog and then click **Show**.

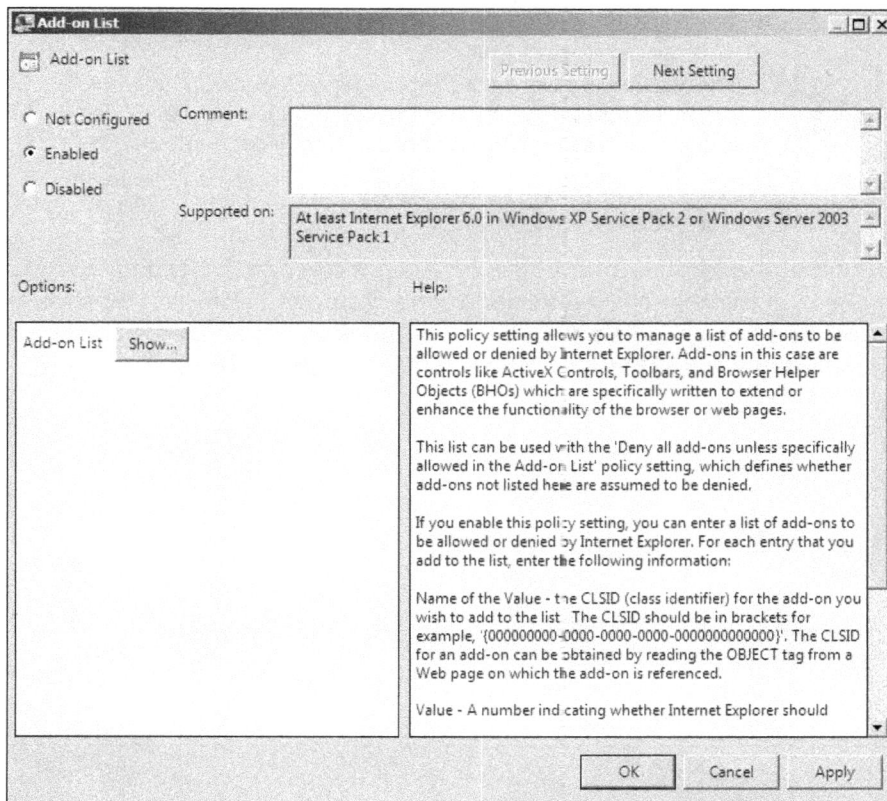

3. In the **Show Contents** dialog, click the empty field under **Value name** and type the Class ID of the Facebook Photo Uploader control including the brackets.

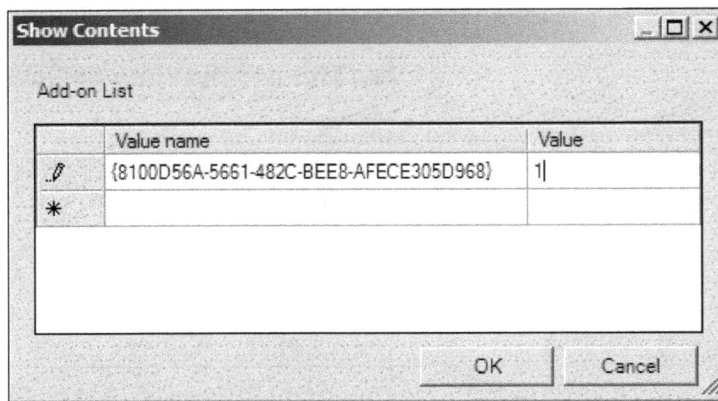

	Value name	Value
✏	{8100D56A-5661-482C-BEE8-AFECE305D968}	1
*		

Show Contents — Add-on List — OK / Cancel

4. Type 1 into the **Value** field and click **OK**.

> The **Value** field can be set to 0 to deny a control, 1 to allow a control, and 2 to allow a control and let the user manage it via the **Manage Add-ons** option in Internet Explorer.

5. Click **OK** in the **Add-on List** dialog.

6. If you now refresh Group Policy on a client machine, by typing `gpupdate /force` at the command line, and reopen Internet Explorer, you should see through **Manage Add-ons** that the Facebook Photo Uploader control status is **Enabled** while all other controls remain disabled.

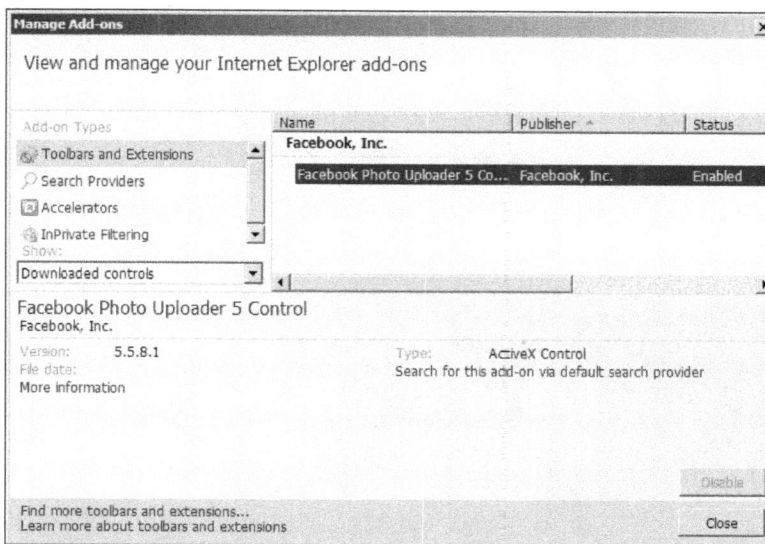

> **Internet Explorer add-on settings**
>
> Sometimes after Group Policy has been refreshed, Internet Explorer must be opened twice before it registers changes in add-on management settings.

Summary

In this chapter we've learned how to leverage the ActiveX Installer Service for installing per-machine ActiveX controls under the context of a standard user account. We've also discussed best practices concerning the management of Internet Explorer add-ons and how to prevent unauthorized controls from running using Group Policy. Before continuing to the next chapter you should:

- Be able to set up and configure the ActiveX Installer Service on multiple computers
- Know how to configure Group Policy to block or enable specific controls
- Understand that controls installed via the ActiveX Installer Service cannot be managed through their full lifecycle without additional software management technology
- Understand the difference between per-user, per-machine, and per-site ActiveX controls

In the next Chapter, we'll discuss strategies and techniques for supporting users running with standard user accounts.

8
Supporting Users Running with Least Privilege

Least privilege user accounts can be a challenge for support staff who are used to working with unmanaged systems. This chapter outlines the changes that we'll need to make to support procedures, and the additional skills that help desk staff will need to work with least privilege user accounts. We will learn about:

- The importance of reliable remote access for supporting least privilege user accounts
- Different techniques for connecting to remote systems with administrative privileges
- Enabling remote access using **Group Policy**
- Configuring **Windows Firewall** to allow remote access

Providing support

IT departments have traditionally relied on users to install approved software and fix problems as directed by the help desk or without any instruction at all. This requires that users have administrative access to PCs, and such access is often granted in the belief that if users can manage their own systems, alone or as guided by the help desk, it will reduce support costs. This *self-service* approach is common, especially in small and medium-sized enterprises, where support staff may not have the necessary skills to help users who don't have full access to their PCs.

As we are aware, the disadvantages of running with administrative access outweigh the advantages in most cases. Here's a quick reminder of some of the drawbacks:

- **Exposure of entire networks to malware, viruses, and denial-of-service (DOS) attacks**: It's often considered that a single machine running with administrative privileges is not a risk to other devices connected to the same network. This is not the case if one device becomes infected with malware; it can launch a denial-of-service attack against other devices, including servers and network hardware, at worst bringing entire networks to a halt or impeding system performance.

- **Data corruption or manipulation**: Malware can cause damage by corrupting data or operating system files, preventing systems from booting.

- **System configuration changes**: Maintaining known configurations across a network is crucial for reliability and reducing support costs.

- **Leakage of sensitive data**: Malware such as key loggers and Trojan horses can reveal sensitive information, including data and login credentials, to systems located outside of your organization.

> Managed systems and standard user accounts can still offer most of the flexibility of unmanaged systems, but in a more controlled manner where only IT-approved applications can be installed. **Group Policy Software Installation** and other technologies, such as **Application Virtualization (App-V)** or OS Virtualization (XP Mode), provide standard users with a secure but flexible environment.

Preparing to support least privilege

So what does least privilege on the desktop mean to the daily operations of the IT department? While in general, support costs will decrease and calls to the help desk should be fewer, IT staff must be able to do the following in order to support standard users:

- **Understand the Windows security model: Access control lists** (ACLs), NT user rights, Integrity Levels, and User Account Control are all components of the security model. With the exception of Integrity Levels and User Account Control, all have been present since Windows NT was released in the mid-1990s. Despite this, many Windows support professionals have a limited understanding of these concepts.

- Using the command line or PowerShell can be essential when supporting standard users over slow network connections. While GUI-based remote access tools can be useful, they are not always the most efficient way to gather data or run commands on remote computers.

- Understand how to work with automated software and patch installation technologies such as Group Policy Software Installation, **Windows Server Update Services (WSUS)**, System Center Configuration Manager, or App-V.

- Be conversant with the management infrastructure, such as Active Directory, Group Policy, or System Center Configuration Manager.

> In addition to the support requirements listed above, IT departments should also have systems management technology such as Group Policy and WSUS in place. In large complex environments, third-party systems management software, such as Systems Center Configuration Manager may also be required.

The points listed above are relevant for help desk staff in any environment, but become more critical when supporting standard users, as a managed infrastructure is required and security technologies play a more vital role. Without the proper infrastructure in place, IT staff will have to "visit" users' desktops, either physically or through remote access, far more often.

Many Windows support professionals solve problems related to standard user accounts by granting users administrative access to their PC, often because the professional doesn't understand how to work with managed systems, or simply doesn't have the time or will to investigate the problem. If a move to standardize user accounts and managed systems is planned and tested carefully, such problems can be avoided.

In this chapter, we'll start off by looking at how each of the remote access methods in Windows works, and how to enable and configure them using Group Policy. The second half of the chapter contains a guide on how to configure Windows Firewall for XP, Vista, and Windows 7 to enable all of the Windows remote access features discussed. I recommend that you start by disabling Windows Firewall on your lab computers and experiment with the remote access features as you read about them.

> Windows Firewall should only be disabled in lab environments for testing purposes. In production, a tested firewall configuration should be deployed that provides the necessary functionality with the maximum possible protection.

Once you're familiar with how the remote access tools work, you should then switch on Windows Firewall and configure Group Policy to enable inbound exceptions for the different remote access features as described, in preparation for deployment in a production environment.

Troubleshooting using remote access

Support tools such as pcAnywhere, VNC, and **Remote Desktop** have long been a staple part of the help desk's tool set, but when users are running with standard user accounts, remote access to systems becomes more critical, because gone is the option of talking a user through a procedure over the phone if it requires administrative access. Unless you create an administrative backdoor to a system, which should only be used as a last resort, you cannot rely on users to perform troubleshooting steps that require a privileged account.

Reliable remote access is critical for supporting standard users.

Troubleshooting for notebook users

Portable computers present a particular support challenge, and more so in cases where users run with least privilege. It's ironic that notebook users are the most in need of standard user accounts to prevent changes to critical system settings and protect against malware and unlicensed software but are the ones most likely to be granted administrative privileges. It's a Catch-22 situation; with standard user accounts, problems are much less likely to arise, but when they do arise will be more difficult to resolve if the help desk can't get remote access.

The notebook challenge

When considering which version of Windows to deploy to notebooks, try to license the latest version, as it will always be the easiest to support. For example, Windows 7 includes **DirectAccess**, which ensures that notebooks are always connected to the corporate network whenever an Internet connection is present, making maintenance and remote troubleshooting much easier. Connecting to the corporate network using a **VPN** or dialer often requires support, and DirectAccess disposes of the need for a dialup VPN.

Providing users with seamless access to the corporate network

Introduced in Windows 7 and Windows Server 2008 R2, DirectAccess aims to provide remote users with seamless access to the corporate intranet. Whenever an Internet connection is available, the remote user has the same experience as if connected directly to the corporate network. No dial-up connections, no VPNs. DirectAccess helps businesses stay in compliance by helping system administrators keep notebooks up-to-date and improves manageability. For more information on DirectAccess visit: http://www.microsoft.com/servers/directaccess.mspx.

Having the right tools in place

Always be prepared for the worst should the regular method of connecting to the corporate intranet stop working. Provide at least one backup remote connection method, such as modem dial-in access or a VPN connection.

Configure GUI-based remote access tools such as Remote Desktop and Remote Assistance, and set up remote access via the command line using **WS-Management** and PowerShell, in case slow network connections prevent the use of the standard GUI tools. Also, enable *Domain* profile inbound remote administration exceptions in Windows Firewall advanced settings to provide an easy way to modify configuration on remote devices.

Notebook users who seldom visit the office

Employees who don't visit the office very often pose additional problems in terms of ensuring their devices stay up-to-date and distributing new software when required. Consider additional technology, such as System Center Configuration Manager, which provides the ability to distribute software and patches over slow network connections. DirectAccess is also a good solution for users who are always on the road or are based in distant locations. **Network Access Protection** (**NAP**) or similar Network Access Control technology can also be used to ensure that returning road warriors are checked for compliance with security policies before allowing them full access to corporate networks.

Setting out IT policy

Set out policies that outline what peripheral equipment notebook users are allowed to connect to their systems. For instance, have an approved list of printers and cable modems to ensure that the help desk can provide effective support. All too often, notebook users go to the local PC store and return with something that may not be suitable or is difficult to support, but nevertheless expect the IT department to assist. Make sure your policy also includes provision for mobile phones and PDAs.

The **Allow non-administrators to install drivers for these device setup classes** Group Policy setting under **Computer Configuration | Policies | Administrative Templates | System | Driver Installation** in Vista and Windows 7 Group Policy allows administrators to stipulate devices that can be installed by standard users according to the device GUID as specified in the driver. **The Group Policy settings contained in the Driver Installation folder under System should not be confused with settings in the Device Installation folder as they serve different purposes.** Device classes can be added generally, that is `{4d36e979-e325-11ce-bfc1-08002be10318}` for printers, or more exact GUIDs used to restrict installation to a specific device. Drivers must be signed according to the Windows Driver Signing Policy or by a publisher that is already trusted by the local computer.

Standard users can install device drivers if:

- A driver that supports the device being connected is included in Windows out of the box.

- A driver for the device has been pre-staged in the local driver store using **Pnputil.exe** or **DISM**.

- A driver signed according to the Windows Driver Signing Policy or by a publisher that is already trusted by the local computer is available on Windows Update or in a location specified in the system's DevicePath registry value (Windows 7 only).

- A driver signed according to the Windows Driver Signing Policy or by a publisher that is already trusted by the local computer is available and the associated device GUID is listed in the **Allow non-administrators to install drivers for these device setup classes** policy setting (Windows Vista and later).

Other functions the help desk might require

When configuring Windows Firewall inbound exceptions, consider what functionality the help desk might require when notebooks are connected to different types of network.

IPsec and Windows Firewall

Starting with Windows Vista, Windows Firewall and IPsec configurations are combined to make the configuration of IPsec rules easier for system administrators. An inbound firewall exception can be created that allows access from devices that have a valid certificate.

For instance, any unknown network will automatically be categorized by Windows as *Public*. Only administrative users can designate an unknown network as *Private* (Work or Home). Windows Firewall's Public profile is very restrictive by design, and you should weigh up the risks before enabling inbound rules for this profile.

Consider a scenario where a user is connected to a public Wi-Fi hotspot but cannot connect to the corporate intranet. The Wi-Fi hotspot is categorized as Public by Windows Firewall and the local **NAT** (**Network Address Translation**) router doesn't pass traffic for L2TP/IPsec VPNs. In such a scenario, it will be impossible for the help desk to offer support using Remote Assistance, as all Public profile inbound firewall exceptions for **Remote Assistance** are disabled by default. Rather than enable Remote Assistance exceptions for the Public firewall profile, a more secure solution would be to invest in an SSL VPN or DirectAccess.

The last resort: An administrative backdoor for notebooks

If a user cannot connect to the corporate intranet, the help desk can't connect to the remote device and all possibilities have been exhausted, this raises the question of how the help desk will provide support should a problem arise. Without least privilege, the solution is to talk to the user through a support procedure over the telephone. However, if the process requires administrative privileges, the only way a standard user can complete the procedure is to provide them with a local administrator username and password.

The good news is that with least privilege enabled, the chances of problems occurring are minimal as users can't change critical system configuration in the first instance, which is the single biggest cause of support calls.

Let's switch off the firewall and grant administrative privileges!
In a well-managed and tested least privilege environment, help desk staff should be aware that PC problems are often the result of factors not connected to standard user accounts or Windows Firewall.

In cases where there is simply no alternative, you should be prepared to provide users with the username and password of a local administrator account. An account with administrative privileges should be created on every portable device with a different password. The help desk can access these credentials should they be required. The help desk should bear in mind that once a user knows the credentials of a local administrator account, the device is likely to fall out of compliance and no longer retain a standard configuration. You should a database of current local administrator account names and passwords for each computer, keyed by asset tag, and by changing passwords on a regular basis.

Enabling and using command-line remote access tools

When supporting remote users over slow network connections, command-line tools can enable system administrators to perform tasks more quickly and even save the day in situations where graphical remote support tools fail due to slow or intermittent network connections.

To use the tools described in the following section, you should temporarily switch off Windows Firewall on all client machines in your lab.

WS-Management

There are various methods for accessing remote machines using the command line, such as OpenSSH and PsExec from the SysInternals support tools on TechNet. As of Windows XP SP2, the supported method is **Windows Remote Management (WinRM)**, sometimes also known as **WS-Management**. WinRM 1.1 is available for Windows XP Service Pack 2 as an additional download, WinRM 2.0 is included in Windows 7 out of the box, and while Vista also includes WinRM, it should be upgraded to version 2.0 to provide useful facilities such as **PowerShell Remoting**.

WS-Management is an open standard for server management, and WinRM is Microsoft's implementation for Windows. Though primarily designed for server management, WinRM is included in Vista and Windows 7 by default, and can be downloaded as an additional component for Windows XP.

Downloading WinRM 1.1 for Windows XP SP2

You can download it from: http://www.microsoft.com/ Downloads/details.aspx?FamilyID=845289ca-16cc-4c73- 8934-dd46b5ed1d33&displaylang=en.

The **Windows Remote Management** components for Vista include WinRM 2.0, PowerShell 2.0, and BITS 4.0.

Downloading Windows Remote Management components for Windows Vista

http://support.microsoft.com/kb/968929

At the time of writing, Microsoft don't plan to back port WinRM 2.0 for Windows XP.

Configuring WS-Management with Group Policy

WinRM is included in Vista and Windows 7 out of the box, but is not enabled or configured for use. As it's likely you'll want to enable WinRM on most of your systems for remote support, you should use **Group Policy** to manage and enable WinRM.

Before enabling WinRM, you should consider the extra attack surface introduced and how best to protect systems from unsolicited remote access requests. **Domain Isolation** can provide devices connected to the corporate intranet with protection from unmanaged systems.

In the following tutorial, we're going to configure WinRM in Group Policy so that it automatically listens for remote access requests on the default port (TCP port 5985 for WinRM 2.0 and TCP port 80 for WinRM 1.1) and set the **Windows Remote Management** service to start automatically.

1. Log in to Windows Server 2008 R2 as a domain administrator and open **Start | Administrative Tools | Group Policy Management**.

2. For the purposes of our lab environment, we'll create a new Group Policy Object and link it to our Clients Organizational Unit. In the **Group Policy Management** window expand your forest; under the **Domains** node you'll find **Clients**. Right-click the **Clients** OU and select **Create a GPO in this domain, and Link it here** from the menu.

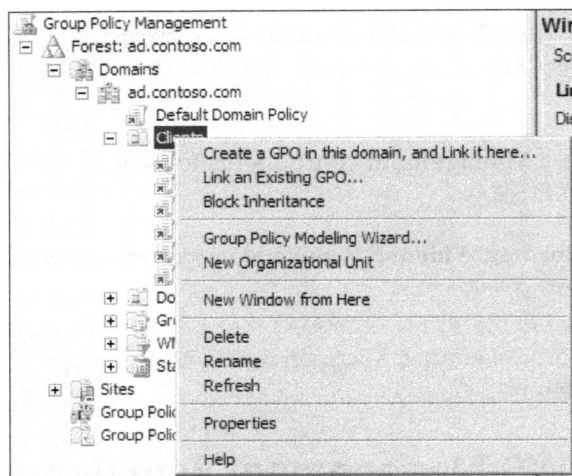

3. Type **Enable WinRM** in the **Name** field of the **New GPO** dialog, leave **Source Starter GPO** set to (**none**), and click **OK**.

4. Right-click the new **Enable WinRM** GPO under the **Clients** OU and select **Edit** from the menu.

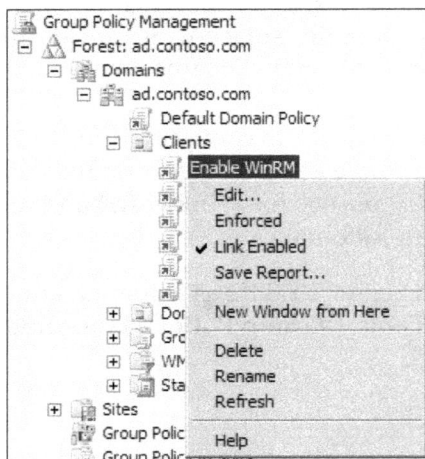

5. In the **Group Policy Management Editor** window, expand **Computer Configuration | Policies | Windows Settings | Security Settings** and click **System Services**.

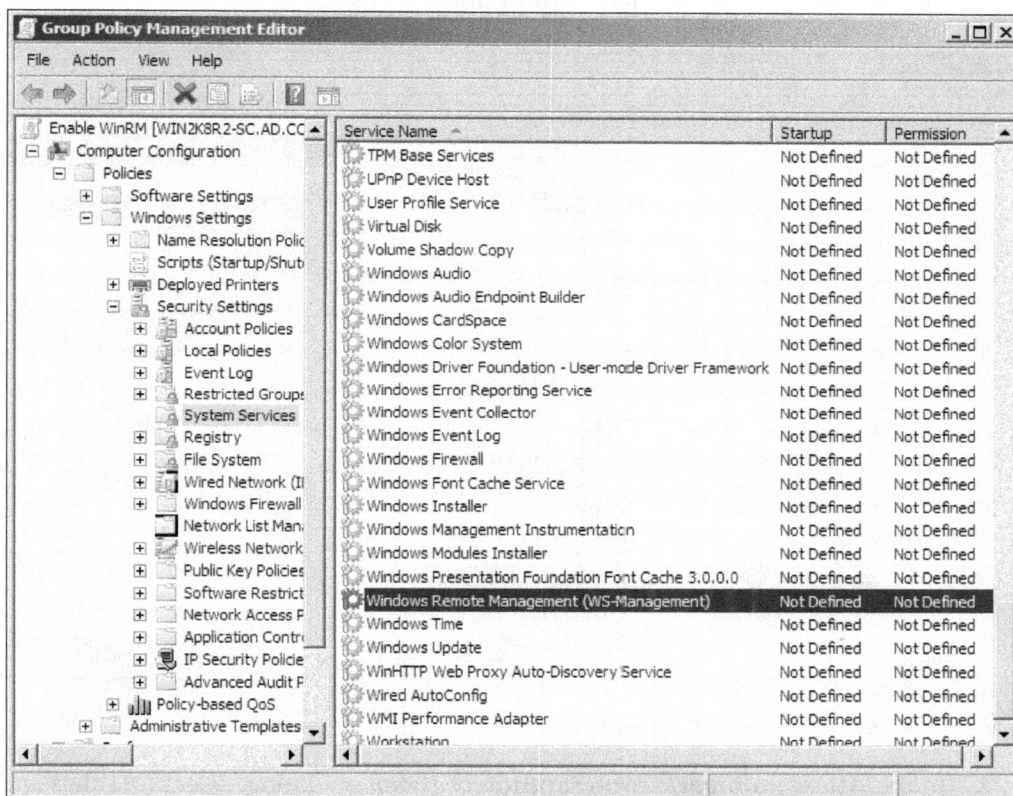

6. In the pane on right-hand side double-click **Windows Remote Management (WS-Management)**.

7. In the **Windows Remote Management (WS-Management) Properties** dialog check the **Define this policy setting** option and set the service startup mode to **Automatic**.

8. Click **OK**. In the left pane under **Computer Configuration | Policies, Administrative Templates | Windows Components | Windows Remote Management (WinRM)** select **WinRM Service** and in the right pane double-click **Allow automatic configuration of listeners**.

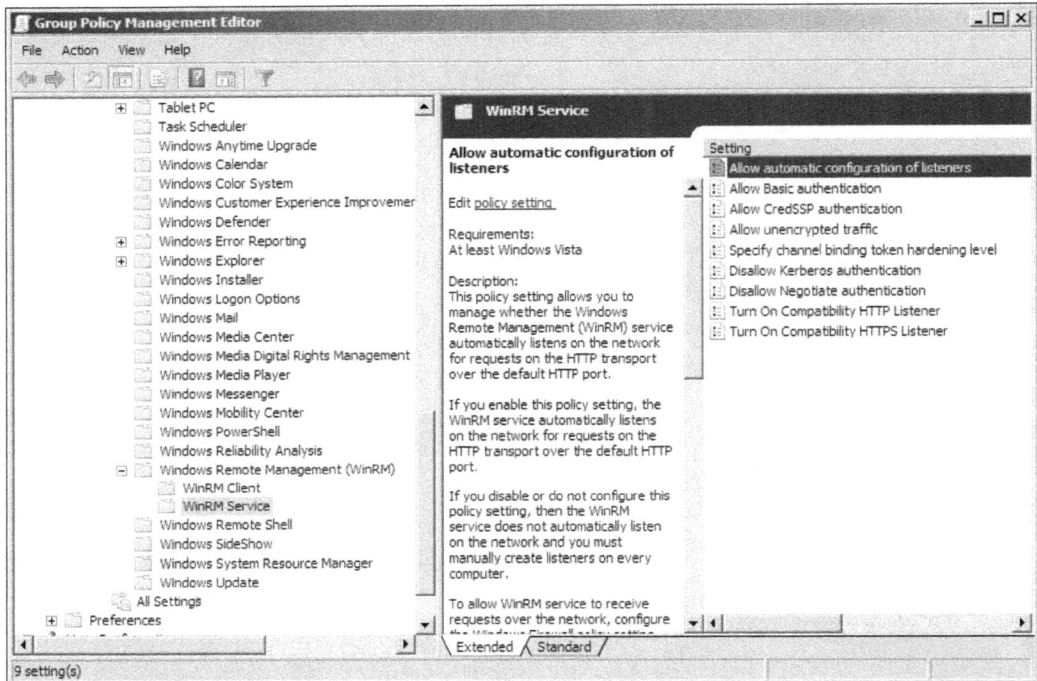

9. In the **Allow automatic configuration of listeners** dialog, select **Enabled** and then under **Options** add "*" (asterik) in the **IPv4 filter** and **IPv6 filter** fields.

> **IPv6 filter**
>
> If you don't use IPv6 on your network, you can leave the **IPv6 filter** field empty, but consider that you may have to issue updates when you do deploy IPv6.

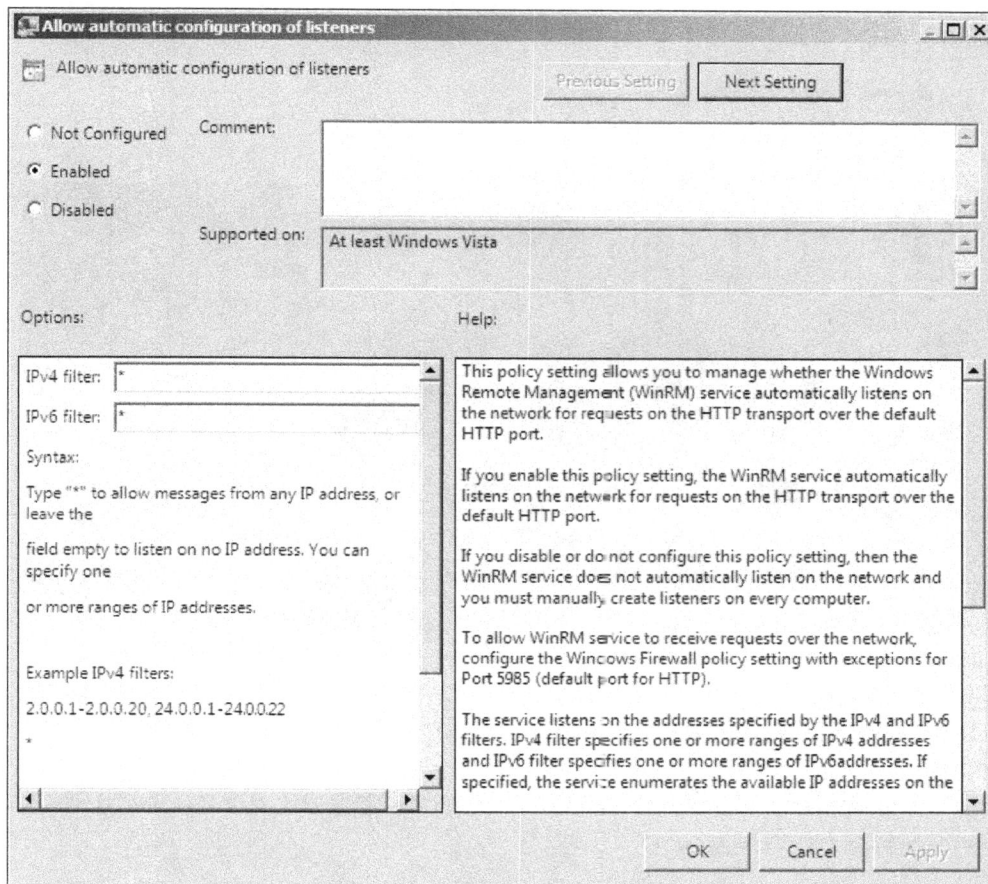

10. Click **OK** and close the **Group Policy Management Editor** window.

Connecting to remote machines using WS-Management

Now that we've got our machines configured with the WinRM service and listening on port 5985 (or port 80 for WinRM 1.1), we need to see if we can connect using the winrs command. Let's start by checking that the WS-Management listener is available on a remote Windows 7 client.

Log in to Windows Server 2008 R2 as a domain administrator and start the command prompt by typing cmd in the **Search programs and files** box at the bottom of the **Start** menu and pressing *Enter*.

2. In the command prompt window type (where WIN7 is the name of your Windows 7 machine):

```
winrm id -remote:WIN7
```

```
Administrator: Command Prompt                                    _ □ X

Microsoft Windows [Version 6.1.7600]
Copyright (c) 2009 Microsoft Corporation.  All rights reserved.

C:\Users\Administrator.AD>winrm id -remote:WIN7
IdentifyResponse
    ProtocolVersion = http://schemas.dmtf.org/wbem/wsman/1/wsman.xsd
    ProductVendor = Microsoft Corporation
    ProductVersion = OS: 6.1.7600 SP: 0.0 Stack: 2.0


C:\Users\Administrator.AD>
```

Here we have some basic information about the remote machine including the exact product version and service pack level.

Running standard Windows commands as an administrator on remote computers

Once you've verified that the WS-Management listener is accessible on the remote computer, you can run standard Windows commands using winrs, either by invoking a remote command prompt or adding the command after winrs. To invoke a remote command prompt type:

```
winrs -r:WIN7 cmd
```

Notice how the command prompt changes from C:\Users\Administrator.AD> to C:\Users\Administrator> when a connection to the remote machine has been made. You can then run a command as if you were sitting at the local terminal.

Alternatively, you can run a command line without invoking a remote command prompt:

```
winrs -r:WIN7 ipconfig
```

```
Administrator: Command Prompt                                          _ □ X
C:\Users\Administrator.AD>winrs -r:WIN7 ipconfig

Windows IP Configuration

Ethernet adapter Local Area Connection:

   Connection-specific DNS Suffix  . :
   Link-local IPv6 Address . . . . . : fe80::a1fe:522e:fc39:f13d%11
   IPv4 Address. . . . . . . . . . . : 192.168.1.30
   Subnet Mask . . . . . . . . . . . : 255.255.255.0
   Default Gateway . . . . . . . . . :

Tunnel adapter isatap.{94A20CDD-C444-45AF-9FC1-A1855842BEDE}:

   Media State . . . . . . . . . . . : Media disconnected
   Connection-specific DNS Suffix  . :

Tunnel adapter Local Area Connection* 11:

   Media State . . . . . . . . . . . : Media disconnected
   Connection-specific DNS Suffix  . :

C:\Users\Administrator.AD>
```

Enumerating information using Windows Management Instrumentation

WS-Management exposes **Windows Management Instrumentation (WMI)** data that can be useful for troubleshooting. The following command shows useful information about the remote machine:

winrm **enumerate** wmicimv2/Win32_OperatingSystem -remote:WIN7

```
Win32_OperatingSystem
    BootDevice = \Device\HarddiskVolume1
    BuildNumber = 7600
    BuildType = Multiprocessor Free
    Caption = Microsoft Windows 7 Ultimate
    CodeSet = 1252
    CountryCode = 44
    CreationClassName = Win32_OperatingSystem
    CSCreationClassName = Win32_ComputerSystem
    CSDVersion = null
    CSName = WIN7
    CurrentTimeZone = 60
    DataExecutionPrevention_32BitApplications = true
    DataExecutionPrevention_Available = true
    DataExecutionPrevention_Drivers = true
    DataExecutionPrevention_SupportPolicy = 2
```

```
Debug = false
Description
Distributed = false
EncryptionLevel = 256
ForegroundApplicationBoost = 2
FreePhysicalMemory = 705316
FreeSpaceInPagingFiles = 860292
FreeVirtualMemory = 1525148
InstallDate
    Datetime = 2009-09-14T15:36:40+01:00
LargeSystemCache = null
LastBootUpTime
    Datetime = 2009-09-24T19:28:12.052017+01:00
LocalDateTime
    Datetime = 2009-09-25T11:35:34.117+01:00
Locale = 0809
Manufacturer = Microsoft Corporation
MaxNumberOfProcesses = 4294967295
MaxProcessMemorySize = 8589934464
MUILanguages = en-US
Name = Microsoft Windows 7 Ultimate |C:\Windows|\Device\
Harddisk0\Partition2
NumberOfLicensedUsers = 0
NumberOfProcesses = 38
NumberOfUsers = 2
OperatingSystemSKU = 1
Organization
OSArchitecture = 64-bit
OSLanguage = 1033
OSProductSuite = 256
OSType = 18
OtherTypeDescription = null
PAEEnabled = null
PlusProductID = null
PlusVersionNumber = null
Primary = true
ProductType = 1
RegisteredUser = rms45
SerialNumber = 00426-065-0022235-86746
```

```
ServicePackMajorVersion = 0
ServicePackMinorVersion = 0
SizeStoredInPagingFiles = 1048576
Status = OK
SuiteMask = 272
SystemDevice = \Device\HarddiskVolume2
SystemDirectory = C:\Windows\system32
SystemDrive = C:
TotalSwapSpaceSize = null
TotalVirtualMemorySize = 2096696
TotalVisibleMemorySize = 1048120
Version = 6.1.7600
WindowsDirectory = C:\Windows
```

WMI Win32 classes

There are lots of Win32 classes that can be used to enumerate information from local or remote machines. To find out more about Win32 classes and associated methods visit http://msdn.microsoft.com/en-us/library/aa394084(VS.85).aspx.

Performing actions on remote computers as an administrator using WMI methods

Many Win32 classes have a set of associated methods that allow you to go beyond simply enumerating information, to performing some kind of administrative action on local or remote computers. For instance, the reboot method of the Win32_OperatingSystem class allows the remote Windows 7 client to be restarted:

```
winrm invoke reboot wmicimv2/Win32_OperatingSystem -remote:WIN7
```

Another useful example is the ability to stop and start system services. Standard users cannot do this for themselves, but using WS-Management a system administrator can easily restart a system service remotely should the need arise. The following command stops the **Print Spooler service** on a remote machine called WIN7:

```
winrm invoke stopservice wmicimv2/Win32_Service?name=spooler -
  remote:WIN7
```

> **Additional WMI classes**
>
> While Win32 classes tend to be the most useful for troubleshooting purposes, there are many other WMI classes that can be used to gather information or perform actions on remote computers as an administrator. Visit `http://msdn.microsoft.com/en-us/ library/aa394554(VS.85).aspx` for more information.

Connecting to WS-Management 1.1 from Windows Server 2008 R2

Windows XP and Vista RTM use WS-Management 1.1, which listens on port 80. Because the WinRM client in Windows Server 2008 R2 expects to find the remote listener on port 5985, you need to specify port 80 when connecting to a WinRM 1.1 listener (where XP1 is the name of the remote machine):

```
winrs -r:XP1:80 cmd
```

In a similar fashion, the `winrm` command also needs to have the port number appended:

```
winrm enumerate wmicimv2/Win32_OperatingSystem -remote:XP1:80
```

```
Administrator: Command Prompt                                    _ □ ×
Microsoft Windows [Version 6.1.7600]
Copyright (c) 2009 Microsoft Corporation.  All rights reserved.

C:\Users\Administrator.AD>winrm enumerate wmicimv2/Win32_OperatingSystem -remote
:XP1:80
Win32_OperatingSystem
    BootDevice = \Device\HarddiskVolume1
    BuildNumber = 2600
    BuildType = Uniprocessor Free
    Caption = Microsoft Windows XP Professional
    CodeSet = 1252
    CountryCode = 1
    CreationClassName = Win32_OperatingSystem
    CSCreationClassName = Win32_ComputerSystem
    CSDVersion = Service Pack 3
    CSName = XP1
    CurrentTimeZone = 60
    DataExecutionPrevention_32BitApplications = true
    DataExecutionPrevention_Available = true
    DataExecutionPrevention_Drivers = true
    DataExecutionPrevention_SupportPolicy = 2
    Debug = false
    Description
    Distributed = false
    EncryptionLevel = 168
```

Working with WS-Management security

WinRM service comes with several different security providers to authenticate requests for remote access. Two are enabled by default—Kerberos and Negotiate. Kerberos is the standard security provider used by **Active Directory** in domain environments. Negotiate sends an authentication request to a server, which then uses Kerberos to authenticate domain accounts (formatted as domain\username) and **NTLM** to authenticate local machine accounts (formatted as server_name\username).

Default security settings can be modified for both WinRM server and client in Group Policy. WS-Management supports HTTPS to add Transport Layer Security (TLS), and should be used in production environments.

You can add authentication parameters to winrm commands if you don't want to use the credentials of the currently logged in user by issuing the following command:

```
winrm id -username:AD\johnd -password:******** -remote:WIN7
```

Automating administration tasks using PowerShell Remoting

PowerShell is a powerful command-line shell and scripting language designed to ease automation of administration tasks and replace standard command-line batch files and Visual Basic scripts. PowerShell version 2.0, which is built-in to Windows 7, supports running commands and scripts on remote computers, and requires WinRM 2.0 and BITS 4.0. PowerShell 2.0 can be downloaded for Windows Vista as part of the Windows Remote Management components.

> **Downloading Windows Remote Management components for Windows Vista**
>
> The components can be downloaded from http://support.microsoft.com/kb/968929.

While we can't cover all the details of using PowerShell in this book, let's open a console in Windows Server 2008 R2 and run some remote PowerShell commands.

1. Log in to Windows Server 2008 R2 as a domain administrator and click the blue Windows PowerShell icon on the task bar.

2. In the PowerShell console, type the following command:

    ```
    Invoke-Command -ComputerName WIN7 {Get-Service}
    ```

```
Select Administrator: Windows PowerShell                                    _ □ ×
Windows PowerShell
Copyright (C) 2009 Microsoft Corporation. All rights reserved.

PS C:\Users\TEMP> invoke-command -ComputerName WIN7 {get-service}

Status     Name             DisplayName                           PSComputerName
------     ----             -----------                           --------------
Stopped    AeLookupSvc      Application Experience                win7
Stopped    ALG             Application Layer Gateway Service      win7
Stopped    AppIDSvc         Application Identity                  win7
Running    Appinfo         Application Information               win7
Stopped    AppMgmt          Application Management               win7
Running    AudioEndpointBu... Windows Audio Endpoint Builder       win7
Running    AudioSrv         Windows Audio                        win7
Stopped    AxInstSV         ActiveX Installer (AxInstSV)          win7
Stopped    BDESVC           BitLocker Drive Encryption Service    win7
Running    BFE             Base Filtering Engine                 win7
Stopped    BITS             Background Intelligent Transfer Ser... win7
Stopped    Browser          Computer Browser                     win7
Stopped    bthserv          Bluetooth Support Service            win7
Stopped    CertPropSvc      Certificate Propagation              win7
Stopped    clr_optimizatio... Microsoft .NET Framework NGEN v2.0.... win7
Stopped    clr_optimizatio... Microsoft .NET Framework NGEN v2.0.... win7
Stopped    COMSysApp        COM+ System Application              win7
Running    CryptSvc         Cryptographic Services               win7
Running    CscService       Offline Files                        win7
Running    DcomLaunch       DCOM Server Process Launcher          win7
Stopped    defragsvc        Disk Defragmenter                    win7
```

3. The output shows a list of services and their state on a remote machine called WIN7. The next command performs the same operation, but on two machines simultaneously; one called WIN7 and the other WIN7-2.

    ```
    Invoke-Command –ComputerName WIN7,WIN7-2 {Get-Service}
    ```

4. The following command restarts the IP Helper service on a remote machine:

    ```
    Invoke-Command –ComputerName WIN7 {restart-Service "iphlpsvc"}
    ```

> For more detailed information on using PowerShell, see Microsoft's site at: http://www.microsoft.com/windowsserver2003/ technologies/management/powershell/default.mspx.

Enabling and using graphical remote access tools

While I can't emphasize enough the importance of making sure you have remote command-line access to devices where least privilege user accounts are deployed, in situations where normal service is available, the help desk is more likely to use graphical remote access tools. This is because they are easier to work with than the command line. Windows includes two such tools; they are:

- Remote Assistance
- Remote Desktop

Enabling Remote Assistance

When users need assistance from the help desk to complete a task or be guided through an unfamiliar process, Remote Assistance allows support professionals to view a user's desktop, or take control if the user gives permission.

Different types of Remote Assistance

You should ensure that the help desk is able to offer Remote Assistance to users on the corporate intranet and to remote workers who are connected via **Direct Access** or a **VPN**. The following table shows the different ways in which users and the help desk can use Remote Assistance to offer and solicit help in corporate environments.

Remote Assistance Connection Method	Description
DCOM	A help desk professional can offer unsolicited Remote Assistance to a machine that's connected to the corporate intranet.
Remote Assistance invitations	Users can create Remote Assistance invitations and send them to the help desk via e-mail, or copy them to a file share to solicit help.
Easy Connect	Though not designed for corporate use, Easy Connect can be used by remote users to solicit Remote Assistance when they are connected to the Internet via their home networks but are unable to get access to the corporate intranet.
Desktop shortcuts	Remote Assistance has a command-line component that can be used to provide shortcuts for quick access to Remote Assistance sessions.

Enabling Remote Assistance via Group Policy

Follow the instructions below to enable Remote Assistance using Group Policy.

1. Log in to Windows Server 2008 R2 as a domain administrator and open **Start | Administrative Tools | Group Policy Management** menu.

2. For the purposes of our lab environment, we'll create a new GPO and link it to our Clients OU. In the **Group Management Policy** window, expand your forest; you'll find the **Domains** node. Right-click the **Clients** OU and select **Create a GPO in this domain, and Link it here** from the menu.

3. Type **Remote Assistance** in the **Name** field in the **New GPO** dialog and click **OK**.

4. Click your domain in the left pane and then right-click the new **Remote Assistance** GPO in the right pane and select **Edit...** from the menu.

5. In the **Group Policy Management Editor** window, expand **Computer Configuration | Policies | Administrative Templates | System** and click **Remote Assistance**.

6. In the right pane double-click **Offer Remote Assistance**.

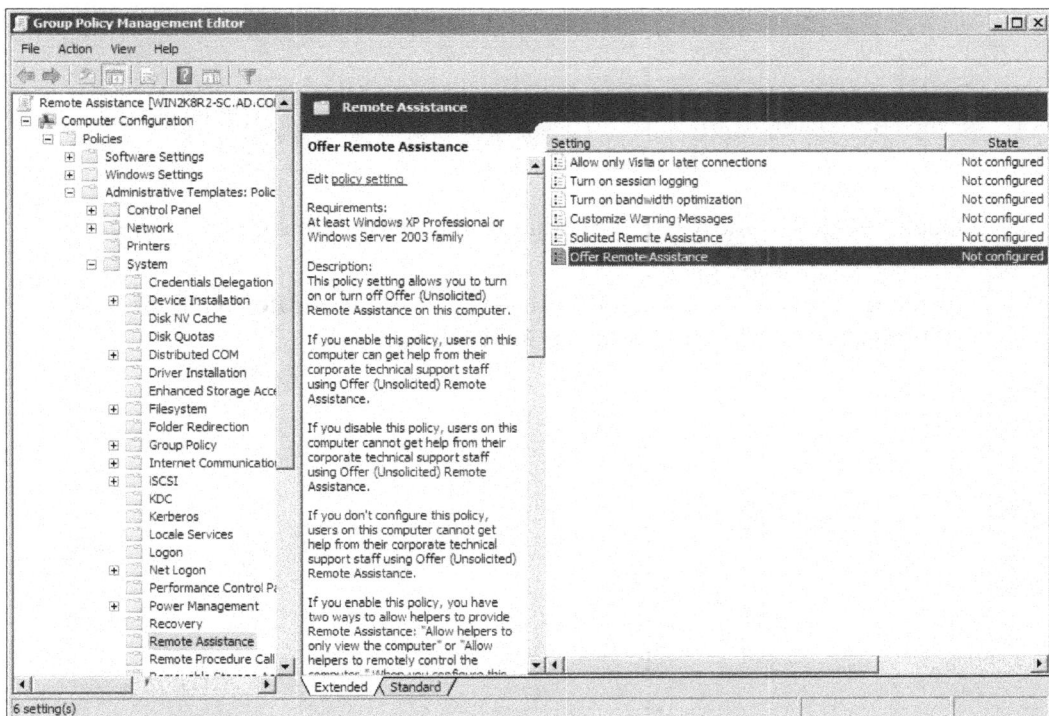

7. In the **Offer Remote Assistance** dialog, check **Enabled** and under **Options** select **Allow helpers to remotely control the computer** from the menu.

8. Click on **Show** next to **Helpers**. In the **Show Contents** dialog that opens under **Value**, type the name of an Active Directory group or user that can offer unsolicited Remote Assistance. In this example, I've already created an Active Directory security group called **Remote Assistance Helpers** for this purpose. You should enter groups or usernames in the format `<domain name> \<group name>` or `<domain name> \<username>`.

Show Contents	_ □ ✕

Helpers:

	Value
🖉	AD\Remote Assistance Helpers|
✱	

OK   Cancel

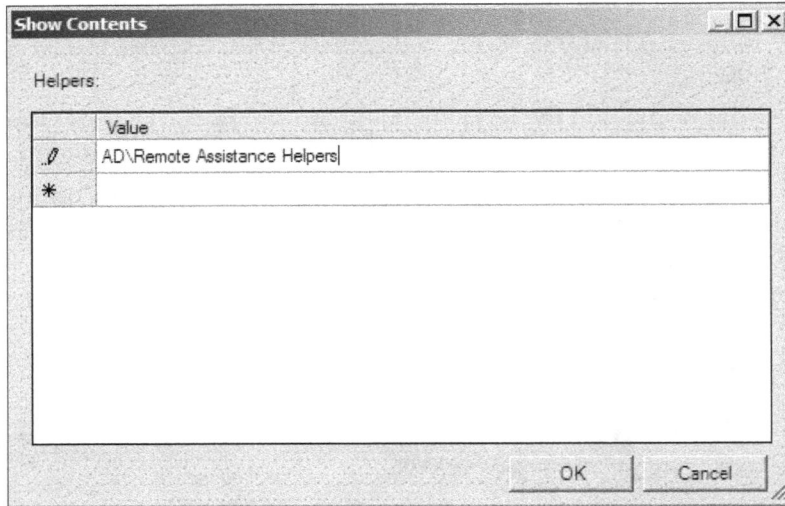

9. Click **OK** in the **Show Contents** dialog and again in the **Offer Remote Assistance** dialog.

10. In the right pane of the **Group Policy Management Editor** window, double-click on **Solicited Remote Assistance**.

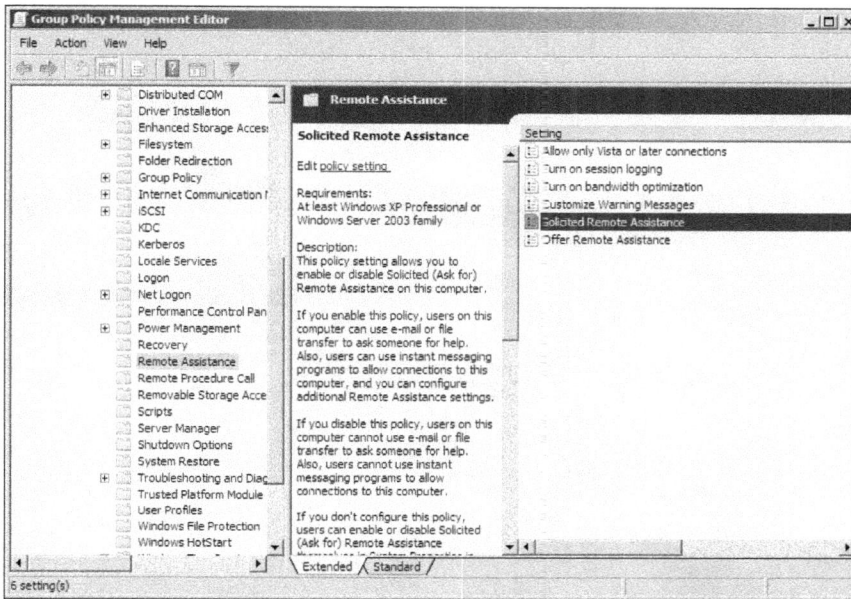

11. In the **Solicited Remote Assistance** dialog, select **Enabled** and click on **OK**.

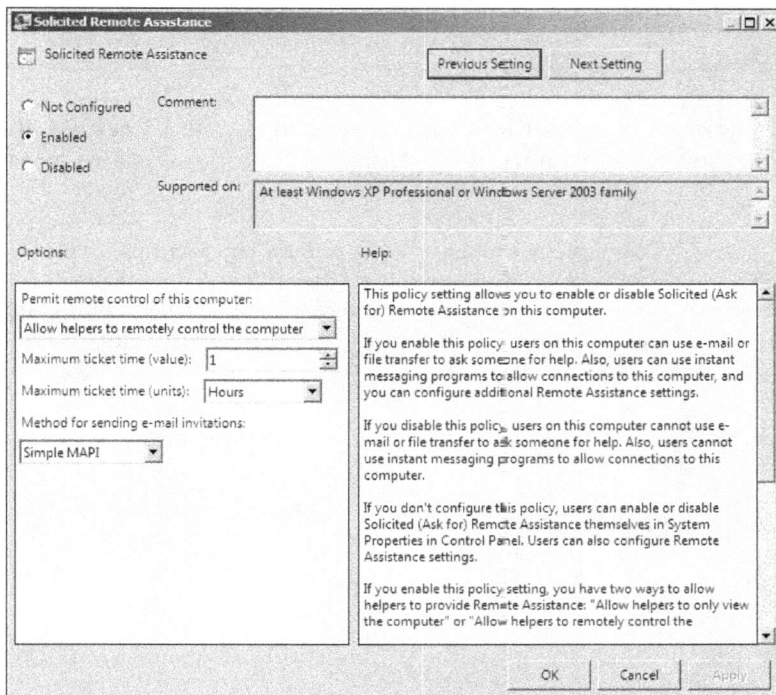

12. In the right pane of the **Group Policy Management Editor** window, double-click **Turn on bandwidth optimization**.

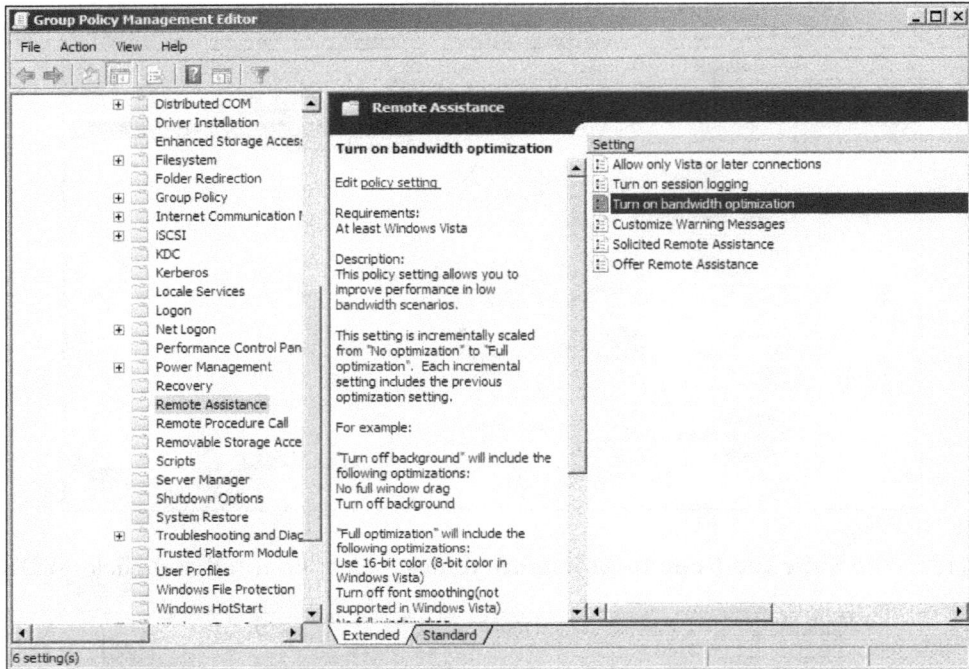

13. In the **Turn on bandwidth optimization** dialog, select **Enabled**, then choose **Full optimization** from the drop-down menu under **Options** and click **OK**.

> If you enable **Allow only Vista or later connections**, Remote Assistance invitations are encrypted and will not work with Windows XP. Additionally, you can **Turn on session logging** if you are required to record all remote access activity.

Offering a computer unsolicited Remote Assistance: DCOM

The help desk can offer users Remote Assistance when requested by simply entering the IP address or name of the remote machine into Remote Assistance. **Distributed Component Object Model (DCOM)** is the most commonly used method for help desks to connect to remote machines. By default, DCOM requires that the remote machine be located on the corporate network—directly connected or via Direct Access, dial-up networking, or VPN. TCP port 135 is open in Windows Firewall only when the firewall's Domain profile is active, hence the previously stated connection requirements. DCOM is the quickest and easiest way for the help desk to offer users Remote Assistance, and requires that the helper (or expert in Remote Assistance terminology) know the name or IP address of the user's computer. To help a user by specifying the IP address or computer name:

1. Log in to Windows 7 as a domain administrator and type `assist` into the **Search for programs and files box** on the **Start** menu and press *Enter*.

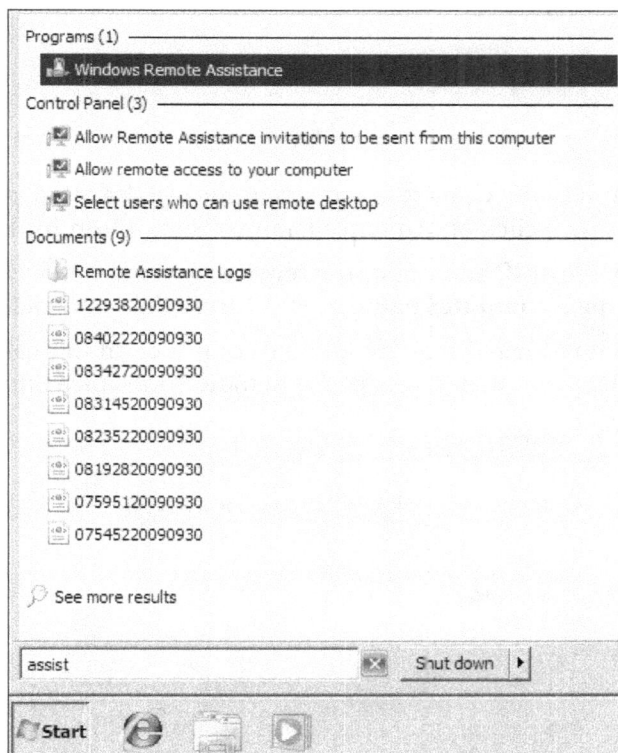

Programs (1)
- Windows Remote Assistance

Control Panel (3)
- Allow Remote Assistance invitations to be sent from this computer
- Allow remote access to your computer
- Select users who can use remote desktop

Documents (9)
- Remote Assistance Logs
- 12293820090930
- 08402220090930
- 08342720090930
- 08314520090930
- 08235220090930
- 08192820090930
- 07595120090930
- 07545220090930

See more results

assist   Shut down ▶

Start

2. In the **Windows Remote Assistance** dialog, click **Help someone who has invited you**.

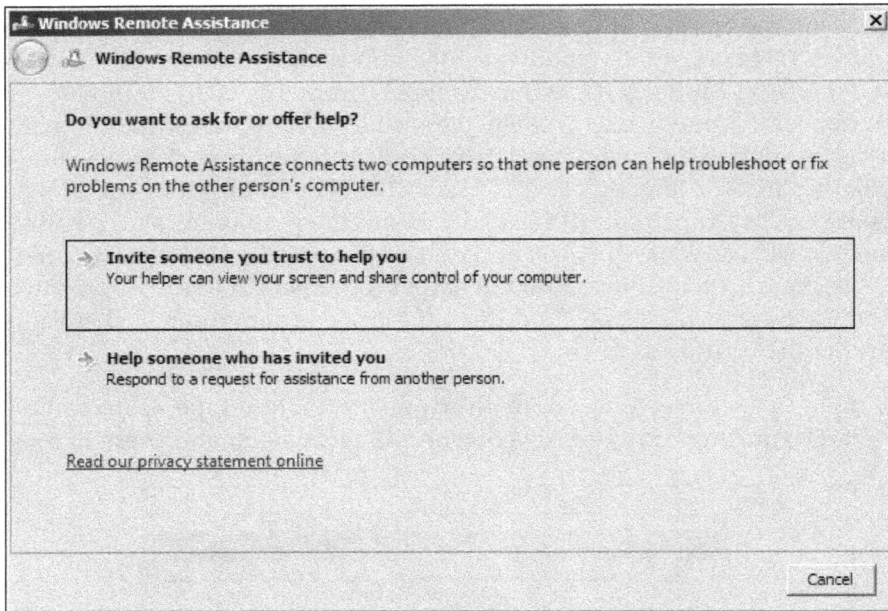

3. At the bottom of the **Choose a way to connect to the other person's computer** screen click on **Advanced connection option for help desk**.

4. Enter the name or IP address of the remote machine you want to connect to in the **Type a computer name or IP address** field and click **Next**.

5. The user, who's logged in to the remote computer, in this case Windows Vista, will be prompted to accept the Remote Assistance offer.

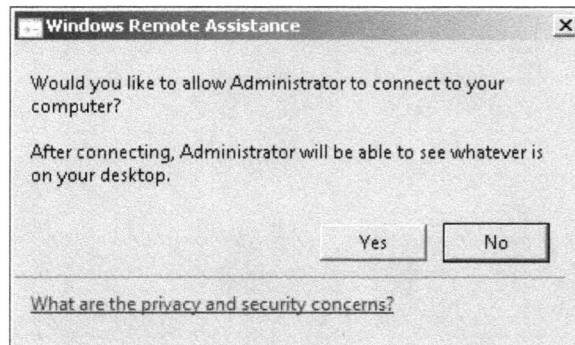

6. Once the remote user has accepted the offer by clicking **Yes** the expert will be able to view the remote desktop, and request remote control if required.

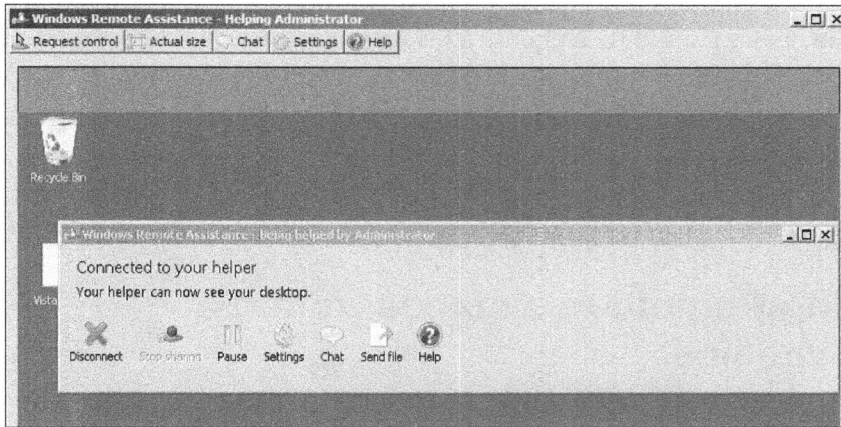

Sending Remote Assistance invitations

Users can solicit help by opening Remote Assistance and creating an invitation file, which can be sent to the help desk via e-mail or copied to a monitored file share. Invitations alleviate the need for the user and help desk to establish the IP address or name of the user's computer. To initiate Remote Assistance without knowing the novice's IP address or computer name:

1. The novice should type `assist` into the **Search for programs and files box** on the **Start** menu and press *Enter*.

2. In the **Windows Remote Assistance** dialog, they should click **Invite someone you trust to help you**.

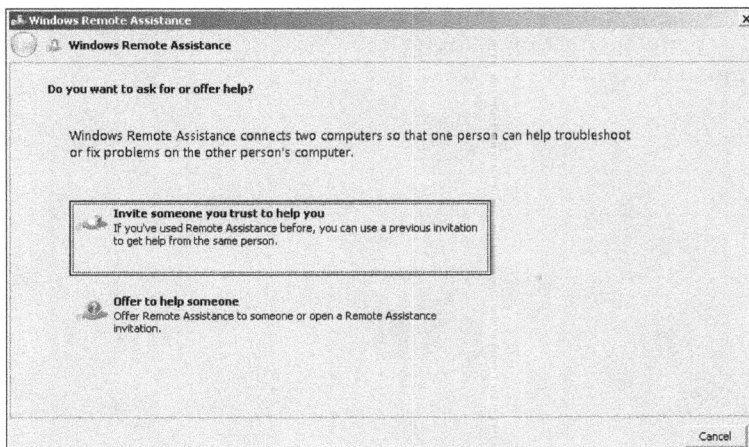

3. They can then either choose to send the invitation by e-mail, use a previous invitation again, or save it as a file. Let's save the invitation as a file by clicking **Save this invitation as a file**.

4. The novice should then choose a location, possibly a file share where users drop Remote Assistance invitations, and then enter and confirm a password before clicking **Finish**.

The help desk expert can then pick up the **Remote Assistance** invitation from the file share and double-click it on their support machine and enter the password to initiate the Remote Assistance session.

Initiating Remote Assistance from the command line

The `msra.exe` application allows help desk experts or users to initiate Remote Assistance sessions quickly and easily from the command line, via desktop shortcuts, or included in scripts. For instance, the following command could be included in a shortcut to provide a user with quick access to Remote Assistance, where `125865e27faa0bd2a442d3e7d864493f0651149b.RAContact` is the address located in the user's `RAContactHistory` XML file.

```
msra.exe /getcontacthelp
    125865e27faa0bd2a442d3e7d864493f0651149b.RAContact
```

RAContactHistory

The `RAContactHistory` file is located in the `appdata\local` folder in the remote user's user profile, for example: `C\users\user\appdata\local`. A Remote Assistance session needs to be established at least once before an `RAContactHistory` file is generated.

For more information on using `msra.exe`, type `msra.exe /?` at the command prompt.

Connecting to remote PCs using Easy Connect

While not intended for enterprise use, Easy Connect can be useful in situations where a remote user cannot get access to the corporate intranet. Easy Connect is only available in Windows 7 and uses IPv6 and Teredo to connect to remote PCs that are located behind NAT routers. Windows Firewall exceptions that allow Easy Connect are disabled by default for the Domain firewall profile, as Teredo UDP packets are often blocked by enterprise edge firewalls, and additionally for the Public profile, which means the help desk can't use Easy Connect to offer Remote Assistance when users are connected to public Internet connections, such as Wi-Fi hotspots in coffee shops.

> **Easy Connect for remote workers**
>
> If you intend to enable Easy Connect for remote users who work at home, you need to ensure that their home network profile is set as Home or Work. This setting can only be changed by a user with administrative privileges and should be configured by a support technician when the notebook is connected to the home network for the first time.

Easy Connect uses **Peer Name Resolution Protocol (PNRP)** and Microsoft P2P Collaboration Services to facilitate offers or requests of Remote Assistance without the need for the help desk to know the IP address or DNS name of the remote computer. Based on IPv6, Easy Connect works with IPv6 global or local-link addresses, and if the help desk's computer has global IPv6 Internet connectivity, either natively or via Teredo, a connection can be established with a remote user on the corporate intranet or to computers with a public IPv6 Internet address behind a NAT router if the Work or Home Windows Firewall profile is active.

> Teredo is a technology built into Vista and Windows 7 that allows computers on NAT'd IPv4 networks to communicate using IPv6 with the help of UDP datagrams.

> **Expert's computer**
>
> The expert's computer can be on a compatible public NAT'd IPv4 network if the novice initiates the request for Remote Assistance via Easy Connect. There is no requirement for the expert's computer to be on a network designated as Work or Home by the Windows Firewall.

To initiate a Remote Assistance session using Easy Connect:

1. To initiate a Remote Assistance session using Easy Connect, the novice user should type `assist` into the **Search for programs and files box** on the **Start** menu and press *Enter*.

2. In the **Windows Remote Assistance** dialog, click **Invite someone you trust to help you**.

3. On the **How do you want to invite your trusted helper?** screen, the novice should select **Use Easy Connect**.

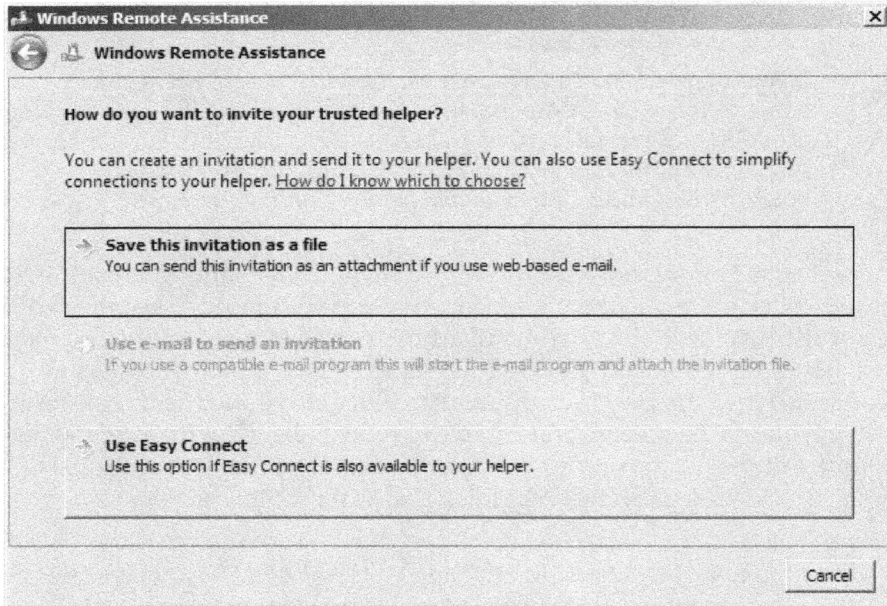

4. An **Easy Connect** password will be generated, which should be given to the help desk expert via telephone.

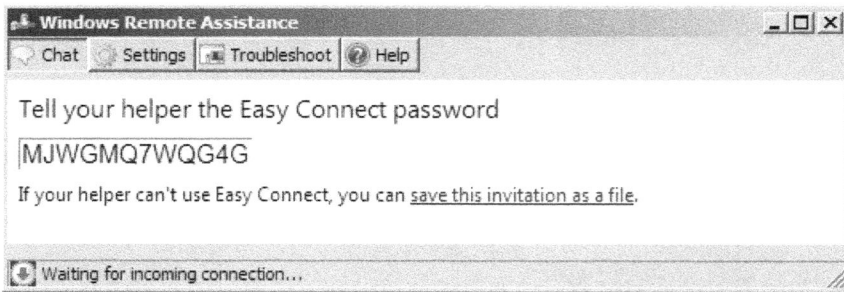

5. The help desk expert should then start **Remote Assistance** on their PC by typing `assist` into the **Search for programs and files box** on the **Start** menu and pressing *Enter*.

6. In the **Windows Remote Assistance** dialog, the expert should click **Help someone who has invited you**.

7. On the **Choose a way to connect to the other person's computer** screen, the expert should select **Use Easy Connect**.

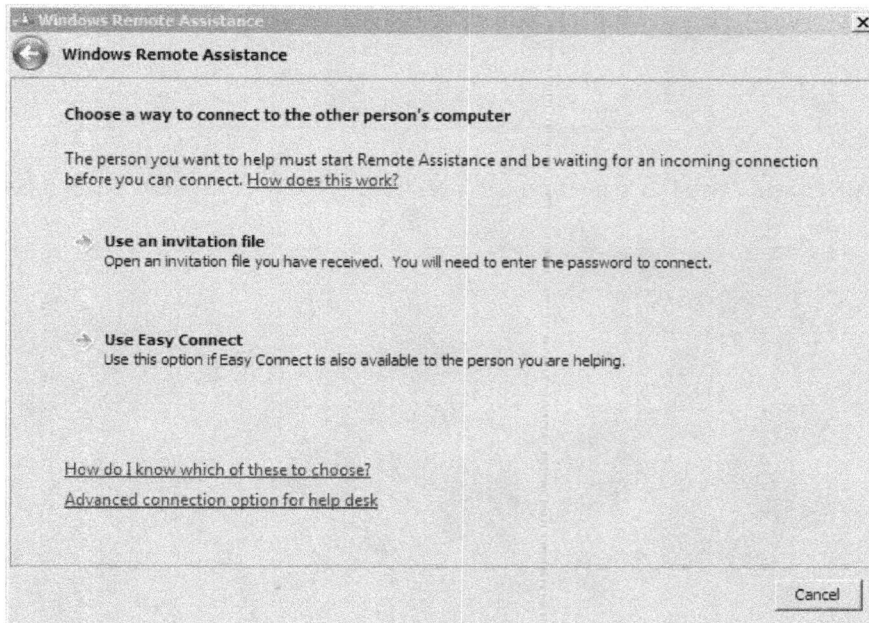

8. The expert will then be required to enter the Easy Connect password as provided by the novice user.

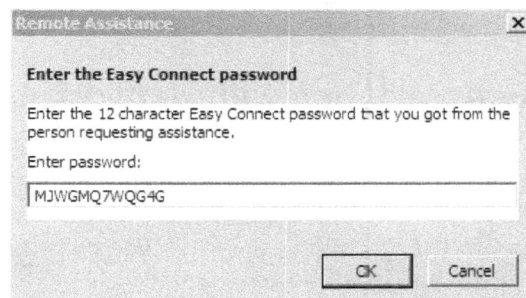

9. The novice user is then required to give permission for the help desk expert to connect.

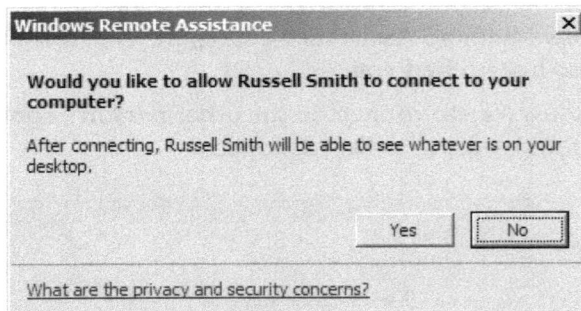

10. A Remote Assistance session initiated using Easy Connect is shown below.

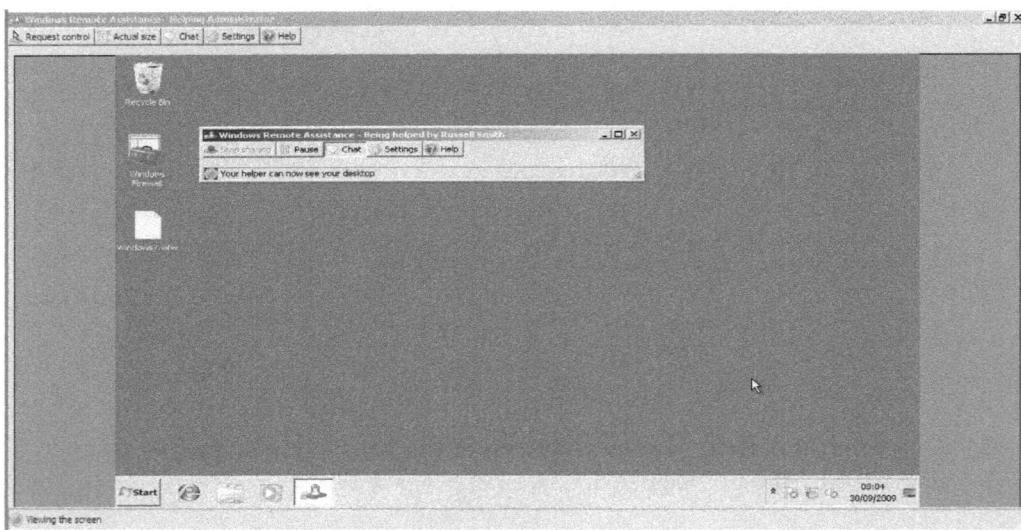

Enabling Remote Assistance with Network Address Translation

Windows 7 and Vista include native support for Internet Protocol version 6 (IPv6), and in conjunction with Teredo, are able to tunnel IPv6 over IPv4 networks, even if endpoints are located behind NAT routers. To establish if a remote user's PC is able to obtain an IPv6 address using Teredo, use `netsh` at the command prompt.

> The remote user's PC should be located on their home or a remote network when running this command.

The ability of a PC to acquire an IPv6 address using Teredo will change depending on the capabilities of the network it is connected to.

```
netsh interface teredo show state
```

Microsoft's Internet Connectivity Evaluation Tool is also useful for establishing whether a network supports **Universal Plug and Play (UPnP)**, IPv6, and Teredo. Though it doesn't support Easy Connect, Remote Assistance in Vista is still able to utilize IPv6 and Teredo, or UPnP to acquire the globally routable external IPv4 address of a UPnP-compliant NAT router.

> **Internet Connectivity Evaluation Tool**
>
> The Internet Connectivity Evaluation Tool can be downloaded from http://www.microsoft.com/windows/using/tools/igd/default.mspx
>
> Switching off Windows Firewall disables Teredo and NAT traversal for Remote Assistance.

Remote Desktop

Based on Windows Terminal Services, Remote Desktop can be used by system administrators or the help desk to connect to remote computers. Remote Desktop is not intended for helping users through a task or shadowing desktop sessions. When a help desk expert who is a member of the Remote Desktop Services group on the remote computer connects to a remote machine using Remote Desktop, any locally logged-on user must log out before the help desk expert can access their remote desktop. A logged-in local user will be prompted to log out so the help desk expert can connect remotely.

To enable Remote Desktop in Group Policy:

1. Log in to Windows Server 2008 R2 as a domain administrator and open **Start | Administrative Tools | Group Policy Management**.

2. In the **Group Management Policy** console expand your forest; you'll find the **Domains** node. Right-click the **Clients** OU and select **Create a GPO in this domain, and Link it here** from the menu.

3. Type **Remote Desktop** in the **Name** field of the **New GPO** dialog and click **OK**.

4. Click your domain in the left pane and then right-click the new **Remote Desktop** GPO in the right pane and select **Edit** from the menu.

5. In the **Group Policy Management Editor** window, expand **Computer Configuration | Policies | Administrative Templates | Windows Components | Remote Desktop Services | Remote Desktop Session Host** and select the **Connections** folder.

6. In the right pane, double-click **Allow users to connect remotely using Remote Desktop Services**.

7. In the **Allow users to connect remotely using Remote Desktop Services** dialog, select **Enabled** and click **OK.**

8. Close the **Group Policy Management Editor** window.

9. Make sure the new policy has applied to a remote client computer in the lab, either by rebooting the machine or issuing a `gpupdate /force` command.

10. Open the **Remote Desktop Client** from the **Search for programs and files** option on the **Start** menu and enter the name or IP address of the remote machine.

If a user is logged in to the remote machine, you see a message like this:

Logon Message

Another user is currently logged on to this computer. If you continue, this user has to disconnect from this computer. Do you want to continue?

Yes   No

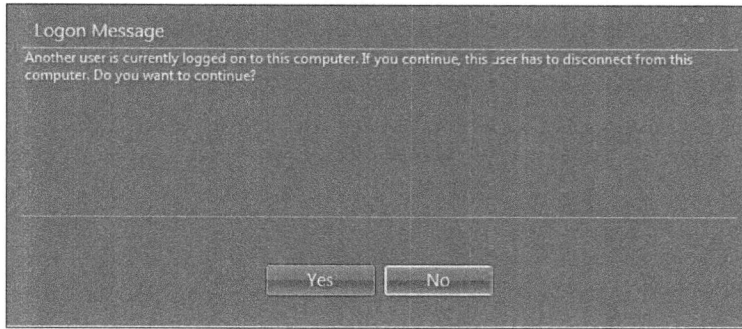

11. Click **Yes** to continue. In the **Windows Security** dialog, enter your username and password and click **OK**.

The Remote Desktop Client will then attempt to create a secure connection.

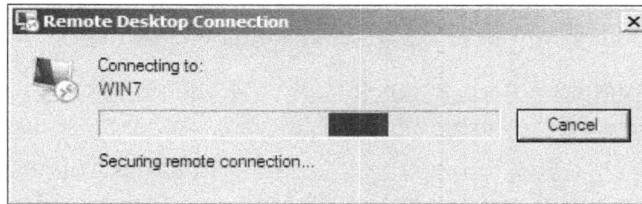

Remote Desktop Connection   ×

Connecting to:
WIN7

Cancel

Securing remote connection...

You will then be presented with a Remote Desktop as shown below.

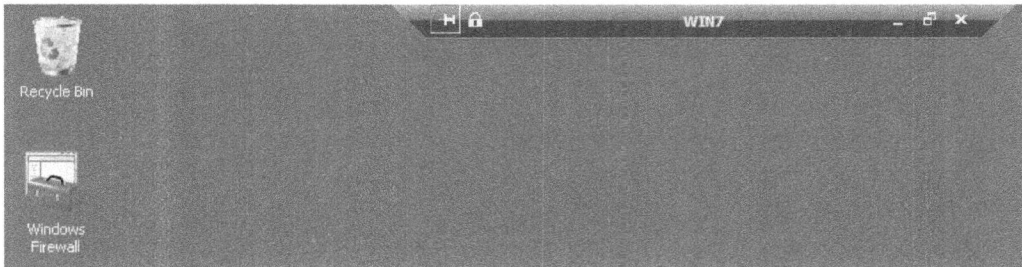

WIN7

Recycle Bin

Windows
Firewall

Connecting to a remote computer using the Microsoft Management Console (MMC)

Where Remote Assistance and Remote Desktop allow help desk experts to observe or control a Remote Desktop session, most of the management consoles in Windows can connect not only to the local computer, but also to a remote computer. Lots can be achieved by the help desk and system administrators without ever having to connect to remote devices with command shells or Remote Desktops, by utilizing management consoles.

> Many management consoles will connect to remote computers by simply enabling the remote administration inbound exceptions in Windows Firewall. Some consoles, like Windows Firewall with Advanced Security, have their own inbound firewall exceptions, which must be enabled separately.

To connect to a remote computer using a management console:

1. Log in to Windows Server 2008 R2 as a domain administrator and type `mmc` in the **Search for programs and files** box on the **Start** menu.

2. In the new console window, press *Ctrl+M* and in the **Add or Remove Snap-ins** dialog, double-click **Device Manager** under **Available snap-ins**.

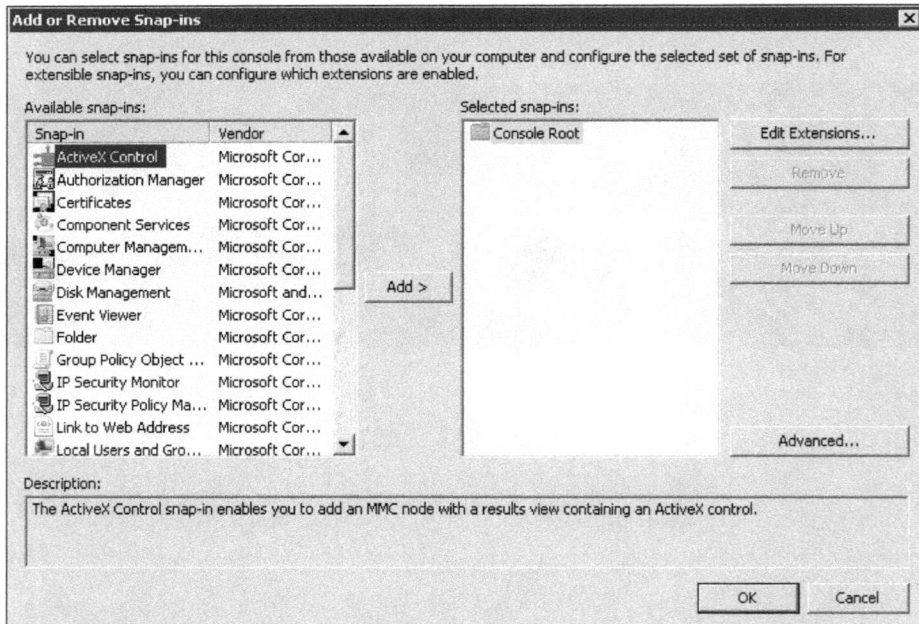

3. In the **Device Manager** dialog, select **Another computer** and either enter the name of a remote computer, or select a computer by clicking **Browse**, and click **Finish**. In this example, **WIN7** is the name of a remote computer.

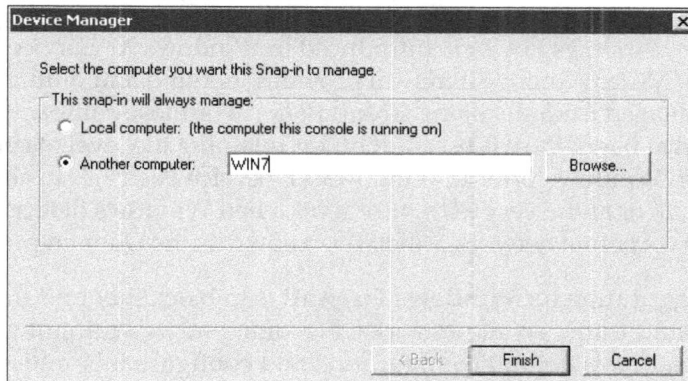

4. Click **OK** in the **Add or Remove Snap-ins** dialog. In the console window, click **Device Manager** under **Console Root** to access the remote device.

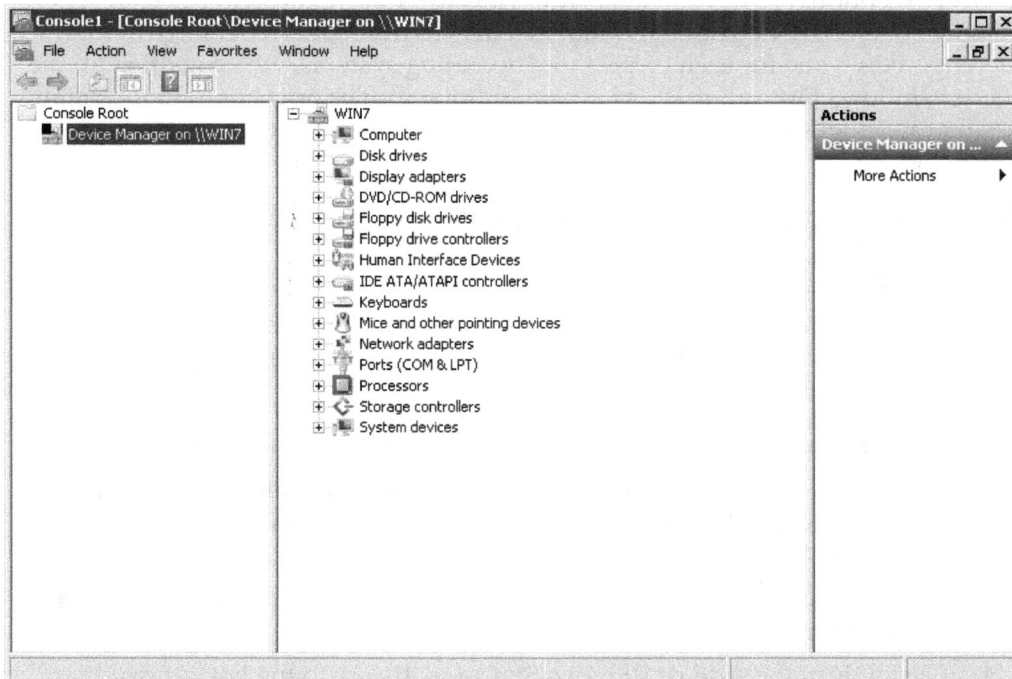

Configuring Windows Firewall to allow remote access

One of the biggest stumbling blocks for many organizations when dealing with remote administration is Windows Firewall. Introduced in Windows XP Service Pack 2, and re-architected for Vista, Windows Firewall provides inbound and outbound filtering, which can be managed centrally using Group Policy. For those companies without skilled personnel at hand, the easiest solution for retaining the level of connectivity that was found in Windows prior to Windows XP Service Pack 2, is to either disable Windows Firewall, or at the very least, turn it off when Windows detects that it is connected to the corporate network, otherwise known as the Domain profile.

The default configuration for **Windows Firewall** is to block inbound traffic, but allow outbound traffic on all networks. I recommend as a minimum, all organizations retain this default configuration and configure inbound exceptions to enable additional functionality as required.

Remote access features can be configured using one Group Policy Object, which works for XP, Vista, and Windows 7. However, the same cannot be said about the inbound exceptions we need to make for Windows Firewall in order to enable these functions. Therefore, I recommend that in a lab environment, we configure three different GPOs—one for each of the three operating systems, which contain all the default Windows Firewall rules, plus any additional rules or changes to the default rules that we might require to enable the desired remote administration features.

Creating a GPO for Windows Firewall in Windows 7

Let's get started and log in to a baseline Windows 7 machine as a domain administrator. First we need to export the default Windows Firewall policy to a file. It is done as follows:

1. In the **Search programs and files** option on the **Start** menu, type mmc.

2. In the console window press *Ctrl+M*. In the **Add or Remove Snap-ins** dialog under **Available snap-ins** double-click **Windows Firewall with Advanced Security**.

3. In the **Select Computer** dialog, check **Local computer (the computer this console is running on)** and click **Finish**.

4. Click **OK** in the **Add or Remove Snap-ins** dialog. In the left pane of the console window, right-click **Windows Firewall with Advanced Security** and select **Export Policy** from the menu.

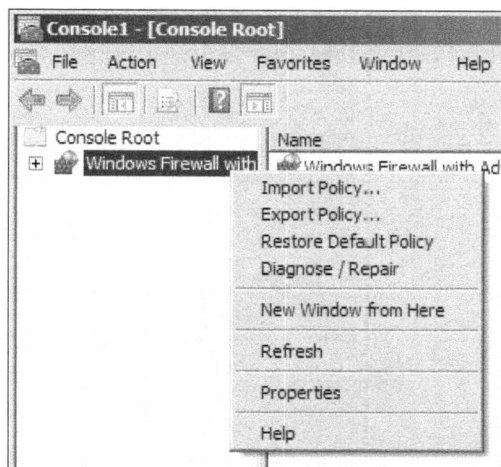

5. In the **Save As** dialog, click on **Desktop** in the left pane, type `Windows7` in the **File name** box, and click **Save**.

6. Click **OK** in the **Windows Firewall with Advanced Security** dialog.

7. Close the console window and in the **Microsoft Management Console** dialog, click **Yes** to save the console.

8. In the **Save As** dialog, select **Desktop** in the left column, and type `Windows Firewall` in the **File name** field and click **Save**.

9. Copy the `windows7.wfw` file to our Windows Server 2008 R2 domain controller.

10. Log in to the domain controller as a domain administrator and open **Start | Administrative Tools | Group Policy Management**.

11. In the left pane, expand your forest and select the **Domains** node. Right-click **Group Policy Objects** and select **New** from the menu.

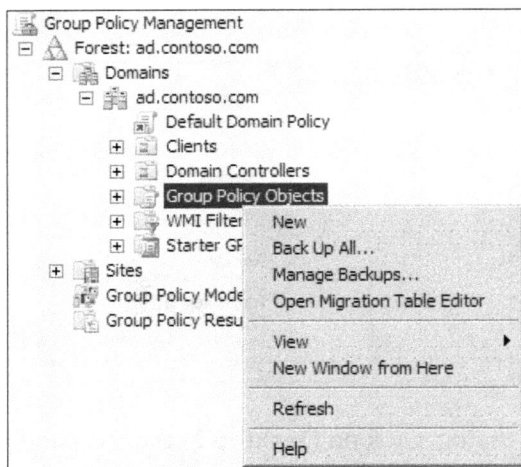

12. In the **New GPO** dialog, type Windows Firewall - Windows 7 in the **Name** field and click **OK**.

13. Expand the **Group Policy Objects** node, right-click **Windows Firewall – Windows 7** and select **Edit** from the menu.

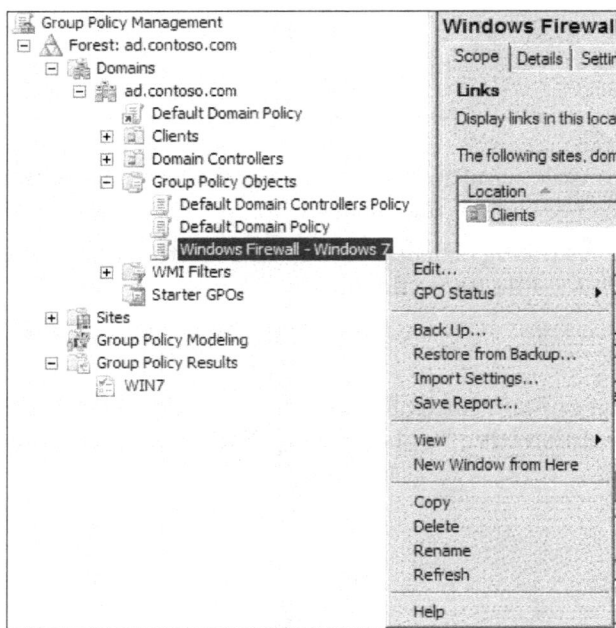

Importing Windows 7 Firewall rules to a GPO

Let's use the Group Policy Management Editor to import Windows 7 Firewall rules.

1. In the **Group Policy Management Editor** window, expand **Computer Configuration | Policies | Windows Settings | Security Settings | Windows Firewall with Advanced Security**. Right-click **Windows Firewall with Advanced Security** and select **Import Policy** from the menu.

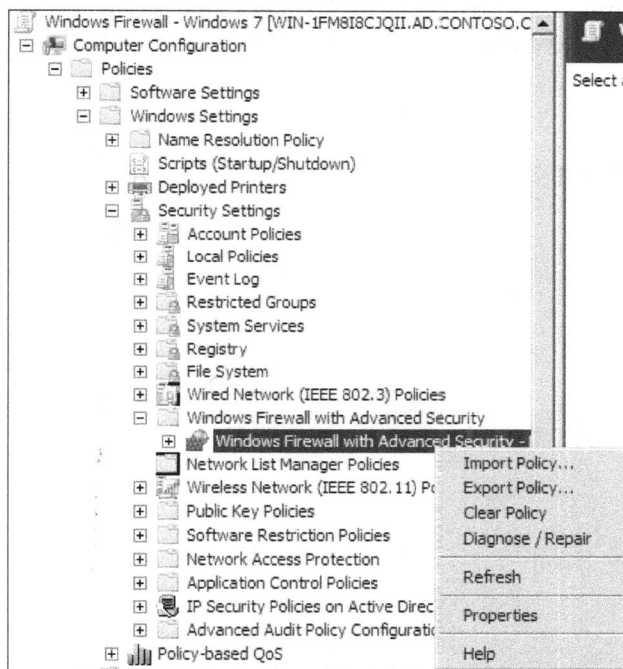

2. Click **Yes** in the **Windows Firewall with Advanced Security** dialog to import the policy we saved in Windows 7.

3. In the **Open** dialog, locate the `windows7.wfw` file you copied to this server from Windows 7, select it in the right pane, and click **Open**.

4. In the **Windows Firewall with Advanced Security** dialog click **OK**.

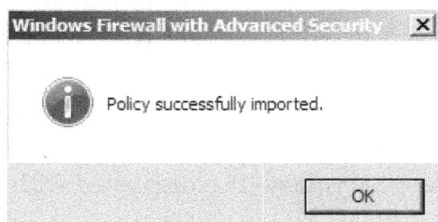

Now we have a set of Windows Firewall rules for Windows 7 in a Group Policy Object that can be used to configure firewall rules on multiple Windows 7 computers in a domain.

Modifying the default Windows Firewall rules

Follow the instructions below to change the default Windows Firewall settings:

1. Expand **Windows Firewall with Advanced Security** and click **Inbound Rules**. In the right pane, click the **Profile** column to order the rules by profile.

2. Scroll down the list of rules until you reach those for the Domain firewall profile.

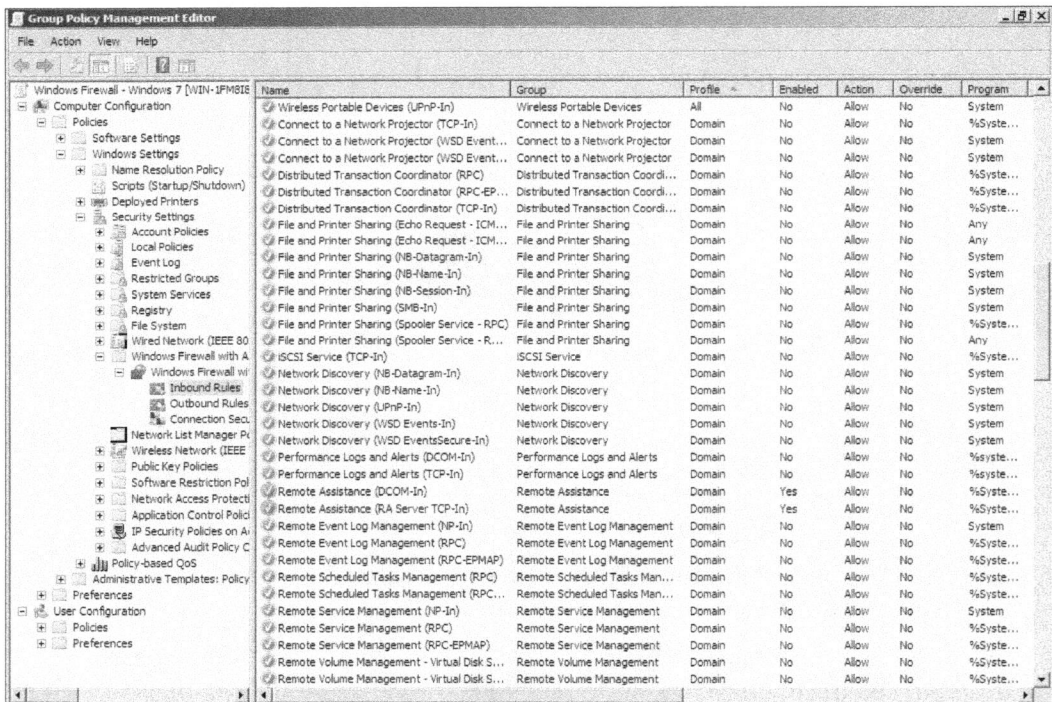

You can see that because this is Windows 7 and **Domain** profile exceptions for Remote Assistance are already enabled. In Vista, these exceptions are disabled by default.

3. Continue scrolling down until you find the **Windows Remote Management (HTTP-In)** exception. Right-click on it and select **Enable Rule** from the menu. Once enabled, the rule will be displayed with a green icon to the left.

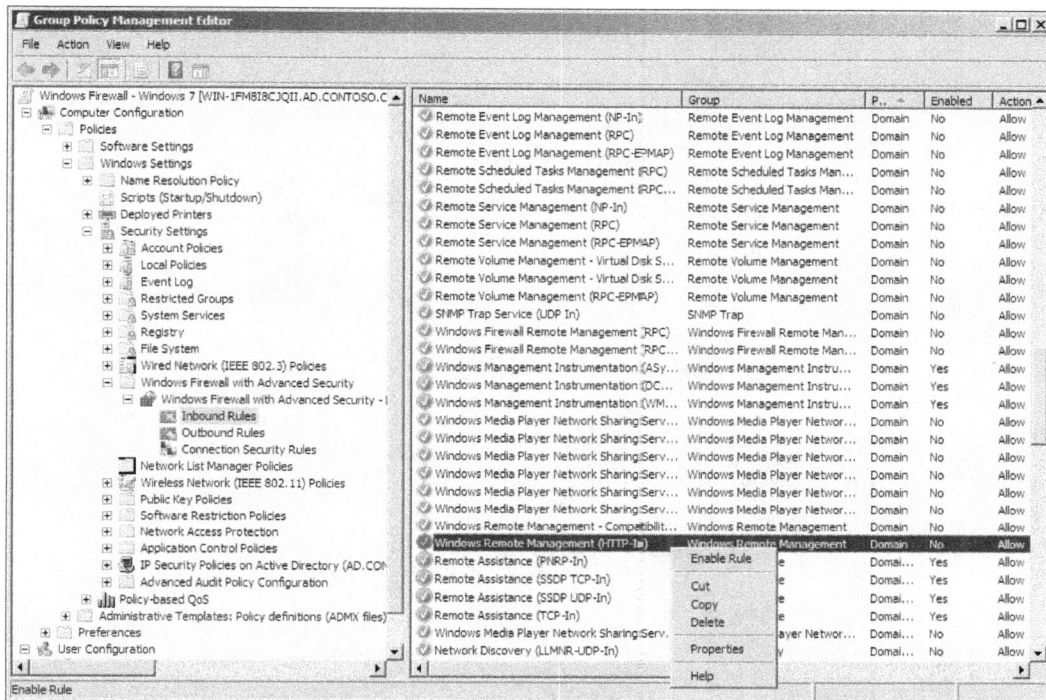

We will limit Remote Desktop to the **Domain** profile to improve security.

4. Find the **Remote Desktop (TCP-In)** inbound rule, right-click on it, and select **Properties** from the menu.

5. Switch to the **Advanced** tab and uncheck the **Public** and **Private** profile boxes under **Profiles**.

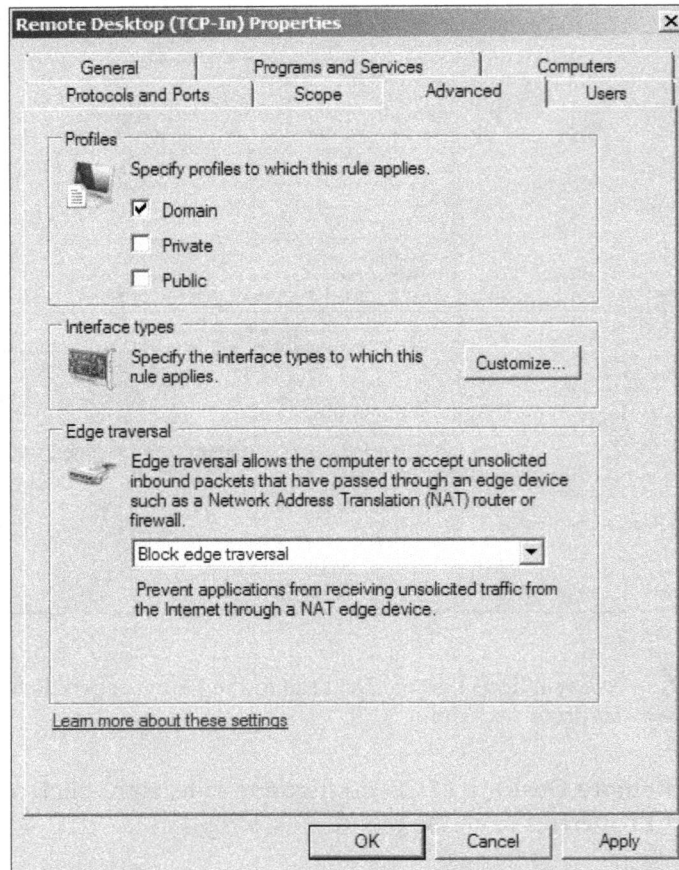

6. Change to the **General** tab, check **Enabled** under **General**, and click **OK**.

Adding additional inbound exceptions for remote administration

Let's add some additional rules that will allow us to connect to Windows 7 clients that are connected to the corporate intranet using Microsoft's management console tools. The steps are as follows:

1. Right-click on **Inbound Rules** in the left pane and select **New Rule** from the menu.

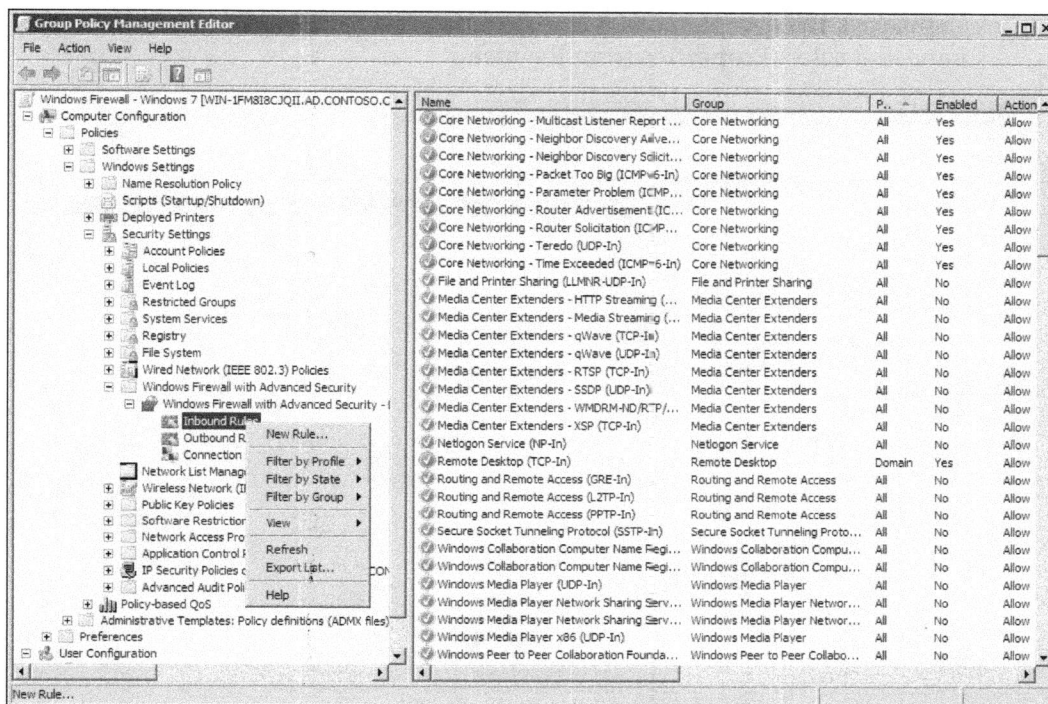

2. In the **New Inbound Rule Wizard** dialog, under **What type of rule would you like to create?** select **Predefined** and **Remote Administration** from the drop-down list. Then click on **Next**.

3. Leave the three default rules selected under **Which rules would you like to create?** and click **Next**.

4. Select **Allow the connection** on the **Action** screen and click **Finish**.

[You should restrict the inbound remote administration exceptions to trusted networks only.]

5. Right-click the new **Remote Administration (RCP-EPMAP)** rule in the right
    pane and select **Properties** from the menu.

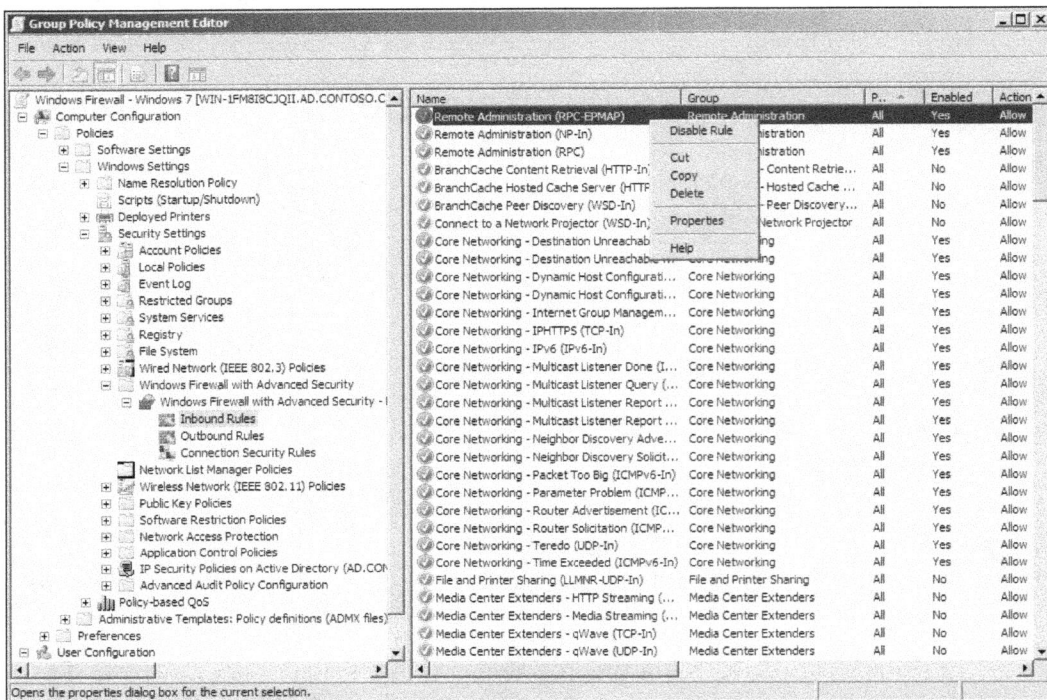

6. Switch to the **Advanced** tab and uncheck **Private** and **Public** under **Profiles**.

7. Repeat this process to restrict exceptions for **Remote Administration (NP-In)**
    and **Remote Administration (RPC)** to the **Domain** profile.

8. Close the **Group Policy Management Editor** window.

The Group Policy Object can now be used to configure Windows Firewall on
Windows 7 computers joined to the domain so that system administrators can
connect using Microsoft's remote management tools.

Creating a WMI filter to restrict the scope of management to Windows 7

Let's create a WMI filter to ensure that the GPO only applies to
Windows 7 computers.

1. In the left pane of the **Group Policy Management** window, right-click **WMI
    Filters** and select **New** from the menu.

2. In the **New WMI Filter** dialog, type `Windows 7` in the **Name** field and then click **Add**.

3. In the **WMI Query** dialog, type the following query, as shown in the following screenshot, into the **Query** field and click **OK**.

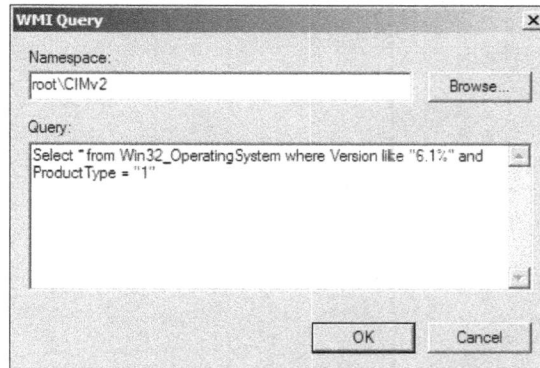

> **Use WMIC to create and check WMI filters**
>
> You can run **WMI** queries from the command line in XP, Vista, and Windows 7 using the `wmic` command-line tool. Type `wmic path win32_operatingsystem` at the command prompt to show all data stored in the `win32_OperatingSystem` class. The following command checks that we'll receive a result from our WMI query used in the filter above:
>
> ```
> wmic path win32_operatingsystem where (Version like
> "6.1%") get Version
> ```

4. Click **Save** in the **New WMI Filter** dialog.

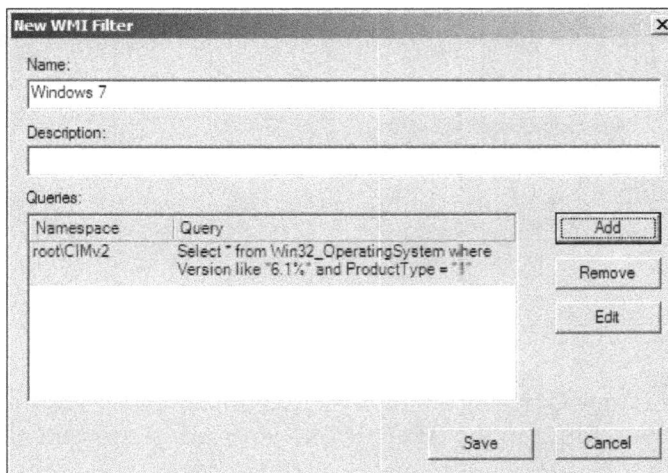

5. In the left pane of the **Group Policy Management** window, expand the **Group Policy Objects** folder and select the **Windows Firewall – Windows 7** GPO.

6. At the bottom of the right pane under **WMI Filtering**, select the **Windows 7** WMI filter from the drop-down list.

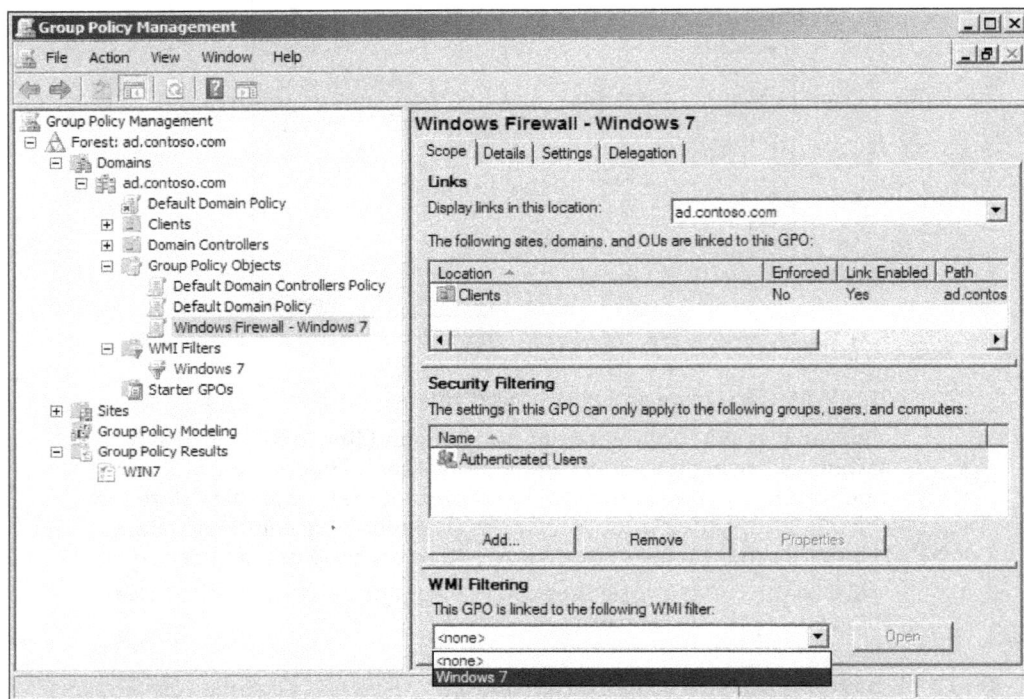

7. In the **Group Policy Management** dialog, click **Yes** to apply the filter to the GPO.

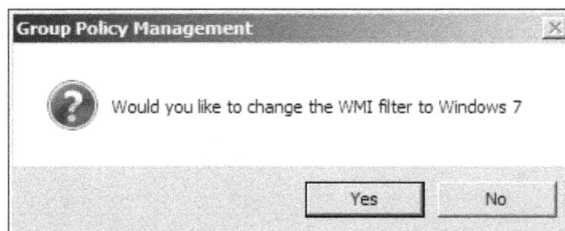

When this Group Policy Object is linked to an Organizational Unit, the WMI filter will ensure that the settings in the GPO are only applied to computers running Windows 7.

Linking the new GPO to the Client OU

Now that everything is configured, let's link the new GPO to our **Clients** OU. In the left pane of the **Group Policy Management** window, right-click the **Clients** OU and select **Link an Existing GPO** from the menu.

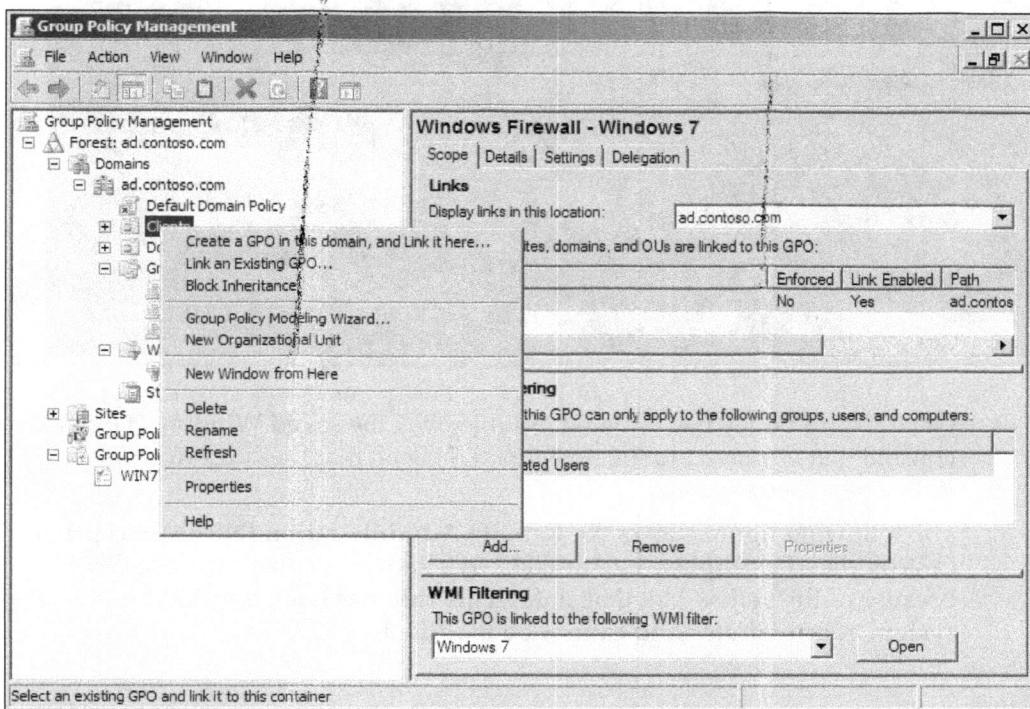

In the **Select GPO** dialog, select **Windows Firewall – Windows 7** under **Group Policy objects** and click **OK**. The settings in this Group Policy Object will now apply to any Windows 7 computers that are located in the Clients Organizational Unit.

Checking the GPO applies to Windows 7

Return to Windows 7 and follow these instructions as follows:

1. Log in to Windows 7 as a domain administrator.
2. Type cmd in the **Search for programs and files** option on the **Start** menu.

3. In the command prompt window type gpupdate /force and press *Enter*.

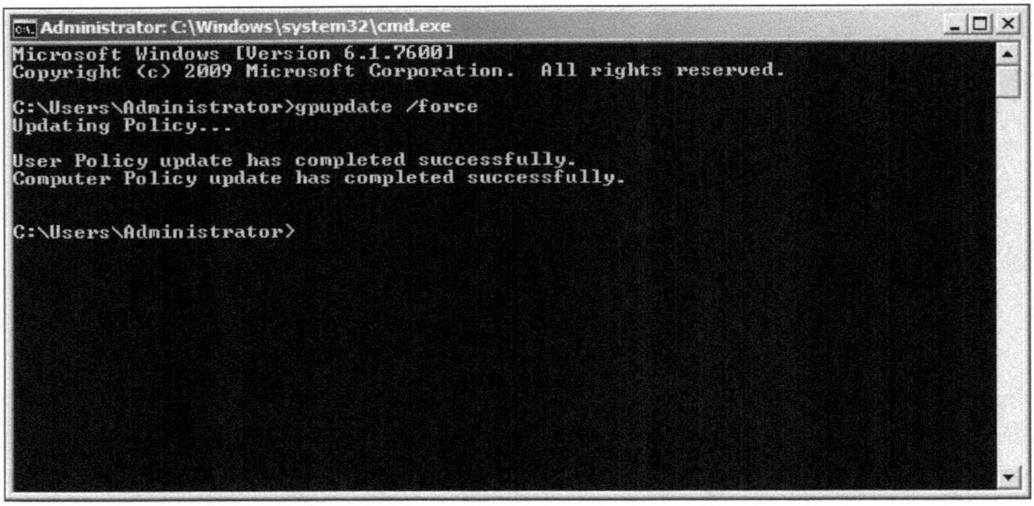

```
Administrator: C:\Windows\system32\cmd.exe                          _ □ ×
Microsoft Windows [Version 6.1.7600]
Copyright (c) 2009 Microsoft Corporation.  All rights reserved.

C:\Users\Administrator>gpupdate /force
Updating Policy...

User Policy update has completed successfully.
Computer Policy update has completed successfully.

C:\Users\Administrator>
```

4. Once Group Policy has updated, double-click the saved Windows Firewall console that we saved to the desktop and check that the rules from Group Policy have been applied.

    The following figure shows the **Remote Administration (NP-In)** exception in Windows 7 as applied by our GPO. We know it's come from the GPO because of the yellow box that states **This rule has been applied by the system administrator and cannot be modified**.

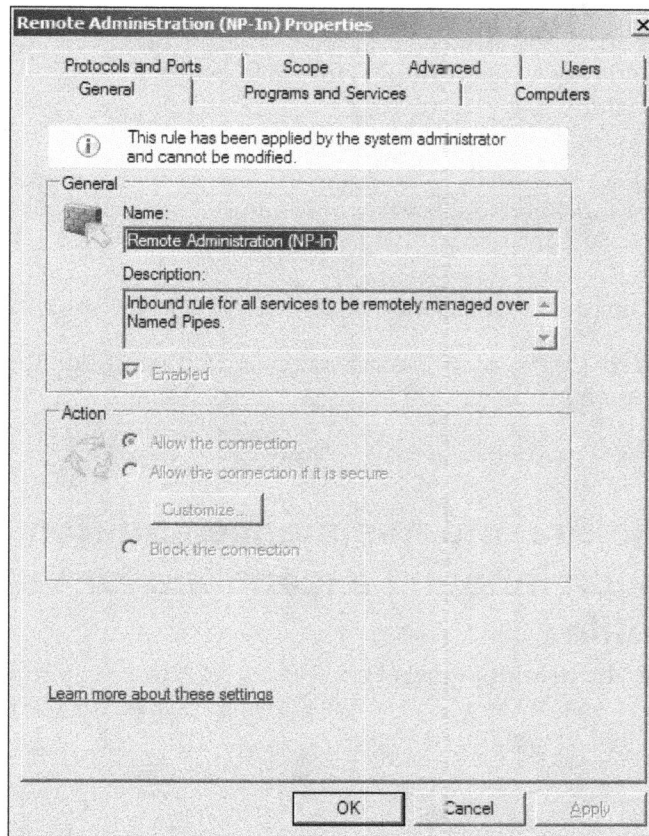

Duplicate rules and local Windows Firewall settings

You might have noticed that firewall rules from Group Policy don't replace the same local rule. This results in twice as many rules on the local computer. Rule merging can be configured in Windows Firewall Properties for each firewall profile. The default setting (Yes) means that a local rule will apply unless a rule defined in Group Policy supercedes it. Selecting No results in local rules being ignored.

Creating a GPO for Windows Firewall in Vista

I recommend configuring a separate GPO for Vista because there are some subtle differences in the default firewall rules.

> Windows Firewall in Vista applies the most restrictive firewall profile to all network interfaces. Starting in Windows 7, firewall profiles can be set per network interface.

You should copy the process for Windows 7 noting the following differences:

1. Enabling Remote Assistance and Remote Administration inbound exceptions for the Domain profile

2. Creating WMI query for Windows Vista

Enabling the Remote Assistance and Remote Administration inbound exceptions for the Domain profile

When customizing the default inbound exceptions for Vista in Group Policy, you need to additionally enable the four Remote Assistance rules for the **Domain** profile, which are not enabled by default in Vista.

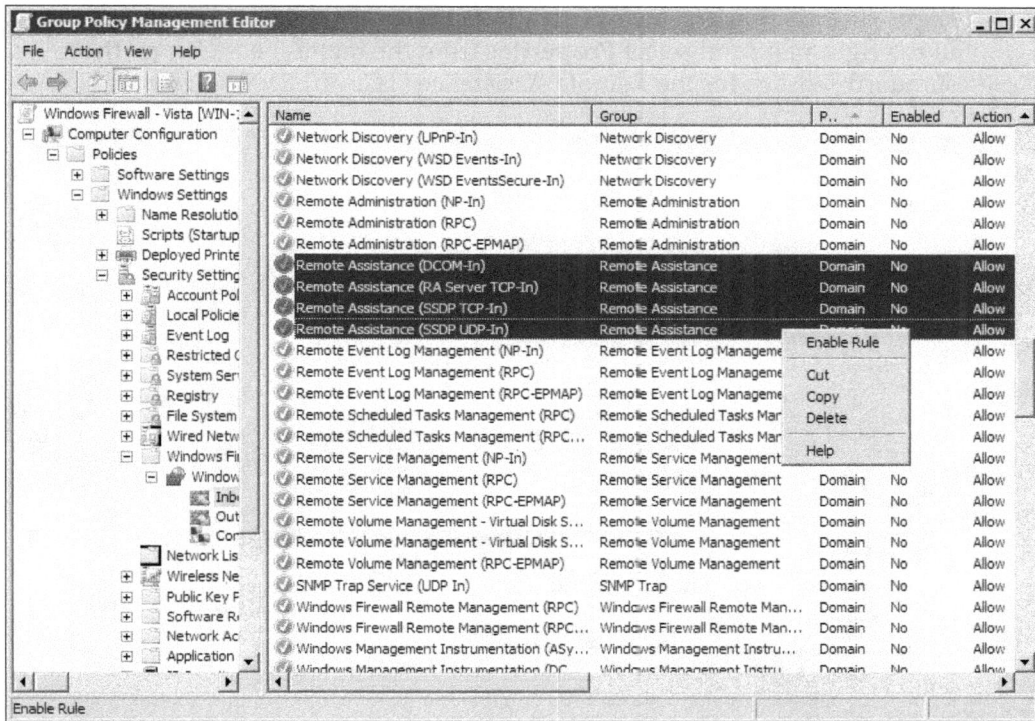

Vista's **Remote Assistance (TCP-In)** inbound exception is configured using two rules—one for the **Domain** and **Public** profiles and another for **Private**. This is as opposed to Windows 7 where this exception is configured using two rules, one for the **Public** profile and another for **Domain** and **Private**. Therefore, in our **GPO** for Vista's firewall, we should enable this exception but change it so that it only applies to the **Domain** profile to ensure that Vista is properly protected when connected to untrusted networks.

1. Right-click on **Remote Assistance (TCP-In)** for the **Domain, Public** profiles in the right pane and select **Properties** from the menu. Let's change the standard settings for the Remote Assistance (TCP-In) firewall rule:

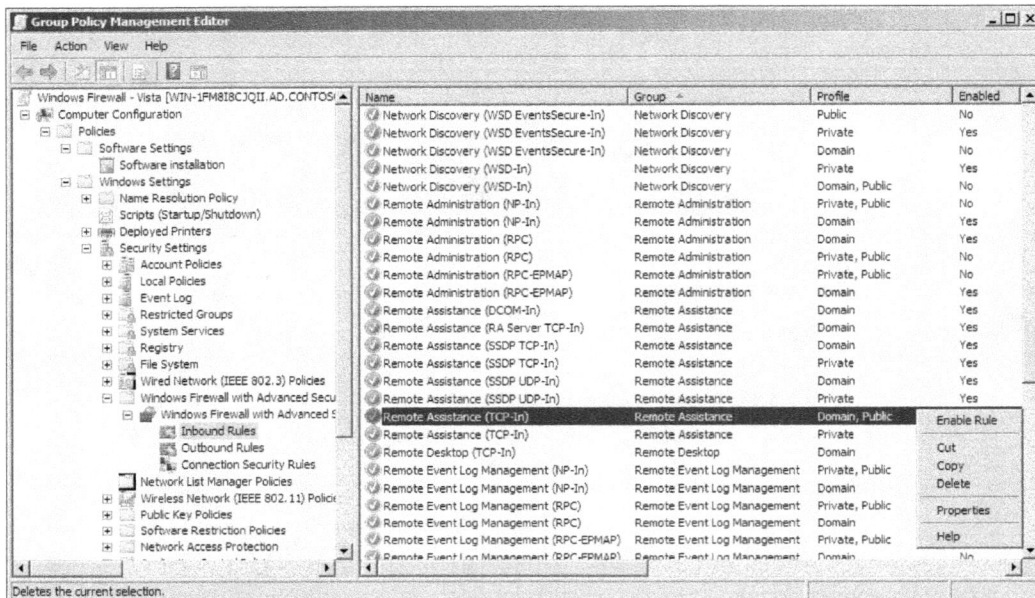

2. Switch to the **Advanced** tab, uncheck **Public** under **Profiles**, and click **Apply**.

3. Change to the **General** tab, check **Enabled** under **General**, and click **OK**.

Vista contains the three Remote Administration exceptions by default, but they need to be enabled for the **Domain** profile.

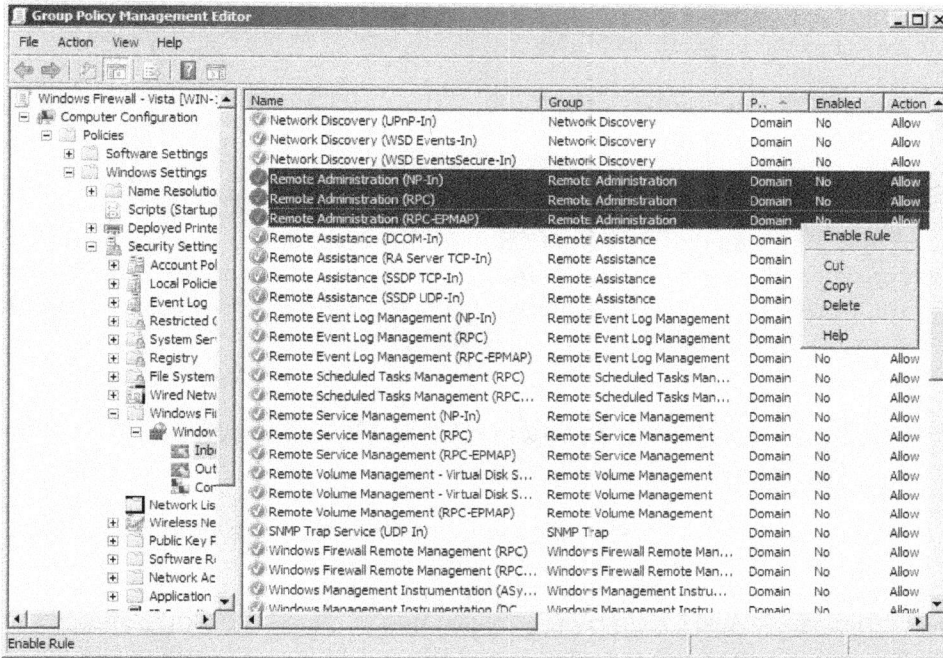

Creating a WMI query for Windows Vista

The WMI query for Windows Vista should look like this:

```
Select * from Win32_OperatingSystem where Version like "6.0%" and
ProductType = "1"
```

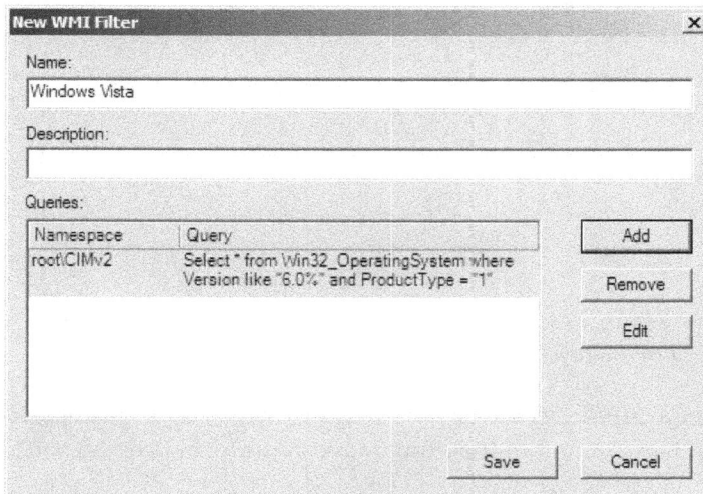

The `ProductType` variable determines what kind of OS will be returned by the query and can be set to the following values:

1. Workstation operating system
2. Domain Controller
3. Member Server

`Version` determines the generation of OS. For instance, version `6.0` refers to Vista and Server 2008, whereas version `6.1` indicates Windows 7 or Server 2008 R2. The version for a given OS can be determined by typing `winver` into the Search programs and files box on the **Start** menu.

Creating a GPO for Windows Firewall in Windows XP

Assuming that we're working with a mixed environment that includes XP, Vista, and Windows 7, we need to create a GPO with settings for XP's firewall. The configuration for Windows Firewall in XP is quite different to that of Vista and Windows 7. Let's create a Group Policy Object that contains firewall settings specifically for Windows XP:

1. Log in to the Windows Server 2008 R2 domain controller as a domain administrator and open **Start | Administrative Tools | Group Policy Management**.

2. In the left pane, expand your forest, under the **Domains** node right-click **Group Policy Objects**, and select **New** from the menu.

3. In the **New GPO** dialog, type `Windows Firewall - Windows XP` in the **Name** field and click **OK**.

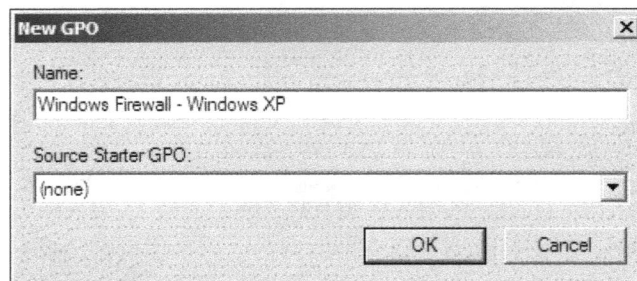

Now we have a Group Policy Object ready for configuring multiple Windows XP computers, which are joined to the domain, with uniform firewall settings.

Configuring GPO settings

Let's load the **Windows Firewall – Windows XP** GFO so we can edit the configuration. It is done as follows:

1. Log in to Windows XP (at least Service Pack 2) as a domain administrator and select **Run** from the **Start** menu.

2. Type mmc into the **Run** dialog and click **OK**.

3. In the console window press *Ctrl+M* and in the **Add/Remove Snap-in** dialog on the **Standalone** tab click **Add**.

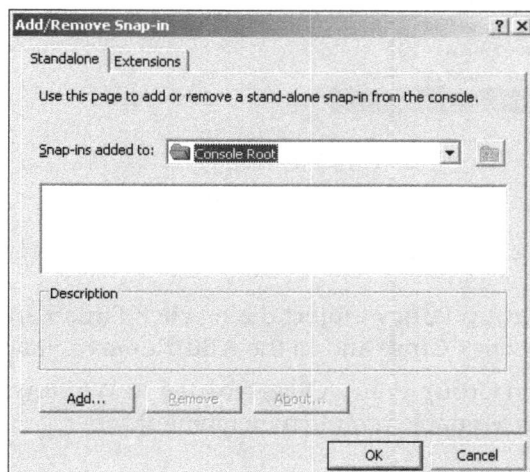

4. In the **Add Standalone Snap-in** dialog select **Group Policy Object Editor** and click **Add**.

5. In the **Select Group Policy Object** dialog click **Browse**.

6. In the **Browse for a Group Policy Object** dialog switch to the **All** tab, select the **Windows Firewall – Windows XP** GPO, and click **OK**.

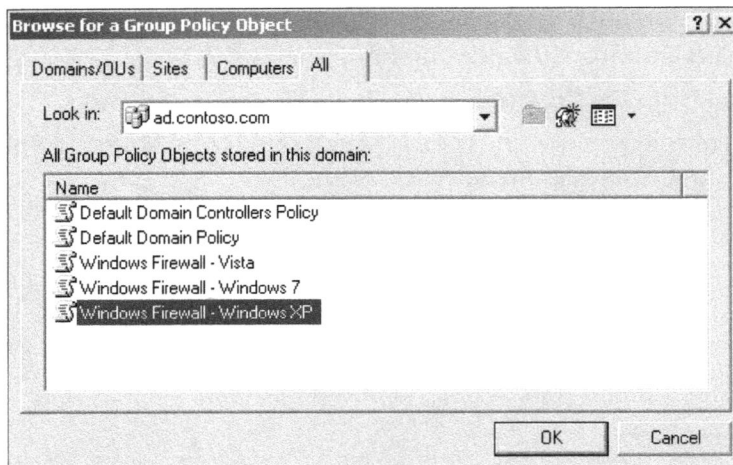

7. In the **Select Group Policy Object** dialog click **Finish**. In the **Add Standalone Snap-in** dialog click **Close** and in the **Add/Remove Snap-in** dialog click **OK**.

Now we have a domain Group Policy Object loaded in Windows XP ready to configure with settings to enable remote management.

Creating an exception for WS-Management

Let's create an inbound firewall rule to allow WS-Management. It is done as follows:

1. In the console window, expand the **Windows Firewall – Windows XP** GPO in the left pane and then **Computer Configuration | Administrative Templates | Network | Network Connections | Windows Firewall** and select **Domain Profile**.

2. In the right pane, double-click **Windows Firewall: Define port exceptions**.

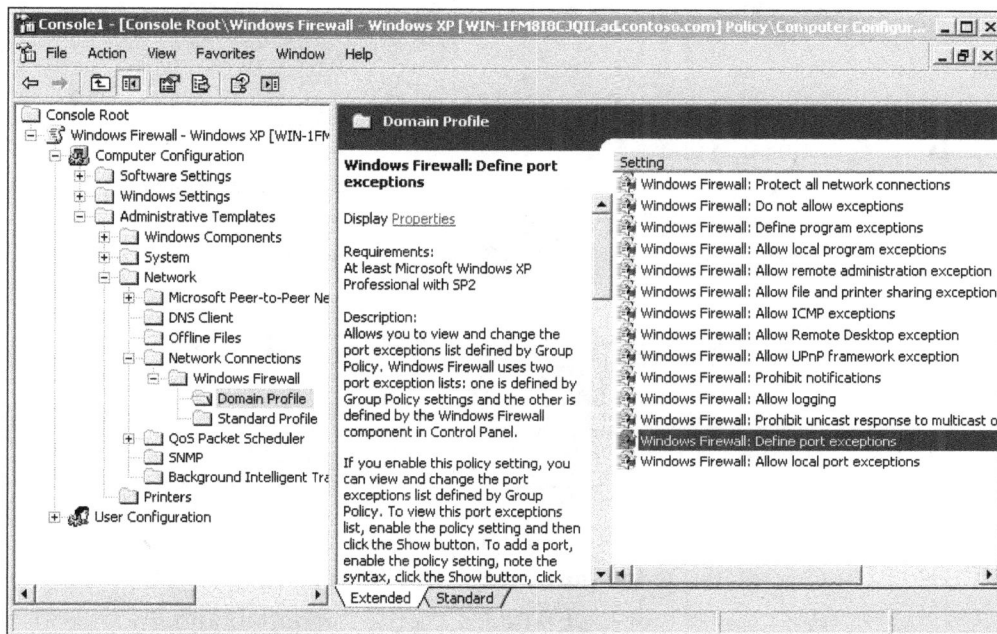

3. In the **Windows Firewall: Define port exceptions Properties** dialog select **Enabled** and then click on the **Show** button

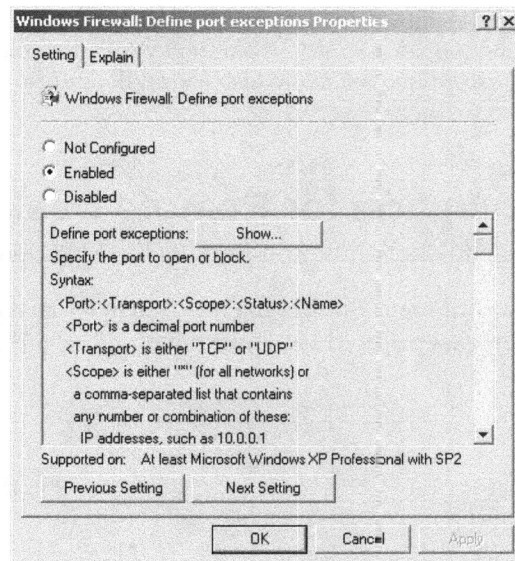

4. Click **Add** in the **Show Contents** dialog.

5. In the **Add Item** dialog, type `80:TCP:localsubnet:enabled:WinRM` and click **OK**.

> **String syntax**
>
> The string syntax used to define port exceptions is as follows, where `Status` can be either `enabled` or `disabled`.
>
> `Port Number:Protocol:Scope:Status:Name`

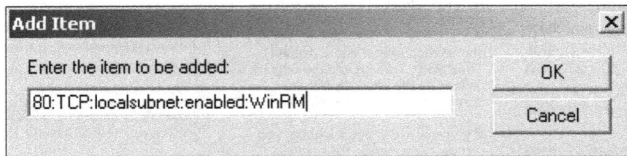

Add Item	✕
Enter the item to be added:	OK
`80:TCP:localsubnet:enabled:WinRM`	Cancel

6. In the **Show Contents** dialog click **OK**, and click **OK** again in the **Windows Firewall: Define port exceptions Properties** dialog.

7. Repeat this procedure for the **Standard Profile** if required and then close the console window.

> While the Vista/Windows 7 Firewall rule restricts inbound access to `svchost.exe` on port 80, you cannot add `svchost.exe` as a program exception for Windows Firewall in Windows XP. Rather than using the `localsubnet` parameter to define the scope of the port exception, you could also use an IP address or list of addresses to improve security.

Creating an exception for Remote Desktop

Let's create a firewall rule to allow inbound Remote Desktop connections.

1. Select **Domain Profile** and double-click **Windows Firewall: Allow Remote Desktop exception** in the right pane.

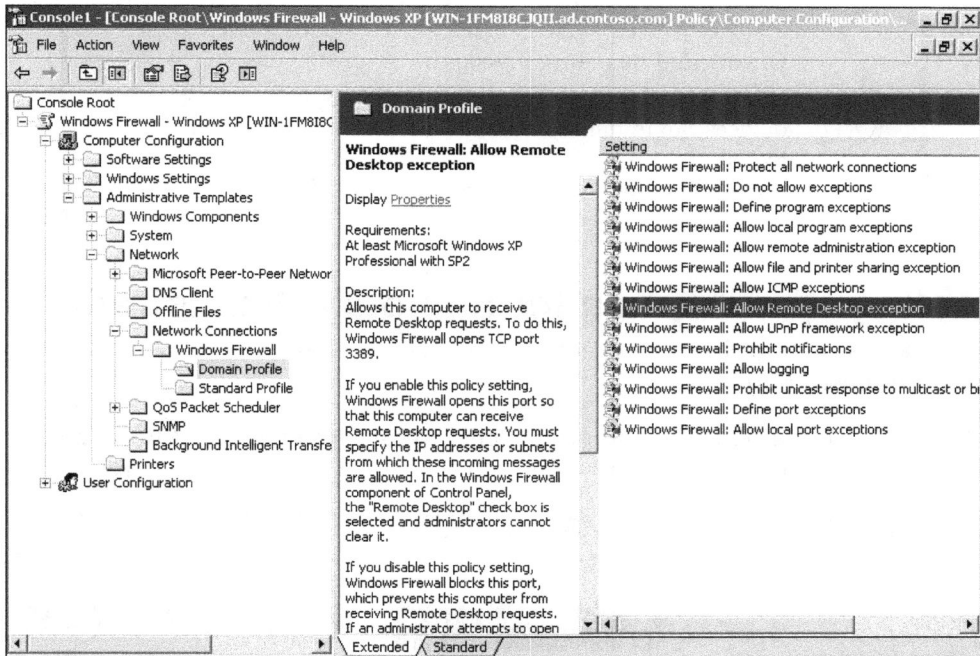

2. In the **Windows Firewall: All Remote Desktop exception Properties** dialog, select **Enabled**, and type ٭ or a set of permitted IP addresses into the box **Allow unsolicited incoming messages from** field and click **OK**.

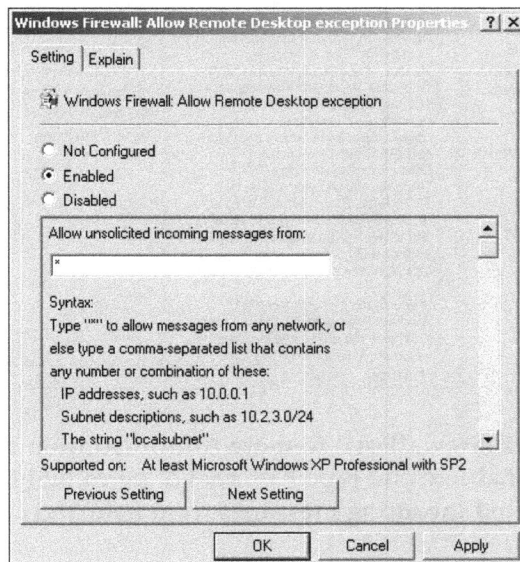

> **Unsolicited incoming messages**
>
> In a production environment, you should restrict which
> devices can initiate a Remote Desktop session to clients
> by entering a list of permitted IP addresses into the **Allow
> unsolicited incoming messages from** field.

Creating an exception for Remote Administration

Follow the instructions below to create a firewall exception for
remote administration.

1. Select **Domain Profile** and double-click **Windows Firewall: Allow remote
   administration exception** in the right pane.

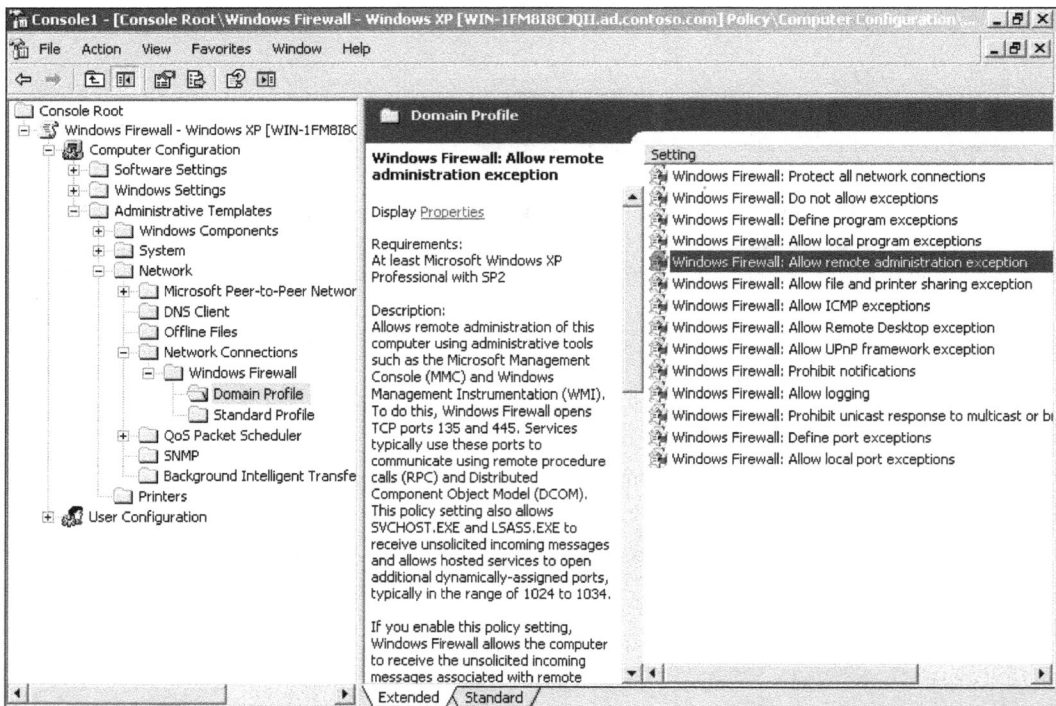

2. In the **Windows Firewall: All Remote Administration exception Properties**
   dialog, check **Enabled**, and type * or a set of permitted IP addresses into the
   Allow unsolicited incoming messages from field and click **OK**.

Creating an exception for Remote Assistance

Follow the instructions below to create a firewall exception for Remote Assistance.

1. Select **Domain Profile** in the console window and double-click **Windows Firewall: Define program exceptions** in the right pane.

2. In the **Windows Firewall: Define program exceptions Properties** dialog, check **Enabled** and then click **Show**.

3. In the **Show Contents dialog**, click **Add**. Type the following string into the **Add Item** dialog and click **OK**.

   ```
   %windir%\system32\sessmgr.exe:*:Enabled:Remote Assistance
   ```

4. Repeat this process for the following two strings:

   ```
   %windir%\pchealth\helpctr\binaries\helpsvc.exe:*:Enabled:Offer
   Remote Assistance
   ```

   ```
   %windir%\pchealth\helpctr\binaries\helpctr.exe:*:Enabled:Remote
   Assistance - Windows Messenger and Voice
   ```

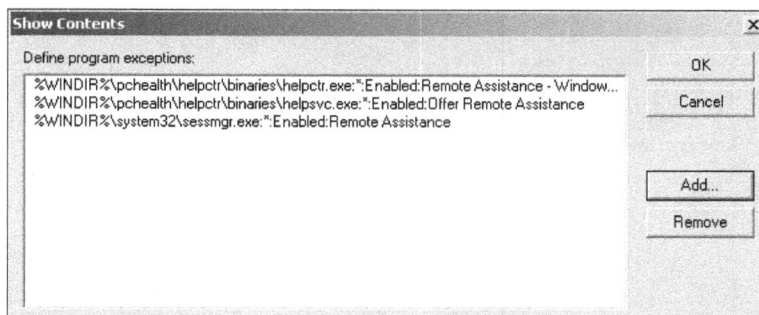

5. In the **Show Contents** dialog and again in the **Windows Firewall: Define program exceptions Properties** dialog click **OK**.

6. In the console window, double-click **Windows Firewall: Define port exceptions** and make sure the policy is set to **Enabled**.

7. In the **Windows Firewall: Define port exceptions Properties** dialog click **Show**.

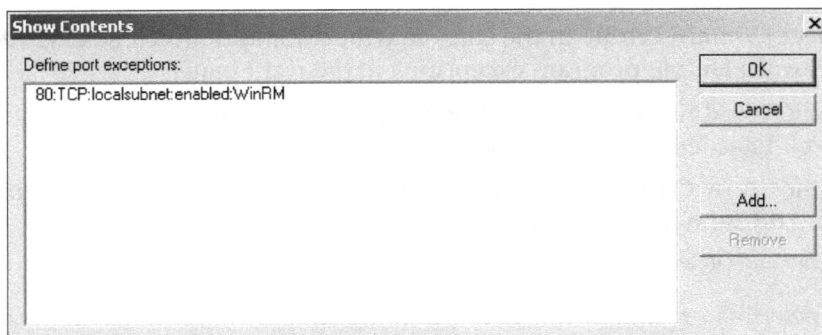

8. In the **Show Contents** dialog, click **Add**. In the **Add Item** dialog, type the following string and click **OK**:

```
135:TCP:*:Enabled:Offer Remote Assistance
```

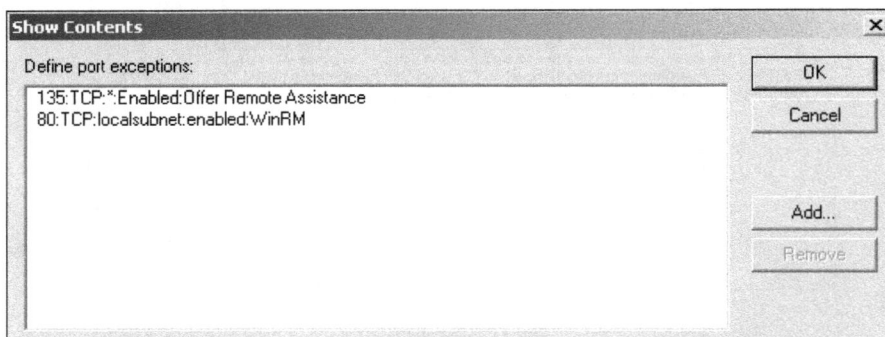

9. In the **Show Contents** dialog and in the **Windows Firewall: Define port exceptions Properties** dialog click **OK** and close the console window.

Creating a WMI filter to restrict the scope of management to Windows XP

Follow the instructions below to create a WMI filter to ensure that a GPO only applies to Windows XP.

1. Log in to Windows Server 2008 R2 as a domain administrator and open **Start | Administrative Tools | Group Policy Management**.

2. In the left pane expand your forest, under the **Domains** container right-click **WMI Filters**, and select **New** from the menu.

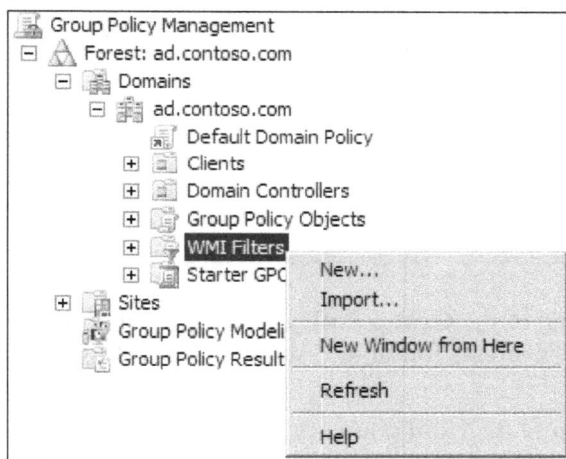

3. In the **New WMI Filter** dialog, type `Windows XP` in the **Name** field and then click **Add**.

4. In the **WMI Query** dialog, type the following query into the **Query** field and click **OK**.

```
Select * from Win32_OperatingSystem where Version like "5.1.2%"
and ProductType = "1"
```

5. Click **Save** in the **New WMI Filter** dialog.

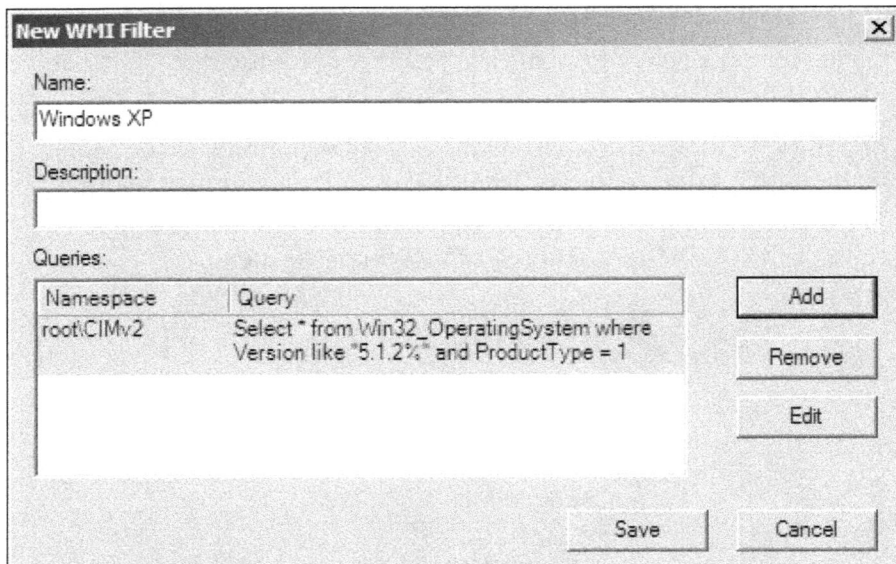

6. In the left pane of the **Group Policy Management** window, expand the **Group Policy Objects** folder and select the **Windows Firewall – Windows XP** GPO.

7. At the bottom of the right pane under **WMI Filtering**, select **Windows XP** from the drop-down list.

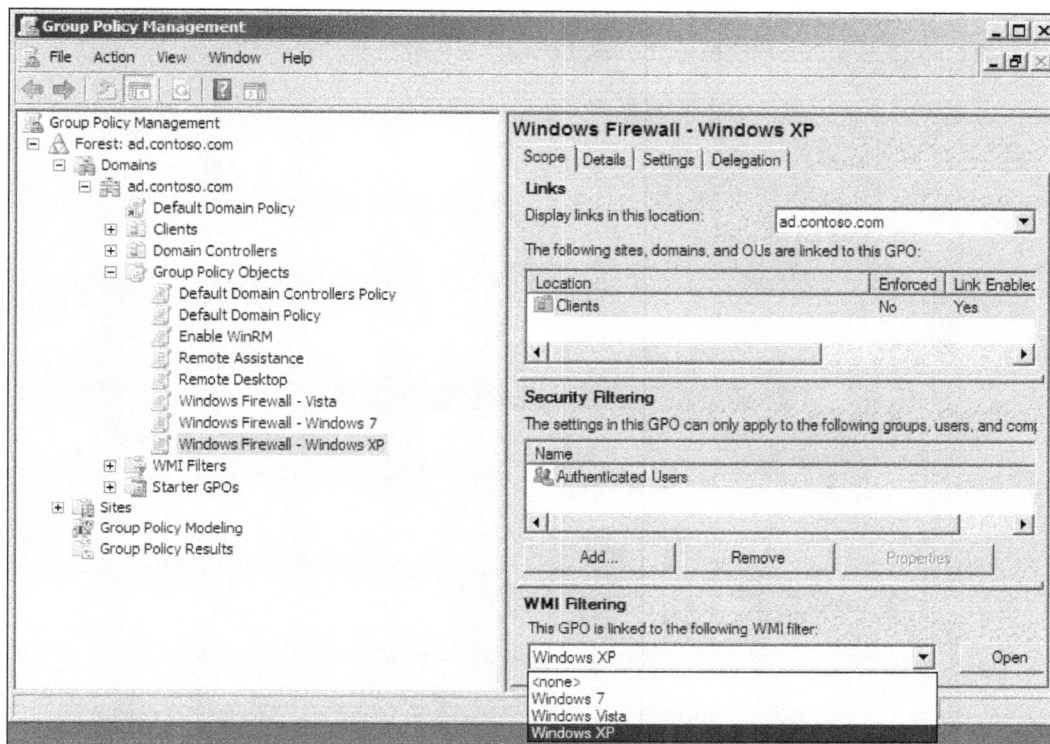

8. In the **Group Policy Management** dialog, click **Yes** to apply the filter to the GPO.

Linking the new GPO to the Client OU

Now that everything is configured, let's link the new GPO to our **Clients** OU.

1. In the left pane of the **Group Policy Management** window, right-click the **Clients** OU and select **Link an Existing GPO** from the menu.

2. In the **Select GPO** dialog, select **Windows Firewall – Windows XP** under **Group Policy objects** and click **OK**.

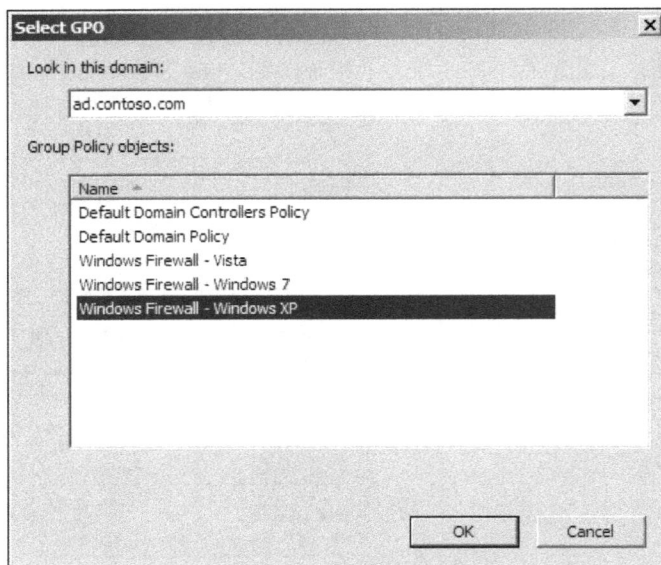

Summary

The most import point to take from this chapter is that reliable remote access is critical when supporting users in a least privilege environment. IT can no longer rely on users undertaking administrative-level actions on the help desk's behalf. From a technical perspective, before continuing to the next chapter we should:

- Be able to configure Windows Firewall to enable all the remote access and administrative features discussed
- Know how to enable remote access tools and features across multiple computers with Group Policy
- Know how to offer support using Remote Assistance
- Be aware of the different connection scenarios for Remote Assistance, and in which versions of Windows they are supported
- Be able to get administrative access to remote machines via the command line

In the next chapter we'll learn how to further secure standard user accounts with **Software Restriction Policies** and **AppLocker**.

9

Deploying Software Restriction Policies and AppLocker

Taking the concept of least-privilege security one step further, in this chapter we'll look at how to make sure that our users are protected from malicious programs, preventing them from running unapproved portable applications, and securing Group Policy by creating a whitelist of allowed applications using Software Restriction Policy and AppLocker. In this chapter we'll learn:

- How to deploy default **Software Restriction Policy (SRP)** or **AppLocker** rules to ensure only programs installed in protected locations can run

- The differences between the different kinds of SRP and AppLocker rules

- How to force an application to launch with standard user privileges even if the user is an administrator

- How to blacklist an application using SRP or AppLocker

Controlling applications

We've already done a lot of work in securing user accounts, ensuring that the applications and functions users need to fulfill everyday duties work, while protecting critical parts of the system from accidental or malicious change. So you'd think that would be enough. However, there are two important reasons why you should look at further securing standard user accounts.

Blocking portable applications

While it may seem that standard users can only run software that is installed by an administrator or a software distribution system, this in fact may not necessarily be the case. Over the past few years, it has become more common for software to be packaged in portable form. This means that no installation is required, and furthermore, administrative rights are not needed to run the software. Users can copy the executable file to their desktop and double-click; and presto, you've got software. These kinds of programs are known as **portable applications**. Installers are more frequently being designed to run under a standard user account, without checking for admin privileges or making system-wide changes. One example of such a program is the popular Google Chrome browser. So even if you run as a standard user, it's perfectly possible that you can run software that isn't located in the protected `Program Files` directory or otherwise approved by your organization's IT department.

Securing Group Policy

Although running as an administrator means that you can easily evade management and security controls such as Group Policy, it's still possible to find your way around Group Policy even as a standard user. Therefore, you should consider applying Software Restriction Policy (Vista and Windows XP) or AppLocker rules (Windows 7) to ensure that users or malware can't circumvent management controls.

Windows applications are responsible for enforcing their own Group Policy settings. Standard users have full permissions over the processes they launch so there's the potential for a user, or malware, to use one running process to modify another to ignore Group Policy. Therefore, you need to make sure that Software Restriction Policy or AppLocker is configured with a whitelist of permitted applications, so the user or other process can't launch applications that are designed to modify the code of programs the user is running and inherently has full permission to change. Blacklisting can also be used to block applications that haven't been approved by IT, but this approach is generally harder to manage.

> DLL injection techniques can be used by a standard user to hijack applications running under their own account, forcing SRP and other Group Policy settings to be ignored.

Preventing users from circumventing Group Policy

Group Policy is not completely infallible, so system administrators should consider implementing some of the following configuration, in addition to other recommendations in this chapter, to help ensure that standard users are not able to override policy settings. Some of these settings result in a tradeoff against convenience or affect system performance. The settings are as follows:

- Set the BIOS to boot only from the local hard disk and set a BIOS password to prevent users from changing system files by booting into another operating system.

- Encrypt the system volume using BitLocker for the highest level of security.

- Use SRP or AppLocker to blacklist Windows executables such as REGEDIT, the command prompt, and the **Microsoft Management Console (MMC)** to stop users accessing important configuration options.

- In high-security environments, assign users read-only mandatory user profiles so users cannot override managed settings.

- Group Policy processing can be configured to reapply settings, even if policy hasn't been changed since the last refresh, in the event that users manually alter settings. Group Policy processing behavior can be changed under **Computer Configuration | Policies | Administrative Templates | System | Group Policy**.

Implementing Software Restriction Policy

First introduced in Windows XP, Software Restriction Policy allows administrators to create whitelists or blacklists, of applications that are permitted or prohibited to run. Software Restriction Policy, sometimes also referred to as **SAFER**, also has the ability to restrict the privilege level of a process. For instance, if you need to log on as an administrator, SRP can be used to launch Internet Explorer with standard user privileges, making the browsing experience considerably "safer".

> **What is a whitelist?**
>
> A **whitelist** is a set of programs, scripts, or processes that are deemed to be trusted and therefore approved to run on your network. It's a good practice to create a whitelist of permitted applications rather than blocking banned programs using a blacklist. It's impossible to include every malicious application in a blacklist, so it's preferable to attempt to define what is allowed in a whitelist.
>
> Software Restriction Policies are available in Vista Business, Enterprise, Ultimate, and Windows XP Professional. SRP is also included in Windows Server 2003, 2003 R2, 2008, 2008 R2, and Windows 7 Professional, Enterprise, and Ultimate editions.

Creating a whitelist with Software Restriction Policy

Rules are used to determine which programs will be included in Software Restriction Policy. By default, each rule can have a security level of *Disallowed*, *Unrestricted*, or *Basic User*. Disallowed blocks a program and Unrestricted allows a program to be launched with the same privileges as the logged in user.

> The **Basic User** security level can be applied to users who log on using an account with administrative privileges. Any application launched by the user that has the Basic User security level enforced will have administrative privileges stripped from its security token. In practice, SRP adds a deny **ACL (Access Control List)** to the process's security token for the local administrators group.

> **Basic User**
>
> The Basic User security level is hidden in Windows XP prior to Service Pack 3. You can enable Basic User by adding a DWORD value called **Levels** with a value of 0x20000 to the following registry key:
>
> HKEY_LOCAL_MACHINE\SOFTWARE\Policies\Microsoft\ Windows\Safer\ CodeIdentifiers

Defining hash rules

A **hash** is a cryptographic, digital finger print that is unique to a given file. Software Restriction Policy can create an MD5 hash for files that aren't digitally signed, or use the SHA-1 or MD5/from the certificate of a signed application to uniquely identify the file. Hash rules are useful for preventing users from running a specific version of an application. Hash rules contain three pieces of information about the given file and are formatted as follows:

```
[MD5 or SHA1 hash value]:[file length]:[hash algorithm id]
```

Defining path rules

A **path** rule can be used to identify the physical location of a file or set of files. Rules can be set using paths defined in the registry (registry path rules) or using file paths. The default SRP rules are defined using registry path rules. The default `HKEY_LOCAL_MACHINE\SOFTWARE\Microsoft\Windows NT\CurrentVersion` and `HKEY_LOCAL_MACHINE\SOFTWARE\Microsoft\Windows\CurrentVersion` keys contain predefined paths to file system locations such as `C:\Program Files`.

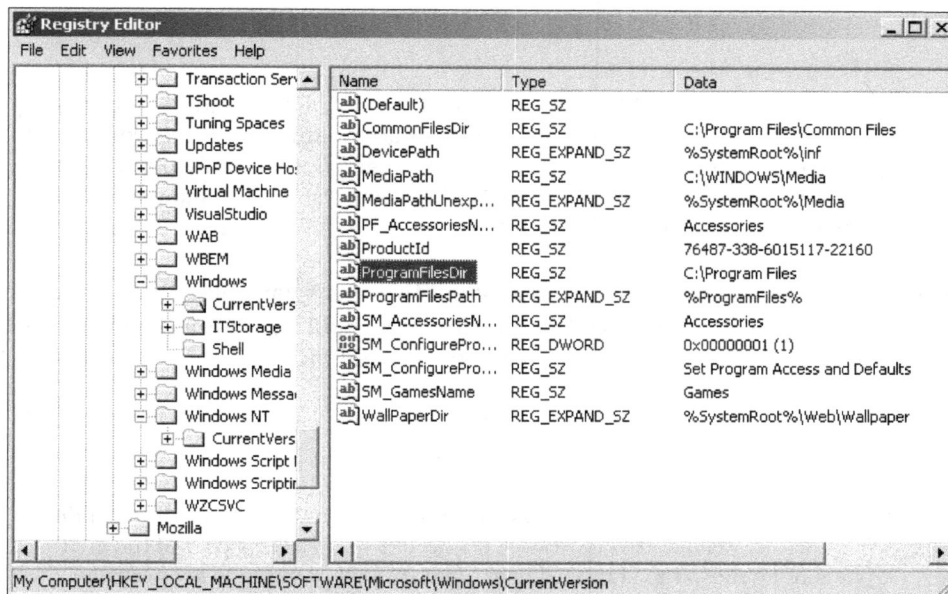

Registry path rules must be enclosed by percent symbols as follows:

```
%HKEY_LOCAL_MACHINE\SOFTWARE\Microsoft\Windows\CurrentVersion\
    ProgramFilesDir%
```

While **environment variables**, such as `%ProgramFiles%`, can be used in SRP path rules, they should be used with caution. If you were to configure an SRP file path rule using an environment variable, such as `%ProgramFiles%\*.*`, a standard user could easily create a personal variable called `%ProgramFiles%` and set the path to something other than `C:\Program Files`; to the path of their desktop for example. This would enable the user to circumvent SRP and run executables and scripts from their chosen path.

> **Environment Variable preferences**
>
> Though `%ProgramFiles%` is considered a system-wide variable, which standard users cannot modify, if two variables with the same name appear in the system-wide and personal lists, the variable in the personal list takes precedence.

> Environment variables are used in scripts and configuration files instead of hard-coded strings and are useful for accounting for differences in system configuration. For instance, `%systemroot%` usually points to the `C:\Windows` path, but could differ between systems if a standard image wasn't used to deploy Windows.

Registry file path rules that avoid the use of environment variables, or use explicit file path rules (that is, those without environment variables), should be employed to ensure that standard users cannot easily circumvent SRP.

> **Setting environment variables**
>
> In Windows XP, standard users can set personal variables through the GUI. In Vista and Windows 7, it's harder to do as this part of the GUI is not exposed to standard users, but it's still possible to set personal variables via the command line.

Trusting software signed by a preferred publisher (Certificate Rules)

Certificate rules are used to trust software signed by a particular publisher's certificate. For instance, you could allow all software signed by Microsoft to run.

Making exceptions for IE zones (Network/Internet Zone Rule)

Identifying executables or scripts by Internet Explorer Zone might be useful in situations where you want to make exceptions for sites listed in IE's *Trusted* zone. For example, maybe users are allowed to launch an application from the company's intranet site.

Creating a whitelist with Software Restriction Policy

Let's create a GPO with a basic Software Restriction Policy that will prevent any executables from being launched that are not located in the trusted locations `C:\Windows` or `C:\Program Files` directories. Log in to Windows Server 2008 R2 as a domain administrator and follow the steps:

1. Open the **Group Policy Management Console** as a domain administrator from **Administrative Tools** on the **Start** menu and expand your **Active Directory** forest and domain in the left pane.

2. Right-click the **Clients** OU and select **Create a GPO in this domain, and Link it here** from the menu. In the **New GPO** dialog, type **SRP** in the **Name** field and click **OK**.

3. Expand the **Clients** OU in the left pane, right-click the **SRP GPO**, and select **Edit** from the menu.

4. In the **Group Policy Management Editor** window, expand **Policies | Windows | Settings | Security Settings** and **Computer Configuration** in the left pane.

5. Right-click **Software Restriction Policies** and select **New Software Restriction Policies** from the menu.

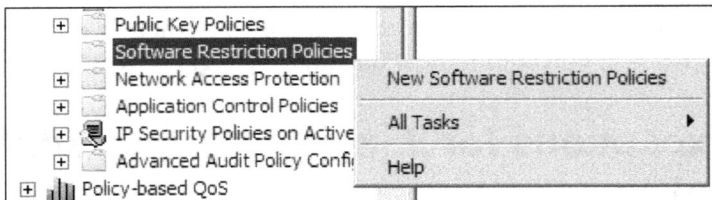

```
 ⊞  Public Key Policies
      Software Restriction Policies
 ⊞  Network Access Protection          New Software Restriction Policies
 ⊞  Application Control Policies
 ⊞  IP Security Policies on Active      All Tasks                      ▶
 ⊞  Advanced Audit Policy Confi         Help
⊞  Policy-based QoS
```

6. Under **Software Restriction Policies**, click **Security Levels**.

7. The default security level is **Unrestricted**. Change the security level to **Disallowed** by right-clicking **Disallowed** in the right pane and selecting **Set as default** from the menu.

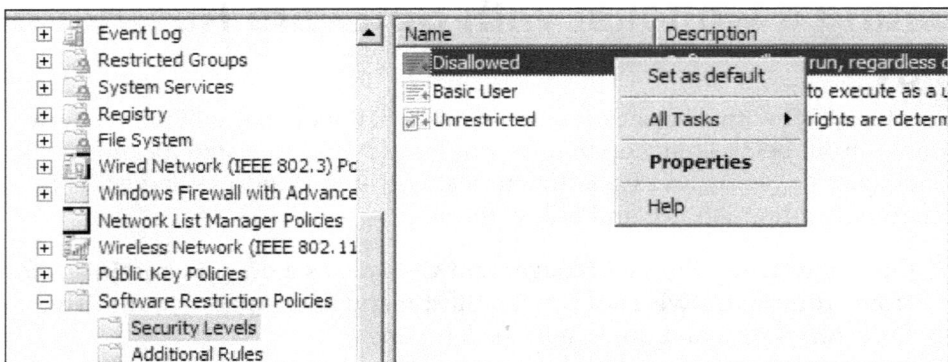

```
⊞  Event Log            ▲   Name              Description
⊞  Restricted Groups         Disallowed                          run, regardless c
⊞  System Services           Basic User         Set as default    to execute as a u
⊞  Registry                  Unrestricted       All Tasks      ▶  rights are detern
⊞  File System
⊞  Wired Network (IEEE 802.3) Pc               Properties
⊞  Windows Firewall with Advance
    Network List Manager Policies              Help
⊞  Wireless Network (IEEE 802.11
⊞  Public Key Policies
⊟  Software Restriction Policies
      Security Levels
      Additional Rules
```

8. In the **Software Restriction Policies** dialog, click **Yes** to continue.

9. Now click **Additional Rules** in the left pane and you'll see the two default path rules set to **Unrestricted** that allow programs in our two trusted locations to run even if the default security level is set to **Disallowed**.

Name	Type	Security Level
%HKEY_LOCAL_MACHINE\SOFTWARE\Microsoft\Windows NT\CurrentVersion\SystemRoot%	Path	Unrestricted
%HKEY_LOCAL_MACHINE\SOFTWARE\Microsoft\Windows NT\CurrentVersion\SystemRoot%*.exe	Path	Unrestricted
%HKEY_LOCAL_MACHINE\SOFTWARE\Microsoft\Windows NT\CurrentVersion\SystemRoot%System32*.exe	Path	Unrestricted
%HKEY_LOCAL_MACHINE\SOFTWARE\Microsoft\Windows\CurrentVersion\ProgramFilesDir%	Path	Unrestricted

Additional rules

It's important not to delete the default additional path rules as you might render machines unusable if the default security level is set to *Disallowed*.

Windows Script Host (WSH) security is tied to Software Restriction Policies by the UseWINSAFER registry value under HKLM\Software\ Microsoft\Windows Script Host\Settings. This means that scripts must also be in a trusted location before they can run.

Name	Type	Security Level
%HKEY_LOCAL_MACHINE\SOFTWARE\Microsoft\Windows NT\CurrentVersion\SystemRoot%	Path	Unrestricted
%HKEY_LOCAL_MACHINE\SOFTWARE\Microsoft\Windows\ CurrentVersion\ProgramFilesDir%	Path	Unrestricted

Shortcuts in Windows XP

In addition to the four default additional path rules in Windows XP, in order to enable users to open programs using shortcuts, you'll need to add the following path rule— *.lnk. You should note that if you add *.lnk as a file path rule, users can circumvent SRP by changing the extension of a script or executable file to .lnk and then launching it from the command line, though not from the **Run** option on the **Start** menu. Therefore, if you must enable compatibility for shortcuts, you should think about restricting access to the command line. **Vista and Windows 7 do not require any additional rules for shortcuts.**

Configuring applications to run as a standard user

For those users who must log in as a local administrator, it may be useful to configure all or certain applications to launch with standard user privilege. The important point to note about logging in as an administrator and then using SAFER to launch an application as a Basic User is that the administrative user's own token is used to launch the application with administrative rights denied thus retaining the ability to use all resources the user has permission to access. Let's configure a GPO for users who run with administrative privileges. Log in to Windows Server 2008 R2 as a domain administrator:

1. Open the **Group Policy Management Console** from **Administrative Tools** on the **Start** menu and expand your **Active Directory** forest and domain in the left pane.

2. Right-click the **Managed Users** OU and select **Create a GPO in this domain, and Link it here** from the menu. In the **New GPO** dialog, type `SRP - Local Admins` in the **Name** field and click **OK**.

> **Choosing between Managed Users or Clients OU**
>
> Depending on how you manage administrative users in your organization, and how **Organizational Units (OUs)** are planned, you may want to configure SRP under the **Computer Configuration** or **User Configuration** node in Group Policy. If you choose **User Configuration**, you must link the GPO to an OU that contains user accounts; and if you choose **Computer Configuration**, you must link the GPO to an OU that contains computer accounts.

3. Expand the **Managed Users** OU in the left pane, right-click the **SRP – Local Admins** GPO, and select **Edit** from the menu.

4. In the **Group Policy Management Editor** window, expand **Policies | Windows | Settings | Security Settings**, and **User Configuration** in the left pane.

5. Right-click **Software Restriction Policies** and select **New Software Restriction Policies** from the menu.

6. Under **Software Restriction Policies**, right-click **Additional Rules** and select **New Path Rule** from the menu.

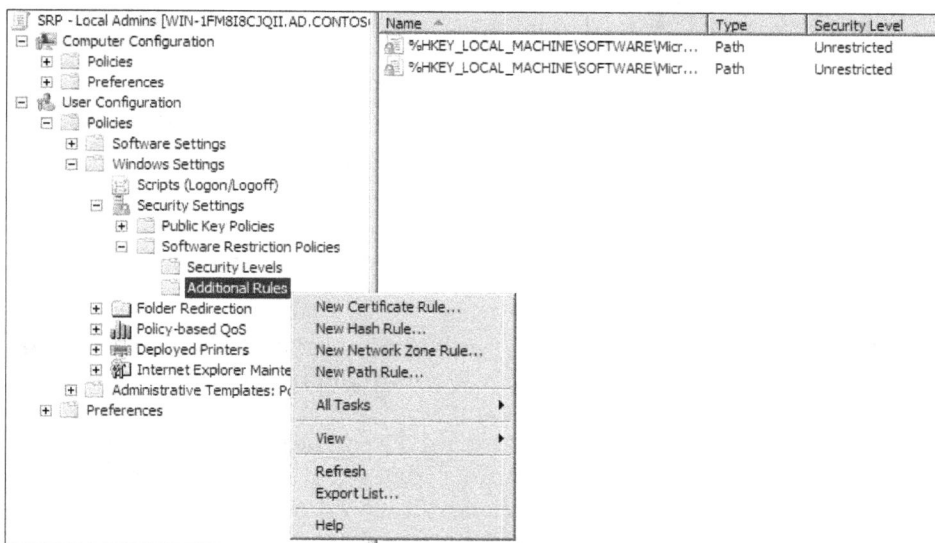

7. In the **New Path Rule** dialog, enter the path for Internet Explorer or find `iexplore.exe` in the `Program Files` folder using **Browse**.

8. Set **Security level** to **Basic User** and click **OK**.

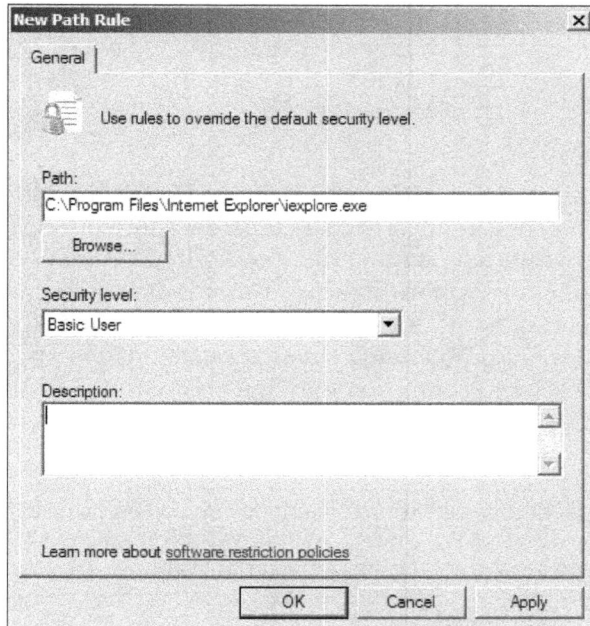

9. Close the **Group Policy Management Editor** window.

Using runas to invoke an application as a Basic User or Unrestricted

You can launch an application from the command line using the `runas` command, as a *Basic User* or *Unrestricted*.

```
runas /trustlevel:"Basic User" iexplore
runas /trustlevel:"Unrestricted" iexplore.exe
```

Now that the **SRP – Local Admins** GPO has been created and linked to the **Managed Clients** OU, you'll likely want to use security group filtering to ensure that the policy is only applied to those users in your organization that are given local administrator rights on their own machines. While it may not do any harm to apply this policy to standard users and those with administrative privileges, for the sake of reducing complexity and ensuring maximum efficiency, it would be best to apply this GPO only where it's necessary. See *Creating a security group to filter a GPO* in *Chapter 6, Software Distribution using Group Policy*.

You should note that while SRP can be used to set a given application to launch by default as a *Basic User*, users running with administrative privileges can start the application configured in SRP to launch as a Basic User, in *Unrestricted* mode from the command line using `runas`.

AppLocker

Designed as a replacement for Software Restriction Policy and introduced in Windows 7, AppLocker is designed to overcome the shortcomings of SRP. Small and medium enterprises rarely deploy SRP, especially in Windows XP. This is due to problems with launching applications from shortcuts, and because path rules are too easy to circumvent in many cases, SRP certificate rules offer limited configuration options and hash rules are problematic when applications are upgraded. AppLocker is more flexible and easier to configure, with the ability to automatically generate rules and apply strong certificate rules based on a variety of different criteria.

AppLocker's complete functionality is only available in Enterprise and Ultimate SKUs of Windows 7. Windows 7 Professional allows AppLocker policies to be created for the purposes of auditing software use, but policies cannot be enforced to prevent software from running.

Automatically generating AppLocker rules

AppLocker includes a wizard that can scan selected directories and automatically create rules to allow applications to run based on publisher or hash rules. Let's see how this works by scanning the executables in the C:\Program Files directory. Log in to Windows Server 2008 R2:

1. Open the **Group Policy Management Console** as a domain administrator from **Administrative Tools** on the **Start** menu and expand your **Active Directory** forest and domain in the left pane.

2. Right-click the **Clients** OU and select **Create a GPO in this domain, and Link it here** from the menu. In the **New GPO** dialog, type **AppLocker** in the **Name** field and click **OK**.

3. Expand the **Clients** OU in the left pane, right-click the **AppLocker GPO**, and select **Edit** from the menu.

4. In the **Group Policy Management Editor** window, under **Computer Configuration** in the left pane expand **Policies | Windows Settings | Security Settings | Application Control Policies | AppLocker**.

5. In the left pane, right-click **Executable Rules** and select **Automatically Generate Rules** from the menu.

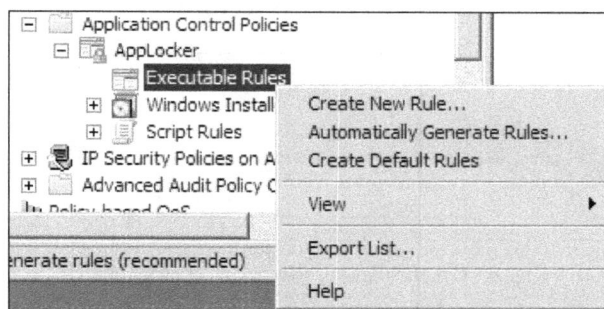

6. In the **Automatically Generate Executable Rules** dialog, accept the default settings on the **Folder and Permissions** screen by clicking **Next** to apply rules to all users for applications located in the Program Files directory.

7. On the **Rules Preferences** screen, accept the default settings by clicking **Next**.

8. On the **Review Rules** screen, click **View rules that will be automatically created**.

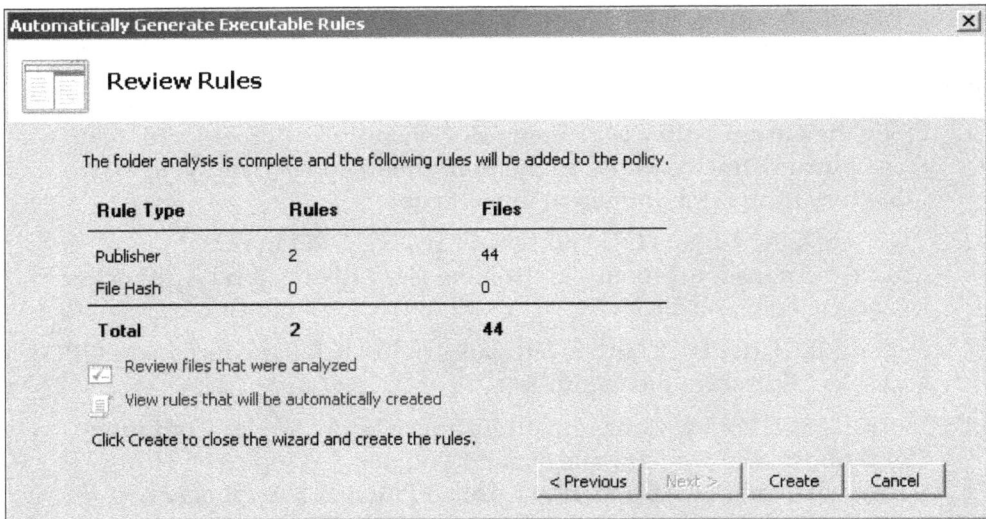

9. You'll see that only two rules have been created despite the large number of executables in the `Program Files` directory.

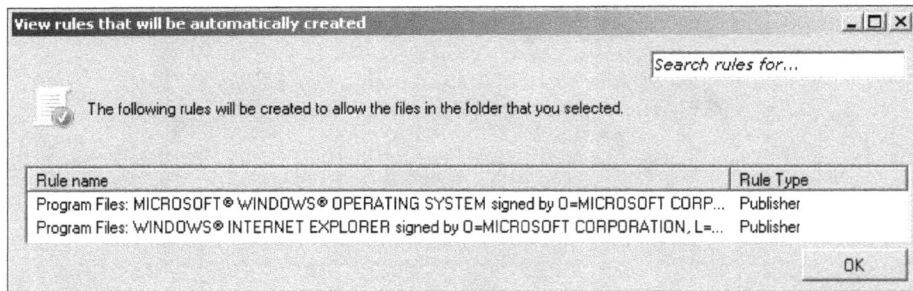

10. In the **View rules that will be automatically created** dialog, click **OK**. Click **Create** on the **Review Rules** screen. In the **AppLocker** dialog, click **Yes** to add the default rules to this list.

Creating default AppLocker rules

The default AppLocker executable rules can also be created by right-clicking **Executable Rules** in the left pane of **Group Policy Management Editor** and selecting **Create Default Rules** from the menu.

Now you'll see the three default rules and the rules we automatically generated in the right pane of Group Policy Management Editor.

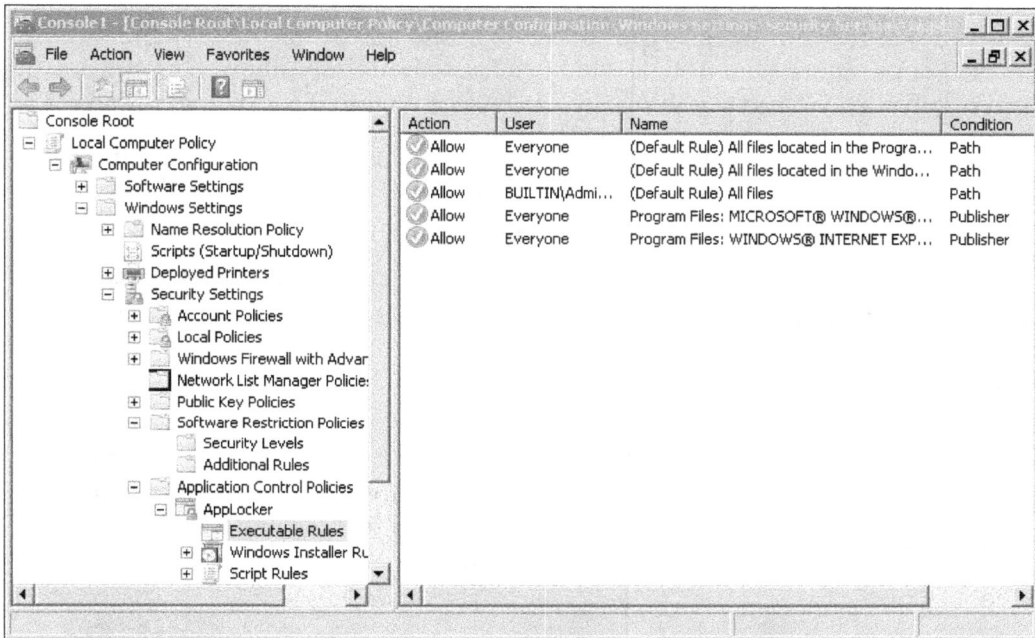

Action	User	Name	Condition
Allow	Everyone	All files located in the `Program Files` folder	Path
Allow	Everyone	All files located in the `Windows` folder	Path
Allow	Everyone	All files	Path

> In this case, the publisher rules automatically generated by the wizard are not needed if the default rules are also enabled. You can now delete the publisher rules by right-clicking them and selecting **Delete** from the menu.

Manually creating an AppLocker rule to blacklist an application

Let's continue configuring our **AppLocker** GPO and add a rule that will block a specified application, even if it's located in a trusted directory allowed by the default AppLocker rules. Continue editing the GPO we created in the previous section:

1. Under **AppLocker** in the left pane of Group Policy Management Editor, right-click **Executable Rules** and select **Create New Rule** from the menu.

2. In the **Create New Rules** dialog, click **Next** on the **Before You Begin** screen.

3. On the **Permissions** screen, under **Action** select **Deny** and click **Next**.

4. On the **Conditions** screen, leave the default rule selection of **Publisher** and click **Next**.

5. On the **Publisher** screen under **Reference file**, click **Browse** and select `iexplorer.exe` in `C:\Program Files\Internet Explorer`. Leaving the slider at the bottom set to **File version** means that the binary must be signed by the publisher (Microsoft in this case), and the three extended attributes of **Product name**, **File name**, and **File version** must match the displayed information. Click **Next** to continue.

> The extended attributes are obtained from the `.exe` file and not the certificate.

> **AppLocker publisher rules**
>
> If you move the slider up the scale, matching requirements are subtracted. So if you move the slider up to **Product name**, the binary must be signed by the publisher and the **Product name** extended attribute must match the displayed information. The two other extended attributes, **File name** and **File version**, will be ignored.

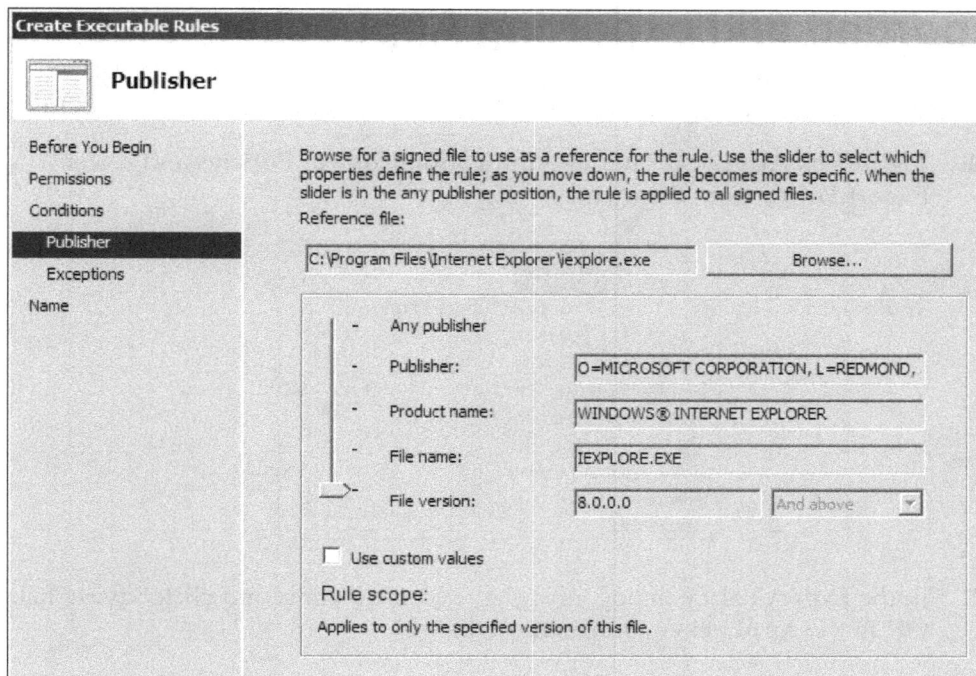

6. In this example we don't want to include any exceptions, so click **Next** on the **Exceptions** screen.

7. Change or accept the rule name on the **Name and Description** screen and then click **Create**.

You'll see the new **Deny** rule appear in the right pane of Group Policy Management Editor.

If you now update Group Policy on a Windows 7 machine in the Clients OU, you'll find that the user is able to run all applications in the `C:\Program Files` directory apart from Internet Explorer.

Importing and exporting AppLocker rules

Finally, if you need to save or copy AppLocker rules then they can easily be imported or exported using Group Policy Management Editor. It's done as follows:

1. Right-click **AppLocker** under **Application Control Policies** and select **Export Policy** from the menu.

2. In the **Export Policy** dialog, give the `.xml` file a name and click **Save**. Click **OK** in the **AppLocker** confirmation dialog.

> **Apply GPOs with AppLocker policy to Windows 7 only**
>
> Use a WMI filter to make sure any GPO objects containing AppLocker policy are applied to Windows 7 machines only. See *Targeting devices using WMI filters and security groups* in *Chapter 6, Software Distribution using Group Policy*. You should retire Software Restriction Policies in most cases, on Windows 7 machines and use AppLocker exclusively. If you must use both, AppLocker policy takes precedence over SRP.

Summary

In this chapter we've learned how to further secure standard users without impacting functionality, and how to give administrative users some of the benefits of running as a standard user by configuring applications to launch with a stripped-down version of their security token. Before proceeding to the next chapter you should be able to:

- Configure the default SRP or AppLocker rules to create a basic whitelist that prevents standard users from running portable applications or launching a process that might hijack a running application

- Prevent an application from running using an SRP or AppLocker blacklist

- Configure applications to run as a *Basic User* for local administrators

The following chapter will help you prepare Windows XP for use in a managed, Least Privilege environment.

10
Least Privilege in Windows XP

Development of Windows Vista was reset in 2004, so that it could be based on security improvements that were to be included in Windows XP Service Pack 2. It was the first Windows operating system to be designed using Microsoft's **Security Development Lifecycle (SDL)**, which includes Least Privilege Security as an important design goal for the system and applications that run on it. User Account Control is intended to make Least Privilege Security a reality for ordinary users. Windows XP and NT-based versions of Windows that came before Vista have a security model similar to the current versions of Windows, but are more difficult to run as a standard user.

Some important functionality, such as changing the time zone, is not permitted under a standard user account in Windows XP—a problem that Microsoft only rectified in Vista. With the trend moving towards portable computing, this is just one example of why system administrators frequently grant users administrative privileges to access a handful of minor, but nevertheless important features.

While Vista makes it realistic for home users to run as a standard user the first time, this has always been possible in enterprise computing since the early days of Windows NT, even if there are some important issues to work around.

In this chapter we'll look at:

- Refreshing Windows XP using the Microsoft Deployment Toolkit
- Using the Application Compatibility Toolkit to identify problems with applications caused by Least Privilege Security
- Understanding limitations that users may face when running with a Least Privilege Security account, and how to mitigate those problems
- Handling ActiveX controls in Windows XP

Installing Windows XP using the Microsoft Deployment Toolkit

Although XP and later versions of Windows use different technologies for the installation process, the Microsoft Deployment Toolkit makes things easy by providing an almost identical deployment process for XP and Vista/Windows 7. Therefore, refer to the previous chapter for the guide to deploy Vista, and you will realize that there is only a single difference while creating a task sequence.

Providing a Volume License product key for an MDT XP Task Sequence

When creating a Task Sequence in MDT to deploy Windows XP, you should specify your Volume License product key in the **Specify Product Key** dialog box. Vista and Windows 7 have a different system for licensing multiple copies of the operating system in a corporate environment, hence the divergence in this step when deploying Windows XP:

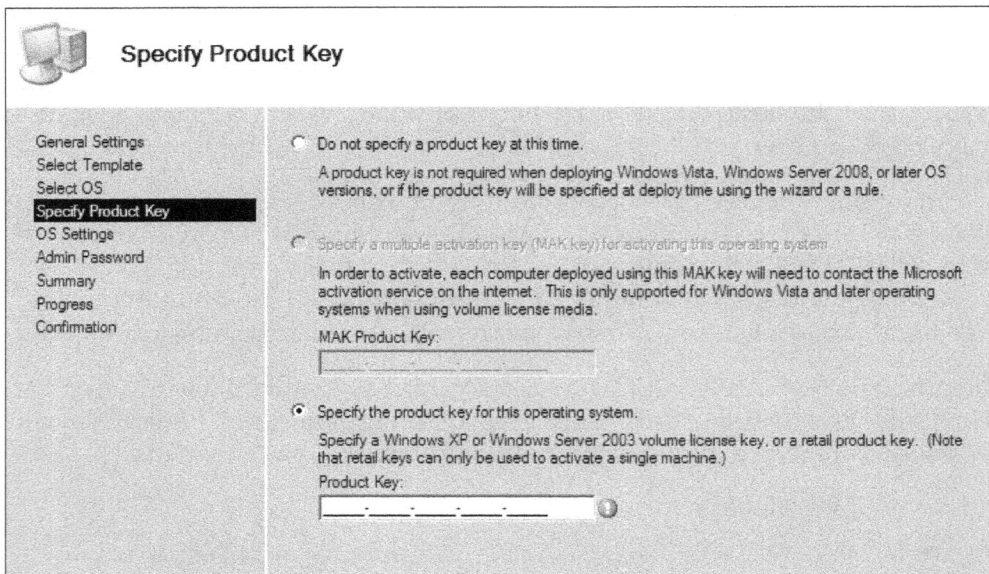

Windows XP security model

While there is no major difference in the underlying security model in XP and Vista, there are many small changes that you should be aware of—the most important being the role of local groups and privileges assigned to them.

> **Privilege**
>
> A privilege is the ability (or *right*) of a user account or group to perform a specified system task. For instance, changing the system time is considered a system task and therefore requires the `Change the system time` privilege.

Power users

In Vista, Microsoft deprecated the role of the Power Users group, which had often been used by system administrators to grant additional privileges to users on their PCs, but was essentially the same as the Administrators group with a few less rights. The group still exists for backwards compatibility, but isn't granted any rights, thus rendering it defunct.

Users would often request that they be made a power user if system administrators didn't want to add them to the Administrators group. The privileges granted to Power Users in Windows XP allow members of this group to make system-wide changes, thereby running most of the same risks as Administrators. In the past, some popular applications required users to be a member of the Power Users group to work correctly, causing additional problems for system administrators.

Network Configuration Operators

Introduced in Windows XP, the **Network Configuration Operators** group allows users to modify TCP/IP settings on *Network Interface Cards* (*NICs*). The Network Configuration Operators group has administrative privileges because it lets users make system-wide changes (but nevertheless has significantly fewer rights than both Power Users and Administrators). Hence, it should be considered in cases where a user needs to modify network settings as part of their everyday tasks. An engineer who's travelling may be an example of a user that fits into this category.

Support_<1234>

Support_<1234> is used for logging on to *Remote Assistance* — a built-in feature that allows help desk professionals to provide assistance to users across the Internet or corporate network. This account appears in Windows XP with a unique number in place of <1234>. The Support_<1234> account is removed in Vista.

User rights

NT rights are divided into logon rights and privileges. There are various command-line tools that can be used to enumerate and modify user rights such as `whoami` and `ntrights`. User rights can also be modified using Group Policy, but care should be taken as any configuration applied from a Group Policy Object overwrites the local settings, as opposed to amending the existing configuration. Therefore, you should audit each machine to check what existing user rights are configured in local settings to avoid accidentally deleting a previously granted right. If a GPO is no longer applied to a computer, the original local settings for user rights are restored.

Modifying logon rights and privileges

Local policy or Group Policy can be used to set or modify NT Rights. To access local policy on XP, log on as an administrator:

1. Click **Run** in the **Start** menu, type **mmc** into the **Run** dialog box, and click **OK**.

2. In the console window, press *Ctrl+M* and select **Group Policy Object Editor** in the **Add or remove Snap-ins** dialog and click **Add**.

3. Click **Finish** in the **Select Group Policy Object** window.

4. Click **OK** in the **Add or Remove Snap-in** dialog.

5. In the console window, go to **Local Computer Policy | Computer Configuration | Windows Settings | Security Settings | Local Policies** and select **User Rights Assignments**.

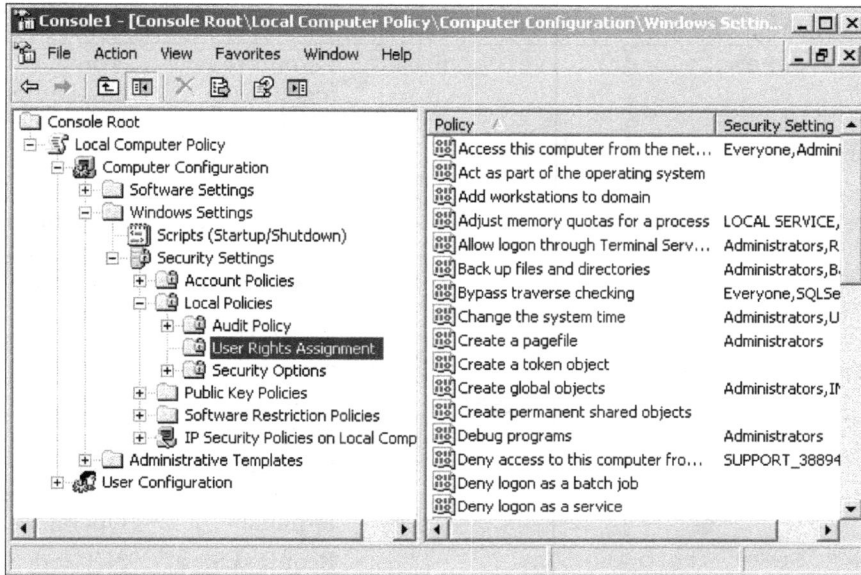

Logon rights

Used to control access to a computer for a given user account or group, logon rights can be set in local or Group Policy for local, remote, and special access such as logon as a batch job for *Task Scheduler*.

> **Allow a group and deny a subset**
>
> When assigning NT Rights, remember that *deny* always takes precedence. Therefore you should broadly set *allow* for a *right* and then deny a smaller group of users.

Windows XP logon rights are as follows:

Right	Programmatic name	Description	Granted to
Access this computer from the network	`SeNetworkLogonRight`	Allows to access the computer from another device across the network.	Administrators, Power Users, Users, Everyone, and Backup Operators

Right	Programmatic name	Description	Granted to
Allow logon through Terminal Services	`SeRemoteInteractiveLogonRight`	Permits remote logon using the Remote Desktop Client.	Administrators and Remote Desktop Users
Log on as a batch job	`SeBatchLogonRight`	Used to execute scripts and batch files run by the task scheduler service.	Administrator, System, and Support_<1234>
Log on locally	`SeInteractiveLogonRight`	Required for basic logon functionality at the local terminal.	Administrators, Power Users, Users, Guest, and Backup Operators
Log on as a service	`SeServiceLogonRight`	Required for a standard user account to log on as a system service.	Network Service
Deny access to this computer from the network	`SeDenyNetworkLogonRight`	Prevents users connecting to local resources from a networked device.	Support_<1234>
Deny logon locally	`SeDenyInteractiveLogonRight`	Prevents logon at the local terminal.	Guest
Deny logon as a batch job	`SeDenyBatchLogonRight`	Prevents an account from running a batch file or script as a scheduled task.	Unassigned
Deny logon as a service	`SeDenyServiceLogonRight`	Prevents a security principle from being used to log on as a service.	Unassigned

Right	Programmatic name	Description	Granted to
Deny logon through Terminal Services	`SeDenyRemoteInteractive LogonRight`	Prevents logon remotely using the Remote Desktop Client.	Unassigned

Privileges

When you configure Least Privilege Security on the desktop, you may need to alter the default system privileges to allow standard users additional access to system settings. I've listed all the privileges in the following two tables. The first lists more useful privileges and the second lists more obscure privileges for completeness.

Commonly used privileges in Windows XP are as follows:

Right	Programmatic name	Description	Granted to
Add workstations to domain	`SeMachineAccountPrivilege`	Must be granted via the Default Domain Controllers GPO when the computer is part of an Active Directory domain.	Unassigned
Back up files and directories	`SeBackupPrivilege`	Allows holders to bypass Access Control Lists so that system files can be backed up or restored.	Administrators and Backup Operators
Bypass traverse checking	`SeChangeNotifyPrivilege`	Allows users to jump (traverse) to a folder, even if they have no permission to access previous folders in the hierarchy.	Administrators, Backup Operators, Power Users, Users, and Everyone

Right	Programmatic name	Description	Granted to
Change the system time	SeSystemTimePrivilege	Allows users to change the system clock and time zone.	Power Users and Administrators
Create a pagefile	SeCreatePagefilePrivilege	Allows users to modify existing and create new pagefiles.	Administrators
Debug programs	SeDebugPrivilege	Allows developers and system administrators to debug programs, but shouldn't be assigned on a permanent basis as it gives access to critical system-wide configuration.	Administrators
Load and unload device drivers	SeLoadDriverPrivilege	Required to install unsigned drivers. Additionally, for this privilege to work, users must be a member of the Administrators or Power Users group.	Administrators

Right	Programmatic name	Description	Granted to
Modify firmware environment values	`SeSystemEnvironmentPrivilege`	Allows users to modify environment values that are found under *Advanced System Settings* in the *System and Security* control panel.	Administrators
Perform volume maintenance tasks	`SeManageVolumePrivilege`	Allows privilege holders to manage disks through *Disk Management*, locally or remotely.	Administrators
Remove computer from docking station	`SeUndockPrivilege`	Lets users remove a notebook from a docking station using the *Eject PC* option on the Start menu.	Administrators, Power Users, and Users
Restore files and directories	`SeRestorePrivilege`	Users can bypass file and folder permissions to back up and restore files.	Administrators and Backup Operators

Vista and Windows 7 NT Rights

The concept of NT Rights still exists in Vista and Windows 7, but you should note that there are some differences from XP in the way rights are assigned to users.

Less commonly used Windows XP privileges are as follows:

Right	Programmatic name	Description	Granted to
Act as part of the operating system	`SeTcbPrivilege`	Used for system services to impersonate another user account and assume the privileges of that account and even add more privileges than owned by the user impersonated.	Unassigned/ Local System
Adjust memory quotas for a process	`SeIncreaseQuota Privilege`	Allows the holder to modify the amount of memory that a process can use.	Administrators, Local Service, and Network Service
Create a token object	`SeCreateTokenPrivilege`	The privilege allows a process to create an access token.	Unassigned/ Local System
Enable computer and user accounts to be trusted for delegation	`SeEnableDelegation Privilege`	Not relevant for desktop/notebook PCs.	Unassigned
Force shutdown from a remote system	`SeRemoteShutdown Privilege`	Allows holders to shut down or restart a system remotely using the `shutdown.exe` command.	Administrators
Generate security audits	`SeAuditPrivilege`	Allows a process to write to the Event Log. This might be necessary for developers.	Local Service and Network Service/Local System
Impersonate a client after authentication	`SeImpersonatePrivilege`	Lets processes assume the logged on user's rights.	Administrators and Local Service

Right	Programmatic name	Description	Granted to
Lock pages in memory	`SeLockMemoryPrivilege`	Used to prevent a process from being paged out of physical RAM.	Unassigned / Local System
Manage auditing and security log	`SeSecurityPrivilege`	Allows users to set auditing on objects such as files and Active Directory objects. Privilege holders can also read and delete items from the security log.	Administrators
Profile single process	`SeProfileSingleProcess Privilege`	This privilege is required for the Performance snap-in to monitor an application process if System Monitor is set to use **Windows Management Instrumentation (WMI)** to gather performance data.	Administrators and Power Users
Profile system performance	`SeSystemProfilePrivilege`	As above, only required if using WMI in System Monitor to monitor a system process.	Administrators
Shut down the system	`SeShutdownPrivilege`	This privilege is mainly of interest in Windows Server.	Administrators, Backup Operators, Power Users, and Users

Right	Programmatic name	Description	Granted to
Synchronize directory service data	`SeSynchAgentPrivilege`	Allows users to bypass security settings and read all objects and properties in Active Directory. This privilege is only relevant on domain controllers.	Unassigned
Take ownership of files or other objects	`SeTakeOwnershipPrivilege`	Allows privilege holders to take ownership of secured objects, such as files and registry keys.	Administrators

CD burning

Windows XP introduced basic CD writing capabilities, and uses the built-in **Image Mastering Application Programming Interface (IMAPI)** service to provision the feature. From Windows Explorer, users can drag files to a compatible CD/DVD-RW drive and use a wizard to start the burning process. Windows Media Player also utilizes IMAPI for burning audio CDs. Curiously, while IMAPI can be updated to version 2.0 in Windows XP to support DVD burning, Windows Explorer still cannot burn to DVD after the upgrade. The update is for third-party software that utilizes IMAPI v2.0.

You can download IMAPI v2.0 for Windows XP SP2 and SP3 from: http://support.microsoft.com/?kbid=932716

Third-party CD/DVD burning software

While everything should be straightforward for standard users who use software that leverages the built-in IMAPI service, some popular third-party products that provide more advanced burning capabilities need modification to run without administrative privileges, as they access low-level drivers to send SCSI or IDE commands directly to the CD/DVD burning hardware. Two of the most popular solutions for Windows XP that need modification to run as a standard user are Nero Burning ROM and CDBurnerXP.

Nero Burning ROM

To correctly run as a standard user, versions 5 and 6 of Nero Burning ROM require additional software called *Nero BurnRights*, which can be downloaded from Nero's website. Once it is installed, system administrators can configure which users are allowed to burn CDs.

> CD authoring software such as Nero and other third-party solutions require direct access to low-level drivers, which send SCSI/IDE commands directly to devices such as hard drives and CD ROMs. However, granting this level of access to standard users allows them to bypass standard security controls, which would permit them to format disks and read data stored by other users of the same machine.
>
> You can download Nero BurnRights from:
>
> `http://www.nero.com/enu/support-nero6-tools-utilities.html`

Installing Nero BurnRights

Log on to Windows XP as an administrator:

1. Double-click `NeroBurnRightsIntaller.exe`. Click **Next** in the **Nero BurnRights Installation Wizard** dialog.

2. Click **Finish** to complete the installation. The **Nero BurnRights** control panel will open and you can select **Everybody** on the **Burn Rights** tab to give all users access to burning. Alternatively, if you want more granular control over who's allowed to burn CD/DVDs, you can select **Members of the group Nero**. Click **OK** to complete the procedure.

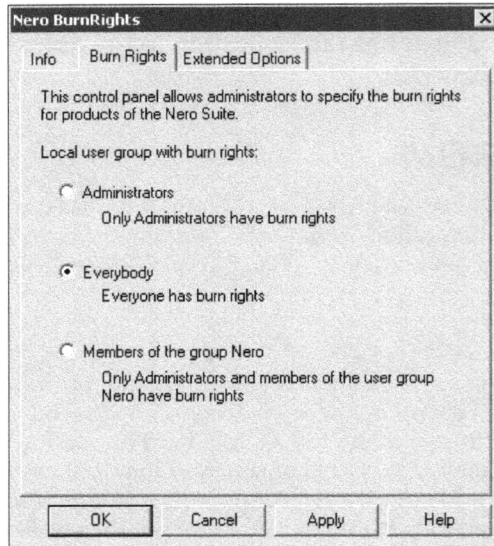

3. If the **Nero** group doesn't exist, you'll be prompted to create the group. Click **Yes** to create the group automatically.

4. You'll then be asked to restart the computer to apply the new settings. Click **Yes** to reboot.

5. Once the computer has rebooted, open **Nero BurnRights** in the **Control Panel** and select the **Extended Options** tab. Here system administrators can apply settings to any additional CD/DVD drives that are added to the system, or reset the configuration.

6. Click **OK** to close the control panel .

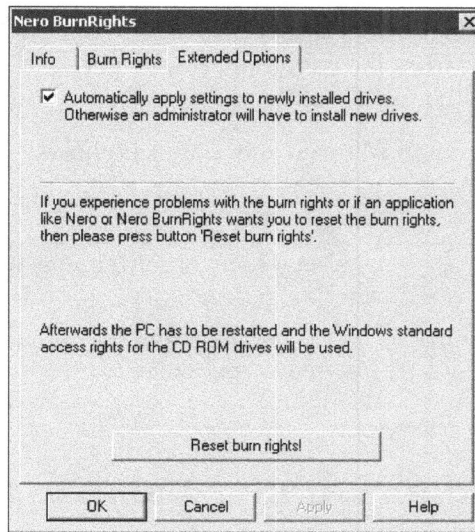

If you opted to grant burn rights to members of the Nero group, you need to add users to the new group in Computer Management:

1. Right-click **My Computer** on the **Start** menu and select **Manage** from the menu. Expand **Local Users and Groups** under the **System Tools** node in **Computer Management** and select **Groups**.

2. In the right pane you'll see a group called **Nero** where you can add users who are permitted to burn CDs or DVDs on this system if you chose to use the Nero group in the Nero BurnRights control panel.

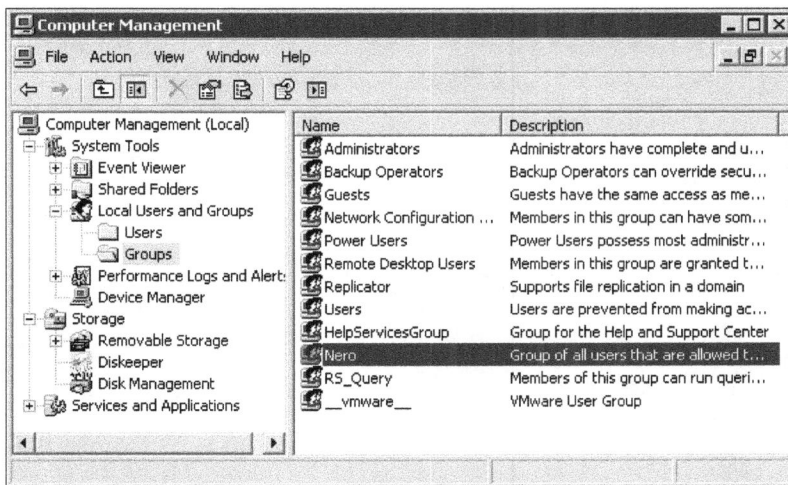

Configuring Nero BurnRights from the command line

If you want to set options from the command line as part of a script, `NeroBurnRights.exe` in the install folder supports four configuration switches.

The Nero BurnRights command-line switches are as follows:

Switch	Action
`/admin`	Allows only administrators to burn discs.
`/all`	Lets all local users write discs.
`/group="<group name>"`	Allows you to specify a pre-created group of users who are permitted to burn discs.
`/reset`	Configures Nero BurnRights to the install defaults.

Allowing non-administrative users to burn discs in CDBurnerXP

CDBurnerXP setup allows system administrators to install Numedia Soft's NMSAccess service, which lets non-administrative users burn discs with software that accesses the hardware using low-level drivers as the following screenshot demonstrates:

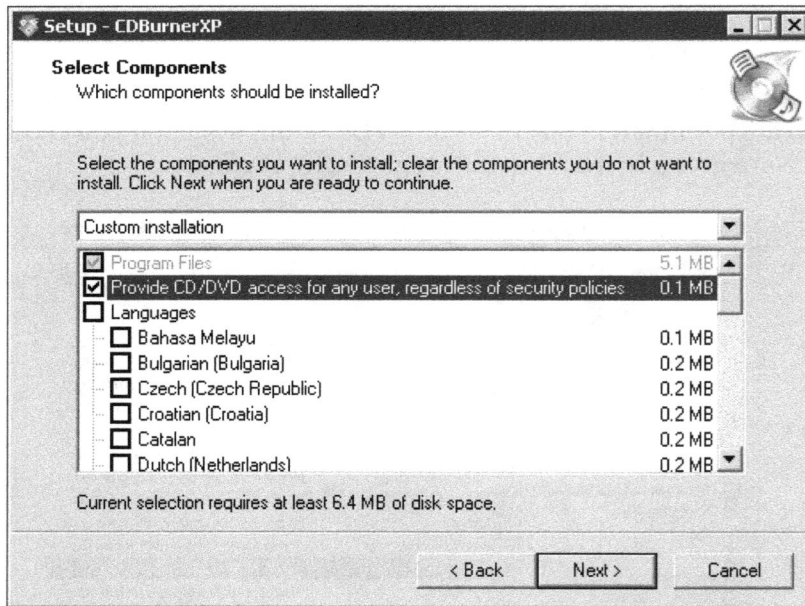

Additional security settings

While the configuration settings that we just discussed for third-party burning applications should be enough, in some cases there are two Windows security settings that you may need to change to get burning to work for standard users.

Restricting access to removable media

The `AllocateDASD` string value in the registry can be configured using local or Group Policy and by default allows only members of the Administrators group to format and eject removable media. This setting can be changed to Administrators and Power Users or Administrators and Interactive Users. Depending on the software users have for burning CDs, you may need to set the `AllocateDASD` string to Administrators and Interactive Users.

To change this setting in local policy, log on to XP as an administrator:

1. Click **Run** on the **Start** menu. Type `gpedit.msc` in the **Run** dialog and click **OK**.

2. In the **Group Policy** window, navigate to **Computer Configuration | Windows Settings | Security Settings | Local Policies | Security Options**.

3. In the right-hand pane double-click **Devices: Allowed to format and eject removable media**.

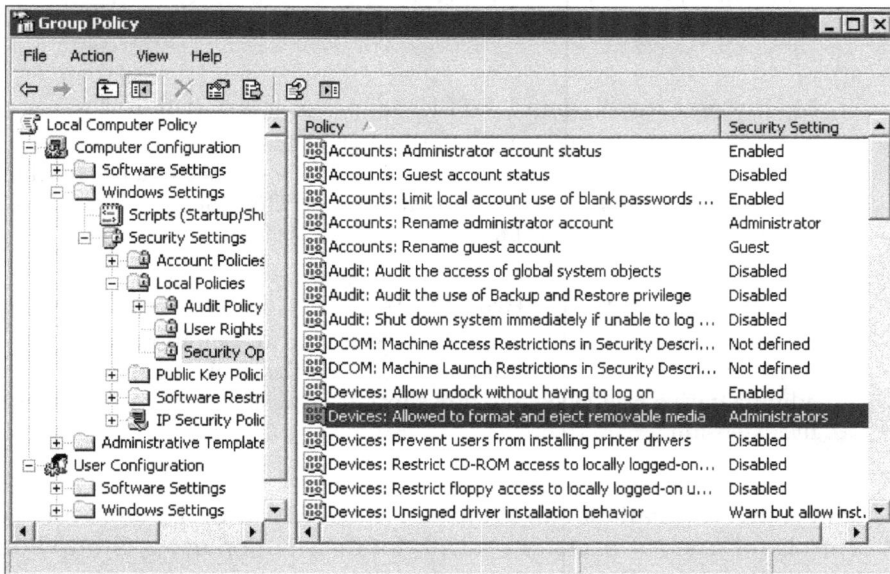

4   On the **Local Security Setting** tab, select **Administrators and Interactive Users** from the drop-down menu and click **OK**.

5. Close the **Group Policy** window.

ActiveX controls

ActiveX controls in Windows XP present a significant problem because administrative privileges are required to install them. Before the release of Internet Explorer 8, ActiveX controls, which are essentially .dll or .ocx files that provide additional browser functionality, were installed in a protected Windows directory. This meant that users needed to be an administrator to install a control. Probably the most common ActiveX control in use today is Adobe's Flash Player. There's barely a site on the Internet that doesn't make use of this control somewhere on its pages.

Internet Explorer 8 introduced the concept of installing ActiveX controls per-user, but unfortunately this is not supported in Windows XP. This allows standard users to run the ActiveX control and install the necessary files to their user profile, significantly reducing the risk of compromising critical system files. However, this requires developers to repackage their controls, and at the time of writing, very few commercially available ActiveX controls could be installed per-user. No doubt this situation will change over time. If you have ActiveX controls that have been developed internally, then changes need to be made to the installer so that the control can be installed per-user, if appropriate.

Modifying ActiveX control .inf files for per-user installation

A new section called [Deployment] can be added to the .inf file, which is embedded inside the control's .cab file, to specify a per-machine or per-user install. For more information on MSDN, you can refer to:
http://msdn.microsoft.com/en-us/library/
dd433049(VS.85).aspx.

Group Policy software installation

Group Policy can be used to distribute software to computers using Windows Installer without the need for the local user to have administrative privileges. Windows Installer packages have .msi as the file extension.

The upshot of ActiveX installation in Windows XP is that administrators must install ActiveX controls for users or package controls for distribution using Group Policy Software Installation or another distribution system.

Flash Player

Adobe provides organizations with different methods for installing Flash Player. You can download Flash as an `.exe` file and run a silent install using a script, or deploy it to standard users by assigning the Flash Player `.msi` file to computers using Group Policy Software Installation. To download the `.exe` or `.msi` installers for Flash Player, you need to apply for a free distribution license.

> You can find the Flash Player distribution license here:
> `http://www.adobe.com/products/players/fpsh_`
> `distribution1.html`

Acrobat Reader

Adobe Acrobat Reader is an example of an application having a browser component that lets users read PDF documents directly in their web browser. You can extract an `.msi` file from the Acrobat Reader installer for use with Group Policy Software Installation, and assign the package to computers so that it can be installed without administrative privileges.

> You can extract the `.msi` package from the installer using the `-nos_ne` switch:
> `AdbeRdr90_en_US.exe -nos_ne`

Silverlight

Not yet as dominant as the omnipresent Flash Player, Silverlight is Microsoft's offering for dynamic web content and is required for some websites. Supplied as an `.exe` file, `.msi` and `.msp` files can be extracted for use with Group Policy Software Installation to assign the package to computers without administrative privileges.

> **Extracting .msi and .msp files from SilverLight.exe**
> Use the following command line to extract Silverlight `.msi` and `.msp` files to a temporary directory:
> `silverlight.exe /x:c:\temp /u`

Other popular ActiveX controls

It's likely that you'll need to provision Flash Player and Acrobat Reader to all users, and possibly Silverlight. There are other applications that use browser components for viewing specific kinds of web content that may also be requested from time to time, including Realplayer, Apple QuickTime, and Sun Java. For users who need only occasional access to websites that require these applications, consider providing remote access to a PC or terminal server where these plug-ins are pre-installed and kept up-to-date. While you should avoid installing the following applications on your network, be prepared just in case a user makes an unexpected request.

RealPlayer

There is some audio and video content on the web that requires RealPlayer. If RealPlayer is needed on a regular basis, consider licensing the enterprise version of the software. There is no `.msi` package for the standard version.

> **RealPlayer Enterprise**
> http://www.realnetworks.com/products/rpe/index.html

QuickTime

It's possible to extract an `.msi` file from the `QuickTime.exe`, but deploying the `.msi` through Group Policy Software Installation isn't straightforward. To extract the `.msi` from `quicktimeinstaller.exe` you need to run the executable, and during the install process copy the `.msi` from `C:\Documents and Settings\username\Local Settings\Temp` or `C:\Documents and Settings\All Users\Application Data\Apple Computer\Installer Cache\QuickTime 7.55.90.70`. The directory name may vary depending on the version of QuickTime being extracted.

Sun Java Runtime Environment

Again, required for viewing content on some websites, the Java Runtime Environment is also needed to run applications coded in Java. You need to run the offline installer for Windows and then grab the `.msi` file from the temporary cache `C:\Documents and Settings\</user>\Local Settings\ApplicationData\Sun\Java\ jre1.6.0_05\jre1.6.0_05.msi`. The directory name may vary depending on the version of Java being extracted. Once you have the `.msi` file, it can be assigned to computers using Group Policy Software Installation.

> **Java Runtime Environment offline installers**
> http://www.java.com/en/download/manual.jsp

Alternatives to QuickTime and RealPlayer

If you don't want to install the QuickTime or RealPlayer applications on your
network, there are Real Alternative and QuickTime Alternative, which play back
the required media files without some of the annoying features of the full version
software. You should install software and codecs only from trusted sources.

Changing the system time and time zone

Giving standard users the ability to change the system time is not recommended.
However, for Windows XP notebook users who travel, you may not have a choice.
Here are the three primary reasons for restricting standard user access to the
system time:

- In a domain environment, PCs must have their time synchronized with
  domain controllers for successful logon.

- Allowing users to modify the system time will put your organization
  beyond some of the regulatory requirements.

- When users control the system time, it can be difficult or impossible to
  investigate security incidents and prove the order of events. This may
  hinder detection of malicious activity..

> **ISO 27001 Information Security Standard**
>
> 10.10.6 Clock Synchronization. The clocks of all relevant information
> processing systems within an organization or security domain shall be
> synchronized with an agreed accurate time source.

Changing the system time

To grant standard users the **Change the system time** privilege in Windows XP:

1. Open the **Group Policy Management Console** on a domain controller as a domain administrator from **Administrative Tools** on the **Start** menu and expand your Active Directory forest and domain in the left pane.

2. Locate your **Clients** OU, right-click it, and select **Create a GPO in this domain, and Link it here...** from the menu.

3. In the **New GPO** dialog, type **Change the system time** privilege in the **Name** field and click **OK**.

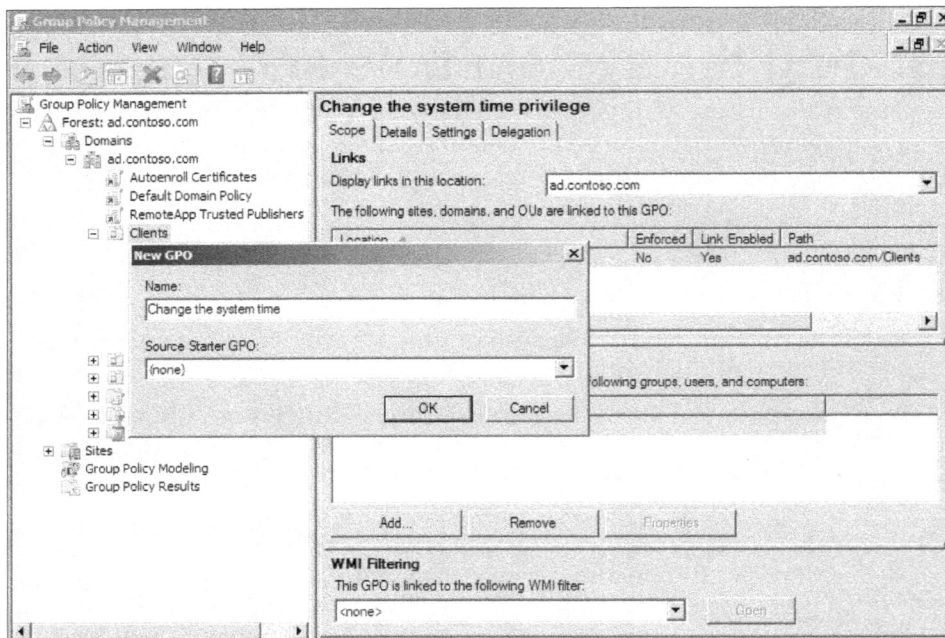

4. Expand the **Clients** OU in the left pane, right-click **Change the system time privilege,** and select **Edit...** from the menu.

5. In the **Group Policy Management Editor** window, go to **Computer Configuration | Policies | Windows Settings | Security Settings | Local Policies| User Rights Assignment**. Double-click **Change the system time** policy in the right pane.

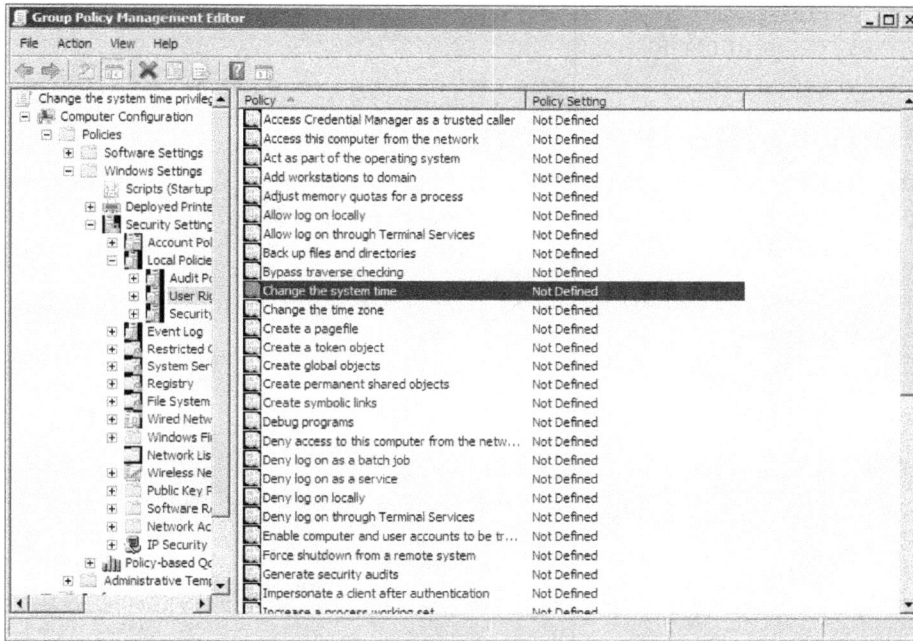

6. On the **Security Policy Setting** tab, select **Define these policy settings** and click **Add User or Group...**.

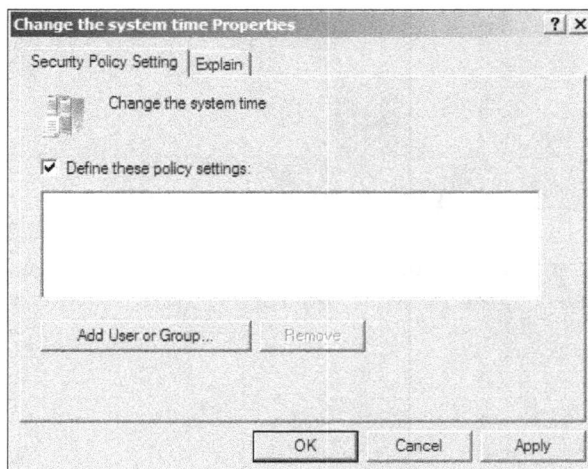

7. Type **users, administrators, power users** in the **Add User or Group** dialog and click **OK**.

8. Click **OK** in the **Change the system time Properties** dialog. You can now close the **Group Policy** window.

Once **Group Policy** has refreshed, you will be able to open the **Date and Time** control panel by double-clicking on the time in the taskbar.

Changing the time zone

To allow standard users to change the time zone, you need to follow the instructions given previously for changing the system time privilege, and then relax permissions on a registry key as follows. Log on to Windows XP as a local administrator and:

1. Click **Run** on the **Start** menu. Type regedit in the **Run** dialog and click **OK**. Navigate to the following registry key:

   HKEY_LOCAL_MACHINE\SYSTEM\CurrentControlSet\Control\
   TimeZoneInformation.

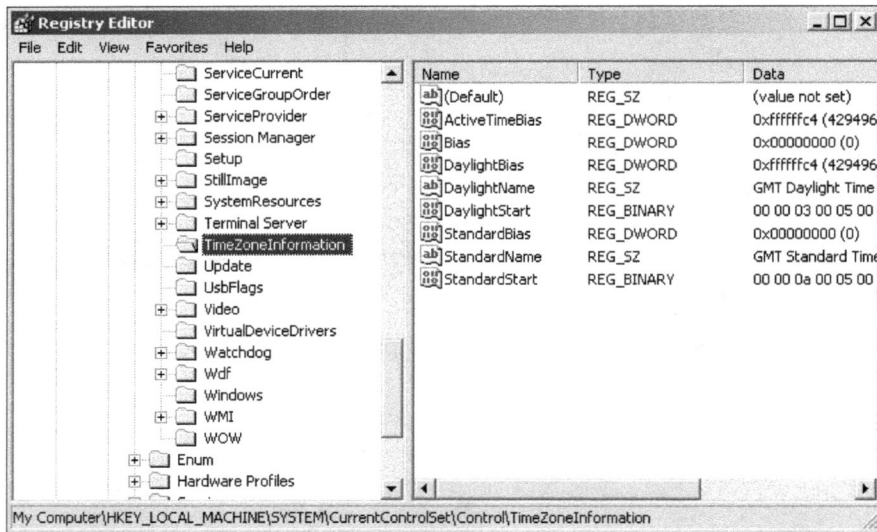

2. Right-click **TimeZoneInformation** and select **Permissions** from the menu. Click **Advanced** in the **Permissions for TimeZoneInformation** dialog.

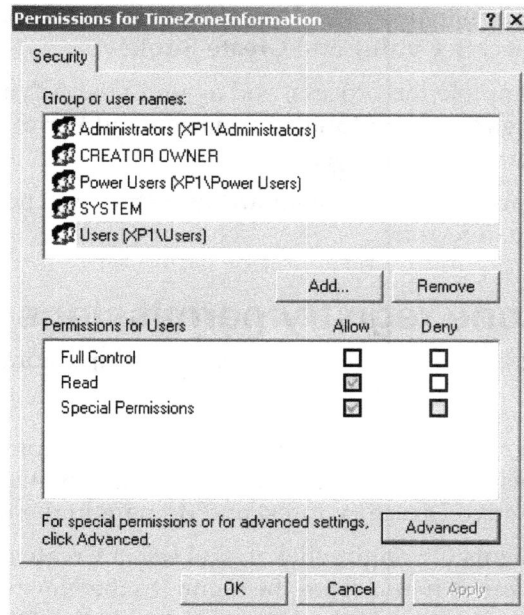

3. On the **Permissions** tab under **Permission entries** select **Users...** and click **Edit...**.

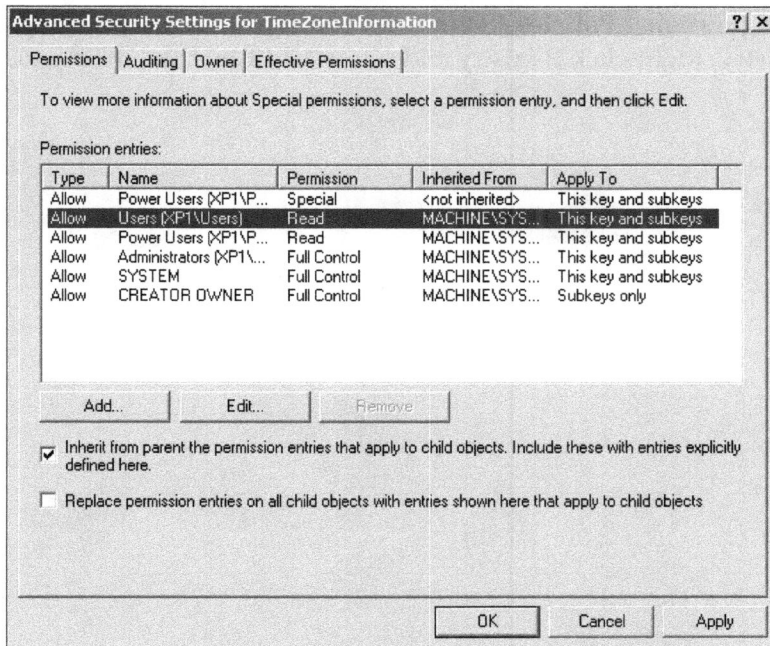

Some of the permissions we need are already granted, but we need to additionally select **Set Value** and **Create Subkey**.

4. Click **OK** to complete the process, and again in the **Advanced Security Settings for TimeZoneInformation** and **Permissions for TimeZoneInformation** dialogs.

Close **Registry Editor** and log on as a standard user. You will now be able to successfully change the time zone.

Setting time zone registry permissions using a GPO

Registry permissions can also be configured across multiple computers using Group Policy.

1. Open the **Group Policy Management Console** on a domain controller as a domain administrator from **Administrative Tools** on the **Start** menu and expand your Active Directory forest and domain in the left pane.

2. Locate your Clients OU, right-click it, and select **Create a GPO in this domain, and Link it here...** from the menu. In the **New GPO** dialog, type **Time Zone Registry** in the **Name** field and click **OK**.

3. Expand the Clients OU in the left pane, right-click the **Time Zone Registry** GPO, and select **Edit...** from the menu.

4. In the **Group Policy Management Editor** window, navigate to **Computer Configuration | Policies | Windows Settings | Security Settings | Registry**. Right-click **Registry** and select **Add Key** from the menu.

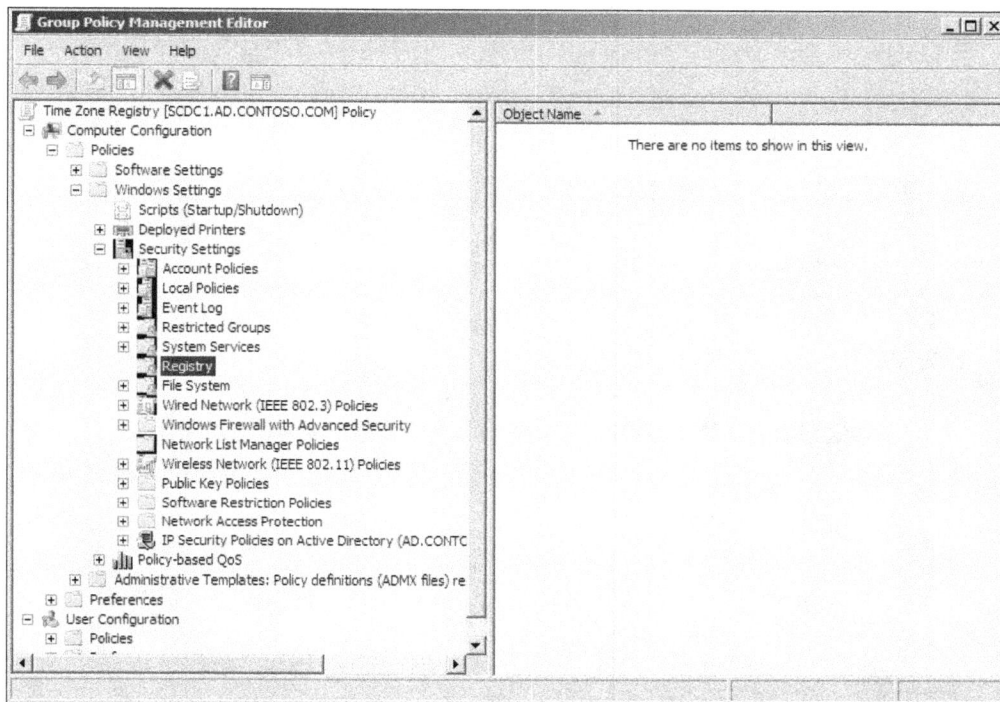

5. Expand the following key and click **OK**:

   ```
   HKEY_LOCAL_MACHINE\SYSTEM\CurrentControlSet\Control\
   TimeZoneInformation
   ```

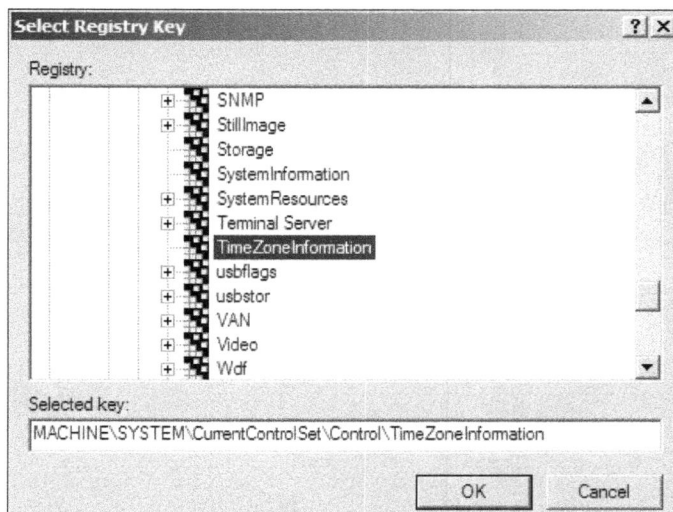

6. Click **Advanced** in the **Database Security for MACHINE\SYSTEM\ CurrentControlSet\Control\TimeZoneInformation** dialog.

7. On the **Permissions** tab under **Permission entries** select **Users...** and click **Edit...**.

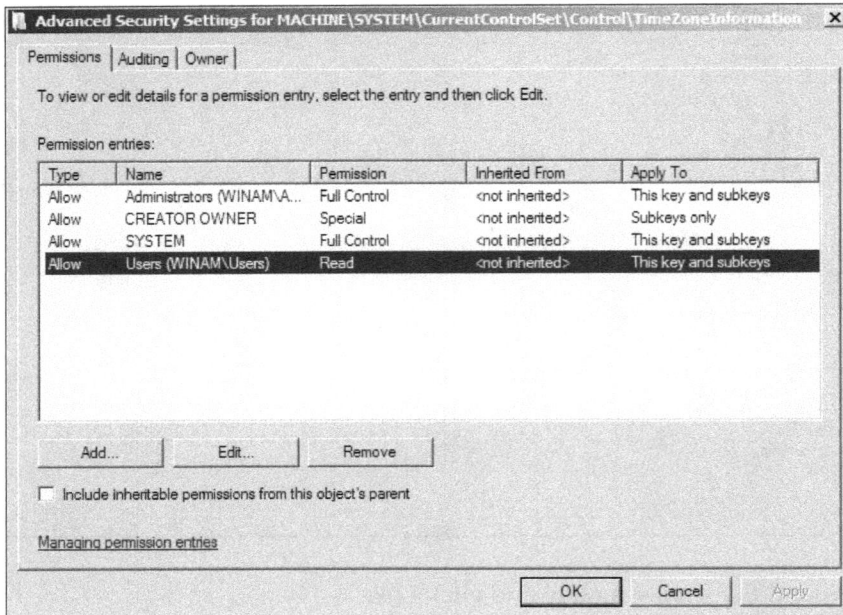

Now we need to select **Set Value** and **Create Subkey**.

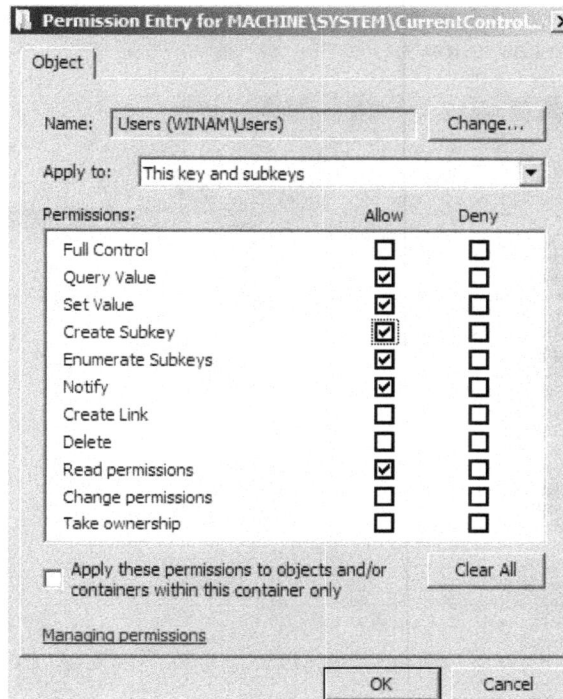

8. Click **OK** to complete the process, and again in the **Advanced Security Settings** for **MACHINE\SYSTEM\CurrentControlSet\Control\ TimeZoneInformation** and **Database Security for MACHINE\SYSTEM\ CurrentControlSet\Control\TimeZoneInformation** dialog boxes.

9. Click **OK** in the **Add Object** dialog to accept the default settings.

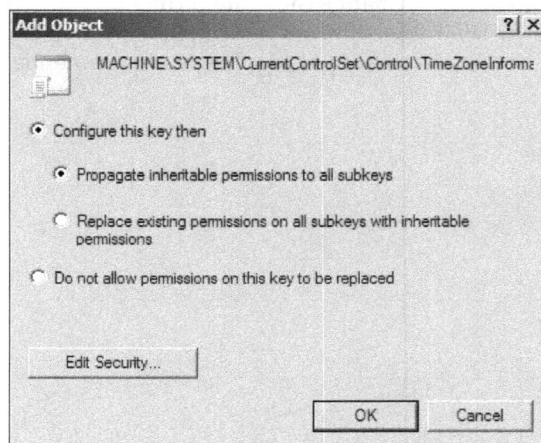

The key will now appear in the right pane of the **Group Policy Management Editor** window as follows:

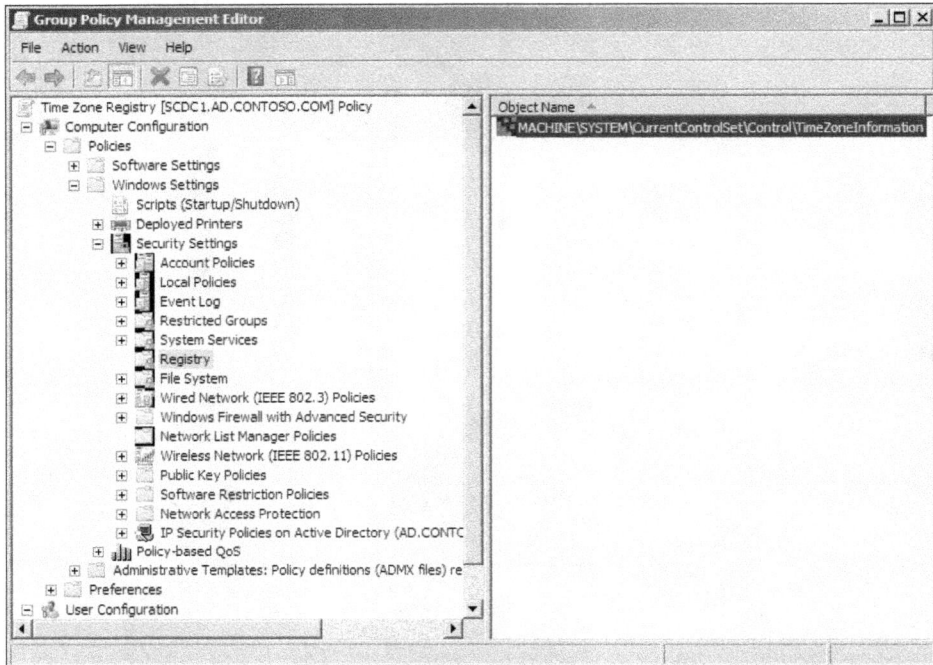

10. Close the **Group Policy Management Editor** window.

Changing the system time privilege required to set the time zone

Unfortunately the **Change the system time** privilege is required to change the time zone in Windows XP, thus potentially leaving your fleet of notebooks outside of regulatory requirements.

Power management

Though in many cases users don't need to change power settings once they've been configured by an administrator, notebook users might want to change the settings when giving a presentation. Windows XP divides power management into per-machine and per-user settings. Unfortunately, the Power Options control panel doesn't allow standard users to change per-user settings unless they have administrative privilege to change per-machine settings. Even worse, Windows XP power settings often get reset when certain Windows patches are applied to the machine, thereby frustrating notebook users who, as standard users, can't reconfigure power settings as desired.

There are several possible solutions to the problem:

- Relax registry security for standard users
- Use Group Policy Preferences
- Run the `powercfg` command-line tool as part of a GPO startup script

Managing power settings with Group Policy Preferences

The preferred method for managing power settings in Windows XP is Group Policy Preferences, which allows system administrators to define initial settings or enforce settings for standard users. As Group Policy Preferences are not natively part of Windows XP, you'll need to install the **Group Policy Preferences Client Side Extensions** from Microsoft. Before doing so, you should ensure that your clients are running Windows XP Service Pack 3. Additionally, to manage GPP settings, you'll need a machine running Vista with Service Pack 1, Windows 7, or Windows Server 2008, along with the Group Policy Management Console, which is part of the **Remote Server Administration Tools (RSAT)** for Windows 7 and Vista.

> **Group Policy Preference downloads**
> The GPP Client Side Extensions for Windows XP, RSAT for Windows Vista, and RSAT for Windows 7 can all be downloaded from http://www.microsoft.com/downloads.

Microsoft doesn't provide the extensions as an `.msi` package, but you can distribute the extensions to Windows XP clients using *Windows Server Update Services (WSUS)* or using a **Group Policy Startup Script** with command-line switches for a silent install.

> **Group Policy Startup Script**
>
> Unlike a logon script, which runs in the context of the logged on user, a Startup Script runs in the context of the computer account and has administrative privileges on the local machine.

> To run a silent install for Windows XP Group Policy Preferences Client Side Extensions type:
>
> `Windows-en-US-KB943729.exe /quiet /passive /norestart`

Creating a GPO startup script to install GPP CSEs

To create a GPO startup script to install GPP CSEs:

1. We will first need to save the following command as a batch file in Notepad and call it KB943729.bat:

```
@REM GP Client Side Extensions
if not exist %systemroot%\KB943729.log %~dp0\Windows-en-US-
KB943729.exe /quiet /passive /norestart
```

> **Variables in batch files**
>
> `%systemroot%` and `%~dp0` are both variables that can be used instead of hard-coded paths to files. `%systemroot%` usually maps to `c:\windows` and `%~dp0` sets the working directory to the same path as the location of the batch file. If we didn't use the `%~dp0` variable we'd have to specify a specific domain controller in the path to `Windows-en-US-KB943729.exe`, which would have looked something like this: `\\<DCname>\sysvol\ad.contoso.com\Policies\{GPO GUID}\Machine\Scripts\Startup`.

2. Open the **Group Policy Management Console** as a domain administrator from **Administrative Tools** on the **Start** menu and expand your Active Directory forest and domain in the left-handed pane.

3. Locate your **Clients** OU, right-click, and select **Create a GPO in this domain, and Link it here...** from the menu.

4. In the **New GPO** dialog, type **GPP CSE startup script** in the **Name** field and click **OK**.

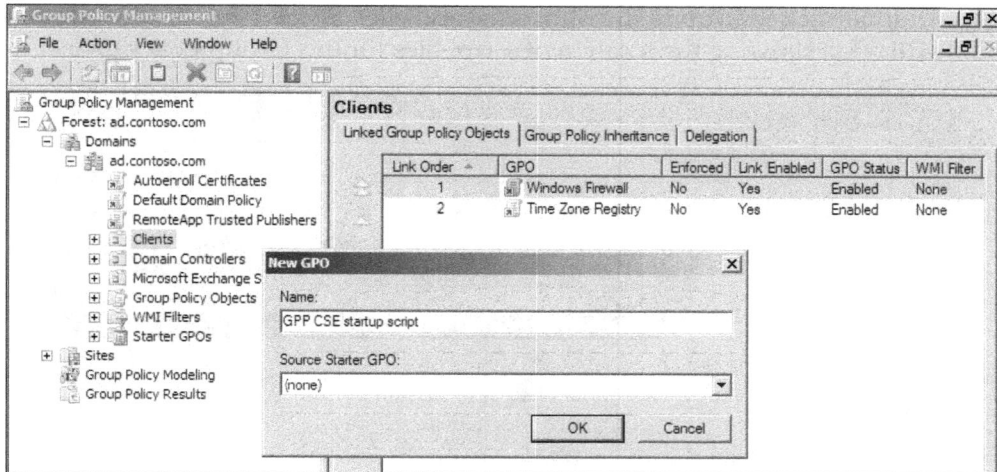

5. Expand the **Clients** OU in the left-hand pane, right-click the **GPP CSE startup script** node, and select **Edit...** from the menu.

6. In the **Group Policy Management Editor** window, expand **Policies** under **Computer Configuration** in the left-hand pane. Expand **Windows Settings** and click **Scripts (Startup/Shutdown)**.

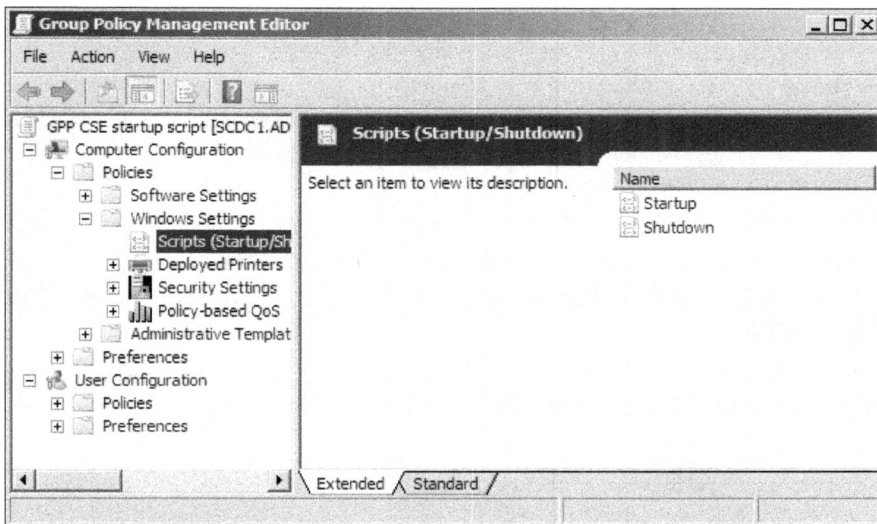

7. Double-click **Startup** in the right pane and click **Show Files**. A new window will open showing the location of script files for this Group Policy Object.

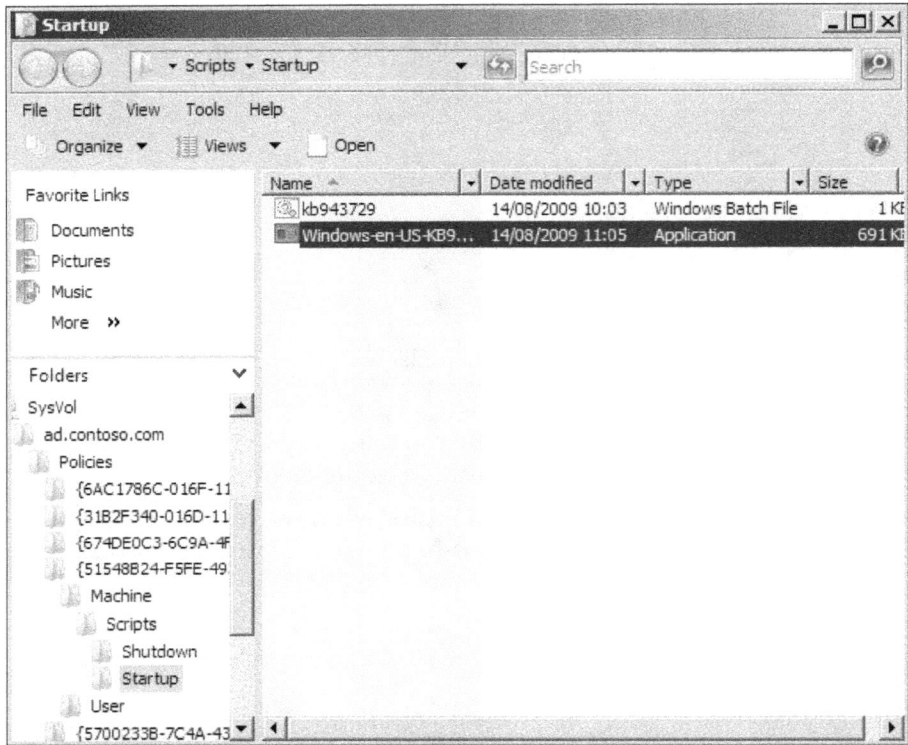

8. Copy the `Windows-en-US-KB943729.exe` package and `KB943729.bat` file to the `Startup` folder, and then close the window.

9. Click **Add...** in the **Startup Properties** dialog and then **Browse** to the right of the **Script Name** field. Select the `kb943729.bat` file in the **Browse** dialog and click **Open**.

10. Click **OK** in the **Add a Script** dialog; the `kb943729.bat` file should now appear in the **Startup Properties** window.

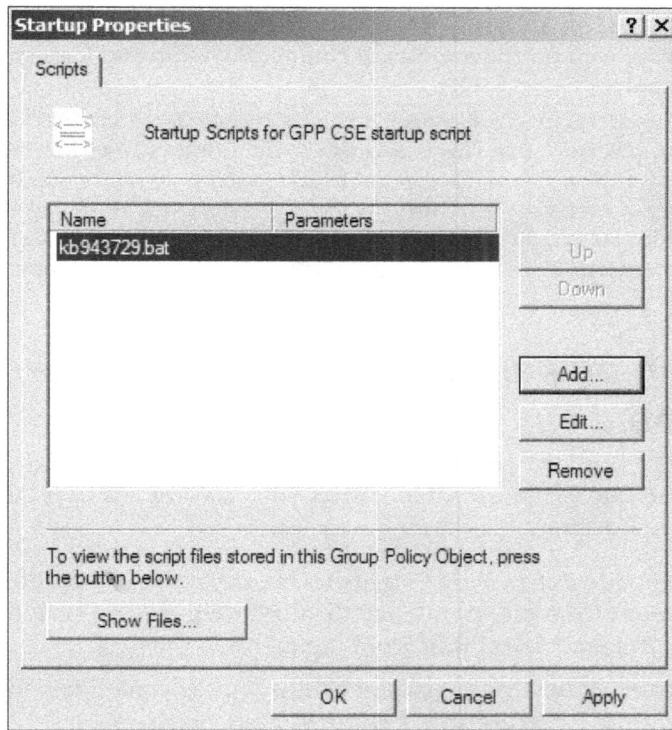

11. Click **OK** in the **Startup Properties** dialog and close the **Group Policy Management Editor**.

Now if you restart an XP machine in the Clients OU, the Startup Script will run as the computer boots as shown in the following screenshot:

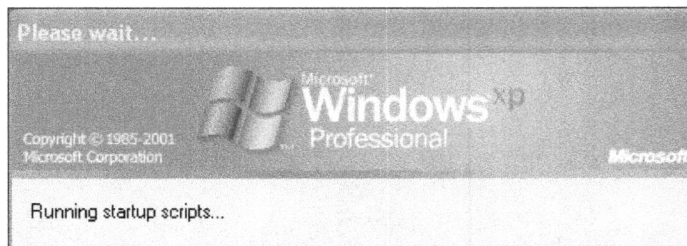

> **Always wait for the network at computer startup and logon to the computer**
>
> Unless configured otherwise, it may take several reboots before the Startup Script runs. This is because by default Windows XP does not wait for the network to respond to all requests, thereby speeding up the boot process. The **Always wait for the network at computer startup and logon to the computer** policy setting is located in **Computer Configuration | Administrative Templates | System | Logon**.

Configuring power options using Group Policy Preferences

For the purposes of our lab, we can reuse the GPO that deployed the Group Policy Preferences Client Side Extensions. Of course, you can create a new GPO and link it to the Clients OU, if desired.

1. We will need to expand the **Clients** OU node in the **Group Policy Management Console**, right-click the **GPP CSE startup script** Group Policy Object, and select **Edit** from the menu.

2. In the **Group Policy Management Editor** window, navigate to **Computer Configuration | Preferences | Control Pane Settings**.

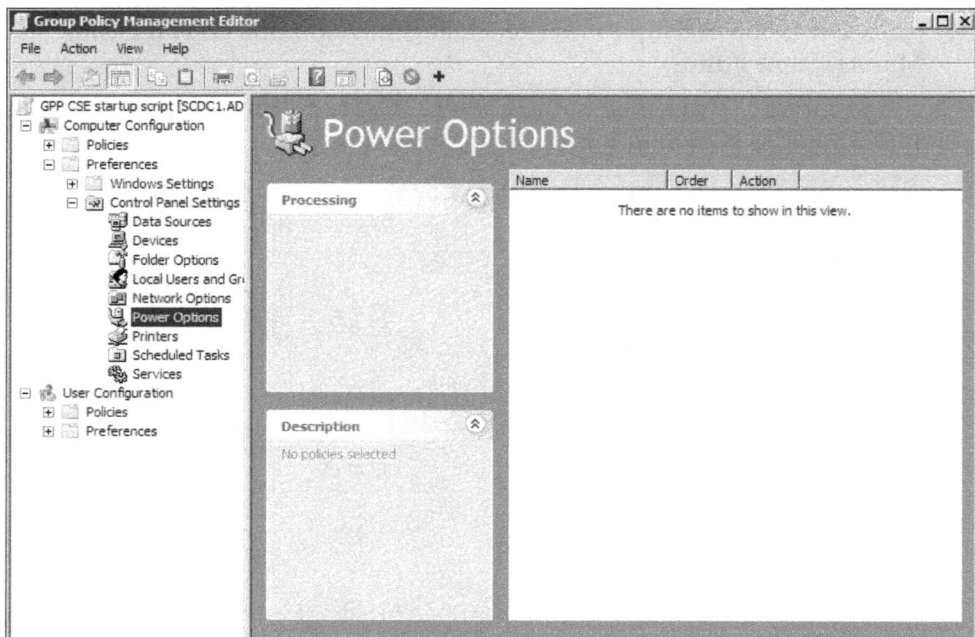

3. Right-click **Power Options**, select **New**, and then click on **Power Options (Windows XP)** from the menu.

> Starting with Vista, Power Options can be set using Group Policy.

4. On the **Power Options** tab, select **Prompt for password when computer resumes from standby**, and click **OK**.

5. Right-click **Power Options** again in the left-hand pane, select **New**, and then click on **Power Scheme (Windows XP)** from the menu. Accept the default scheme settings on the **Power Scheme** tab by clicking **OK**.

> **Power options** can also be set in user configuration.

Configuring the registry for access to power settings

To allow standard users to modify power settings, we need to change the permissions on the `GlobalPowerPolicy` and `PowerPolicies` registry keys in the following hive: `HKEY_LOCAL_MACHINE\SOFTWARE\Microsoft\Windows\CurrentVersion\Controls Folder\PowerCfg`.

1. Open the **Group Policy Management** Console as a domain administrator from **Administrative Tools** on the **Start** menu and expand your Active Directory forest and domain in the left-hand pane.

2. Locate your **Clients** OU, right-click it, and select **Create a GPO in this domain, and Link it here...** from the menu.

3. In the **New GPO** dialog, type **Power Options Registry** in the **Name** field and click **OK**.

4. Expand the **Clients** OU in the left pane, right-click the **Power Options Registry** node, and click **Edit...** from the menu.

5. In the **Group Policy Management Editor** window, in the left-hand pane navigate to **Computer Configuration | Policies | Windows Settings | Security Settings**, right-click **Registry**, and select **Add Key** from the menu.

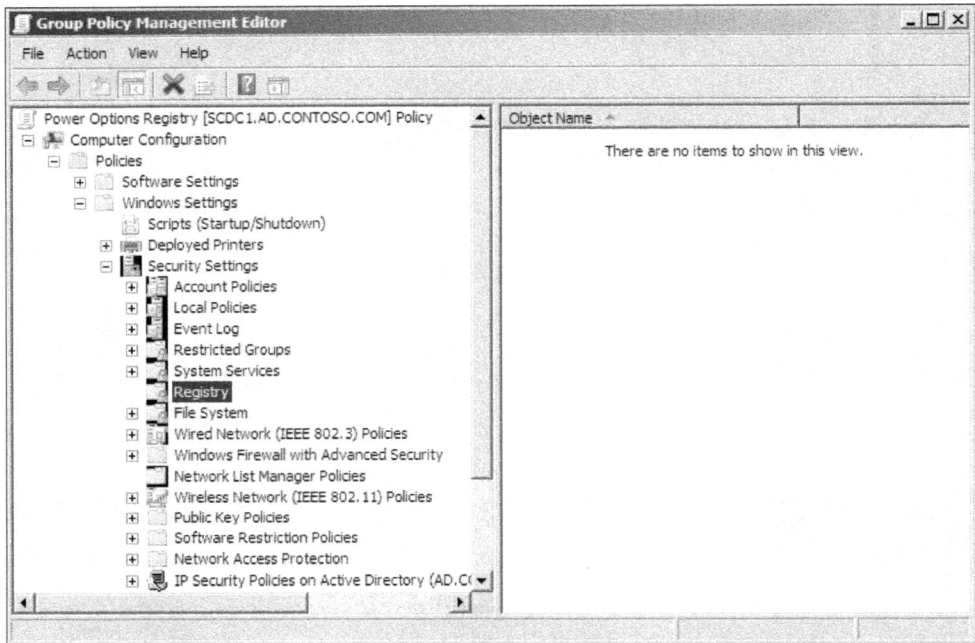

6. Expand the HKEY_LOCAL_MACHINE hive in the **Select Registry Key** dialog, go to the GlobalPowerPolicy key, and click **OK**.

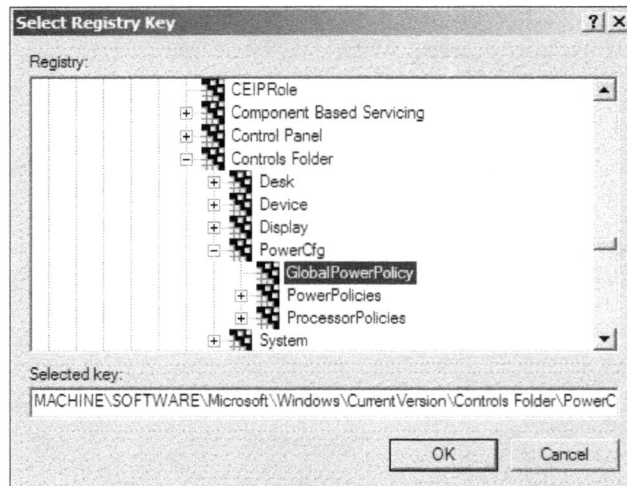

7. Click **Advanced** in the **Database Security for...** dialog.

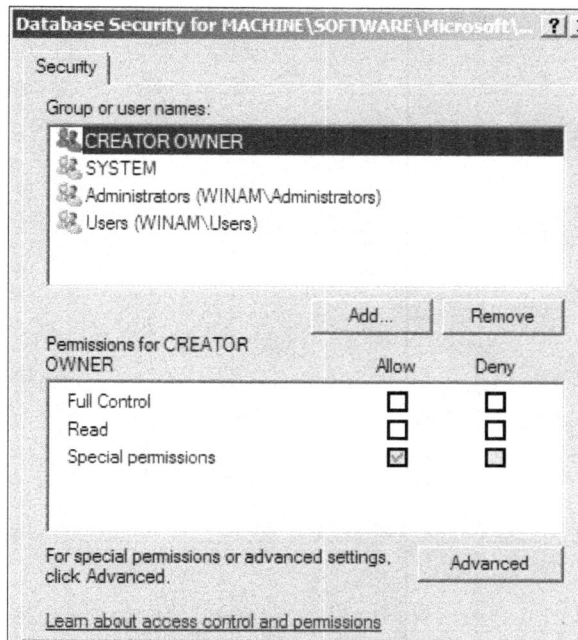

8. Select **Users...** under **Permission** column, and click **Edit...**.

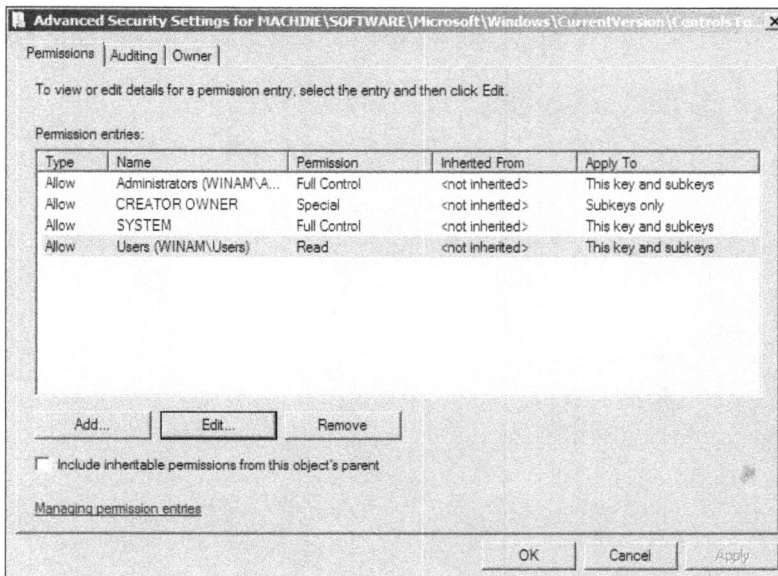

9. In the **Permission Entry...** dialog, select the **Set Value** and **Create Subkey** boxes in the **Allow** column and click **OK**.

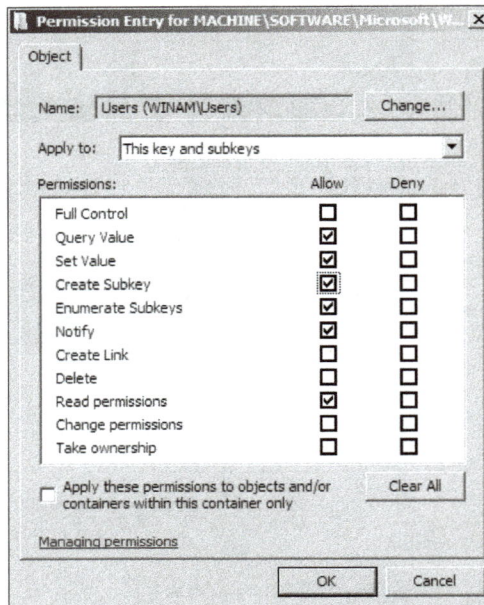

10. Click **OK** in the **Advanced Security Settings...** dialog and in the **Database Security...** dialog.

11. Accept the default settings in the **Add Object** dialog by clicking **OK**.

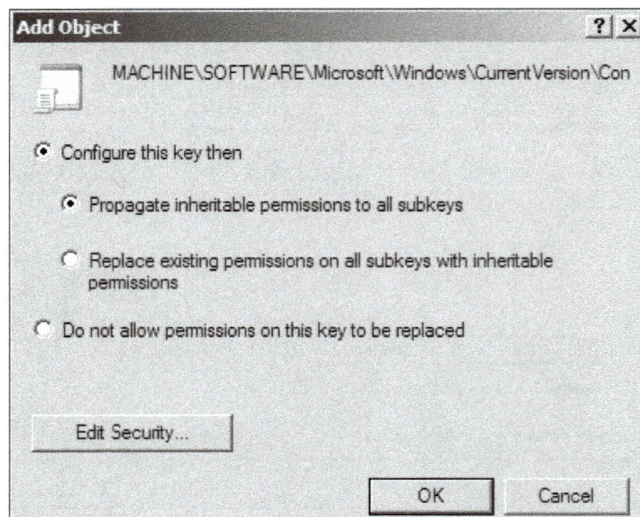

12. Repeat the process given previously and add the same permissions for the `PowerPolicies` key. When you've finished, you should see both the new policies in the **Group Policy Management Editor** window as shown in the following screenshot:

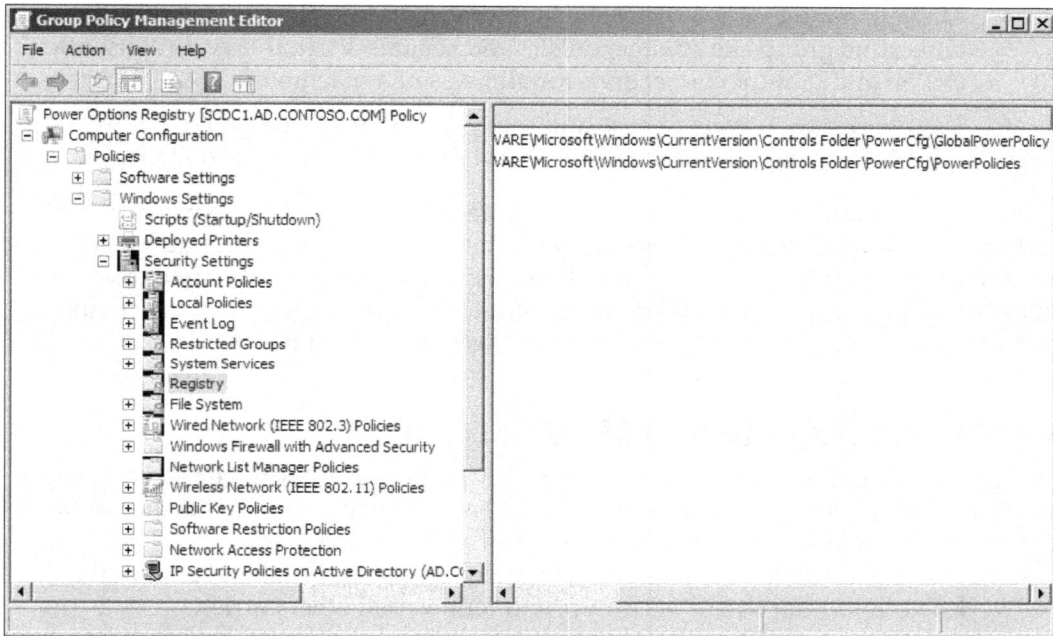

13. Close the **Group Policy Management Editor** window.

Once Group Policy has been refreshed on the machines in the Clients OU, users will be able to successfully modify settings in the Power Options control panel.

Managing network configuration

Windows XP introduced a new group called **Network Configuration Operators**, and as members of this group can modify system-wide settings, it is considered to be a group with administrative privileges. However, if you want users to run with Least Privilege Security, it's far better to add users to this group rather than make them administrators or members of the Power Users group. Network Configuration Operators can:

- Change TCP/IP settings for local network adapters: This is useful in situations where engineers might need to assign themselves a static IP address to connect to a network or specific device when on the road.

- Rename network connections: If a machine has a lot of network connections, the ability to rename connections is useful simply for identification purposes.

- Enable or disable a connection: This is useful in testing and troubleshooting scenarios.

- Manage remote access connections: Members of the Network Configuration Operators group can change, delete, and rename **Virtual Private Network (VPN)** and dial-up connections for all users of a machine.

- Use `ipconfig` to issue release and renew commands: Useful for troubleshooting **Dynamic Host Control Protocol (DHCP)** problems.

While being a member of the Network Configuration Operators group has benefits for certain users, for the average employee, being able to modify network settings can lead to connectivity problems that are difficult for help desk staff to troubleshoot remotely. In the worst case, a user can render their computer completely useless if they're unable to connect to the corporate network because of a configuration problem.

Configuring Restricted Groups

For any of the built-in local groups on a client PC, Group Policy can be used to control the membership. Here, we'll look at how to add a domain group called *Engineers* to the Network Configuration Operators group on all PCs in the Clients OU. This Group Policy setting ensures that only the domain group Engineers is a member of the Network Configuration Operators group, and removes all other entries.

1. Open the Group Policy Management Console as a domain administrator from **Administrative Tools** on the **Start** menu and expand your Active Directory forest and domain in the left-hand pane.

2. Locate your **Clients** OU, right-click it, and select **Create a GPO in this domain, and Link it here...** from the menu.

3. In the **New GPO** dialog, type **Network Configuration Operators** in the **Name** field and click **OK**. The new GPO will appear linked to the **Clients** OU as shown in the following screenshot:

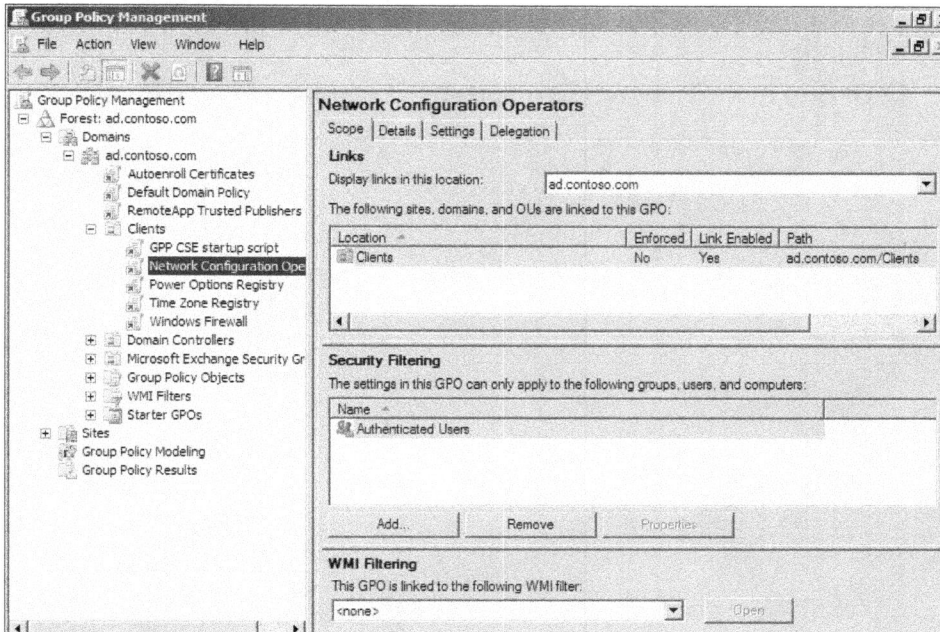

4. Expand the **Clients** OU in the left-hand pane, right-click on the **Network Configuration Operators** node, and select **Edit...** from the menu.

5. In the **Group Policy Management Editor** window, navigate to **Computer Configuration | Policies | Windows Settings | Security Settings**. Right-click on **Restricted Groups**, and select **Add Group** from the menu.

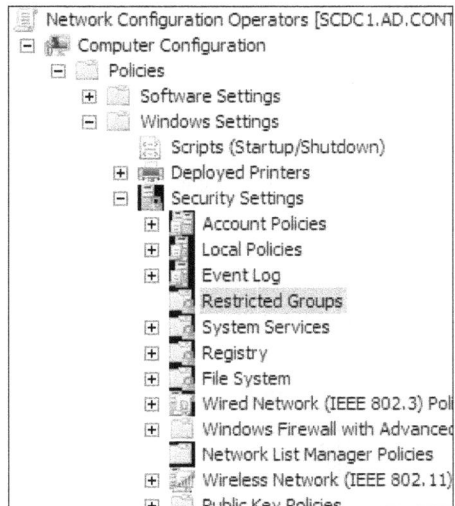

6. Type **Network Configuration Operators** in the **Add Group** dialog and click **OK**.

7. Click **Add** in the **Network Configuration Operators Properties** dialog.

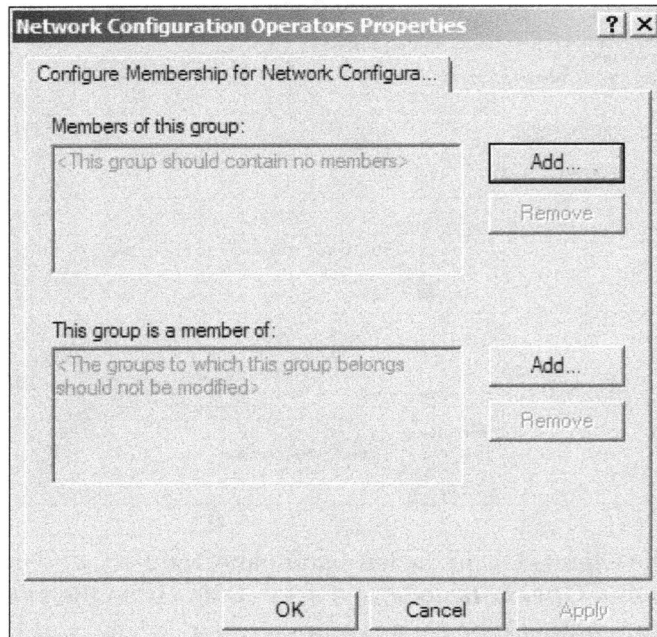

8. Type CONTOSO\Engineers in the **Add Member** dialog and click **OK**.

CONTOSO\Engineers group

You should replace CONTOSO with the name of your domain and Engineers with any domain group that you want to add to the Network Configuration Operators group on each PC in the Clients OU. Alternatively, you can click **Browse** and use the **Select Users or Groups** dialog to find an Active Directory group.

9. The group will now appear in the **Members of this group** field in the **Network Configuration Operators Properties** dialog. Click **OK** to continue.

10. Your domain group will appear in the right-hand pane of the Group Policy Management Editor window and you can close it.

When this policy is refreshed on the machines in the Clients OU, your domain group will become a member of the local Network Configuration Operators group.

Identifying LUA problems using Standard User Analyzer

If you don't have any Vista or Windows 7 PCs on your network, you might consider using the Standard User Analyzer to identify conflicts when running software as a standard user. The Standard User Analyzer can also be used for applications running on Vista or Windows 7 and gives more comprehensive results than agents deployed using Application Compatibility Manager.

In the following example, despite the fact that we're looking at identifying compatibility issues in Windows XP, we're going to run the problem application and the Standard User Analyzer on Vista. When the Standard User Analyzer runs on Vista or Windows 7, more functionality is enabled that helps system administrators solve application compatibility problems and generates more comprehensive results.

Application Verifier

Before using the Standard User Analyzer, you'll need to download and install Application Verifier, (which is not included in ACT) from the Microsoft download center: `http://www.microsoft.com/downloads`.

Log on to Vista as a standard user:

1. Open **Standard User Analyzer** from **Start | All Programs | Microsoft Application Compatibility Toolkit | Deployment and Tester Tools**.

2. Click **Browse** in the **App Info** tab, select the application you want to test (in this case `maxthon.exe`) in the **Browse for Application** dialog, and click **Open**.

3. Under **Launch Options**, deselect **Elevate**, and select **Disable Virtualization**.

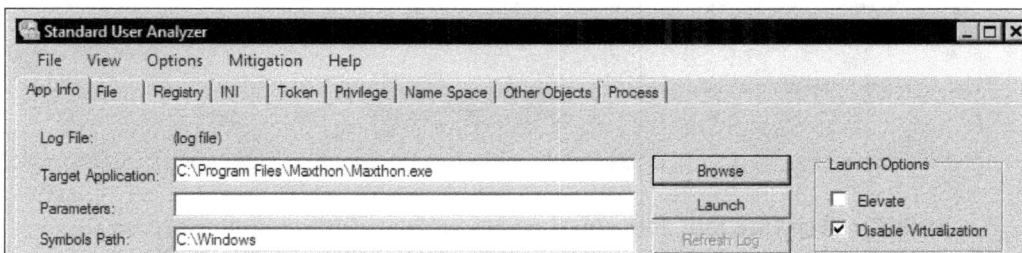

4. Click **Launch** in the **App Info** tab to start monitoring Maxthon. A User Account Control dialog will appear to elevate the Standard User Analyzer process. Maxthon will run as a standard user.

5. Enter administrator credentials and click **OK**.

6. Click **Yes** in the **Warning** dialog to delete existing AppVerifier logs.

7. Perform a task in the application that you know fails when logged on as a standard user and then close the program. In this case, I modified a user preference in Maxthon's options that I know can't be modified when logged on as a standard user. Wait for debugging to complete on the **App Info** tab.

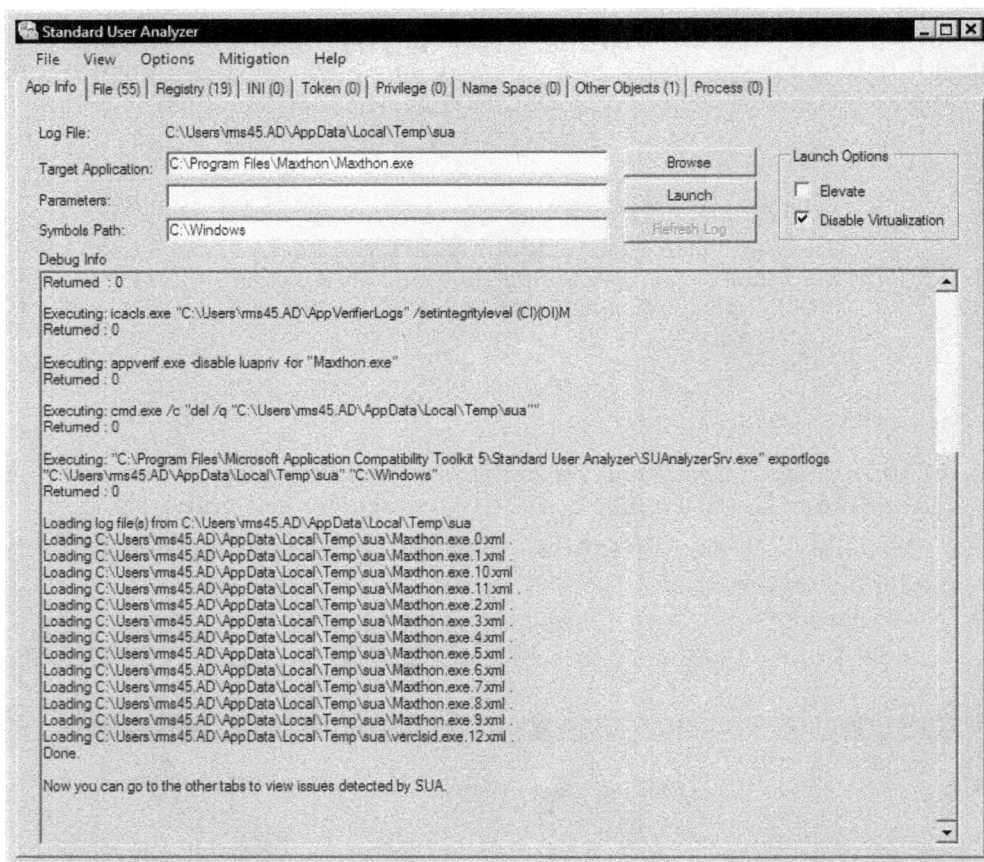

8. Switch to the **File** tab, and you'll be able to see all the registry access operations that couldn't be completed successfully as a standard user.

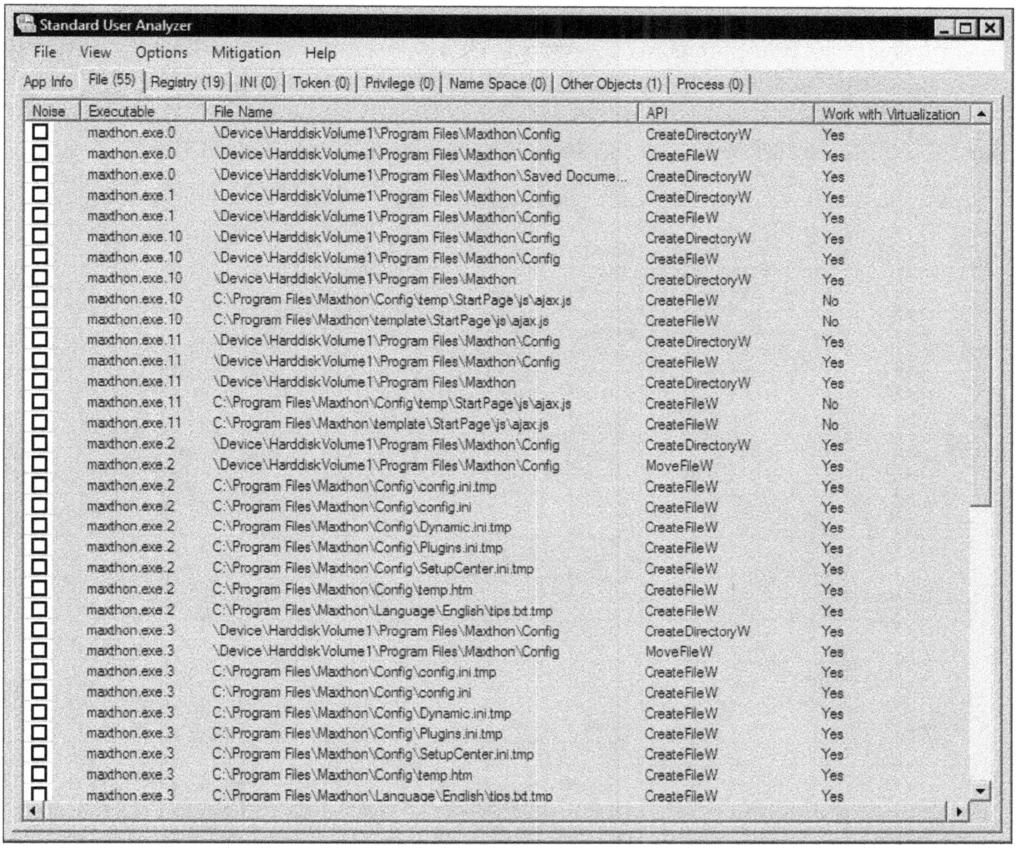

Noise	Executable	File Name	API	Work with Virtualization
☐	maxthon.exe.0	\Device\HarddiskVolume1\Program Files\Maxthon\Config	CreateDirectoryW	Yes
☐	maxthon.exe.0	\Device\HarddiskVolume1\Program Files\Maxthon\Config	CreateFileW	Yes
☐	maxthon.exe.0	\Device\HarddiskVolume1\Program Files\Maxthon\Saved Docume...	CreateDirectoryW	Yes
☐	maxthon.exe.1	\Device\HarddiskVolume1\Program Files\Maxthon\Config	CreateDirectoryW	Yes
☐	maxthon.exe.1	\Device\HarddiskVolume1\Program Files\Maxthon\Config	CreateFileW	Yes
☐	maxthon.exe.10	\Device\HarddiskVolume1\Program Files\Maxthon\Config	CreateDirectoryW	Yes
☐	maxthon.exe.10	\Device\HarddiskVolume1\Program Files\Maxthon\Config	CreateFileW	Yes
☐	maxthon.exe.10	\Device\HarddiskVolume1\Program Files\Maxthon	CreateDirectoryW	Yes
☐	maxthon.exe.10	C:\Program Files\Maxthon\Config\temp\StartPage\js\ajax.js	CreateFileW	No
☐	maxthon.exe.10	C:\Program Files\Maxthon\template\StartPage\js\ajax.js	CreateFileW	No
☐	maxthon.exe.11	\Device\HarddiskVolume1\Program Files\Maxthon\Config	CreateDirectoryW	Yes
☐	maxthon.exe.11	\Device\HarddiskVolume1\Program Files\Maxthon\Config	CreateFileW	Yes
☐	maxthon.exe.11	\Device\HarddiskVolume1\Program Files\Maxthon	CreateDirectoryW	Yes
☐	maxthon.exe.11	C:\Program Files\Maxthon\Config\temp\StartPage\js\ajax.js	CreateFileW	No
☐	maxthon.exe.11	C:\Program Files\Maxthon\template\StartPage\js\ajax.js	CreateFileW	No
☐	maxthon.exe.2	\Device\HarddiskVolume1\Program Files\Maxthon\Config	CreateDirectoryW	Yes
☐	maxthon.exe.2	\Device\HarddiskVolume1\Program Files\Maxthon\Config	MoveFileW	Yes
☐	maxthon.exe.2	C:\Program Files\Maxthon\Config\config.ini.tmp	CreateFileW	Yes
☐	maxthon.exe.2	C:\Program Files\Maxthon\Config\config.ini	CreateFileW	Yes
☐	maxthon.exe.2	C:\Program Files\Maxthon\Config\Dynamic.ini.tmp	CreateFileW	Yes
☐	maxthon.exe.2	C:\Program Files\Maxthon\Config\Plugins.ini.tmp	CreateFileW	Yes
☐	maxthon.exe.2	C:\Program Files\Maxthon\Config\SetupCenter.ini.tmp	CreateFileW	Yes
☐	maxthon.exe.2	C:\Program Files\Maxthon\Config\temp.htm	CreateFileW	Yes
☐	maxthon.exe.2	C:\Program Files\Maxthon\Language\English\tips.txt.tmp	CreateFileW	Yes
☐	maxthon.exe.3	\Device\HarddiskVolume1\Program Files\Maxthon\Config	CreateDirectoryW	Yes
☐	maxthon.exe.3	\Device\HarddiskVolume1\Program Files\Maxthon\Config	MoveFileW	Yes
☐	maxthon.exe.3	C:\Program Files\Maxthon\Config\config.ini.tmp	CreateFileW	Yes
☐	maxthon.exe.3	C:\Program Files\Maxthon\Config\config.ini	CreateFileW	Yes
☐	maxthon.exe.3	C:\Program Files\Maxthon\Config\Dynamic.ini.tmp	CreateFileW	Yes
☐	maxthon.exe.3	C:\Program Files\Maxthon\Config\Plugins.ini.tmp	CreateFileW	Yes
☐	maxthon.exe.3	C:\Program Files\Maxthon\Config\SetupCenter.ini.tmp	CreateFileW	Yes
☐	maxthon.exe.3	C:\Program Files\Maxthon\Config\temp.htm	CreateFileW	Yes
☐	maxthon.exe.3	C:\Program Files\Maxthon\Language\English\tips.txt.tmp	CreateFileW	Yes

9. Switch to the **Registry** tab. Also note the **Work with Virtualization** column, that shows whether UAC File and Registry Virtualization will automatically solve the problem.

As before, it's likely that some of the problems flagged don't really impact standard user operation. You can check such issues in the **Noise** column, and they'll be excluded from the mitigations.

10. Click the **Mitigations** menu at the top of Standard User Analyzer and select **Export Mitigations as MSI** from the menu. You'll see that in the **Migrate AppCompat Issues** dialog, all mitigations are selected apart from **Loosen ACLs**. You should only enable the **Loosen ACLs** mitigations as a last resort. Redirecting file system and registry writes is more secure than loosening ACLs.

11. If you scroll down through the list of mitigations in the **Migrate AppCompat Issues** dialog, you'll see **CorrectFilePaths** mitigations also listed and selected. Scroll horizontally to examine the complete information.

The correct file paths consist of strings listed in two halves, delimited by semi colons. The first half of the string shows the original file path, in this case the protected Program Files directory; the second half is the path for the virtualized copy of the `config.js` file.

```
&quot;%SystemDrive%\Program Files\Maxthon\Config\temp\StartPage\
config.js;%UserProfile%\AppData\Local\VirtualStore\Program Files\
Maxthon\Config\temp\StartPage\config.js&quot;
```

While you can export these mitigations by clicking **Export MSI** in the **Migrate AppCompat Issues** dialog, the resulting Windows Installer package cannot run on Windows XP. The Standard User Analyzer can only be used to identify problems with an application running as a standard user, and not to automatically deploy mitigations to XP machines. In Chapter 7, we'll look at how to use the information generated by the Standard User Analyzer to create an Application Compatibility Shim for Windows XP.

Summary

In this chapter, we've learned how to identify and mitigate many of the most important restrictions for standard users in Windows XP. Before continuing to the next chapter you should now be able to:

- Deploy Windows XP using the Microsoft Deployment Toolkit
- Identify application compatibility issues for programs running as a Standard User with the Standard User Analyzer
- Use Group Policy to set access control lists on registry keys and files or folders
- Develop a strategy for deploying ActiveX controls to Windows XP users

The next chapter will guide you through preparing your environment for Least Privilege Security.

11

Preparing Vista and Windows 7 for Least Privilege Security

There's a lot of groundwork involved in a successful move to Least Privilege Security on the desktop, and in this chapter we'll look at how to implement a **desktop refresh** project including Least Privilege. If the thought of reinstalling the operating system across your fleet of PCs fills you with dread, you'll be pleased to know that Microsoft provides tools to simplify the process and eliminate the risk of losing data.

In the chapter, we will cover:

- Using Microsoft's Application Compatibility Toolkit (ACT) to collect and analyze data to identify any potential compatibility problems with Least Privilege Security and software installed on networked PCs

- Analyzing logon scripts for Least Privilege compatibility

- Preparing a desktop image with Least Privilege Security enabled from the get go

- Deploying the new image while preserving users' files and settings

This chapter focuses on moving from an unmanaged environment (where users log on with administrative privileges) to a managed environment, where UAC is enabled and users log on with standard user privileges. However, some of the information in this chapter is also relevant to Windows XP.

The Application Compatibility Toolkit

Before we begin the process of creating a new desktop image, we need to have a good understanding of what applications are installed on PCs across the organization and identify any potential software compatibility problems with Least Privilege Security.

Although designed primarily to help system administrators migrate legacy applications to new versions of Windows, the Microsoft **Application Compatibility Toolkit (ACT)** can be useful when designing a desktop image for Least Privilege Security. ACT has two core applications:

- **Application Compatibility Manager**: This application is for performing software inventories and identifying compatibility problems with Least Privilege Security and new versions of Windows.

- **Compatibility Administrator**: This application is for creating fixes to address problems identified with the Application Compatibility Manager.

Application Compatibility Manager

ACT's Application Compatibility Manager can be used to dispatch **Data Collection Packages (DCPs)** to PCs. DCPs consist of several components that feed data back to an ACT server for analysis. To identify potential Least Privilege Security compatibility problems with our software, we're interested in the following two DCP components:

- **Inventory Collector**: Used to create software and hardware inventories on networked PCs

- **User Account Control Compatibility Evaluator (UACCE)**: For identifying potential software compatibility issues with UAC and standard users in Vista or Windows 7

> **64-bit Windows**
> ACT 5.5 **Compatibility Evaluators** don't support 64-bit versions of Windows.

In this chapter, we're interested in the software installed on PCs across our network, and the **Inventory Collector** will automate that job for us. In *Chapter 4, User Account Control,* We will also require data about potential application conflicts with User Account Control and standard user accounts, so at this point we'll also dispatch the UACCE.

Installing and configuring ACT

ACT 5.5 can be installed on Windows XP (Service Pack 3) or later and Windows Server 2003 (Service Pack 1), and requires Microsoft SQL 2005 (full or express edition) or later. In this example we're going to install ACT with a local instance of SQL Server 2008 Express running on Windows Vista.

1. Start by installing the ACT and SQL Server Express binaries. Launch the Application Compatibility Manager located in the `Microsoft Application Compatibility Toolkit` folder in **Start | All Programs**.

2. Click **Next** on the **Welcome to the ACT Configuration Wizard** screen.

3. You will then need to select **Enterprise configuration** and click **Next**.

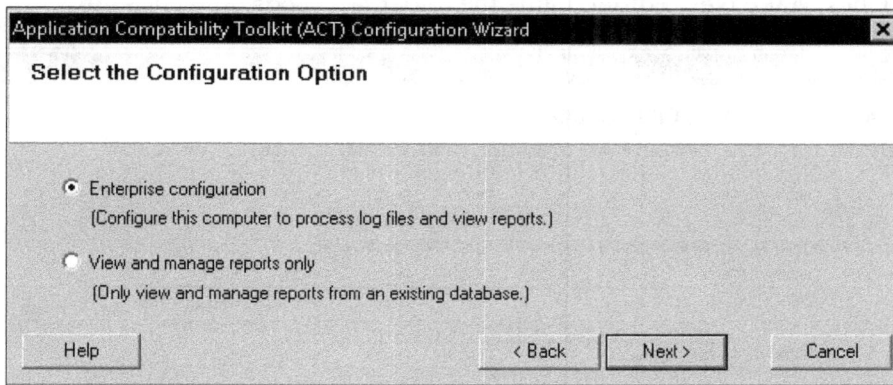

4. Click the **SQL Server** drop-down menu and select `(local)\SQLEXPRESS`.

5. Now, click **Connect** and **(local)**, and the **SQL Server** field will change to the local PC name, in this case `VISTA1`. The **Database** field will turn white.

6. Type ACT in the **Database** field and click **Create**.

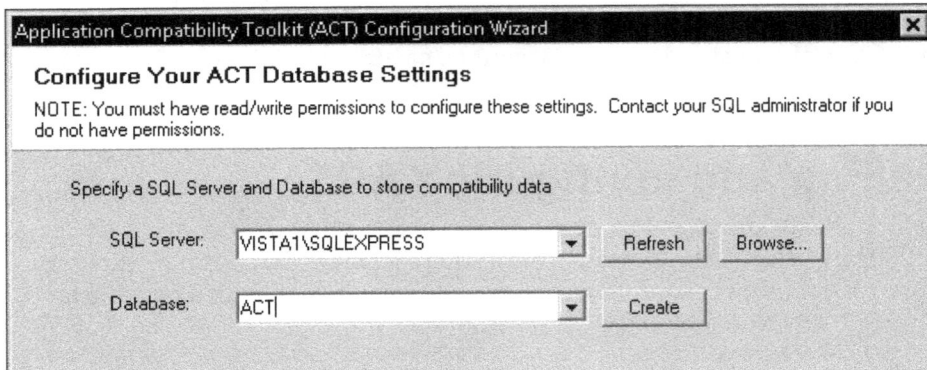

Application Compatibility Toolkit (ACT) Configuration Wizard ☒

Configure Your ACT Database Settings

NOTE: You must have read/write permissions to configure these settings. Contact your SQL administrator if you do not have permissions.

Specify a SQL Server and Database to store compatibility data

SQL Server: `VISTA1\SQLEXPRESS` ▼ | Refresh | Browse... |

Database: `ACT` ▼ | Create |

7. Once the database has been created, click **Next**.

8. Click the **Browse** button appearing to the right of the **Path** field, and choose a location on a local disk where you will create a new folder for storing ACT log files.

9. Click **Make New Folder**, name the folder ACT Logs, and click **OK**.

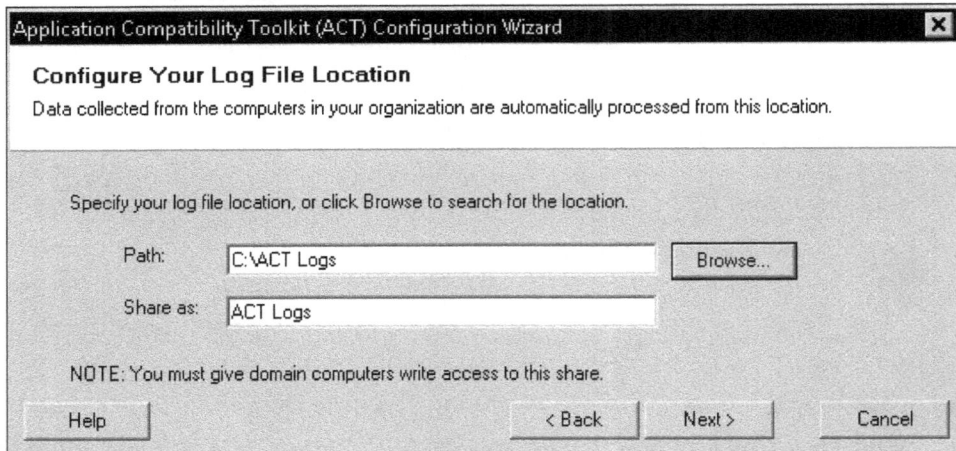

Application Compatibility Toolkit (ACT) Configuration Wizard ☒

Configure Your Log File Location

Data collected from the computers in your organization are automatically processed from this location.

Specify your log file location, or click Browse to search for the location.

Path: `C:\ACT Logs` | Browse... |

Share as: `ACT Logs`

NOTE: You must give domain computers write access to this share.

| Help | | < Back | Next > | Cancel |

10. Click **Next**. Select **Local System** on the **Configure Your ACT Log Processing Service Account** screen, and click **Next** again.

11. Click **Finish** on the **Congratulations** screen, and the Application Compatibility Manager will start automatically.

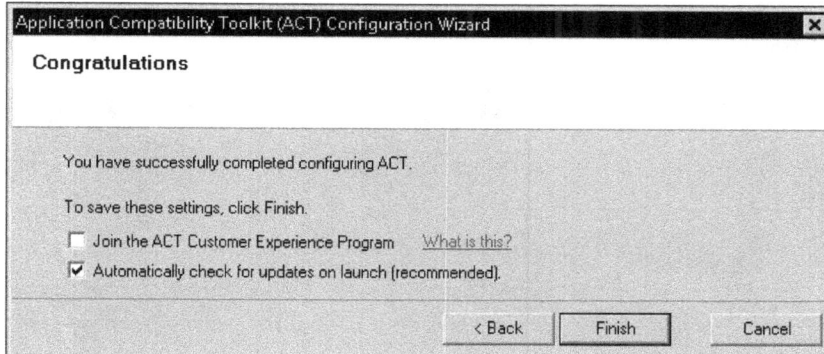

Creating a Data Collection Package

After the Application Compatibility Manager has been configured, the next stage is to create a Data Collection Package to gather inventory and UAC compatibility data from PCs.

1. Select **New** in the **File** menu.

2. Name the package Least Privilege testing, and in the **Evaluation compatibility when** section, click **Advanced**.

3. Deselect **Windows Compatibility Evaluators** and click **OK.**

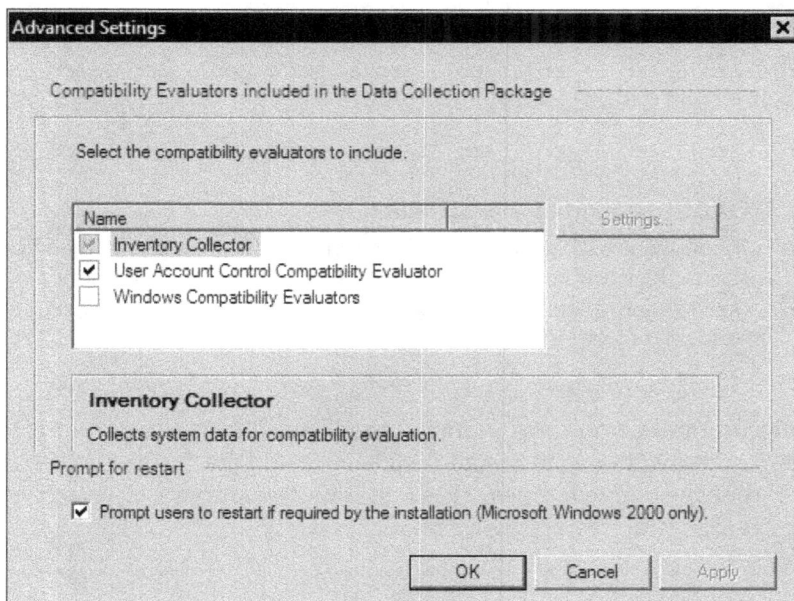

4. Under **When to monitor application usage**, set the **Upload data every** to **2 hours**.

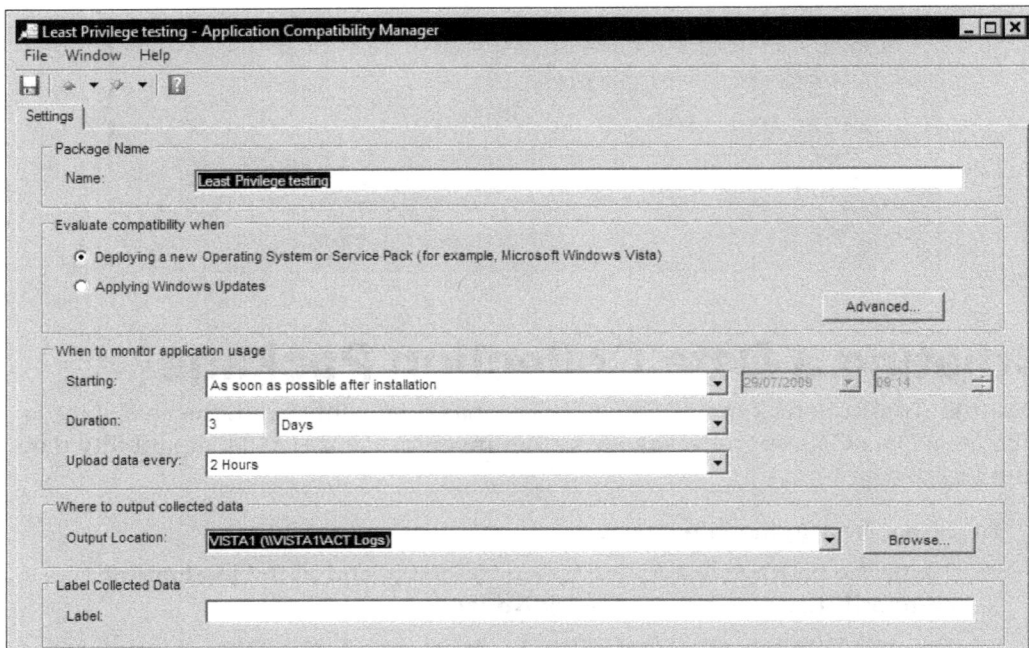

5. Select **Save and Create Data Collection Package** in the **File** menu.

6. Save the `Least Privilege testing.msi` package to your desktop and close the Data Collection Package window.

> **UACCE supported user accounts**
>
> If you want to deploy the UACC Compatibility Evaluator, then you should be running Vista or Windows 7 using a standard user or protected administrator account. UACCE enables UAC logging and sends data from local event logs to ACT.

To begin collecting data, you need to install the Least Privilege testing MSI package on your PCs. You may choose to install the DCP on all PCs, but it may be sufficient to carefully target specific machines. This will limit the amount of data collected by ACT, thereby making the results easier to analyze.

> **Trial period usability testing**
>
> While ACT does a good job of collecting and presenting relevant data, you shouldn't assume that it will identify every problem. In conjunction with ACT, you should perform application usability testing during a trial period, using PC images with Least Privilege Security enabled.

DCPs can be distributed by copying the `Least Privilege testing.MSI` file to each machine and manually installing it, or using software distribution technology such as Group Policy or **System Center Configuration Manager (SCCM)**.

> **Data Collection Packages**
>
> You should note that DCPs are only intended to collect data for a limited period of time, and are not intended to be used as a software inventory system on a permanent basis.

Analyzing data collected by ACT

An inventory of our client PCs should be created as soon as the Data Collection Package is installed. We can use the Application Compatibility Manager to view the log files and organize the collected data. Over the course of three days, any software problems caused by Least Privilege Security will be identified and added to the ACT logs by UACCE.

To keep the logs to a minimum size, let's install our Data Collection Package on just two PCs: one running Windows 7 and the other Windows XP. In addition to my standard Microsoft Office suite applications, I've installed an old version of Maxthon on both PCs. Maxthon is a replacement shell for Internet Explorer (IE), which I know in advance has limited functionality when running as a standard user. We'll be able to see in the Application Compatibility Manager logs how ACT is able to identify compatibility problems with Maxthon when run as a standard user in Windows 7.

> **Standard User Analyzer (SUA)**
>
> As UACCE does not install in Windows XP, we'll use the Standard User Analyzer to indentify Least Privilege Compatibility software conflicts in Windows XP. The Standard User Analyzer also runs on Vista and Windows 7, and provides more detailed information than UACCE. However, it is more difficult to interpret the information SUA provides, and it cannot be distributed to remote computers.

Analyzing Windows XP compatibility

If you have a mixed environment, that is, a combination of Windows XP and Vista, or Windows 7, Data Collector Packages should be targeted at Windows Vista. Data collected by UACCE can be used to identify and resolve standard user compatibility issues in Windows XP. Data collected by UACCE is more general than that collected by the Standard User Analyzer tool.

For UACCE to detect potential compatibility problems, applications need to be executed and tested thoroughly to ensure that all issues are caught by the DCP. Before we return to the Application Compatibility Manager, we need to run Maxthon a few times to ensure errors show up in the ACT logs and then wait as DCPs send information periodically.

Like many legacy applications, Maxthon stores user preferences in what are deemed protected areas of the Windows system such as the `Program Files` folder and restricted areas of the registry. This causes problems when Maxthon is run as a standard user. In Windows XP, these problems manifest themselves when users customize Maxthon's browser options. When the application is closed, it forgets users' customizations, as it can't write to protected system areas.

Windows Vista solves most of these problems using UAC's **File and Registry Virtualization**, which is designed to mitigate application compatibility problems when running as a standard user, by redirecting reads and writes in protected locations to a per-user virtualized filesystem and registry. Though this system is effective, it's intended to be a temporary solution for organizations that are migrating from XP to Vista or Windows 7. For an application to be certified for Vista or Windows 7, it mustn't rely on UAC File and Registry Virtualization to operate correctly.

Install and configure applications before running Data Collection Packages

We'll get less redundant information in the ACT logs and be able to analyze the data more easily if all applications are installed and configured for first use before deploying Data Collection Packages. In the demonstration that follows, we'll install an application after a Data Collection Package is deployed, to show the extra information logged and how to resolve any related issues.

Now that we've been using our application for a couple of days, and waited for the logs to be uploaded to our `ACT Logs` share, let's go back to the Application Compatibility Manager to analyze the results.

1. Go to **Start | Application Compatibility Manager.**

2. Make sure that the **Analyze** tab is selected in the left pane. Under **Quick Reports,** click the **Applications** node beneath **Windows 7** or **Vista SP1/SP2. Maxthon Browser** appears in the **Application Report** window showing five active issues.

Windows Vista SP1/SP2 - Application Report

Application Nam	Version	Compan	My Asse	Send	Vendor A	Community Assessm	Active Iss	Compute
2007 Microsoft Offi...		Microsoft	✓				0	1
2007 Microsoft Offi...	12.0.64...	Microso...	✓				0	0
Maxthon Browser (...				**✓**			**5**	**1**
maxthon1setup.exe			✓				5	1
Microsoft Applicati...	5.5.676...	Microso...	✓				2	2
Microsoft Office On...	12.0.64...	Microso...	✓				0	1
Microsoft Office Pr...	12.0.64...	Microso...	✓				0	1
Microsoft Office To...	12.0.45...	Microso...	✓				0	1
MSN			✓				0	1
Office Diagnostics...	12.0.64...	Microso...	✓				0	1
Office Source Engi...	12.0.45...	Microso...	✓				0	1
Windows Messeng...			✓				0	1

3. Double-click your program in the **Application Report,** and switch to the **Issues** tab to view more detailed information.

Maxthon Browser (remove only) -

File   View   Actions   Window   Help

Assessment   Issues   Application Properties   Computers   Labels

Status	Provider	Subprovider	Seve	Title
	Compatibility Eva...	Uacce	2	The application attempted to store a file in a restricted location.
	Compatibility Eva...	Uacce	3	The application attempted to store a file in a system location that was virtualized by Windows.
	Compatibility Eva...	Uacce	2	The application attempted to open a restricted registry key.
	Compatibility Eva...	Uacce	2	The application attempted to write to a restricted registry location.
	Compatibility Eva...	Uacce	3	The application attempted to store information under the HKEY_LOCAL_MACHINE\SOFTWARE

Let's deal with each issue one by one. Some of the problems detected by UACCE need to be solved, and others we can safely ignore.

> [💡 Issues identified by UACCE on Vista or Windows 7 may require different solutions in Windows XP.]

The application attempted to store a file in a restricted location

Let's deal with the first issue.

1. Double-click the first issue in the list. We can see that the problem presents a potentially major loss of functionality and must be fixed. The **Title** field shows us that Maxthon attempted to create a file in a protected system location.

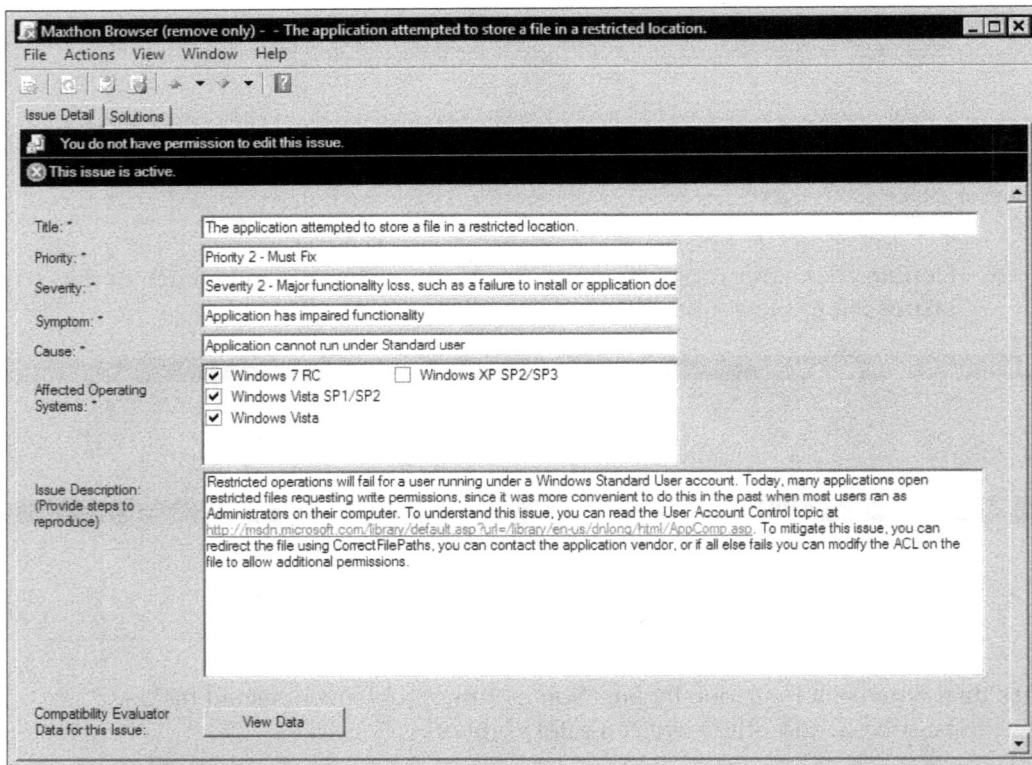

2. For more information about what the application was trying to do, click **View Data** at the bottom of the window. A new window appears showing exactly the file paths that Maxthon was trying to access.

```
API Name:              CreateFileW
User's Account Group:  Administrators
Path:                  C:\Program Files\Maxthon\template\StartPage\js\ajax.js
Restricted by ACL:     TRUE
Additional Path:
Requested Access:      0x40000000

API Name:              CreateFileW
User's Account Group:  Administrators
Path:                  C:\Program Files\Maxthon\template\StartPage\js\feed.js
Restricted by ACL:     TRUE
Additional Path:
Requested Access:      0xC0000000

API Name:              CreateFileW
User's Account Group:  Administrators
Path:                  C:\Program Files\Maxthon\template\StartPage\js\md5.js
Restricted by ACL:     TRUE
Additional Path:
Requested Access:      0x40000000

API Name:              CreateFileW
User's Account Group:  Administrators
Path:                  C:\Program Files\Maxthon\template\StartPage\js\feed.js
Restricted by ACL:     TRUE
Additional Path:
Requested Access:      0x40000000

API Name:              CreateFileW
User's Account Group:  Administrators
Path:                  C:\Program Files\Maxthon\template\StartPage\js\app.js
Restricted by ACL:     TRUE
Additional Path:
Requested Access:      0xC0000000

API Name:              CreateFileW
User's Account Group:  Administrators
Path:                  C:\Program Files\Maxthon\template\StartPage\js\ajax.js
Restricted by ACL:     TRUE
Additional Path:
```

Closer inspection of these files and usability testing of the application shows that the `template` folder and associated files are added when Maxthon is launched for the first time. Therefore, as long as Maxthon is run at least once using an account with administrative privileges, these files will be created successfully and need not be modified thereafter.

With sufficient usability testing, we can write off this problem and make appropriate notes in ACT, so that if the application is added to an image, the sysadmin or engineer responsible can run the application before putting the image into production.

3. Click the **Solutions** tab and then the **Add Solution** icon.

4. Add details of the solution into the dialog and click **Save**.

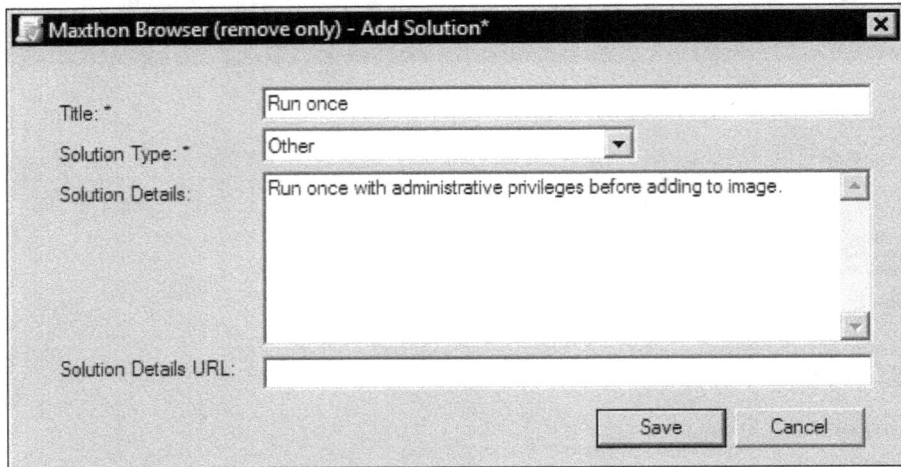

5. Switch back to the **Issue Detail** tab, click the **Resolve Issue** icon, and close the window.

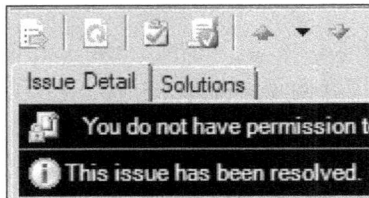

The application attempted to store a file in a system location that was virtualized by Windows Vista

You'll notice that the next issue in the list has a severity rating of **3**, which means it's not as serious as the first, at least on Vista and Windows 7, as UAC File Virtualization will automatically redirect any reads and writes to a special per-user area of the filesystem.

As UAC File and Registry Virtualization is intended only as a temporary measure to counteract Least Privilege Security compatibility issues, ACT flags our error as *nice to fix*. While it would be preferable to modify the application, it's not worth our time trying to change the application code ourselves or create a compatibility shim, unless Windows XP is the predominant OS. It's likely that the latest version of the application will resolve the issue, and if the application was written internally, you should refer the problem to the development team.

```
API Name:                 CopyFileW
User's Account Group:     Administrators
Path:                     C:\Program Files\Maxthon\Config\config.ini
Restricted by ACL:        TRUE
Additional Path:
Requested Access:         0x40000000
```

We can see that Maxthon is trying to copy the `config.ini` file to the protected `Program Files` directory. As Maxthon stores user settings in this file, as a result on Windows XP as a standard user, all settings are lost every time the application is closed. The failure to store user preferences on closing the application will be a major headache for users, so this problem should be a top priority to fix. For now, let's assume that we're not going to run this application on Windows XP, and mark it as resolved. If you need to implement a fix for this problem, refer to *Chapter 10, Least Privilege in WIndows XP*, for possible solutions.

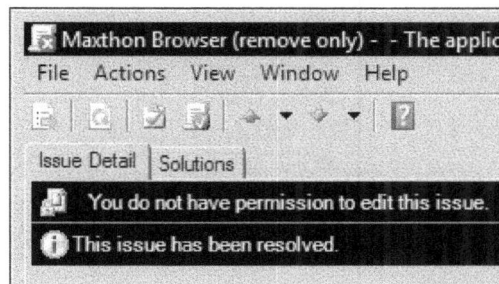

```
Maxthon Browser (remove only) - - The applic
 File   Actions   View   Window   Help

 Issue Detail | Solutions |
    You do not have permission to edit this issue.
    This issue has been resolved.
```

The application attempted to open a restricted registry key and write to a restricted registry location

Before jumping to the conclusion that these errors must be fixed, let's click **View Data** to find out exactly what's going on. All the registry keys listed here are related to Maxthon offering to make itself the PC's default browser. As long as the **default browser** setting is changed the first time the application is run, no further write access to these keys should be required. However, standard users won't be able to change this setting later.

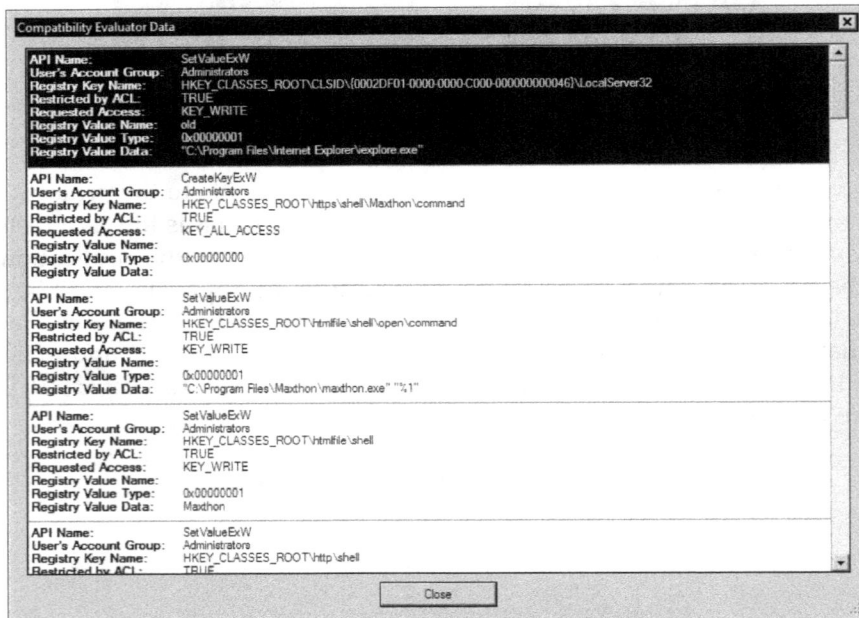

Inside the registry

HKEY_CLASSES_ROOT is a merged view of HKEY_LOCAL_MACHINE\
Software\Classes and HKEY_USERS_Classes. HKEY_CLASSES_
ROOT comes from a time when file associations were per-machine only,
that is, individual users couldn't associate file types with a program.
HKEY_CLASSES_ROOT also stores information about **context handlers**
and other settings connected with specific applications. While in new
applications this information should be written to HKEY_LOCAL_
MACHINE during the installation and to HKEY_USERS_Classes when
it is run for the first time or during usual operation, legacy applications
assume everything should be written to HKEY_CLASSES_ROOT, causing
software compatibility issues when running as a standard user.

In this example, let's mark both these issues as resolved, with the caveat that either Maxthon must be set as the default browser when run for the first time by a sysadmin, or thereafter will be limited to functioning as a secondary browser.

> If you need to implement a fix for this problem, refer to *Chapter 10, Least Privilege in WIndows XP*, for possible solutions.

The application attempted to store information under the HKEY_LOCAL_MACHINE\SOFTWARE registry hive

According to the details listed under **Issue Detail**, we can assume that UAC File and Registry Virtualization will automatically solve this problem for us. Again, the registry paths indicate that the changes Maxthon is trying to make are related to default browser settings.

Printers and Least Privilege Security

Not only are printers the bane of most system administrators' lives, but they present several complex problems when shared as a network resource, and adding Least Privilege Security to the equation further complicates matters. Let's look at the two main methods of configuring network printers:

- **Windows Print Server**: Sometimes referred to as *shared printers*. The traditional method for granting PCs access to network printers is to install the printer on a Windows Server as a *local printer* using a TCP/IP port, and then share the printer as a network resource. Users can then install the printer without administrative privileges.

- **TCP/IP**: Enterprise-class printers come with their own built-in TCP/IP print server, and don't require the printer to be installed and shared through Windows Server at the expense of centralized management. PCs are able to communicate directly over the network with the printer using the TCP/IP protocol. This has three major advantages:

  ○ Windows Server is removed as a single point of failure.

  ○ Network traffic is reduced (as data is sent across the network only once).

  ○ There are no concerns about running out of disk space on the server for large print jobs.

In least privilege environments, using Windows Print Services to deploy and manage printers offers several advantages over direct TCP/IP printing. **Point and Print** is a feature of Windows Print Services that ensures users always have the latest driver software installed, and should any settings or features on the printer change, the necessary updates are automatically made to PCs. Point and Print works without administrative privileges, but TCP/IP printer connections require an administrator to update drivers. Though it's an important feature of Point and Print that PCs don't require administrative privileges, there are numerous other advantages of using Windows Print Services such as:

- Prioritization and scheduling
- Driver administration
- Controlling access permissions to printers
- Printer pooling and print server clustering
- Auditing and tracking
- Integration with Active Directory

Installing printers using Group Policy Preferences

Shared printers and TCP/IP printers can be deployed using **Group Policy Preferences (GPP)**. A prerequisite for deploying TCP/IP printers using Group Policy Preferences is that the printer must be installed locally and shared on a Windows Server. The share must be enabled for a TCP/IP printer connection to install on a PC successfully using Group Policy Preferences, but once installed, the share is not referenced again unless the printer needs to be reinstalled or the settings need to be updated.

Installing printers using Windows Server 2003 Print Management and Group Policy

If you're not running a Windows Server 2008 domain, *Windows Server 2003 Release 2* introduced the Print Management Console and the ability to deploy printers using Group Policy. The Print Management Console can be used to add per-machine or per-user printer deployment information to a **Group Policy Object (GPO)**. It uses a small executable to deploy the printers (PushPrinterConnections. exe), as part of a logon script for per-user connections or as a startup script for per-machine connections.

> The PushPrinterConnections.exe program is not required in Windows Vista or later.

Installing printers using a script

If your printers are shared through Windows Print Services, users will be able to search Active Directory and add printers without any administrative privileges. To deploy printers automatically to users, you can use a Visual Basic script to add per-user printer connections, or printui.dll to add per-machine printer connections.

> **printui.dll**
>
> For information about calling printui.dll from a script to add per-machine printer connections, download PrintUIUsers.doc from http://download.microsoft.com/download/8/2/c/82cffcfa-56f6-4fc3-bfa5-80cd84793871/PrintUIUsersGuide.doc.

Windows Script Host (WSH) has two methods as part of the **WshNetwork Object** that can be used to map printer connections.

- **AddPrinterConnection** maps a remote printer to a local port.
- **AddWindowsPrinterConnection** adds a shared windows-based printer.

Here's an example of how you can map a printer connection using WSH with Visual Basic script:

```
Set WshNetwork = WScript.CreateObject("WScript.Network")
Printer1 = \\WIN01PS\OfficePrinterHP
WshNetwork.AddWindowsPrinterConnection Printer1
```

Logon scripts

Many organizations use logon scripts to configure users' environments every time they log on to a PC. In the past, with limited management technology included in Windows out of the box, scripting was the favored method for managing settings. Some typical tasks that logon scripts perform are listed as follows:

- Synchronizing the system time
- Updating antivirus definitions
- Changing protected system configuration
- Mapping network drives
- Mapping printers
- Creating desktop shortcuts

I would encourage you to use scripting as a last resort. Logon scripts have been superseded by Group Policy Preferences, which is a management technology that was introduced in Windows Server 2008. Most of the common functions that logon scripts perform can be achieved using Group Policy Preferences, so there should be no need to write and maintain scripts in most cases. However, to take advantage of Group Policy Preferences, you need to be running a Windows Server 2008 domain.

Synchronizing the system time

This is common function found embedded in logon scripts, but in Windows 2000 and later, the **Windows Time Service** synchronizes the time of all domain-joined computers. Therefore, you should be able to remove any time synchronization functionality in your logon scripts for all PCs running NT-based Windows, starting with Windows 2000 Professional.

Windows Time Service

Windows 2000 introduced the Windows Time Service, which can be controlled from the command line using the `w32tm` command. Most functions require the user to have administrative privileges. In standard domain-based environments, you usually don't need to worry about configuring the system time, as the Windows Time Service handles this automatically.

Updating antivirus definitions

Many legacy antivirus applications offered the ability to update antivirus scanning engines and definitions by calling a remote application from a logon script. This was often the easiest way for system administrators to configure corporate antivirus systems, but required users to have administrative privileges on the local machine.

New enterprise-class antivirus solutions are compatible with Least Privilege Security, and calling executables from a logon script is considered a legacy means of updating definitions or scanning engines. Check the administrators' guide of your antivirus solution and ensure that logon scripts are not being used to update client components.

Changing protected system configuration

Logon scripts are sometimes used to add, modify, or remove protected files or registry keys. Batch files may also be called to install third-party hotfixes or make other system modifications. If you really need to modify the registry and if you have a Windows Server 2008 domain, use Group Policy Preferences. Group Policy Preferences run, by default, in the context of the Local System account, so they can perform actions that are usually restricted for a standard user. If Group Policy Preferences are not an option, you can use **Group Policy Startup Scripts**. Similar to the concept of a logon script, a startup script runs before users log on, and most importantly runs in the security context of the local computer account. As such, startup scripts can make modifications to the system as if they were a local administrator.

If you need to distribute hotfixes or software to your PCs automatically, you should consider using **Group Policy Software Installation** or a third-party product. Group Policy Software Installation is a free component of Active Directory, and can be used to install software on PCs where Least Privilege Security is used. Windows patches should be managed centrally by **Windows Server Update Services**. Updates can be installed automatically and controlled by system administrators from a central management console.

Mapping network drives and printers

Group Policy Preferences can provide users with network driver and printer connections every time they log on and should be used in preference to scripting. However, if you need to use legacy logon scripts, no administrative privileges are required to map a network drive.

Mapping per-user printer connections from a Windows Print Server doesn't require administrative privileges. If you use a script to create local printer ports for TCP/IP printers, you will run into compatibility problems with Least Privilege Security. Use of a Windows Print Server is recommended for least privilege environments.

Creating desktop shortcuts

As with network drives, Group Policy Preferences can be used to provide users with desktop shortcuts, and as long as shortcuts are created on individual user desktops and not on the desktop of the Default User Profile or All Users, no administrative privileges are required when using a legacy logon script.

Why do a desktop refresh from a technical perspective?

In *Chapter 2, Political and Cultural Challenges for Least Privilege Security*, we discussed the political reasons for integrating a move to Least Privilege Security with a desktop refresh project. However, there are also sound technical justifications why you should consider installing a new OS image at the same time as implementing least privilege.

Though we could simply apply Least Privilege Security to an existing system and reap some benefit, a new standardized image with built-in Least Privilege Security allows us to ensure a problem-free experience, and provides additional benefits such as the extra performance gained from a new install and elimination of undetected viruses, software, and configuration errors that might impede performance.

Testing images before production

If you intend to undertake a desktop refresh project, you must thoroughly test the images you create before they are used in your production environment.

One of the many advantages of Least Privilege Security is that it prevents problems from manifesting themselves by blocking unwanted changes to system configuration. If we apply Least Privilege to an existing system without a new image, we freeze any existing configuration errors into the system, and users won't experience the full benefit of Least Privilege. We'll discuss reinstalling the existing operating system rather than upgrading to something new, as it has its own set of concerns and requires extra planning.

> For the purposes of this book, unless stated otherwise, Least Privilege Security on the desktop assumes running with a standard user account. Vista and Windows 7 also have an account type called *Protected Administrator* that provides many of the benefits of a standard user, but is not ideal in a corporate setting as it still allows users to modify critical system settings.

Different methods of reinstalling Windows

Pre Vista, when installing a fresh version of Windows from the DVD media, it was best practice to reformat the disk and then proceed with the install. It's inevitable that in an unmanaged environment, there will be data stored on PC hard disks, so reformatting introduces the risk of losing important data.

Manual, non-destructive install

The **Windows Imaging Format** (**WIM**) introduced in Vista can install OS images non-destructively, leaving existing data on the disk intact. Provided that you're working with Vista or Windows 7, WIM file-based imaging technology provides system administrators with the option to leave all user files and settings in place, and application binaries are retained on the local disk, though not installed in the new operating system.

Automated install

If you choose to automate the process, the **Microsoft Deployment Toolkit** (**MDT**) automatically migrates users' files and settings to the new operating system and optionally backs up the entire OS before reinstalling.

Reinstall Vista or Windows 7 with Least Privilege Security

It's important to understand that the default install of Vista or Windows 7 is configured for Least Privilege Security. In many organizations, system administrators add the Domain Users group or individual user accounts to the local administrators group and switch off User Account Control to ensure that all applications work correctly. This is known as an unmanaged environment, where users install their own software, change settings, and use PCs that don't work properly—which requires a lot of attention from IT to keep PCs working.

> In the demo that follows, we're going to reinstall Windows 7. The procedure is the same for Windows Vista.

We want to reinstall Windows 7, preserving all user files and settings, and ensure that any applications that were previously installed get added back to the new system. This process is known as a desktop refresh.

> **Thin versus fat images**
>
> A **thin image** has little or no OS customization, thereby giving more flexibility when settings and applications need to be changed or updated on a regular basis. A **fat image** contains all the applications and configuration settings from the get go.

As creating custom images is not within the scope of this book, we're going to use a thin image and MDT to install core applications such as Microsoft Office, and back up the old image and preserve users' settings and files. Other applications and configuration settings can be added later using Group Policy.

> **Where is all the important data?**
>
> Group Policy should be used to enforce storage of all important data on servers. Windows contains a feature called *Offline Files* that synchronizes users' files stored on servers with notebooks, and vice versa. So, when disconnected from the network, users always have access to their files.

Installing the Microsoft Deployment Toolkit

Install MDT on Vista or Windows 7, making sure that you have enough disk space to store at least one WIM image (7 or 8 GB should be more than enough). The **Windows Automated Installation Kit (WAIK)** is a prerequisite component.

> **Downloads**
>
> **MDT 2010** — `http://www.microsoft.com/downloads/ details.aspx?FamilyId=3BD8561F-77AC-4400-A0C1- FE871C461A89&displaylang=en`.
>
> **Windows Automated Installation Kit (WAIK)** — `http://www. microsoft.com/downloads/details.aspx?familyid=696DD665- 9F76-4177-A811-39C26D3B3B34&displaylang=ena`

Once the two main tools are installed, we'll need to add the **User State Migration Tool (USMT 3.0.1)** to the list of downloaded components. Log on to the machine where MDT is installed as a local administrator:

1. Start `Deployment Workbench` from the `Microsoft Deployment Toolkit` folder in **Start | All Programs**.

2. In the left pane, expand **Infosrmation Center** and click **Components**.

3. Under **Components** in the central pane, click **User State Migration Tool 3.0.1,** choosing the **x86** or **x64** version as appropriate, and click **Download** at the bottom of the screen.

Components			
Description	Architecture	Version	Status
Available for Download			
User State Migration Tool 3.0.1 (x64)	X64	3.0	
MSXML 6.0	X64	6.0	
KMS 1.1 for Windows Server 2003 x86	X86	1.1	
KMS 1.1 for Windows Server 2003 x64	X64	1.1	
KMS Management Pack for MOM 2005	Any	1.0	
Volume Activation Management Tool	Any	1.0	
Office Migration Planning Manager	Any	1.0	
Microsoft Assessment and Planning (MAP) x86	X86	3.2	
Microsoft Assessment and Planning (MAP) x64	X64	3.2	
Security Compliance Management Toolkit	Any	2.0	
Unavailable for Download			
Windows Automated Installation Kit (x64) 2.0	X64	6.1.0.0	
Filter manager rollup package for Windows XP SP2...	X86	KB 914882	
Offline servicing kernel patch for Windows XP SP2...	X86	KB 926044	
Offline servicing kernel patch for Windows Server ...	X86	KB 926044	
Offline servicing kernel patch for Windows Server ...	X64	KB 926044	

Details

You can use the User State Migration Tool (USMT) 3.0 to migrate user files and settings during large deployments of Microsoft Windows XP and Microsoft Windows Vista operating systems. USMT captures desktop, and application settings, as well as user accounts and user files, and then migrates them to a new Windows installation. Using USMT can help you improve and simplify your migration process. You can use USMT for both side-by-side and wipe-and-load migrations. If you are only upgrading your operating system, USMT is not needed.

Applicable OS versions:

Download

Creating a deployment share

Once MDT and all the required components are installed, we need to create a deployment share. Our existing Windows 7 client will connect to this share when installing the new image:

1. Launch **Deployment Workbench** from the **Start** menu.

2. Right-click **Deployment Shares** in the left pane and select **New Deployment Share** from the menu.

3. Accept the default deployment share path (`c:\DeploymentShare`) and click **Next**.

> Note that the `DeploymentShare` folder must exist before you can continue.

4. Leave `DeploymentShare$` as the **Share Name** and click **Next**. Do the same for **Deployment share description**.

5. Click **Next** through the **Allow Image Capture**, **Allow Admin Password**, and **Allow Product Key** screens, thus accepting the default settings.

6. Check the information on the **Summary** screen and click **Next**.

7. Click **Finish** on the **Confirmation** screen once all tasks are complete.

Adding an operating system image

Now that we've created our deployment share, we need to add a Windows 7 image. We'll use the default image from the Windows 7 installation media and configure the OS later using Group Policy.

1. Expand **Deployment Shares | MDT Deployment** and right-click **Operating Systems**.

2. Select **Import Operating System** from the menu. The Import Operating System Wizard will start.

3. On the **OS Type** screen, select **Full set of source files** and click **Next**.

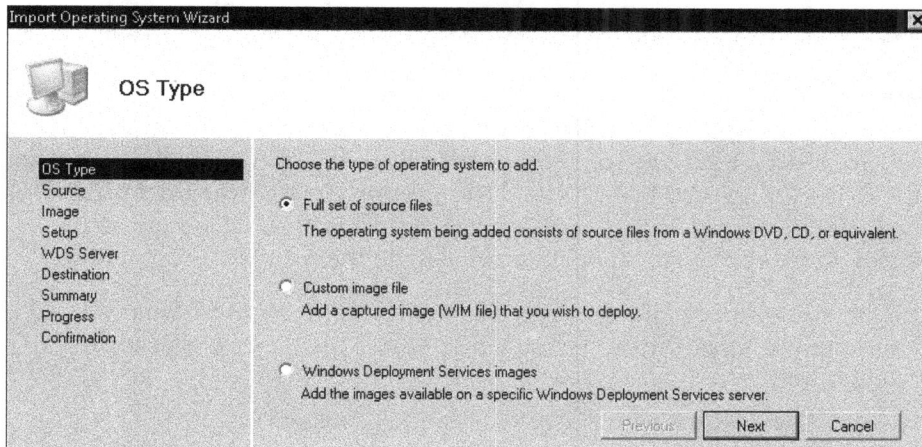

4. Insert the Windows 7 media into the local DVD-ROM drive and
    click **Browse**.

5. Select your DVD-ROM drive in the **Browse for Folder** window and click **OK**.
    The **Source directory** field will show the path to your DVD-ROM drive.

6. Click **Next** to continue.

7. The wizard should automatically detect the Windows 7 images on the
    DVD and suggest an appropriate destination directory name.

8. Click **Next** to continue.

9. The **Summary** screen appears, showing details of the pending operation.
    Click **Next** to continue.

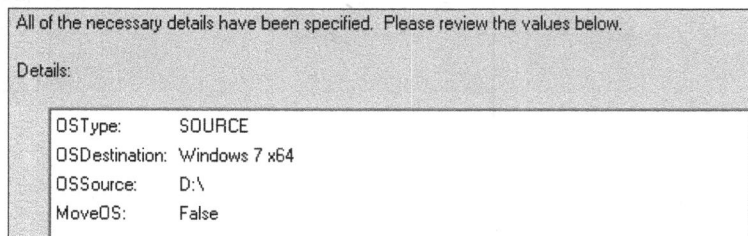

10. Importing the image to our deployment share may take some time, so
    be patient! Once completed, **Operating system import complete** will be
    displayed and you can click **Finish**.

Adding core packages to our Lite Touch installation

Although we're going to rely on Group Policy to distribute most of our software, let's add Microsoft Office 2007 as a core application, which we can choose to include when the OS is deployed. MDT will add the application after the operating system has been installed, maintaining the concept of a thin image and giving us the opportunity to make changes quickly and easily in the future.

1. Right-click **Applications** under the **MDT Deployment Share** node, select **New Application** from the menu, and the **New Application Wizard** will start.

2. Select **Application with source files** and click **Next**.

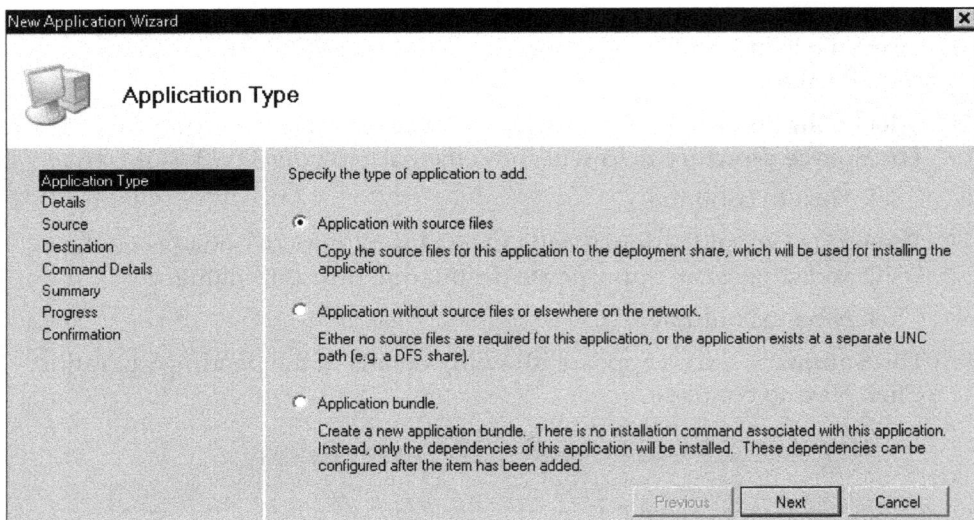

3. On the **Details** screen, type a name for the application and click **Next**.

4. Browse to the source files for Office 2007, in this case a folder called O_2007 on a network share called distribution, and click **OK**.

> **Microsoft Office 2007 administrative installation point**
>
> If you don't already have an administrative installation point for Office, you can find more information on customizing Office 2007 at Microsoft's website: http://technet.microsoft.com/en-us/library/cc179097(office.12).aspx.

5. On the **Destination** screen, accept the default directory name and click **Next**.

6. Enter setup.exe in the **Command line** field, leave the path for the working directory as default, and click **Next**.

7. Click **Next** on the **Summary** screen and wait for the application source files to be copied to our deployment share.

8. Click **Finish** on the **Confirmation** screen.

Creating a Lite Touch task sequence

Now that we've got our operating system image and main application added to the MDT deployment share, we need to create a **task sequence** to install the new image and application(s) while at the same time giving the sysadmin some options such as the ability to create a full backup and preserve users' settings and files.

1. Right-click **Task Sequences** under the **MDT Deployment Share** node and select **New Task Sequence** from the menu. The **New Task Sequence Wizard** will start.

2. Enter a Task Sequence ID, a name, and click **Next**.

3. Select **Standard Client Task Sequence** from the drop-down menu and click **Next**.

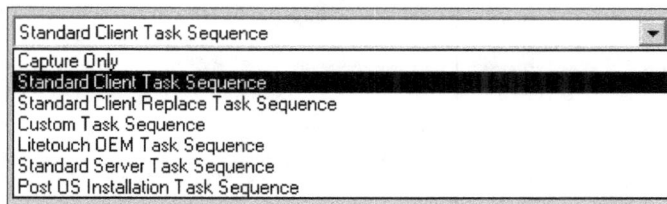

4. Our WIM image contains all the available SDKs of Windows 7, so here we need to decide which one we are going to deploy. This will largely depend on your licensing agreement with Microsoft, but you definitely don't want to use any of the *Home* versions. Select either **Windows 7 PROFESSIONAL** or **Windows 7 ULTIMATE** and click **Next**.

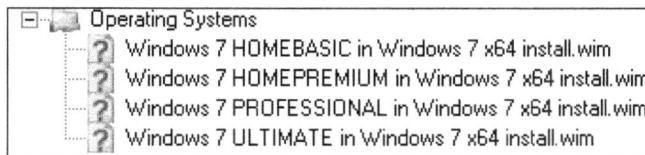

> **Windows 7 SDKs**
>
> If you're a Microsoft Volume License customer, use the *Enterprise Edition* of Windows 7.

5. Select **Do not specify a product key at this time** on the **Specify Product Key** screen and click **Next**. For more information about license keys and product activation in a production environment, see the following information at Microsoft's website: `http://www.microsoft.com/licensing/existing-customers/product-activation.aspx`.

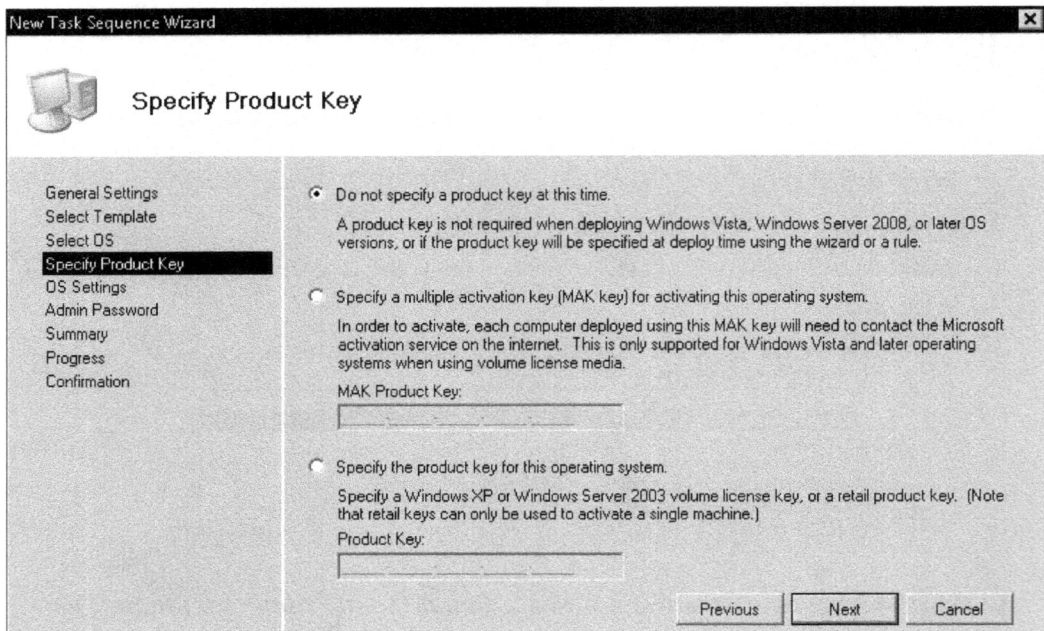

6. Complete the **Full Name, Organization**, and **Internet Explorer Home Page** fields on the **OS Settings** screen and click **Next**.

7. On the **Admin Password** screen, select **Do not specify an Administrator password at this time** and click **Next**.

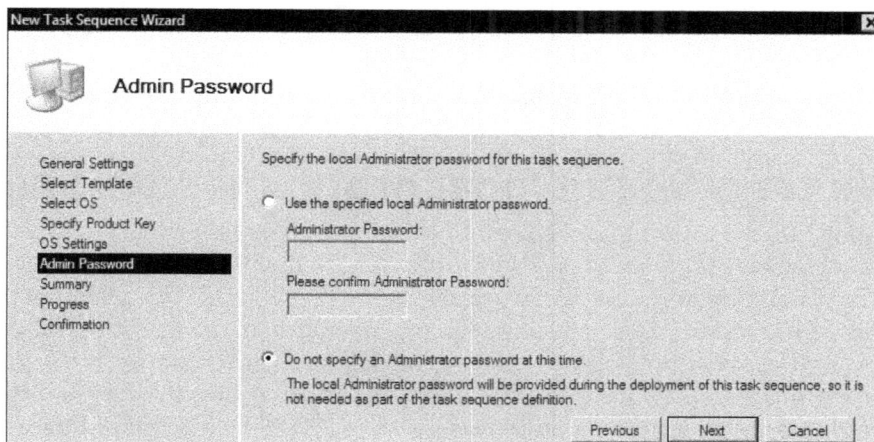

As a best practice, you should specify a different local administrator password for each client PC.

8. Click **Next** on the **Summary** screen and then **Finish** on the confirmation screen.

Updating our deployment share

Now that we've added an OS image, applications, and a task sequence, we need to update the deployment share that we created earlier.

1. Select the **Deployment Share** node in the left pane, right-click the **MDT Deployment Share** in the central pane, and select **Update Deployment Share** from the menu.

2. The **Update Deployment Share Wizard** will start. Check **Optimize the boot image updating process** and click **Next**.

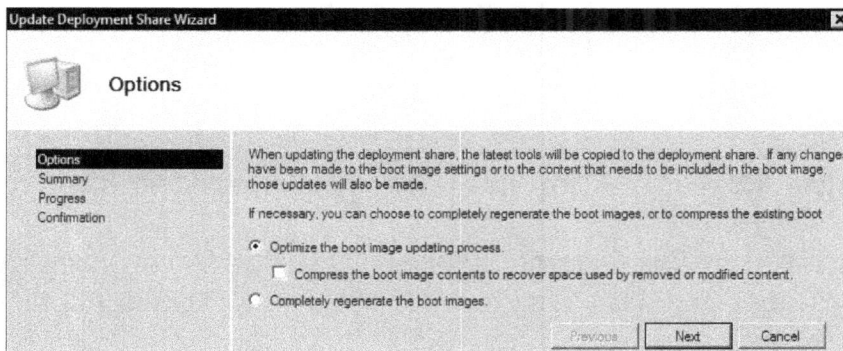

3. Check the details on the **Summary** screen and click **Next**. The update process may take some time, so be patient.

4. Once the process is complete, click **Finish** on the **Confirmation** screen.

Preserving default local group membership

The **Standard Client Task Sequence** restores local group membership by default when the operating system is re-installed. We want to ensure that the local Administrators, Power Users, and Network Operators groups are not populated with accounts that should run as a standard user. If you don't have the option of using Group Policy to control group membership, you can prevent the task sequence from restoring groups, thereby ensuring that users log on with standard user privileges, by disabling the **Restore Groups** script. Expand **Deployment Shares**, **MDT Deployment Share**, and select **Task Sequences** in the left pane of **Deployment Workbench**.

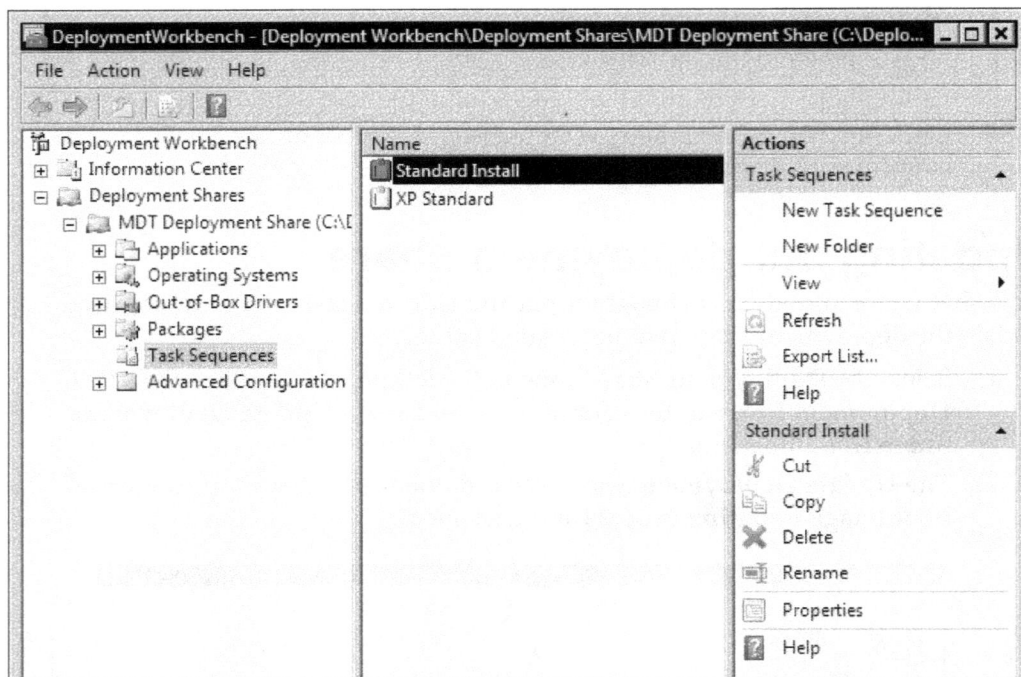

1. Right-click your **Task Sequence** in the central pane and select **Properties** from the menu.

2. Switch to the **Task Sequence** tab and select **Restore Groups** on the left.

3. Go to the **Options** tab on the right-hand pane, select **Disable this step,** and click **OK**.

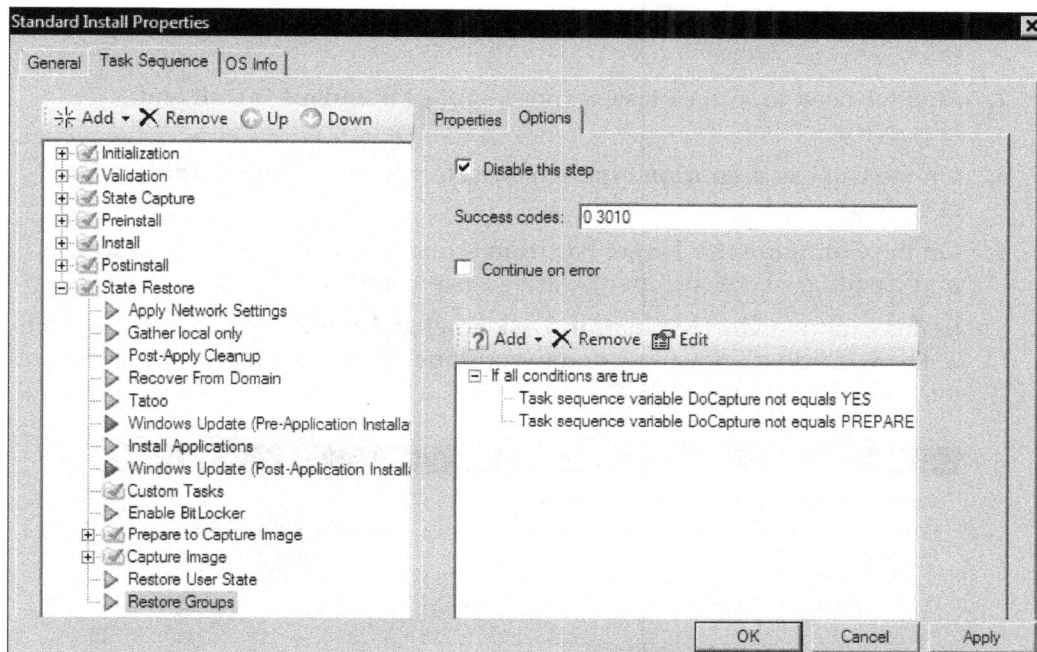

Standard Install Properties

General | **Task Sequence** | OS Info |

⁜ Add ▾ ✕ Remove ⟲ Up ⟳ Down | Properties | **Options** |

- ⊞ Initialization
- ⊞ Validation
- ⊞ State Capture
- ⊞ Preinstall
- ⊞ Install
- ⊞ Postinstall
- ⊟ State Restore
  - ▷ Apply Network Settings
  - ▷ Gather local only
  - ▷ Post-Apply Cleanup
  - ▷ Recover From Domain
  - ▷ Tatoo
  - ▷ Windows Update (Pre-Application Installa
  - ▷ Install Applications
  - ▷ Windows Update (Post-Application Install
  - ▷ Custom Tasks
  - ▷ Enable BitLocker
  - ⊞ Prepare to Capture Image
  - ⊞ Capture Image
  - ▷ Restore User State
  - ▷ Restore Groups

☑ Disable this step

Success codes: `0 3010`

☐ Continue on error

? Add ▾ ✕ Remove ▦ Edit

- ⊟ If all conditions are true
  - Task sequence variable DoCapture not equals YES
  - Task sequence variable DoCapture not equals PREPARE

[OK]   [Cancel]   [Apply]

Local group membership dependencies

If you choose not to restore local group membership in the task sequence, you should test line of business functionality after the OS has re-installed, as there may be local group membership dependencies in your environment.

Refreshing our OS with the Windows Deployment Wizard

Let's run our Lite Touch installation from an existing Windows 7 PC. To complete the installation process successfully, your environment must have a properly configured *DHCP* and *DNS* server, so that the machine can pick up a new IP address when it reboots and locate our MDT deployment share using DNS resolution. Log on to the Windows 7 machine that you want to refresh as a domain administrator.

1. Browse to the remote MDT deployment share. Run `LiteTouch.vbs` in the `Scripts` folder.

2. First we need to select a task sequence. Select **Standard Install** and click **Next**.

3. On the **Choose migration type** screen, select **Refresh this computer** and click **Next**.

4. On the **Configure the Target Partition** screen, select the destination disk and partition of the current operating system and click **Next**.

    In this example, the **Destination Disk** is set to **0** and **Destination Partition** to **2**. The wizard will not allow you to continue if you can't identify the disk and partition of the current OS.

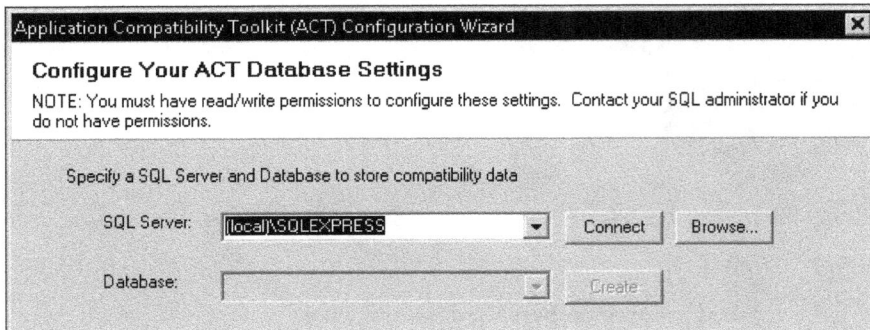

Determining the disk and partition

If you're unsure about which disk and partition the current operating system is installed on, you can use the `diskpart` command to enumerate the local disks and partitions. Log on to your PC as a local or domain administrator and open a command prompt from the **Start** menu.

Type `list disk` at the `DISKPART>` prompt. The chances are you'll have only one physical disk and it will show as disk 0. Type `select disk 0` in the prompt and then `list partition`. Take a look at the partition table and try to determine where the OS is likely to be installed. In this case, I think that partition 2 contains the OS boot files. To check, type `select partition 2` at the prompt and then `detail partition`. The command output confirms the drive letter as `C` and that it's a bootable partition.

5. Next, enter a computer name on the **Configure the computer name** screen and click **Next**.

6. Decide whether you want to join this machine back to your domain or leave it as a *workgroup* machine, and enter the necessary details on the **Join the computer to a domain or workgroup** screen. In order to keep it simple, I've decided not to join the computer to a domain at this time. Click **Next** to continue.

7. We want to preserve users' settings and files, so select **Automatically determine the location** and click **Next**.

Specify where to save your data and settings.

    • Automatically determine the location.
        Let the system determine the best location based on available disk space.

        ☑ Allow data and settings to be stored locally when possible.

    ○ Specify a location.
        Save all configuration information for later restoration.

        Location:

        [   ] Browse

    ○ Do not save data and settings.
        All user data and settings will be lost.

8. To be on the safe side, you should create a backup. Again for simplicity, I've chosen not to back up the computer, and continue by clicking **Next**.

9. Choose appropriate **Locale** and **Keyboard** options from the drop-down menus and click **Next** to continue.

10. Choose the appropriate time zone and click **Next**.

11. Now we get the opportunity to add applications. Select **Office 2007 Professional** and click **Next**.

12. As this is not a notebook and the PC will be physically secure, I'm not going to enable BitLocker. Click **Next** to continue.

13. When the PC reboots, it will need to connect back to our MDT deployment share to complete the installation. Enter credentials that have permission to connect to the deployment share and click **Next**.

> **Deployment share credentials**
>
> Make sure you get the details right here, as the wizard doesn't perform any checks to verify the credentials, and if the share cannot be reached during the installation process, the entire procedure will fail.

14. You can check the installation details on the **Ready to begin** screen by clicking **Details**.
15. Once you're happy that everything's correct, click **Begin**.

The first phase of installation captures user settings and files, and stores them in a file on the local hard disk. They are then applied back to the machine once the OS has reinstalled.

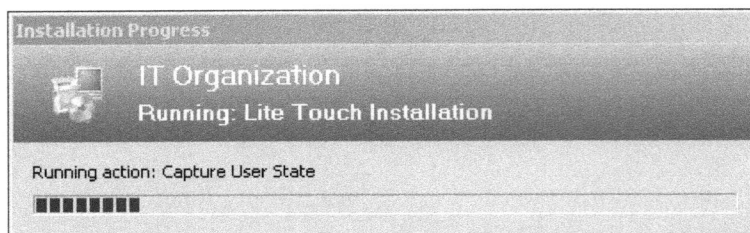

The machine will reboot and, assuming Windows PE is able to successfully connect back to our deployment share, the installation will continue according to the options you selected using the **Windows Deployment Wizard**.

Summary

In this chapter, we've seen how to prepare Vista or Windows 7 for use in an environment with Least Privilege Security. By the end of the chapter, you should be able to:

- Create an inventory of all the software installed on our network
- Identify potential issues with User Account Control and Least Privilege Security on PCs running on Vista and Windows 7
- Prepare, or even eliminate, legacy logon scripts for Least Privilege Security
- Create an automated MDT task sequence to refresh Windows 7

In the next chapter, we'll look at how Terminal Services can be used to help solve application compatibility and distribution problems faced when working with standard user accounts.

12
Provisioning Applications on Secure Desktops with Remote Desktop Services

As one of the key pain points of Least Privilege Security is distributing and updating applications on desktops, the next three chapters are dedicated to different technologies that can be used to get applications to users quickly and easily without the need for administrative rights on the local machine. This chapter focuses on one of the oldest but still commonly used technologies, *Terminal Services*, and is intended to give a basic overview of the technology and how it might be used to overcome some of the challenges of Least Privilege Security on the desktop. In this chapter we'll learn how to:

- Install the core server roles for Remote Desktop Services in Windows Server 2008 R2 using Windows PowerShell
- Set up and understand Remote Desktop Licensing
- Configure Remote Desktop Gateway for secure remote access to applications over HTTPS
- Advertise published Remote Applications on Windows 7's Start menu using Remote Desktop Web Access

Consider a scenario where a user requests that a trial application be installed so that it can be evaluated. In a managed environment where standard user accounts are implemented, simply installing the application on the user's PC could be problematic, as the application hasn't been tested for compatibility with Least Privilege, and also could conflict with line-of-business applications. Remote Desktop Services gives system administrators the opportunity to quickly install an application on a remote server, at the same time giving users access as if it was installed locally without making any changes to the user's PC.

Introducing Remote Desktop Services

The name for a collection of service roles in Windows Server, Remote Desktop Services — formerly known as Terminal Services — provides access to applications or complete desktops hosted on remote servers over the network using the **Remote Desktop Protocol (RDP)**.

The ability to centrally install and manage applications, as opposed to distributing and installing programs on individual PCs, has several **advantages**:

- Application workload is transferred to the server, allowing low-powered devices to run applications that might not be supported if installed locally
- No special privileges are required by users to run applications
- Application updates and patches need only be applied to programs installed on the Remote Desktop Server(s)
- Data can be stored exclusively on the Remote Desktop Server, reducing the risk that sensitive information could be compromised from a stolen or hacked device

While Remote Desktop Services can provide organizations with much flexibility, it's not without its **disadvantages**:

- Remote connections to Remote Desktop Servers require each user to have a **Client Access License (RDS CAL) in addition to a standard Windows CAL to access the server**. The typical list price for a single CAL is $85 on Microsoft's Open License for Business program, which requires you to buy a minimum of five licenses, but prices can vary considerably depending on the license scheme used. **Windows 2000 and XP Professional clients can access a Windows 2000 Terminal Server without a TS CAL.**
- A network link is required to make a connection to a Remote Desktop Server.
- Some applications, especially those with heavy graphics or multimedia requirements, don't perform well when running across the Remote Desktop Protocol. Windows Server 2008 Service Pack 1 will include **Microsoft RemoteFX**, a technology that's designed to improve RDS performance for media-rich applications.

Installing Remote Desktop Session Host and Licensing roles

Session Host is the server role for Remote Desktop Services that enables system administrators to give users remote access to applications or desktops hosted on a Remote Desktop Server. While a limited number of administrators can access any Windows Server without installing RD Session Host, to use the full functionality of Remote Desktop Services, the Session Host server role must be installed.

Remote Desktop Services can be used without CALs for 120 days, but after that period, to continue use, you must install the RD Licensing role and purchase the necessary quantity of licenses. Let's start off with the basics and get the RD Session Host and Licensing roles installed in Windows Server 2008 R2.

1. Log in to the Windows Server 2008 R2 system that you want to designate as a Remote Desktop Server with a domain administrator account.

2. Install the Remote Desktop Service roles using PowerShell, which can be launched from the taskbar or by typing `PowerShell` into the **Search programs and files** box on the Start menu.

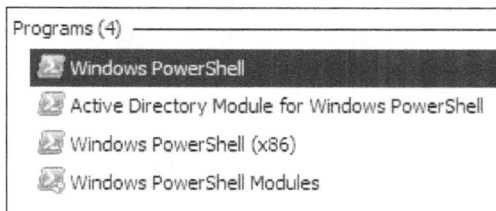

3. Before running the following commands, you'll need to import the Server Manager module into PowerShell by typing `Import-Module servermanager` and pressing *Enter*. First add the Remote Desktop Services feature:

```
Add-WindowsFeature RDS-RD-Server
```

4. You will now need to restart the server before you can install any more roles or features. Once the server has rebooted, install the RD Licensing role:

```
Add-WindowsFeature RDS-Licensing
```

Controlling access to the Remote Desktop Server

Now that the core Remote Desktop Services roles are installed, we need to grant access to domain users who want to connect to the server remotely, and we need to enable inbound access for the Remote Desktop Protocol. Access is controlled via membership of the local Remote Desktop Users group on the Remote Desktop Server. Start by adding a domain user to the Remote Desktop Users group from the command line.

1. In the PowerShell window, type `net localgroup "Remote Desktop Users" AD\User /ADD` into the command prompt, replacing `AD\User` with the name of your domain and user account, and press *Enter*.

2. Now we'll enable the Remote Desktop inbound firewall rule that exists by default in the Windows Firewall advanced firewall settings. Type `netsh advfirewall firewall set rule name="Remote Desktop (TCP-In)" new enable=yes` and press *Enter*.

3. Now go to a Windows 7 client in your domain, start the **Remote Desktop Connection** client from the **Start** menu and enter the DNS name of the Remote Desktop Server and credentials of the user we added to the Remote Desktop Users group in Step 1.

Installing the Remote Desktop Gateway

Standard Remote Desktop Server access uses the Remote Desktop Protocol over TCP port 3389. This is fine if all users are located on the corporate intranet, but for mobile Internet users who are using a public Internet connection, outbound access is often restricted to HTTP (TCP/80) and HTTPS (TCP/433). The RD Gateway server role provides access to your Remote Desktop Servers over HTTPS on TCP port 443, ensuring that remote users can get access to any Remote Desktop Servers you choose to publish on the Internet.

Log in to your Remote Desktop Server using a domain administrator account before performing the following steps:

1. Open PowerShell from the **Start** menu and type `Import-Module servermanager` and press *Enter*.

2. Type `Add-WindowsFeature RDS-Gateway` and press *Enter*.

3. Once the RD Gateway role has installed successfully, open **Remote Desktop Gateway Manager** from **Start | Administrative Tools | Remote Desktop Services**.

4. In the RD Gateway Manager window in the left pane, right-click your Remote Desktop Server and select **Properties** from the menu.

5. In the **Properties** dialog window, click **Create and Import Certificate**.

6. In the **Create Self-Signed Certificate** dialog box, accept the default settings and click **OK**.

SSL Certificates

In a production environment, it is best practice to use a certificate issued by an internal or external **Certification Authority** (**CA**). The CA server role can be installed in Windows Server (Standard, Enterprise, and Datacenter editions) and issues X.509 certificates. Self-signed certificates are intended for testing purposes only. Any self-signed certificate issued through this dialog box will expire after six months and must be replaced.

7. Click **OK** in the **RD Gateway** dialog box, confirming the creation and location of the certificate, and then click **OK** in the **Properties** dialog box.

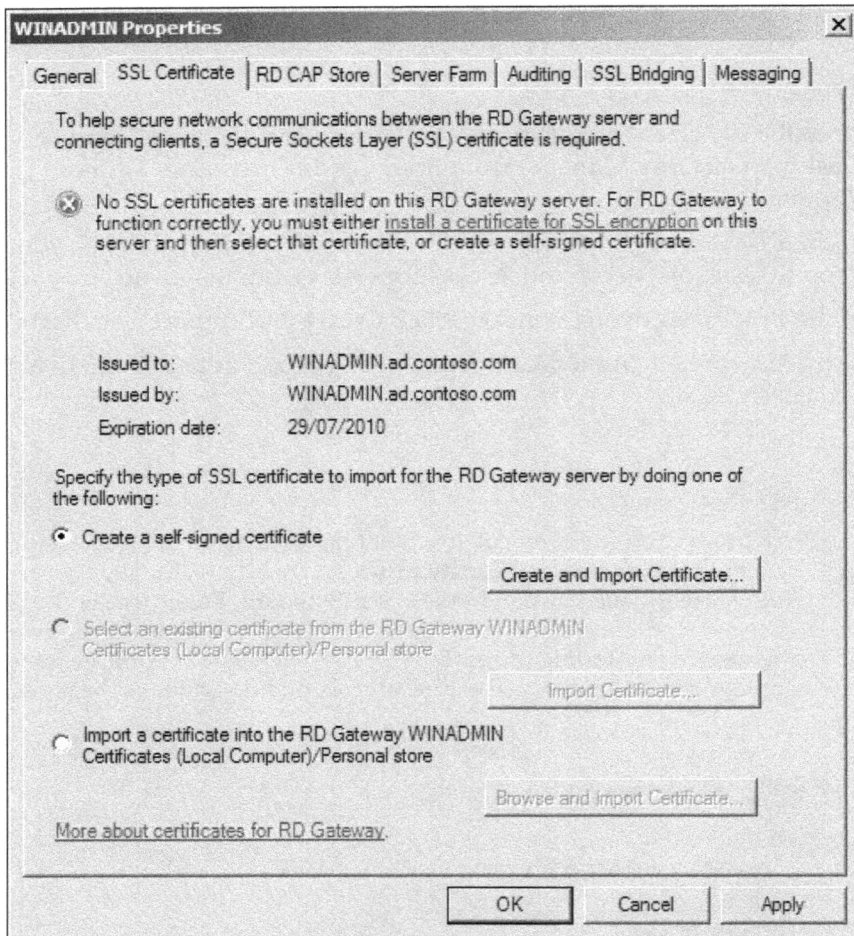

8. Close RD Gateway Manager.

Creating Connection (CAP) and Resource (RAP) Authorization Policies

Before users can connect to an RD Gateway Server, Network Policy Server, which is installed automatically when RDS is set up, must be configured with CAP and RAP policies.

1. In **RD Gateway Manager**, select the RD Gateway Server in the left pane and then click **Create connection authorization policy** in the central pane.

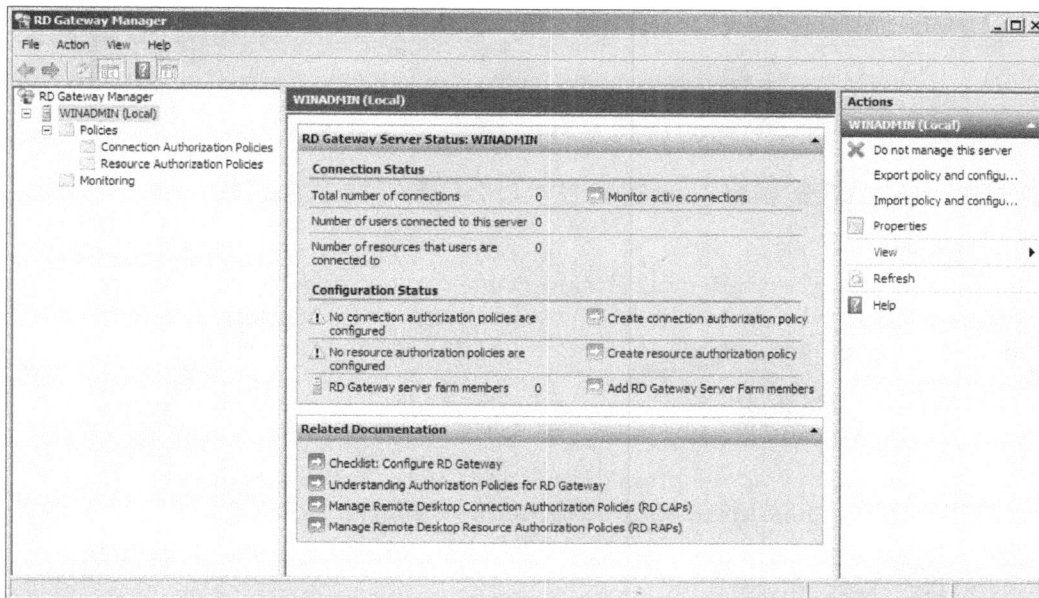

2. In the **New RD Cap** dialog box, name the policy RD_CAP_01 on the **General** tab.

3. Switch to the **Requirements** tab and click **Add Group** to the right of **User group membership (required)**.

4. In the **Select Groups** dialog box, click **Locations** and in the **Locations** dialog box, select the RD Gateway server and click **OK**.

5. In the **Select Groups** dialog box, type `Remote Desktop Users` into the **Enter the object names to select** box, click **Check Names** and then **OK**.

6. Click **OK** in the **New RD Cap** dialog box.

7. In RD Gateway Manager, select the RD Gateway Server in the left pane and then click **Create resource authorization policy** in the central pane.

8. In the **New RD Rap** dialog box, name the policy RD_RAP_01 on the **General** tab.

9. Switch to the **User Groups** tab and click **Add**.

10. In the **Select Groups** dialog box, type `Remote Desktop Users` into the **Enter the object names to select** box, click **Check Names** and then **OK**.

11. Switch to the **Network Resource** tab and check **Allow users to connect to any network resource** and click **OK**.

> In a production environment, you should limit the servers to which users can connect on the Network Resource tab.

Installing the RD Gateway SSL Certificate in Windows 7

Before clients can access a Remote Desktop Gateway server, you must import the server's SSL certificate to Windows 7's computer certificate store. Log in to Windows 7 as a domain administrator:

1. Type MMC into the **Search programs and files** box on the **Start** menu and click **Yes** in the UAC prompt.

2. In the MMC window, press *Ctrl+M* and select **Certificates** under **Available snap-ins** in the **Add or Remove Snap-ins** dialog box.

3. Click **Add** and, in the **Certificates snap-in** dialog box, select **Computer**. Click **Next**.

4. Leave the default selection of **Local computer** and click **Finish**.

5. In the **Add or Remove Snap-ins** dialog box, click **OK**.

6. In the MMC window, expand **Certificates (Local computer)** in the left pane.

7. Right-click **Trusted Root Certification Authorities** and select **All Tasks | Import** from the menu.

8. In the **Certificate Import Wizard**, click **Next**.

9. Browse to the .cer file created in the previous steps and click **Next**.

10. Ensure that **Trusted Root Certification Authorities** is selected as the store and click **Next**.

11. Click **Finish**.

12. Click **OK** on the **Import was successful** dialog box.

13. In the MMC window, click **Certificates** under **Trusted Root Certification Authorities** and you should see the certificate for our Remote Desktop Gateway Server.

14. Close the MMC window.

[⟡ In a production environment, the certificate should be issued to the RD Gateway Server by a Certification Authority and distributed to clients using Group Policy.]

Connecting to a Remote Desktop Server via an RD Gateway from Windows 7

Now, all we need to do is configure the Remote Desktop Connection client in Windows 7 to connect using our Remote Desktop Gateway. Log in to Windows 7 as a domain user:

1. Start the **Remote Desktop Connection** client from the **Start** menu, and on the **General** tab enter the DNS name of the Remote Desktop Server and username of a user that's a member of our Remote Desktop Users group on the RD Server.

2. Switch to the **Advanced** tab, and click **Settings** under **Connect from anywhere**.

[⟡ For testing purposes, we're going to manually configure RD Gateway Server settings in the Remote Desktop Connection client. In a production environment, you should leave **Automatically detect RD Gateway server settings** selected and configure Group Policy to provide the necessary server settings: **User Configuration | Policies | Administrative Templates | Windows Components | RD Gateway**.]

3. In the **RD Gateway Server Settings** dialog box, check **Use these RD Gateway server settings**.

4. In the **Server name** box, type the full DNS name of the RD Gateway server.

5. Uncheck **Bypass RD Gateway server for local addresses** if you're testing the connection on the local intranet.

6. Under **Logon settings**, check **Use my RD Gateway credentials for the remote computer** and click **OK**.

7. Back in the Remote Desktop Connection client window, click **Connect** and then enter the password for the selected user in the **Windows Security** dialog box and click **OK**.

Installing applications on Remote Desktop Servers

Not all applications are compatible with Remote Desktop Servers, and you should always test programs and consult the developers to check if the application is supported for use on a Remote Desktop Server. Before you install an application on your Remote Desktop Server, you should turn on Install Mode to ensure that the program works correctly for multiple users who log in to the server remotely.

1. In the PowerShell window, or from a standard command prompt, type `change user /install` and press *Enter*.

2. Install the application on the Remote Desktop Server.

3. Once the install process has completed, type `change user /execute` and press *Enter* in the PowerShell window.

Publishing applications using Remote Desktop Services

After configuring access to the Remote Desktop Server, we were able to access a remote desktop using the Remote Desktop Connection client. Remote Desktop Services can also be used to publish individual applications, using a specially crafted Remote Desktop Connection (`.rdp`) file, or via Remote Desktop Web Access. Assuming you've installed at least one application on your Remote Desktop Server, let's start by looking at how to publish it using the Remote Desktop Connection client.

> RemoteApps can also be accessed via an RD Gateway Server.

Adding applications to the RemoteApp Manager

Logged in to your Remote Desktop Server as a domain administrator, complete the following steps:

1. Open **RemoteApp Manager** from **Start | Administrative Tools | Remote Desktop Services**.

RemoteApp Deployment Settings ⊠

| RD Session Host Server | RD Gateway |
| Digital Signature | Common RDP Settings | Custom RDP Settings |

You can sign .rdp files that are used for RemoteApp connections by using a digital certificate. This will allow clients to recognize and trust remote resources from your organization.

☑ Sign with a digital certificate

Digital certificate details:

Signing as: WINADMIN.ad.contoso.com

Issued by: WINADMIN.ad.contoso.com

Valid until: 29/07/2010

[Details]   [Change]

More about digitally signing files for RemoteApp connections

[OK]   [Cancel]   [Apply]

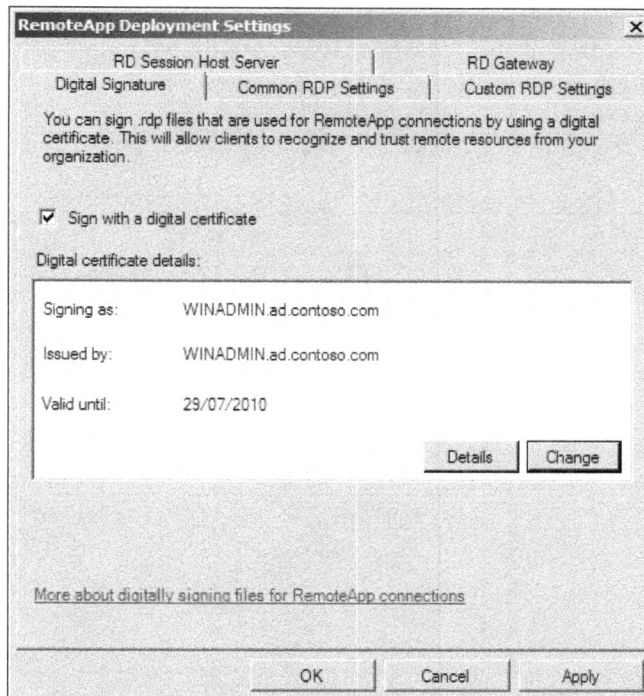

2. In the **RemoteApp Manager** window, click **Add RemoteApp Programs** in the **Actions** pane on the right.

3. In the **RemoteApp Wizard** dialog box, click **Next** to start the process.

4. Select an installed application from the list and click **Next**.

5. On the **Review Settings** screen, click **Finish**.

6. Make sure that the selected application is selected in the **RemoteApp Programs** section at the bottom of **RemoteApp Manager** and under **Other Distribution Options**, select **Create .rdp File**.

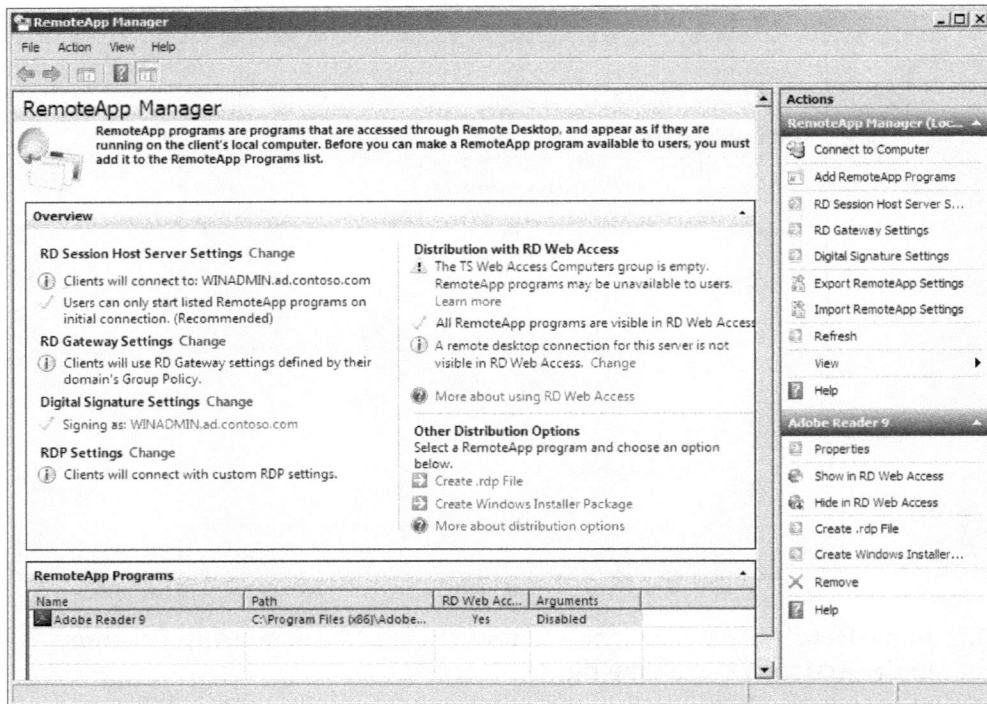

7. In the **RemoteApp Wizard**, click **Next**.

8. On the **Specify Package Settings** screen, click **Next** to accept the default settings.

RemoteApp Wizard ☒

Specify Package Settings
You can specify the location to save the packages, and configure RemoteApp connection and authentication settings.

Enter the location to save the packages:

C:\Program Files\Packaged Programs   [Browse...]

RD Session Host server settings

| Server: | WINADMIN.ad.contoso.com |
| Port: | 3389 |

[Change...]

RD Gateway settings

RD Gateway server settings will be automatically detected.

[Change...]

Certificate settings
No files will be signed by a certificate.

[Change...]

[< Back] [Next >] [Cancel]

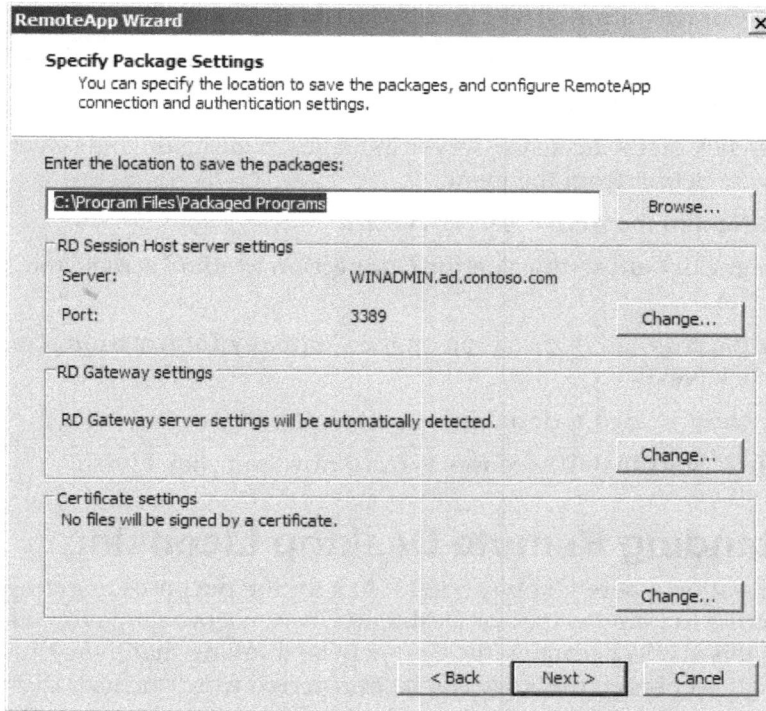

9. On the Review Settings screen, click **Finish**.

We can now run the .rdp file from a remote Windows 7 computer.

> In a production environment, you should use **RemoteApp Manager** to sign your .rdp files and configure Group Policy to only allow remote applications to run from trusted publishers.

Managing Remote Desktop Services licenses

Before you can purchase Remote Desktop licenses, you need to activate your licensing server with Microsoft's clearing house:

1. Open **Remote Desktop Licensing Manager** from **Start | Administrative Tools | Remote Desktop Services**.

2. Right-click the licensing server in the left pane and select **Review Configuration** from the menu.

3. In the **Configuration** dialog box, click **Add to Group**.

4. In the **RD Licensing Manager** dialog box, click **Continue** and then **OK**.

5. In the **Configuration** dialog box, click **OK**.

6. Right-click on the licensing server in the left pane again and select **Activate Server** from the menu.

7. Click **Next** in the **Active Server Wizard**.

8. Leave the default settings on the **Connection Method** screen and click **Next**.

9. Enter the required information on the **Company Information** screen and click **Next**.

10. Click **Next** on the **Optional Information** screen.

11. Uncheck **Start Install Licenses Wizard now** and click **Finish**.

Understanding Remote Desktop Licensing

Consider a situation where you buy 5 RD CALs for the purposes of giving users temporary access to RemoteApps or Desktops. These users change frequently and none require this access permanently. You may be thinking that there must be some way to manage licenses so that they can be transferred from one user to another (or one machine to another in the case of Per Device CALs). The answer to this question is yes and no.

Remote Desktop CALs manage themselves under most circumstances. CALs are issued from your pool of available licenses for a period of between 52-89 days, and if the client does not connect to the Remote Desktop Server, are transferred back to the license pool. If there are no available licenses, a temporary license is issued for 90 days, and by the time it's expired, a CAL must be available in the license pool to replace the previously issued temporary license. If not, you must purchase more CALs, as you have more CALs active simultaneously than available in your license pool.

Per User or Device CALs

If the number of users will outnumber the devices, then Per Device CALs will work out less expensive, and vice versa.

Revoking Per Device Remote Desktop Services Client Access Licences

While it shouldn't be necessary to revoke RDS CALs and return them to your license pool in most cases, as of Windows Server 2008, it is possible to revoke Per Device RDS CALs. This might come in useful if a machine that was issued a Per Device RDS CAL is to be retired and that RDS CAL is required in the license pool so that it can be immediately reissued. You can only revoke 20% of the total number of licenses available. Once the limit is reached, you must wait for revoked RDS CALs to expire, at which point more RDS CALs can be revoked.

Tracking Per User Remote Desktop Services Client Access Licences

Windows Server 2008 and Windows Server 2008 R2 can track their corresponding RDS CALs in a domain environment via RD Licensing Manager.

1. In RD Licensing Manager, expand your licensing server and right-click **Reports**. Select **Create Report | Per User CAL Usage** from the menu.

2. Select the scope for the report in the **Create Per User CAL Usage Report** dialog box and click **Create Report**.

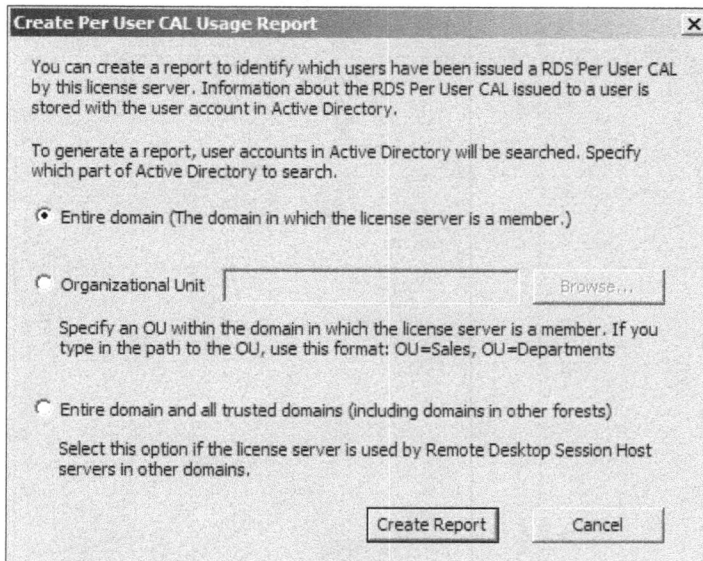

3. Click **OK** in the RD Licensing Manager dialog box once the report has been generated.

4. Right-click the report in the right pane of RD Licensing Manager and select **Save As** from the menu.

5. Save the report to a convenient location. Reports are saved in `.csv` format, which can be viewed using Microsoft Excel.

Installing Remote Desktop Web Access

We've covered the basic methods for accessing RemoteApps and Desktops, but it's also possible to configure a website from which users can connect to published RemoteApps, and in the case of Windows 7, which can be used to advertise published RemoteApps on the **Start** menu using a **Really Simple Syndication (RSS)** feed. Log in to your Remote Desktop server as a domain admin to install the RD Web Access server role:

1. Open a PowerShell prompt and type `Import-Module servermanager` and press *Enter*.

2. Type `Add-WindowsFeature RDS-Web-Access` and press *Enter*.

3. Open **Remote Desktop Web Access Configuration** from **Start | Administrative Tools | Remote Desktop Services**.

4. Internet Explorer will open taking you to the RD Web Access page. Log in using a domain administrator account.

5. On the **Configuration** tab, check **One or more RemoteApp sources** and enter the DNS name of the Remote Desktop Server in the **Source name** box and click **OK**.

Remote Desktop Services Default Connection
RemoteApp and Desktop Connection

RemoteApp Programs   **Remote Desktop**   Configuration   Help   Sign out

You must configure RD Web Access to provide users access to RemoteApp and Desktop Connection. Use these settings to specify the source that provides the RemoteApp programs and desktops that are displayed to users through RemoteApp and Desktop Connection. Users can access RemoteApp and Desktop Connection through the Start menu on a computer that is running Windows 7 or through the RD Web Access Web site.

Select the source to use: ○ An RD Connection Broker server

○ One or more RemoteApp sources

Source name: WINADMIN.ad.contoso.com

Enter the NetBIOS name or fully qualified domain name (FQDN) of the RemoteApp source. If you are using an RD Session Host server farm as the RemoteApp source, specify the DNS name of the farm. If you are specifying multiple RemoteApp sources, separate each name with a semicolon.

OK   Cancel

---

6. You'll be automatically transferred to the **RemoteApp Programs** tab, where you should see any applications that you previously published using RemoteApp Manager. RemoteApps can be launched from this tab by standard users.

Configuring RSS for advertising RemoteApps in Windows 7

RemoteApps can be advertised directly on users' Start menus if they're running Windows 7. This can be configured manually or using Group Policy. To configure RemoteApp and Desktop Connections manually, log in to Windows 7 as a standard user:

1. Type RemoteApp into the **Search programs and files** box on the Start menu and press *Enter*. The **RemoteApp and Desktop Connections** control panel will open.

2. Click **Set up a new connection with RemoteApp and Desktop Connections** in the control panel window.

3. In the **Set up a new connection with RemoteApp and Desktop Connections** window, enter a **Connection URL** for the RD Web Access server. This should be in the format: `https://<servername>/RDWeb/Feed/webfeed.aspx`. Click on **Next**.

> The URL should be prefixed with HTTPS, meaning that the RD Web Access server must have a valid SSL certificate and Windows 7 clients must trust the RD Web Access server's certificate.

4. Click **Next** on the **Ready to set up the connection** screen and then **Finish** once the connections have been successfully added to Windows 7.

5. The RemoteApp and Desktop Connections control panel will show the new connection and the number of published RemoteApps and/or desktops.

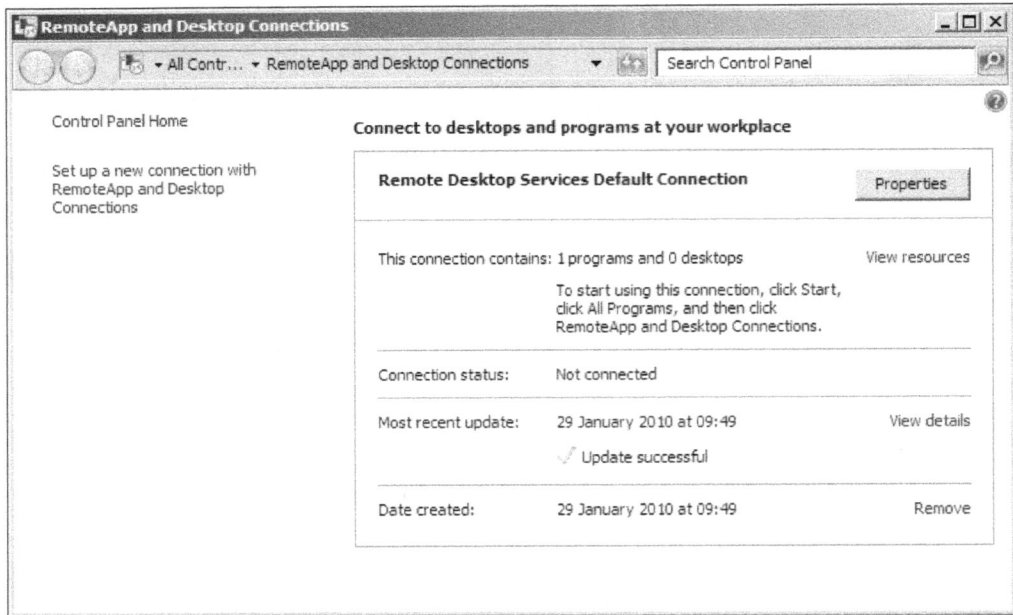

You'll now find any published RemoteApps and Desktops on the Start menu under **All Programs | RemoteApp and Desktop Connections**.

Understanding Remote Desktop and Virtual Desktop Infrastructures

As you may have guessed, it's also possible to give users access to remote virtual machines. A system that automatically connects and provisions virtual machines for users is known as a **Virtual Desktop Infrastructure** (**VDI**). In Windows Server 2008 R2, Microsoft integrated Remote Desktop Services and Hyper-V R2, Microsoft's hypervisor for server virtualization, to provide a basic VDI.

With Microsoft's VDI, Virtual Machines can be automatically started or resumed as needed, saving Hyper-V server resources, and users reconnected to sessions that they were previously connected to. Virtual Machine pools allow users to be randomly assigned an available virtual machine, or Active Directory can be used to assign users a specific VM.

The Remote Desktop Virtualization Host server role installs on a Hyper-V server (and if Hyper-V is not pre-installed, installing the RD Virtualization Host role will install it) and provides integration with Remote Desktop Services. The Remote Desktop Connection Broker server role, as well as managing user sessions in Remote Desktop Server farms, is at the center of Microsoft's VDI solution and sends instructions to the RD Virtualization Host for controlling and connecting to virtual machines.

Microsoft's VDI solution is designed for small and medium sized organizations that need to provide their users with occasional access to remote virtual machines. Microsoft VDI in Windows Server 2008 R2 is not intended to be used as a complete desktop replacement. VDI solutions are also about providing users with a complete, dedicated desktop and operating system, and are not intended for publishing individual applications, as with RemoteApps.

Nevertheless, Microsoft's VDI solution could prove to be useful in situations where users log in with standard user rights but temporarily need the freedom of a virtual machine for installing and experimenting with different configurations or software, but you don't necessarily want to install a virtualization solution locally.

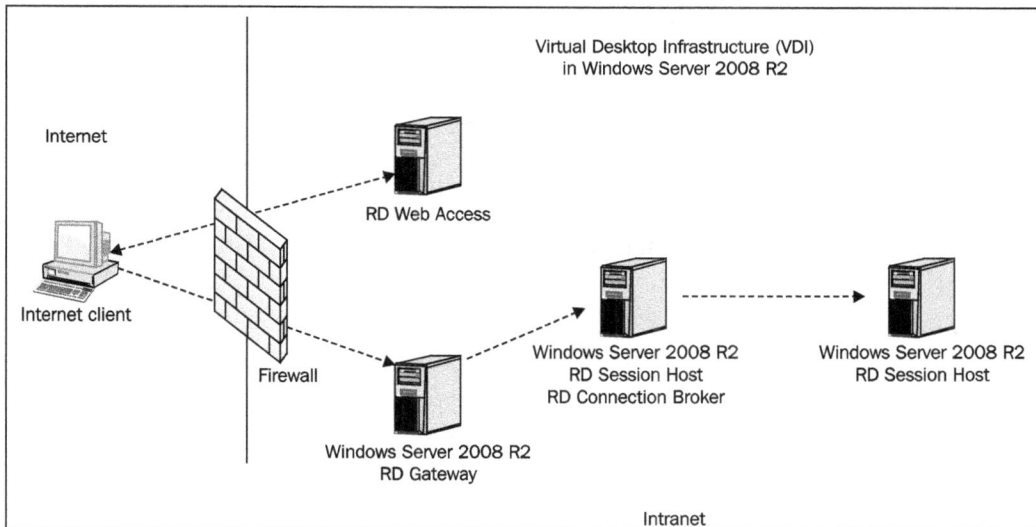

Scaling with Remote Desktop Services

Remote Desktop Services is based on tried and trusted technology and can be scaled to provide remote application access for tens of thousands of users by configuring Remote Desktop Server farms. Application Virtualization technology, which we'll discuss in more detail in the next chapter, allows sysadmins to install applications independently from each other, potentially increasing the number of applications that can be installed on any one Remote Desktop Server, and makes updating and servicing those applications easier.

Summary

In this chapter we've learned about the role Remote Desktop Services can play in providing flexible but secure access to applications and remote desktops. Before continuing to the next chapter you should be able to:

- Configure the main Remote Desktop Server roles using PowerShell
- Configure basic access to RemoteApps and Desktops from the Remote Desktop Connection client, the Remote Desktop Web Access home page, and from the Start menu in Windows 7
- Configure secure access to RemoteApps and Desktops over HTTPS using Remote Desktop Gateway

In the next chapter, we'll look at application virtualization technology that allows system administrators to install applications in secured virtualization layers on users' PCs without disturbing system configuration or other applications installed on the system.

13
Balancing Flexibility and Security with Application Virtualization

Continuing the theme of pain points that users and system administrators experience in organizations that deploy Least Privilege Security on desktops, application compatibility, installation, and maintenance has to be top of the list. In *Chapter 6, Software Distribution using Group Policy*, we looked at different methods for distributing applications and updates to standard users. **Application Virtualization** (**App-V**) is a technology that allows applications to be deployed in virtualization layers that are isolated from each other and the host operating system, so that applications can be installed without the need for regression testing and as a standard user. In this chapter we'll look at:

- The different deployment models for App-V
- How to **sequence** an application for streaming and virtualization
- Setting up the App-V client to work with a server-less deployment model
- VMware ThinApp, an alternative to App-V

Microsoft Application Virtualization 4.5 SP1 for Windows desktops

Application Virtualization technology, previously known as SoftGrid, is now part of Microsoft's product portfolio and renamed to App-V. SoftGrid was purchased from Softricity in 2006 and is now a component of the **Microsoft Desktop Optimization Pack (MDOP)**, which can be licensed by organizations with Software Assurance. MDOP has proved to be one of Microsoft's most popular products.

With App-V, system administrators can virtualize applications in dedicated virtualization layers without the need to deploy virtual machines, unlike the MED-V and XP Mode solutions (refer to *Chapter 14, Deploying XP Mode VMs with MED-V*). App-V programs can be streamed from a server on the corporate network or across the Internet, but unlike terminal services, are also available offline. App-V applications can be managed centrally, so that if an application is updated on an App-V server, those changes are automatically streamed to App-V clients.

Isolating applications with SystemGuard

App-V provides a virtualized *bubble* for each application using a technology called **SystemGuard**. Each bubble isolates an application from the host operating system and from other applications. System services (Windows services, COM, OLE, printers, fonts, cut and paste), files (DLLs, .ini files, and so on), and registry keys are all virtualized in separate bubbles.

SystemGuard is a patented technology and works by monitoring virtualized programs and redirecting calls to virtualized resources, such as system services, files, and registry keys. This enables programs to run without actually installing them on the host operating system. Using this technology on the desktop we can:

- Eliminate conflicts with other applications running on the same host OS
- Allow legacy applications that require administrative privileges to run under a standard user account
- Run different versions of the same application on the same host OS
- Update applications on a central server and stream the changes to desktops
- Allow standard users to run applications on demand without the need to elevate to administrative privileges
- Stream only the required elements of an application suite
- Enable applications to follow users who work on multiple devices

In addition to these benefits, App-V can be useful for terminal server environments as follows:

- Virtual applications deployed across multiple terminal servers can be updated and managed centrally
- Programs that were previously not compatible with terminal services, because they were not designed for multi-user mode, will run under App-V
- Terminal servers can be consolidated as App-V allows applications to run side-by-side, which may not have been possible in the past

Inside each virtualized bubble, there are no **Access Control Lists (ACLs)** that prevent a standard user from modifying the application's virtual registry or filesystem. This means that most programs that fail to run due to restricted access to the registry and filesystem as a standard user when directly installed to the operating system will work in App-V without any additional modifications, effectively making the user a local administrator in the application's virtual registry and file system. If an App-V program is allowed to pass through to the host OS to read or write to a file or registry key, ACLs apply to the logged in user as if the application was running locally on the host OS.

Deploying App-V

There are several models for deploying App-V in an organization, from streaming applications using an existing file or web server to a fully managed system that provides comprehensive management and distribution over geographically distributed networks.

- Standalone model
- Streaming model
- Full infrastructure

Deploying App-V using the standalone model

The simplest model that we'll cover in this chapter is the standalone model, where applications can be streamed over **SMB (Server Message Block)** from a file server, over HTTP from a web server, or distributed using removable media. Small businesses might consider using the standalone model if there's no infrastructure in place to host streaming servers, or they do not want the complexity of managing additional servers.

> Applications can be streamed from IIS 6.0 or 7.0 using HTTP(S).

> **Publishing applications using SFTMIME**
>
> The App-V Client includes the SFTMIME command-line application that can be used to publish applications to users' desktops in cases where an App-V Management Server is not deployed.

Deploying App-V using the streaming model

Providing a partly-managed infrastructure, the streaming model doesn't require the backend support of Active Directory or SQL servers, and permission to install applications is controlled using ACLs. Streaming servers can also be managed using System Center Configuration Manager 2007 SP1.

> App-V Streaming Servers cannot publish applications and support only RTSP(S).

Deploying App-V using the full infrastructure

An App-V Management Server can be used to publish application shortcuts on users' desktops, and/or **Start** menus, and file associations. A management server can also stream applications to users on the same LAN. Streaming servers should be deployed in remote locations to work in conjunction with a management server. Management servers are also required to:

- Deploy applications based on Active Directory group membership
- Enforce concurrent and per-user licensing
- Enable reporting

> **Publishing versus Streaming**
>
> App-V Management Servers publish shortcuts and file associations to clients but this does not necessarily mean that an application has been streamed to the client. The application's bits are streamed on demand. **App-V Management Servers only support RTSP(S).**

Creating a self-service system with App-V for standard users

Due to the isolation that App-V provides, system administrators can provide a self-service system where users can choose which applications to install and when to install them, and most importantly, without administrative privileges or assistance from the help desk. Many applications can be installed side-by-side without affecting the integrity of the image build.

Application Virtualization provides organizations with the ability to deploy secure, but at the same time, flexible systems. One major concern for organizations is that security often reduces usability and flexibility. With Application Virtualization, businesses can have the best of both worlds.

Office 2010 Click-To-Run

If you want a quick demonstration of App-V technology, the latest trial edition of Microsoft Office 2010 Click-To-Run downloads the App-V client to your desktop and then streams the individual suite apps on demand. This technology allows users to try the new software quickly and easily without disrupting current Office installs or the need to uninstall Outlook, which cannot run side-by-side with a different version.

Enforcing security descriptors

When monitoring an application installation during the sequencing process, it is possible to detect ACLs on captured files and enforce those ACLs. See the section *Sequencing an application for App-V* for more information on sequencing. ACLs should be enforced unless you can't find any other way to make the application run correctly.

ACLs on registry keys are not captured when an application is sequenced for App-V. Users can change all registry keys except those associated with system services. Changes a user makes to an application are stored locally and specifically for that user, ensuring that other users of the application are not affected. If an application stops working due to changes a user has made to the application's files or registry keys, it must be redeployed to that user.

> **Can App-V applications write to the host OS?**
>
> In short, yes. While I stated earlier that App-V programs are isolated from each other and the host operating system, to enable full functionality so that the virtualized program can communicate with the OS and other virtualized programs running on the host, it must be able to write to the OS for the purposes of cut and paste, OLE, and printing. Virtualized programs can also write to a user's profile. Complete isolation would severely limit a program's functionality.

Emulating Application Programming Interface (API)

App-V does not emulate APIs, therefore if a virtualized application makes a call to Windows to check if the logged in user has administrative privileges, the program may still fail to run as Windows reports back correctly that the user doesn't have the necessary privileges.

Solving App-V compatibility problems with shims

The application compatibility engine in Windows cannot see shims that are sequenced as part of a virtualized application. Shims for virtualized applications must be installed on the host OS. A virtual application's **Import Address Table (IAT)** is constructed directly in the host OS and shims can still be used to change or redirect API calls for the virtual program.

Sequencing an application for App-V

All applications that will be virtualized using App-V must be sequenced. Sequencing is the process of monitoring an application as it's installed onto a clean system to detect changes made to the filesystem, registry, and system services. The application is then configured for first use and packaged by the sequencer so that it can be distributed to desktops where the App-V client component is preinstalled. Whether you intend to use an App-V server to stream applications to desktops, deploy using Windows Installer, or use a static network drive, all applications must be sequenced before they can be virtualized by App-V.

Sequencing is very similar to the process of repackaging an application by monitoring the installation process or creating before and after snapshots. As such, you're likely already aware that sequencing is somewhat of an art and you might find that some applications are easier to sequence than others. Microsoft Office, for example, is one of the hardest applications to sequence.

If you don't have access to MDOP to install App-V 4.5 SP1, App-V 4.2 is available for download at http://support.microsoft.com/kb/941408. The instructions in this chapter are for App-V 4.5, so requirements for installing and sequencing applications with an older version of the software may vary slightly.

Installing the sequencer

In this chapter we'll need two virtual machines running Windows 7, 32-bit. Support for 64-bit operating systems is included in the next version of App-V, version 4.6.

App-V Sequencer and Client

You **cannot** install the App-V Client and Sequencer on the same machine, hence the need for two VMs (Virtual Machines).

The machine on which you install the Sequencer should comply with the following configuration:

- A clean install of Windows 7 with no pre-installed software
- Anti-virus and Windows Defender software should be disabled
- Turn off Windows Update and the automatic disk defragmentation engine
- Create a disk (Q\:) with enough free space to install applications to be sequenced

Creating a Q Partition with Disk Management in Windows 7

Before you can start sequencing an application, you must have a disk formatted with the drive letter "Q". In Windows 7, this can be easily created using the Disk Management console. You can shrink your existing system partition and use the freed-up space to create a new volume and assign it the drive letter Q.

Log in to Windows 7 as a local or domain administrator and insert the MDOP installation media into the CD/DVD-ROM. Then follow the steps as follows:

1. Click **Application Virtualization for Desktops** on the **Desktop Optimization Pack for Software Assurance 2009 R2** screen.

2. On the **Application Virtualization for Desktops** screen, click **Install Microsoft Application Virtualization Sequencer 4.5 SP1**.

[![note] Before continuing, you may be prompted to install Microsoft Visual C++ 2005 SP1 Redistributables.]

3. Click **Next** in the InstallShield Wizard welcome screen.

4. Accept the license agreement and click **Next**.

5. Accept the default install location and click **Next**.

6. Click **Install** to begin the installation.

7. Check **Launch the program** and click **Finish**.

Let's sequence Adobe Acrobat Reader 9, which can be downloaded from `http://get.adobe.com/uk/reader/enterprise/`. For the purposes of sequencing Acrobat Reader, it's better to use the download that's intended for enterprise distribution.

[![note] **Sequencing for different versions of Windows**
Despite the fact that we're sequencing Acrobat Reader in Windows 7, any version of Windows that supports the App-V client will be able to run our sequenced package without modifications.]

1. In the **Microsoft Application Virtualization Sequencer** window, select **New Package** from the **File** menu.

2. In the **Sequencing Wizard** window on the **Package Information** screen, type **Acrobat Reader 9** in the **Package Name** field and click **Next**.

3. On the **Monitor Installation** screen, click **Begin Monitoring**.

4. In the **Browse for Folder** dialog, select the `Q:` drive and click **Make New Folder**. Name the new folder **ACREAD9**, make sure it's selected, and click **OK**.

[![note] The folder name must conform to 8.3 file naming conventions, which means no spaces or special characters, and a maximum length of eight characters.]

5. Wait for the virtual environment to load. When **Monitoring started. Please being installation.** is displayed on the **Monitor Installation** screen, start the Acrobat Reader installer.

6. Follow through the Acrobat Reader installation process, changing the destination folder for Acrobat Reader from the default `C:\Program Files\Adobe\Reader 9.0\` to `Q:\ACREAD9\`.

7. Once the installation is complete, click **Stop Monitoring** on the **Monitor Installation** screen.

8. Click **Next** on the **Monitor Installation** screen.

9. Click **Next** on the **Add Files to Virtual File System** and **Configure Applications** screens.

10. On the **Launch Applications** screen, click **Launch All**.

11. Acrobat Reader should start. Accept the license agreement, configure the application as you would like it to be on users' machines, and then close the application.

12. The Sequencer should automatically detect that Acrobat Reader has closed. This may take a couple of minutes. Click **Next** on the **Launch Applications** screen.

13. Once sequencing is complete, click **Finish** on the **Sequence Package** screen.

14. In the main Sequencer window, switch to the **Deployment** tab and under **Server URL** select FILE from the **Protocol** menu. In the path field, you'll need to enter a URL specifying the location of the ACREAD9 folder as it will be available on your network. In this example, the name of the server where I'll copy the sequenced package is SERVER1, to a share called Packages.

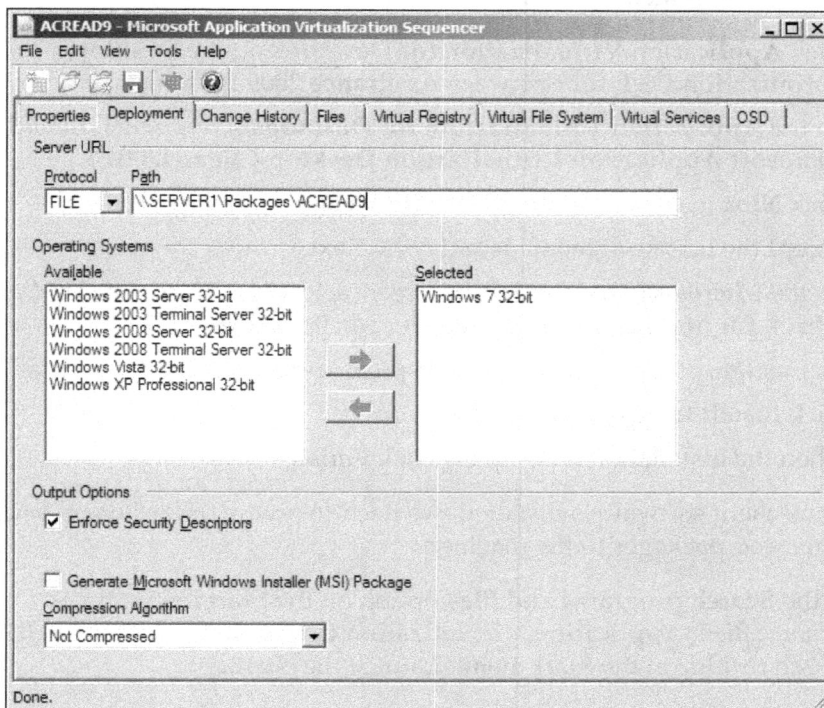

15. In the main Sequencer window, select **Save** from the **File** menu. In the **Save As** dialog, create a new folder ACREAD9 on the desktop for saving the project files. Name the project ACREAD9 and click **Save**.

16. Copy the ACREAD9 folder to the file server specified in Step 14 where it will be accessible to all users.

> The App-V Sequencer can also generate Microsoft Installer (.msi) files so that applications can be distributed using Group Policy Software Installation or System Center Configuration Manager.

> **Running App-V Sequencer .msi files as a standard user**
>
> While the .msi files generated by the App-V sequencer require administrative privileges to run, it is possible to edit .msi files to remove this requirement using a separate MSI editor such as Orca.

Installing the client

Now log in to your second Windows 7 machine as a local or domain administrator and insert the MDOP media into the CD/DVD-ROM:

1. Click **Application Virtualization for Desktops** on the **Desktop Optimization Pack for Software Assurance 2009 R2** screen.

2. On the **Application Virtualization for Desktops** screen, click **Install Microsoft Application Virtualization Desktop Client 4.5 SP1**.

3. Click **Next** in the InstallShield Wizard welcome screen.

4. Accept the license agreement and click **Next**.

5. On the **Microsoft Update Opt In** screen, select **Use Microsoft Update when I check for updates (recommended)** and click **Next**.

6. On the **Setup Type** screen, select **Typical** and click **Next**.

7. Click **Install** to begin the installation.

8. When the installation is complete click **Finish**.

Now that the client software is installed, we need to give standard users permission to add sequenced packages to the machine.

1. In the **Search programs and files** option on the **Start** menu, type *virtualization*. **Application Virtualization Client** should appear in the search results on the **Start** menu. Launch the client.

2. In the left pane of the **Application Virtualization Client** window, right-click **Application Virtualization (Local)** and select **Properties** from the menu.

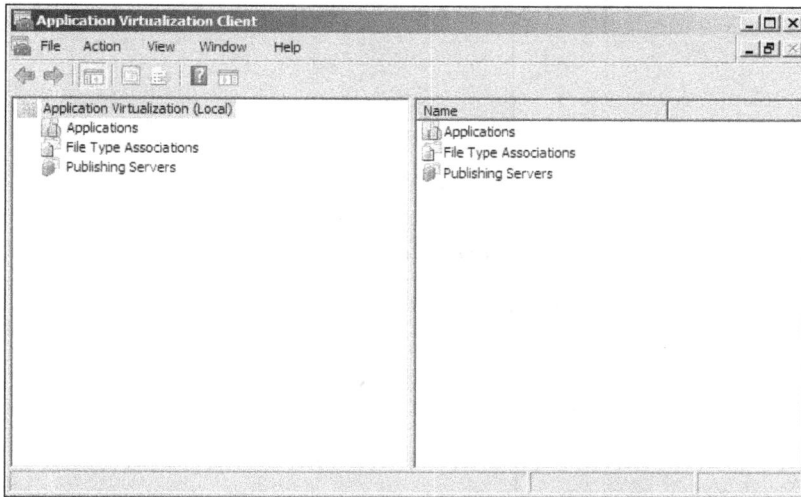

3. In the **Application Virtualization (Local) Properties** dialog select the **Permissions** tab.

4. Check the **Add applications** permission option and click **OK**.

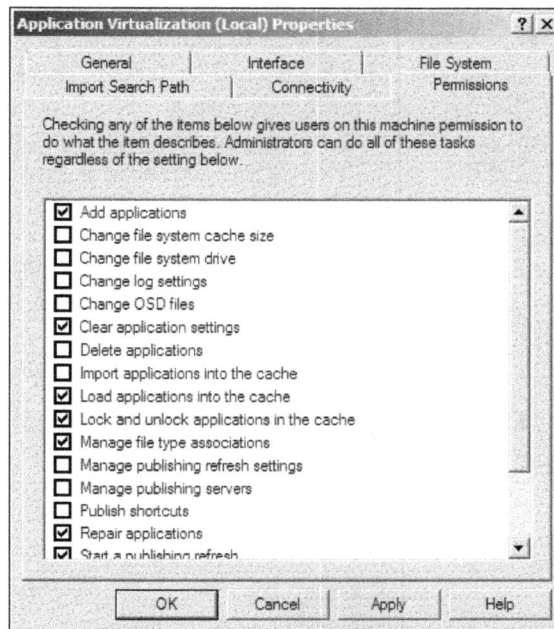

5. We need to set one more permission that cannot be configured using the Application Virtualization Client console and will allow us to stream from a file as we have no server set up on the network. In the **Search programs and files** option in the **Start** menu, type *regedit*, and press *Enter*. In the left pane of **Registry Editor**, navigate to the following key: HKLM\SOFTWARE\Microsoft\ SoftGrid\4.5\Client\Configuration\.

6. Change the AllowIndependentFileStreaming value to 1 and close the window.

Let's log in as a standard user and see if we can launch the Acrobat Reader package that we copied to SERVER1 in the last section:

1. Log in to Windows 7 as a standard user and browse to the ACREAD9 folder on the file server.

2. Double-click the **Adobe Reader 9 9.0.0.332** Application Descriptor file and Acrobat Reader should launch.

ACREAD9 Icons	12/02/2010 10:07	File folder	
ACREAD9.sft	12/02/2010 10:07	SFT File	212,046 KB
ACREAD9.sprj	12/02/2010 10:07	SPRJ File	13 KB
ACREAD9_manifest	12/02/2010 10:07	XML Document	1 KB
Adobe Reader 9 9.0.0.332	12/02/2010 10:07	Application Descriptor	2 KB

Streaming applications with an App-V Server

Through an optional component, App-V Streaming Servers store and stream applications to App-V clients on demand. Streaming is the process of distributing applications to clients on demand in the same way that video files are streamed to users on YouTube using HTTP or the **Real Time Streaming Protocol (RTSP)**. When an application is streamed to a user, they can start to use it before all the code has been transferred to their desktop. When the user disconnects from the Internet or corporate network, the application is stored in a local cache so that it can be used without a connection to the App-V Server. Sequencing is the process of packaging an application to be streamed to clients from an App-V Server.

Installing Microsoft System Center Application Virtualization Streaming Server

Let's install the App-V Streaming Server in Windows Server 2008 R2. Log in as a domain administrator and insert the MDOP media into the CD/DVD-ROM:

1. Click **Application Virtualization for Desktops** on the **Desktop Optimization Pack for Software Assurance 2009 R2** screen.

2. On the **Application Virtualization for Desktops** screen, click **Install Microsoft System Center Application Virtualization Streaming Server 4.5 SP1**.

3. Click **Next** in the InstallShield Wizard welcome screen.

4. Accept the license agreement and click **Next**.

5. On the **Microsoft Update Opt In** screen, select **Use Microsoft Update when I check for updates (recommended)** and click **Next**.

6. Enter the relevant information on the **Customer Information** screen and click **Next**.

7. Accept the default settings on the **Installation Path** screen and click **Next**.

8. On the **Connection Security Mode** screen, uncheck **Use enhanced security** and click **Next**. If you have a PKI in your production environment, you can leave this setting checked.

9. Leave the default RTSP port 554 selected on the **TCP Port Configuration** screen and click **Next**.

10. On the **Content Root** screen, you can either leave the default path or change the path to the shared folder created in the previous section: `c:\packages`. Click **Next** to continue.

11. Accept all the default values on the **Advanced Settings** screen and click **Next**.

12. Finally, click **Install** on the **Ready to Install the Program** screen.

13. Once the installer has completed, click **Finish**. You will then be prompted to restart the server.

Once a server is installed, the App-V Client can be configured to connect to the server and load any available applications:

1. In the App-V Client, right-click **Publishing Servers** in the left pane and select **New Server** from the menu.

2. Enter a **Display Name** for the server and choose a server **Type** from the menu. In this case we need to select **Application Virtualization Server** as there is no enhanced security configured on the streaming server.

3. Enter the streaming server's DNS **Host Name** and click **Finish**.

4. Select the server in the right pane of the App-V client and select **Refresh Server** from the **Action** menu to update the available applications.

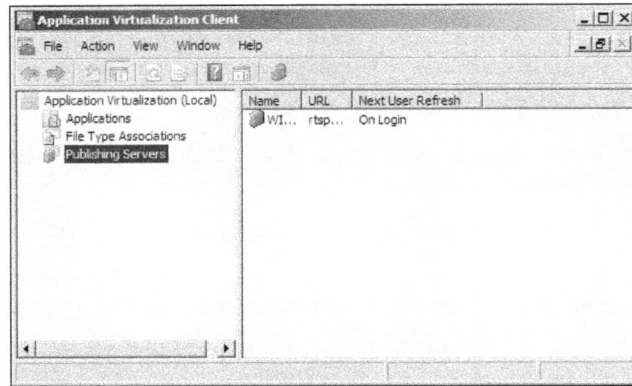

Deploying and managing applications for users who never connect to the corporate intranet

Application virtualization technology can also be made available directly over the Internet, which comes in handy for users who never make a VPN connection to the corporate intranet. Such users pose a particular problem when it comes to keeping devices up-to-date. App-V ensures that users are always running the latest version of an application.

Updating applications and Differential Streaming

The different App-V deployment models support varying update methods, including Active Update and Override URL.

Active Update

In a streaming or full infrastructure model, App-V Streaming Servers support **Active Update**, a technology that allows system administrators to place an updated application on the server and the server automatically detects that App-V clients requesting the old version of the application should be updated, and streams the necessary changes to the clients. This is known as **Differential Streaming**.

Override URL

In a standalone deployment of App-V, clients must be reconfigured to point to new versions of applications that are streamed from IIS or a file server. This essentially means republishing the application on the client using the Override URL setting to point to the location of the updated bits on the server. Once the updated application is published and loaded on the client, IIS and file servers support Differential Streaming to update the bits in the local App-V Client cache.

VMware ThinApp

App-V is just one of several enterprise-grade systems that virtualize and stream applications to Windows clients. If you already have **Software Assurance (SA)** for your Windows clients, the Microsoft Desktop Optimization Pack is a cost-effective management solution that provides many tools in addition to App-V.

VMware's ThinApp system is similar to App-V, but the client is embedded into the sequenced package, otherwise known as a **Virtual Operating System (VOS)**, and doesn't require that the client be "installed" like App-V's kernel-mode client. This makes ThinApp virtualized packages potentially easier to deploy to secured desktops. Independent testing also shows that ThinApp is less resource-intensive than App-V. ThinApp additionally supports 64-bit clients, though App-V 4.6 updates the client components to support 64-bit Windows hosts.

Other alternatives

Citrix XenApp and Symantec SVS Pro also deploy a kernel-based agent like App-V for application virtualization and streaming.

One other major difference between ThinApp and App-V is that ThinApp requires one or more servers in all deployment scenarios. ThinApp can also generate Microsoft Installer (.msi) files for use with existing software deployment systems such as System Center Configuration Manager, and enforcement can be configured via Active Directory.

Summary

This chapter has provided a summary of application virtualization technology, with specific details of how to sequence an application using App-V, deploy the App-V Client, and stream applications from a Windows file server using the SMB protocol. Before continuing to the next chapter you should:

- Understand the difference between a virtual machine and application virtualization
- Be familiar with the different deployment models for App-V
- Be able to sequence an application for use with App-V
- Know how to set up the App-V Client to stream applications from a Windows file server

In the next chapter, we'll look at Microsoft's other virtualization offerings, Windows XP Mode for Windows 7, and MED-V — a managed VM solution for enterprises and also part of MDOP.

14
Deploying XP Mode VMs with MED-V

This chapter focuses on what is probably recognized as the most common virtualization technology — virtual machines. Microsoft's Virtual PC and VMware's Workstation software have long provided technical enthusiasts and developers with access to virtualization technology. Unlike application virtualization covered in Chapter 13, this technology virtualizes an entire operating system environment producing what is known as a **virtual machine** (**VM**). This chapter includes details on how to use the latest virtualization technologies to:

- Deploy legacy applications that are not compatible with newer versions of Windows
- Set up Windows XP Mode for Windows 7
- Configure the different components of MED-V for managing and deploying VMs in a large corporate environment
- Prepare VMs for use with MED-V

Solving least privilege security problems using virtual machines

Microsoft pitches Windows 7 XP Mode as a way of solving application compatibility problems by allowing users to run programs in a pre-configured virtual machine in Windows XP Service Pack 3. In addition, as part of the Microsoft Desktop Optimization Pack, a technology called **Microsoft Enterprise Desktop Virtualization** (**MED-V**) for larger organizations allows system administrators to deploy and manage virtual machines across an enterprise network.

Virtual PC and Windows 7 XP Mode

Windows XP Mode is intended for small businesses and home users who need a quick way of making applications that are not compatible with Windows 7 run on the platform. While it's always best to avoid virtualization technologies or compatibility fixes, in the real world that's not always possible. XP Mode provides organizations that don't have the technical resources or time to solve compatibility with a fast and elegant, if not ideal, solution. As a bonus, XP Mode provides a quick and easy way to run an application as a local administrator while providing some integration with the logged in user's session on the host operating system.

Differentiating between App-V and XP Mode

Though both App-V and XP Mode are virtualization technologies, they are designed to solve different problems. The core technology in App-V, SystemGuard, is for isolating virtual applications from each other and virtual applications from the host OS, allowing programs to be deployed without extensive regression testing for conflicts. The streaming and deployment technology in App-V also provides standard users with an on-demand installation service for corporate applications without the need for administrative privileges.

In contrast, XP Mode is specifically for running legacy applications in Windows 7. Both XP Mode and App-V have the potential to allow programs that don't usually run under a standard user account to function correctly without any specific modification to the application itself.

XP Mode provides a certain amount of integration with the host operating system, such as the ability to launch applications installed in the guest VM from the host's **Start** menu and save files created in the guest VM to the host.

Setting up Windows 7 XP Mode

Windows 7 XP Mode is supported in Windows 7 Professional, Enterprise, and Ultimate SKUs only. The host will also need a minimum 2 GB of memory and a 1 GHz (32 or 64-bit) processor. You can download the necessary files from Microsoft's Virtual PC website: http://www.microsoft.com/windows/virtual-pc/download. aspx. On supported WIndows 7 SKUs, the XPMode VM is licensed for free, i.e. no additional license is required to run this preconfigured Windows XP virtual machine.

Two files are required, Windows6.1-KB958559 and WindowsXPMode_en-us. Log in to Windows 7 as a local administrator:

1. Run Windows6.1-KB958559 and follow the onscreen instructions and reboot the computer when prompted.

2. Once the computer has restarted, log in as an administrator and run `WindowsXPMode_en-us`.

3. Click **Next** on the welcome screen.

4. Accept the default installation location and click **Next**; XP Mode will now install. You may be required to accept UAC prompts during the installation process.

5. Once installation has completed, check **Launch Windows XP Mode** in the setup dialog and click **Finish**.

6. In the **Windows XP Mode Setup** dialog, check **I accept the license terms** and click **Next**.

7. On the **Installation folder and credentials** screen, enter and confirm a password for the **XPMUser** account and click **Next**.

> The XPMUser account is used to log in to Windows XP and run any applications installed in the VM. Applications installed in the VM have access to the stored credentials for this account.

8. On the **Help protect your computer** screen, select **Help protect my computer by turning on Automatic Updates now** and click **Next**.

9. On the **Setup will share the drives on this computer with Windows XP Mode** screen, click **Start Setup**.

> Windows XP Mode drive sharing options can be changed after installation.

10. Once setup has completed, the new virtual machine will appear on the screen, logged in with the XPMUser account.

Launching applications installed in XP Mode from the Windows 7 Start menu

Now that you have Virtual PC and XP Mode set up in Windows 7, applications that are installed inside the XP Mode virtual machine and have a shortcut published to XP's **Start** menu will appear in Windows 7's **Start** menu under **Windows Virtual PC | Windows XP Mode Applications**. In this example, I've installed Adobe Acrobat Reader in the XP Mode VM. Once I've logged off the XPMUser and closed the VM, Acrobat Reader appears in Windows 7's **Start** menu.

[✎ The XPMUser account is placed in the local administrators group in
the XP Mode virtual machine by default, and as such, all applications
installed in the VM run in the security context of a local administrator.]

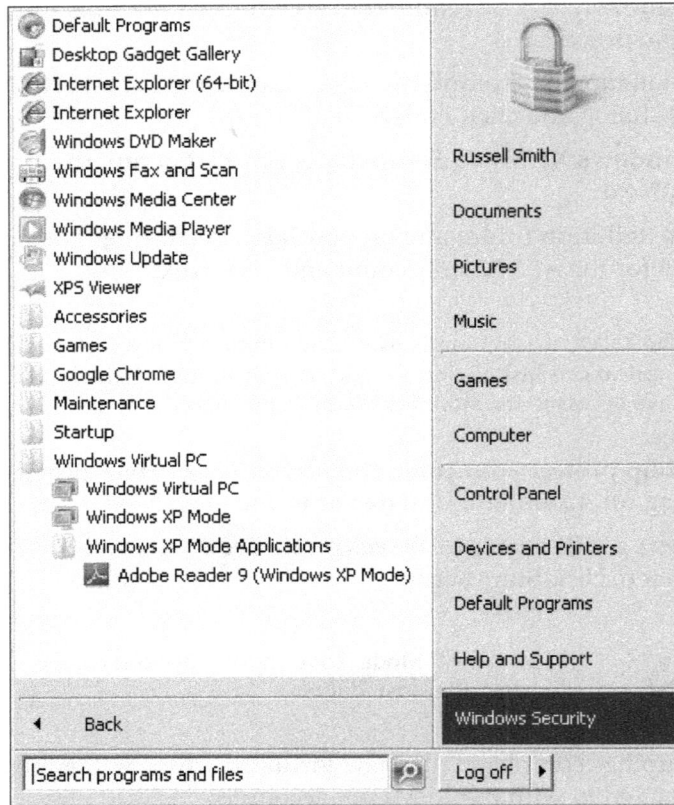

I can click on the shortcut for Acrobat Reader and it will launch in its own seamless
window independently of the VM's desktop environment, giving the impression that
the application is not virtualized but running directly on the Windows 7 desktop.
This ability to publish applications to the host operating system's **Start** menu is a
feature of Virtual PC.

[✎ Virtual applications cannot be run when the XP Mode virtual
machine desktop is running.]

The integration features included in Virtual PC allow users to run applications installed in VMs but save or open files on the host operating system. The host operating system's disks appear as mapped network drives.

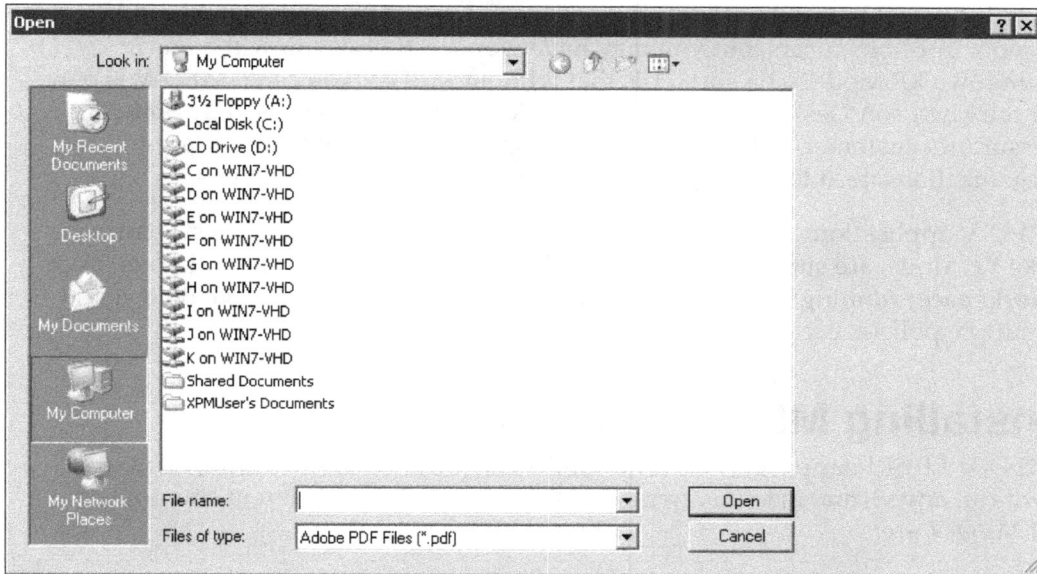

Security concerns when running XP Mode

Windows XP Mode is a quick and integrated solution for running applications in seamless windows that are installed in a virtual machine. However, you shouldn't forget that running a virtual machine on each desktop across your network increases management and administrative overhead, especially in large corporate environments where VMs may not be powered on all the time. For each copy of XP Mode installed you need to additionally configure:

- Antivirus software
- Windows Update
- Third-party software updates
- Management and security settings

Microsoft Enterprise Desktop Virtualization (MED-V)

Windows XP Mode provides a good solution for small businesses, without IT support, or home users, but you may have wondered how you will manage Windows XP Mode? The answer is that without MED-V you can't. MED-V is part of the Microsoft Desktop Optimization Pack, which can be licensed by Software Assurance customers. MED-V provides all the management features large organizations need to manage XP VM images and Virtual PC settings.

MED-V applications run in seamless windows on the host operating system, and like XP Mode, are supported by a fully virtualized operating system (known as a **workspace**) running in the background. Each workspace has a usage policy, and multiple policies can be assigned to a single Virtual PC image.

Installing MED-V 1.0 SP1

MED-V 1.0 SP1 supports Windows 7 and Vista (32 and 64-bit edition) hosts and will run any virtual machine created with Virtual PC. The different components of MED-V are:

- **MED-V Server**: Manages the central configuration and management point for storing usage policies and controlling access to VM images.

- **MED-V Image Repository**: This is an IIS Virtual Directory, which is configured on a server. It must be configured independently of the MED-V Server.

- **MED-V Client**: This is installed on users' desktops and is used to access MED-V workspaces.

- **Virtual PC 2007 SP1**: Installed on a system administrator's desktop and is used to create VM images for use with MED-V. The MED-V Client and MED-V Management Console are also installed on a system administrator's desktop. The management console is used to manage VM packages (compressed VM images) that are uploaded to the Image Repository and configure usage policies stored on the MED-V Server.

Installing the Image Repository

The MED-V Image Repository is hosted by an Internet Information Services (IIS) Virtual Directory and must be installed and configured manually. To install IIS and the necessary dependent components in Windows Server 2008, log in as a local or domain administrator and follow these steps:

1. Install the Internet Information Services role from Server Manager, ensuring that the following role services are included:
    -   Basic Authentication
    -   Windows Authentication
    -   Client Certificate Mapping Authentication

2. Install the **Background Intelligent Transfer Service (BITS)** feature from Server Manager, making sure the **IIS Server Extension** is also selected.

3. In Server Manager's left pane, expand your server's roles, find **Web Server (IIS)**, and click **Internet Information Services**.

4. In the central pane of Server Manager, the **IIS Manager** will now be displayed. Expand your server, **Sites**, right-click **Default Web Site**, and select **Add Virtual Directory** from the drop-down menu.

5. In the **Add Virtual Directory** dialog, type MEDVImages into the **Alias** field and then click the browse icon to locate the physical location where the MED-V images will be stored. Click **OK** to complete the process.

6. Make sure the new virtual directory is selected and then in the central pane of **IIS Manager** double-click **Directory Browsing** in **Features View**. In the right pane of **IIS Manager** under **Actions**, click **Enable**.

7. In the left pane of **IIS Manager**, click the **MEDVImages** virtual directory again. In the central pane of **IIS Manager**, double-click **BITS Uploads** in **Feature View**.

8. Check **Allow clients to upload files** and then click **Apply** in the **Actions** pane.

9. In the left pane of **IIS Manager**, click the **MEDVImages** virtual directory. In the central pane of IIS Manager, double-click **MIME Types** in **Feature View**.

10. In the **Actions** pane click on **Add**. In the **Add MIME Type** dialog, type .ckm into the **File name extension** field and application/octet-stream into **MIME type** and click **OK**.

11. Repeat Step 10 but this time type .index into the **File name extension** field and application/octet-stream into **MIME type** and click **OK**.

12. In the left pane of **IIS Manager**, right-click the **MEDVImages** virtual directory and select **Edit Permissions** from the menu. Make sure that the **Everyone** group has READ permission and click **OK**.

Installing the MED-V Server component

Log in to the Windows Server 2008 that will act as a MED-V Server with an administrator account and insert the MDOP 2010 media into the CD/DVD-ROM:

1. On the MDOP welcome screen, click **Enterprise Desktop Virtualization**.

2. On the **Enterprise Desktop Virtualization** screen, click **Install the Server component of Microsoft Desktop Virtualization**, choosing the right architecture (32-bit or 64-bit) for your server operating system.

3. The installer will check for prerequisites such as .NET Framework, and so on. On the welcome screen, click **Next** to start the install wizard.

4. Accept the license agreement and click **Next**.

5. On the **Destination Folder** screen, accept the default install location and click **Next**. Click **Install** on the next screen.

6. On the completion screen, check **Launch MED-V Server Configuration Manager** and click **Finish**.

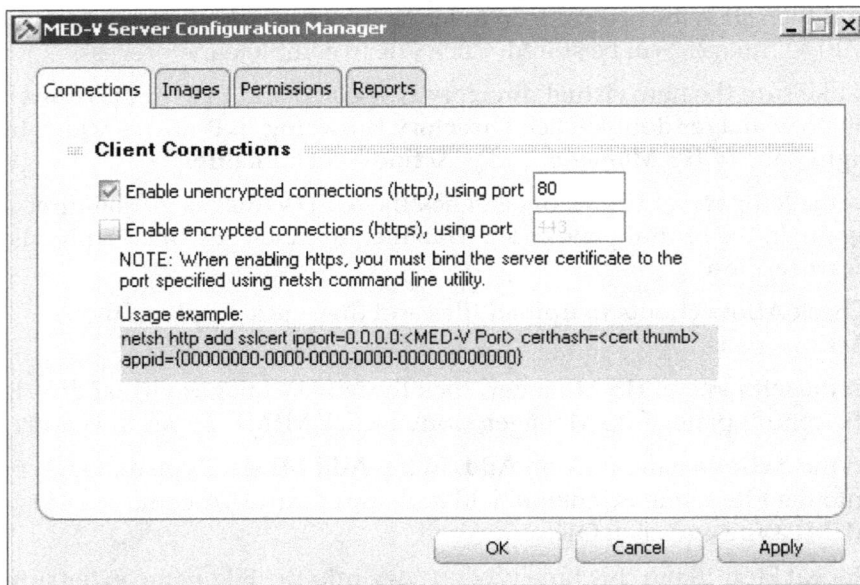

7. In the **MED-V Server Configuration Manager** window, click the **Images** tab.

8. In the **VMs URL** option, type the URL for the Image Repository and accept all the other default settings by clicking **Apply**.

9. Click on **OK** to complete the process.

10. Click **Yes** to start the MED-V Server when prompted.

Installing the MED-V Management Console

The management console cannot be installed on a server operating system, so you must install the console in Windows Vista. The installer for the management console is not available from the main install screen that starts automatically when you insert the MDOP media into a CD/DVD-ROM. To start the installer, log in to Vista as a domain administrator and follow the steps:

> Note that the MED-V Client is installed by default on the same machine as the Management Console.

1. Run `MED-V_1.0.72.msi` in the `MED-V\Installers` folder on the MDOP 2010 installation media.

2. On the welcome screen click **Next**.

3. Accept the license agreement and click **Next**.

4. On the **Destination Folder** screen, accept the default install location and click **Next**.

5. On the **MED-V Settings** screen, check **Install the MED-V management application**.

6. In the **Server address** field, type the full DNS name of the Windows 2008 Server where you installed the MED-V Server component and click **Next**.

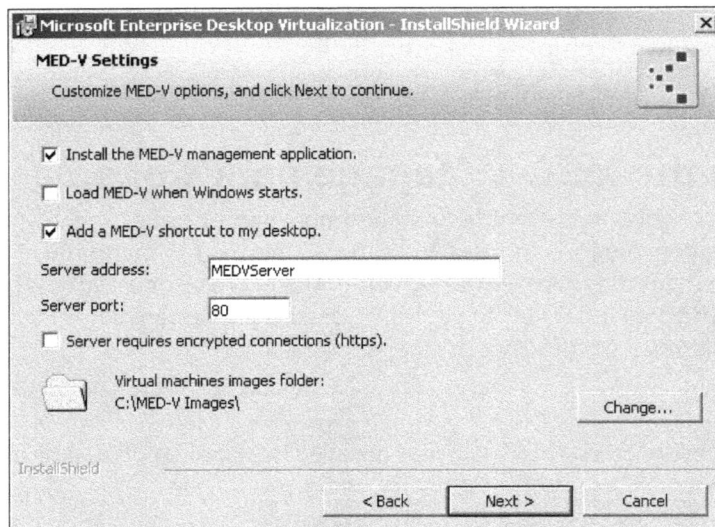

7. On the **Ready to Install the Program** screen, click **Install**.

8. Once the install process has completed, uncheck **Launch Microsoft Enterprise Desktop Virtualization** and click **Finish**.

Preparing a virtual machine for use with MED-V

MED-V 1.0 SP1 uses Virtual PC, which is included on the MDOP 2010 media and can be installed on Windows XP Professional (32-bit), Vista (Business, Enterprise, or Ultimate 32-bit) or Windows 7 (Professional, Enterprise, or Ultimate 32 and 64-bit). Before following the instructions here, you should install Virtual PC and the KB958162 update that's included on the MDOP media on the host OS, and then create a VM with a volume license version of Windows XP Professional with Service Pack 3. This VM will then be prepared for use with MED-V. In this example, **install Virtual PC 2007 SP1 on the same machine as the MED-V Client and Management Console**. Once XP has installed follow these steps:

> If you want to test this procedure in a lab, you must use a volume license key when installing Windows XP. The MED-V VM Prerequisites Tool will not install on retail versions of XP.

1. Make sure the Windows XP SP3 VM is started and in the Virtual PC window, select **Install or Update Virtual Machine Additions** from the **Action** menu.

2. Click **Continue** in the warning dialog.

3. In the **Virtual Machines Additions** dialog, click **Next**.

4. Once setup has completed, click **Finish** and reboot the VM as prompted.

5. When the VM has rebooted, download and install .NET Framework 3.5 SP1 from the following link: `http://download.microsoft.com/download/2/0/e/20e90413-712f-438c-988e-fdaa79a8ac3d/dotnetfx35.exe`.

6. Next we need to install the MED-V Workspace in the VM, which includes the components to prepare the virtual machine for use with MED-V. From the `MED-V\Installers` directory on the MDOP media, copy the `MED-V_Workspace_1.0.72.msi` file to the VM and run it.

7. On the **Microsoft Enterprise Desktop Virtualization** welcome screen click **Next**.

8. Accept the license agreement and click **Next** and then **Install**.

9. On the completion screen, check **Launch VM Prerequisites Tool** and click **Finish**.

10. In the **MED-V Prerequisite Wizard** dialog, click **Next**.

11. On the **Windows Settings** screen, leave the default settings and click **Next**.

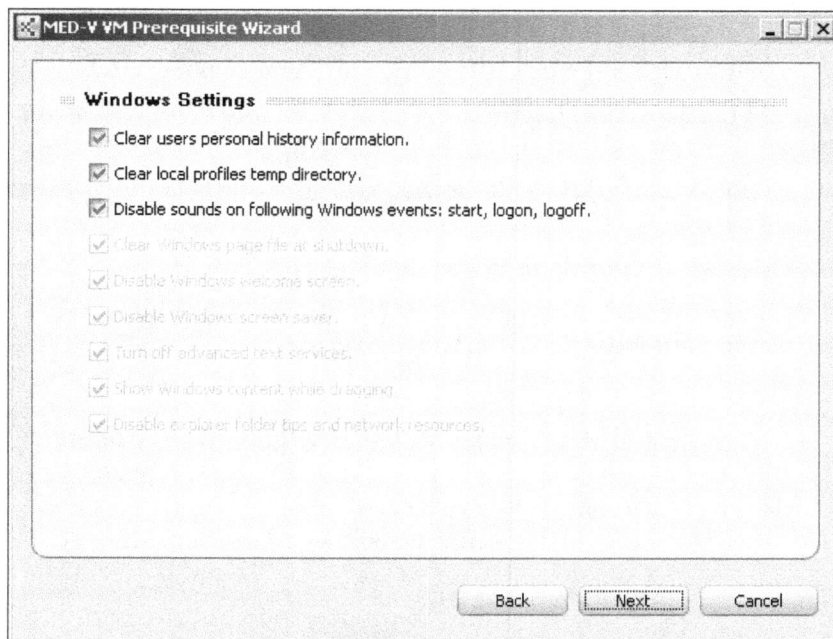

12. On the **Internet Explorer Settings** screen accept the defaults again by clicking **Next**.

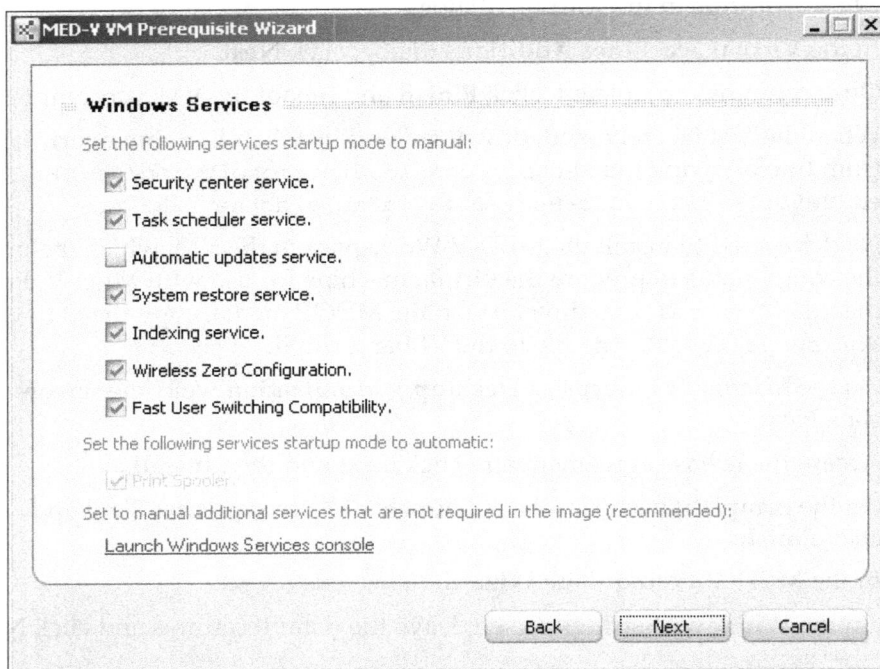

13. Click **Next** to accept the default settings for **Windows Services**.

14. On the **Windows Auto Logon** screen, check **Enable Windows Auto Logon**, enter a username and password, and click **Apply**.

15. In the **MED-V** dialog, click **Yes** to **Are you sure you want to apply these changes now?**

16. In the **MED-V Prerequisite Wizard** dialog, click **Finish**.

17. Select **Close** from the **Action** menu in the **Virtual PC** window and select **Shut down Windows XP** in the **Close** dialog.

> **Preparing a MED-V image for use in a domain environment**
> You should prepare the VM using standard Windows deployment tool **Sysprep** if it's going to be joined to an Active Directory Domain to ensure that each VM has a unique **Security Identifier** (**SID**).

Working with the MED-V Management Console

Now we need to start the MED-V Management Console on Vista so we can test the VM created in the last section, apply usage policies, and package the VM for use with the MED-V Server.

Importing a VM for testing

Before we package and upload a VM to the MED-V Server, we can import the VM created in the previous section to the local MED-V Management Console and test it. This is done as follows:

1. Start the MED-V Management Console from **Start | All Programs | MED-V | MED-V Management**.
2. Log in to the MED-V Management Console using the same account credentials as are valid on the MED-V Server.
3. In the **MED-V Management** window, switch to the **Images** tab and select **New** under **Local Test Images**.

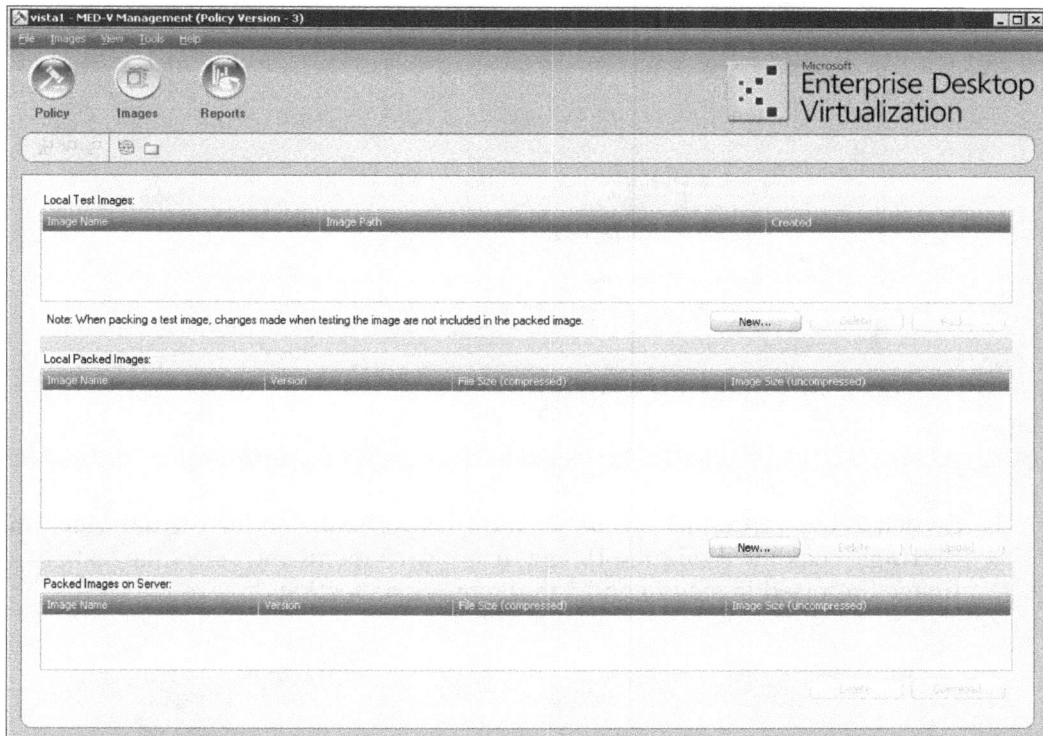

4. In the **Test Image Creation** dialog, select the .vmc file for the VM created in the previous section.

5. Enter a name for the image in the **Image name** field and click **OK**.

Creating a usage policy

Let's create a usage policy that can be used in conjunction with the VM we've just imported into the MED-V Management Console:

1. In the **MED-V Management** window, switch to the **Policy** tab and let's modify the default **Workspace** policy.

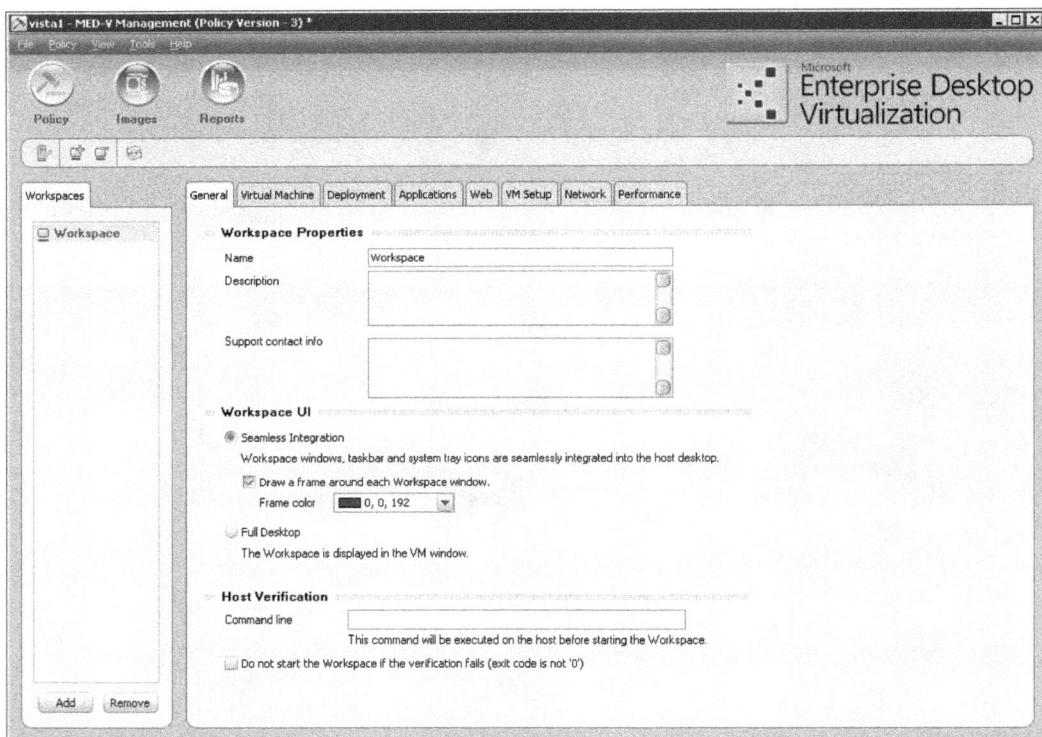

2. Switch to the **Virtual Machine** tab and click **Refresh**. Under **Virtual Machine Settings**, click the **Assigned Image** drop-down menu and select the test image imported in steps 4 and 5 in the previous section.

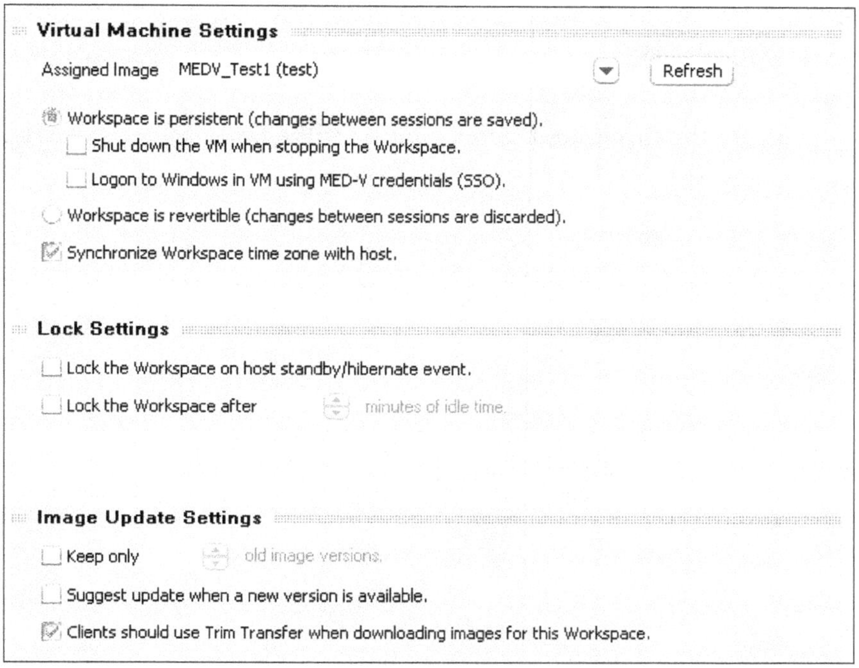

Virtual Machine Settings

Assigned Image   MEDV_Test1 (test)   ▼   [Refresh]

⦿ Workspace is persistent (changes between sessions are saved).
   ☐ Shut down the VM when stopping the Workspace.
   ☐ Logon to Windows in VM using MED-V credentials (SSO).
◯ Workspace is revertible (changes between sessions are discarded).
☑ Synchronize Workspace time zone with host.

Lock Settings

☐ Lock the Workspace on host standby/hibernate event.
☐ Lock the Workspace after   [↕] minutes of idle time.

Image Update Settings

☐ Keep only   [↕] old image versions.
☐ Suggest update when a new version is available.
☑ Clients should use Trim Transfer when downloading images for this Workspace.

3. Now switch to the **Deployment** tab. Here we can select which users have access to the workspace and set an expiry date. Let's leave the default settings as shown in the following screenshot.

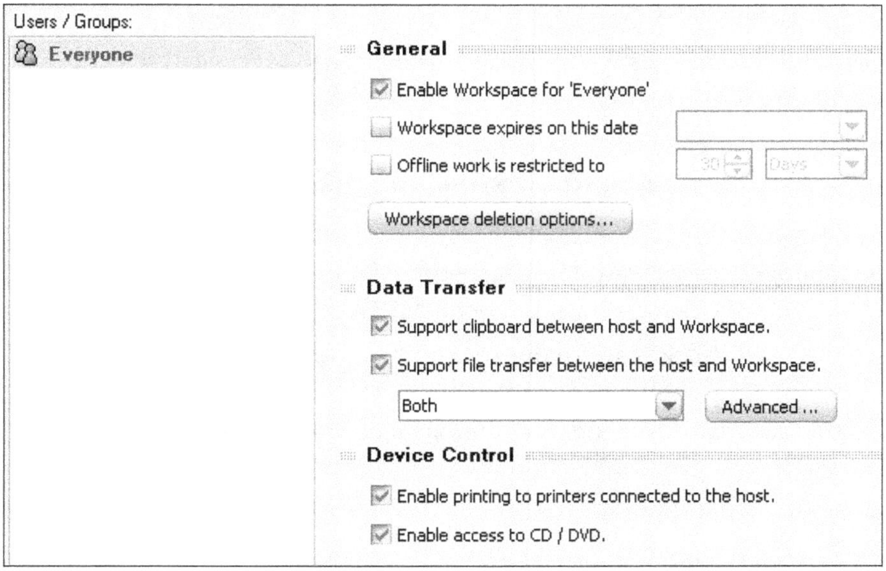

Users / Groups:

👥 Everyone

General

☑ Enable Workspace for 'Everyone'
☐ Workspace expires on this date   [▼]
☐ Offline work is restricted to   [30 ↕] [Days ▼]

[Workspace deletion options...]

Data Transfer

☑ Support clipboard between host and Workspace.
☑ Support file transfer between the host and Workspace.
[Both   ▼] [Advanced...]

Device Control

☑ Enable printing to printers connected to the host.
☑ Enable access to CD / DVD.

4. Switch to the **Applications** tab and under **Published Applications** click **Add**.

5. Click under the **Display Name** column for the new application entry and type **Notepad**.

6. Click under the **Command Line** column for the new application entry and type c:\windows\system32\notepad.exe.

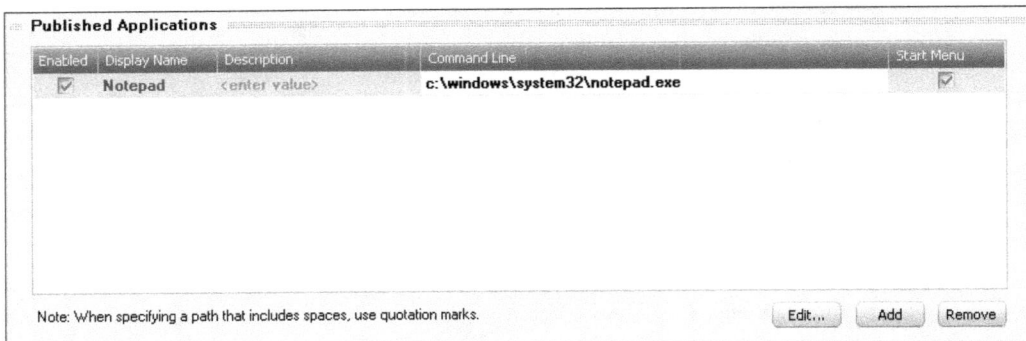

Published Applications

Enabled	Display Name	Description	Command Line	Start Menu
☑	Notepad	<enter value>	c:\windows\system32\notepad.exe	☑

Note: When specifying a path that includes spaces, use quotation marks.   [Edit...] [Add] [Remove]

> The Web tab allows us to specify that certain websites that are opened in the host OS must be transferred to the browser in the MED-V workspace and opened in the browser installed in the guest VM. This allows system administrators to force certain websites to be opened in different versions of IE for compatibility reasons.

7. To save the changes we've made to the workspace policy, select **Commit** from the **Policy** menu.

Testing the workspace and usage policy

Now we'll test the workspace and usage policy:

1. Start the MED-V Client from the MED-V folder from the **Start** menu. The MED-V Client is simply named **MED-V**.

2. In the **Start Workspace** dialog, enter a username and password that are valid on the MED-V Server and click **OK**.

3. In the **Confirm Running Test** dialog, click **Use Test Image**.

4. Once the workspace has started, **go to the Start menu on the host OS** and look for the MED-V Applications folder. There you should see **Notepad** as a published application. Start Notepad and you'll see that it opens in a window marked by a border, denoting it as a MED-V application.

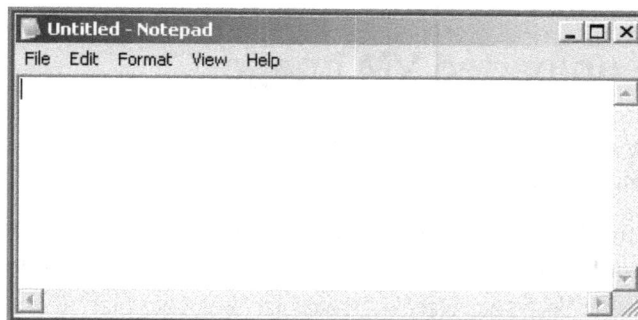

Now right-click the MED-V icon on the taskbar and select **Stop Workspace** from the menu. Click **Yes** when prompted **Are you sure you want to stop the Workspace?**

Packing the VM for use with the MED-V Server

Now that we've tested the workspace and usage policy, we need to package the VM so it can be uploaded to the MED-V Server. This is done as follows:

1. In the MED-V Management Console, switch to the **Images** tab.
2. Select the imported VM under **Local Test Images** and click **Pack**.
3. Click **OK** when the image has been successfully packed.

Uploading the VM image to the MED-V Server

Now that the VM image has been packed, you'll notice that the compressed file size displayed in the MED-V Management Console under **Local Packed Images** is considerably smaller than the original file size.

File Size (compressed)	Image Size (uncompressed)
44.1 GB	56.93 GB

Now we need to upload this image to the Image Repository:

1. Select the VM image to upload under **Local Packed Images** and click **Upload**.

2. Click **OK** once the transfer is complete.

Testing the uploaded VM image

Now that the image has been uploaded to the Image Repository, you should go back to the usage policy called Workspace that we configured earlier and change the VM to the uploaded image rather than the local test image on the **Virtual Machine** tab.

Now you can fire up the MED-V Client and start the workspace. If there are multiple usage policies stored on the MED-V Server, you have the option to select which workspace to connect to.

> **Trim Transfer**
>
> MED-V Clients check the Image Repository every 15 minutes for new and updated images. MED-V Trim Transfer technology is used to compare the files on the MED-V Client with those in any updated images to ensure that only the necessary files are transferred to the client machine.

Summary

In this chapter, we've learned how to set up Windows XP Mode for Windows 7 and how to configure a basic MED-V system for deploying Windows XP VMs to Windows Vista clients. You should now be able to:

*   Understand the differences between MED-V and Application Virtualization
*   Set up Windows XP Mode for Windows 7
*   Understand and set up a basic MED-V infrastructure
*   Configure and upload VMs to a MED-V Server

That brings us to the end of the book.

Index

[PACKT] PUBLISHING enterprise
professional expertise distilled

Thank you for buying
Least Privilege Security for Windows 7, Vista and XP

About Packt Publishing

Packt, pronounced 'packed', published its first book "Mastering phpMyAdmin for Effective MySQL Management" in April 2004 and subsequently continued to specialize in publishing highly focused books on specific technologies and solutions.

Our books and publications share the experiences of your fellow IT professionals in adapting and customizing today's systems, applications, and frameworks. Our solution based books give you the knowledge and power to customize the software and technologies you're using to get the job done. Packt books are more specific and less general than the IT books you have seen in the past. Our unique business model allows us to bring you more focused information, giving you more of what you need to know, and less of what you don't.

Packt is a modern, yet unique publishing company, which focuses on producing quality, cutting-edge books for communities of developers, administrators, and newbies alike. For more information, please visit our website: www.packtpub.com.

About Packt Enterprise

In 2010, Packt launched two new brands, Packt Enterprise and Packt Open Source, in order to continue its focus on specialization. This book is part of the Packt Enterprise brand, home to books published on enterprise software – software created by major vendors, including (but not limited to) IBM, Microsoft and Oracle, often for use in other corporations. Its titles will offer information relevant to a range of users of this software, including administrators, developers, architects, and end users.

Writing for Packt

We welcome all inquiries from people who are interested in authoring. Book proposals should be sent to author@packtpub.com. If your book idea is still at an early stage and you would like to discuss it first before writing a formal book proposal, contact us; one of our commissioning editors will get in touch with you.

We're not just looking for published authors; if you have strong technical skills but no writing experience, our experienced editors can help you develop a writing career, or simply get some additional reward for your expertise.

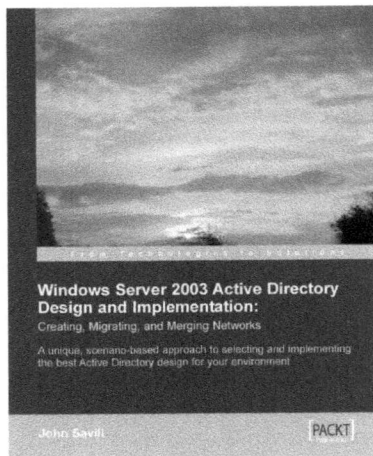

Windows Server 2003 Active Directory Design and Implementation: Creating, Migrating, and Merging Networks

ISBN: 978-1-904811-08-4   Paperback: 372 pages

A unique, scenario-based approach to selecting and implementing the best Active Directory design for your environment

1. Create new networks or evolve existing Active Directory installations

2. Create the best Active Directory design for a broad range of business environments

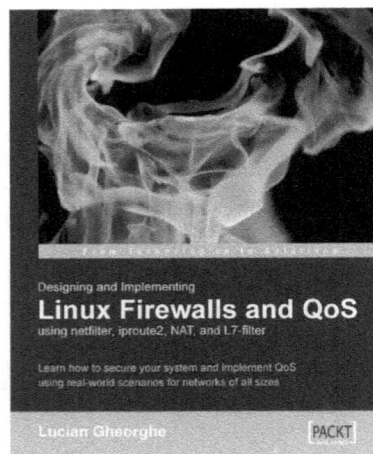

Designing and Implementing Linux Firewalls and QoS using netfilter, iproute2, NAT and l7-filter

ISBN: 978-1-904811-65-7   Paperback: 288 pages

Learn how to secure your system and implement QoS using real-world scenarios for networks of all sizes

1. Implementing Packet filtering, NAT, bandwidth shaping, packet prioritization using netfilter/iptables, iproute2, Class Based Queuing (CBQ) and Hierarchical Token Bucket (HTB)

2. Building intelligent networks by marking, queuing, and prioritizing different types of traffic

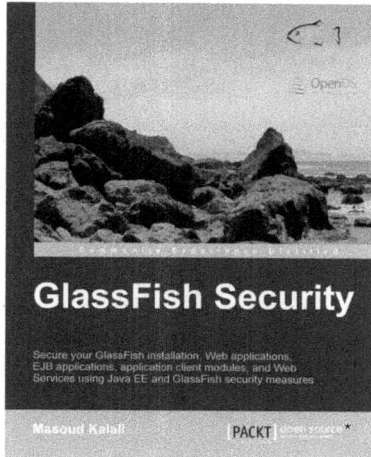

GlassFish Security

ISBN: 978-1-847199-38-6   Paperback: 296 pages

Secure your GlassFish installation, Web applications, EJB applications, Application Client modules, and Web services

1. Secure your GlassFish installation and J2EE applications

2. Develop secure Java EE applications including Web, EJB, and Application Client modules

3. Secure web services using GlassFish and OpenSSO web service security features

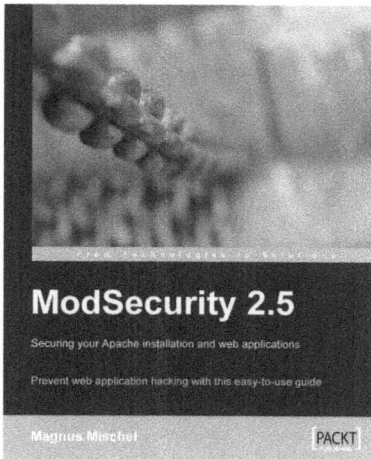

ModSecurity 2.5

ISBN: 978-1-847194-74-9   Paperback: 280 pages

Prevent web application hacking with this easy to use guide

1. Secure your system by knowing exactly how a hacker would break into it

2. Covers writing rules in-depth and Modsecurity rule language elements such as variables, actions, and request phases

3. Covers the common attacks in use on the Web, and ways to find the geographical location of an attacker and send alert emails when attacks are discovered

Please check **www.PacktPub.com** for information on our titles